MIGRANT WORKERS IN SINGAPORE

Lives and Labour in a Transient Migration Regime

Highly Recommended Titles

Globalisation, Migration and Health: Challenges and Opportunities
edited by Andre M N Renzaho
ISBN: 978-1-78326-888-7

Migration in East and Southeast Asia
edited by Samuel C Y Ku and Kristina Kironska
ISBN: 978-981-3141-66-7

World Scientific Handbook of Global Migration
In 3 Volumes
edited by Robert M Sauer
ISBN: 978-981-124-793-4 (Set)
ISBN: 978-981-124-900-6 (Vol. 1)
ISBN: 978-981-124-901-3 (Vol. 2)
ISBN: 978-981-124-902-0 (Vol. 3)

MIGRANT WORKERS IN SINGAPORE

Lives and Labour in a Transient Migration Regime

Edited by

Brenda S. A. Yeoh
National University of Singapore, Singapore

Kellynn Wee
National University of Singapore, Singapore & University College London, UK

Theodora Lam
National University of Singapore, Singapore

World Scientific

NEW JERSEY • LONDON • SINGAPORE • BEIJING • SHANGHAI • HONG KONG • TAIPEI • CHENNAI • TOKYO

Published by

World Scientific Publishing Co. Pte. Ltd.
5 Toh Tuck Link, Singapore 596224
USA office: 27 Warren Street, Suite 401-402, Hackensack, NJ 07601
UK office: 57 Shelton Street, Covent Garden, London WC2H 9HE

Library of Congress Cataloging-in-Publication Data
Names: Yeoh, Brenda S. A., editor. | Wee, Kellynn, editor. | Lam, Theodora, editor.
Title: Migrant workers in Singapore : lives and labour in a transient migration regime / edited by Brenda S.A. Yeoh, Kellynn Wee, Theodora Lam.
Description: New Jersey : World Scientific, [2022] | Includes bibliographical references.
Identifiers: LCCN 2022011162 | ISBN 9789811255021 (hardcover) | ISBN 9789811255038 (ebook) | ISBN 9789811255045 (ebook other)
Subjects: LCSH: Foreign workers--Singapore. | Foreign workers--Singapore--Social conditions--21st century. | Foreign workers--Health and hygiene--Singapore. | Construction workers--Singapore. | Construction workers--Singapore--Social conditions--21st century. | Construction workers--Health and hygiene--Singapore.
Classification: LCC HD8700.67 .M54 2022 | DDC 331.095957--dc23/eng/20220407
LC record available at https://lccn.loc.gov/2022011162

British Library Cataloguing-in-Publication Data
A catalogue record for this book is available from the British Library.

For any available supplementary material, please visit
https://www.worldscientific.com/worldscibooks/10.1142/12798#t=suppl

Desk Editor: Jiang Yulin

Typeset by Stallion Press
Email: enquiries@stallionpress.com

About the Editors

Brenda S.A. Yeoh FBA is Raffles Professor of Social Sciences at the National University of Singapore (NUS) and Research Leader of the Asian Migration Cluster at the Asia Research Institute, NUS. She was recently awarded the prestigious Vautrin Lud Prize (2021) for her outstanding achievements in the field of Geography. Her research interests include the politics of space in colonial and postcolonial cities, and she has considerable experience working on a wide range of migration research in Asia, including key themes such as cosmopolitanism and highly skilled talent migration; gender, social reproduction, and care migration; migration, national identity, and citizenship issues; globalising universities and international student mobilities; and cultural politics, family dynamics, and international marriage migrants. She has published widely on these topics and her recent books include *Asian Migrants and Religious Experience: From Missionary Journeys to Labor Mobility* (Amsterdam University Press, 2018 with Bernardo Brown) and *Handbook of Asian Migrations* (Routledge, 2018 with Gracia Liu-Farrer).

Kellynn Wee is a PhD candidate at University College London's Department of Anthropology, where she is studying the intersections between collaborative narrative, contingency, and play in tabletop role-playing games in Southeast Asia. She also worked at the Asia Research Institute for five years, where she researched extensively on the migration industry for migrant domestic workers in Singapore and Indonesia.

Theodora Lam is Senior Research Fellow in Asia Research Institute, National University of Singapore (NUS). She obtained her PhD in Geography from NUS and her dissertation focused on understanding changing gender subjectivities, webs of care, and relationships within the family in the wake of transnational labour migration. Her research highlights the voices of return migrants as well as carers and children who have remained in the home countries. Theodora's research interests cover transnational migration, family dynamics, children's geographies, and gender studies. She has co-edited several special journal issues and has also published on themes relating to migration, citizenship, and education in various journals and edited books including *American Behavioral Scientist*, *Asia Pacific Viewpoint*, *Environment and Planning A*, *Journal of Ethnic and Migration Studies*, and *Population, Space and Place*.

Contents

Acknowledgements

We are grateful to all the contributors of this volume, without whom this publication would not have been possible.

We would also like to thank Franchesca Rose Morais, Karen Anne Sun Liao and Wang Jun Hao for all their hard work and editorial assistance behind the scenes.

At World Scientific Publishing, we are grateful to Mr Max Phua and Mr Jiang Yulin, who found this project interesting and relevant, and for being unceasingly patient with us.

Singapore's past, present, and future are inextricably interwoven with the lives and labour of migrant workers. We acknowledge and thank in particular those who have generously shared their time and experiences in each of the studies brought together in this volume.

As Singapore, the region, and the world continue to grapple with the challenges of the COVID-19 pandemic, we hope that migration as a livelihood strategy can emerge a more humane and sustainable strategy for all.

Migrant Construction Workers in Singapore: An Introduction

Kellynn Wee

Department of Anthropology
University College London
and
Department of Sociology
National University of Singapore

Theodora Lam

Asia Research Institute
National University of Singapore

Brenda S.A. Yeoh FBA

Asia Research Institute and Department of Geography
National University of Singapore

Initially upheld as a bastion of success in curbing the spread of COVID-19 in the first few months of 2020, Singapore found itself home to the highest number of coronavirus cases in Southeast Asia by the middle of the same year. Over 90 per cent of its cases occurred among the 300,000 migrant construction workers primarily from Bangladesh, India, and China who live as part of a transient population in this city-state. This collection looks beyond the immediacy of heightened concerns surrounding the migrant worker population in the time of the COVID-19 crisis. It gives attention to broader questions of migrant lives and labour in a city-state that has thrived on migration since its beginnings as a colonial entrepôt. Serving as a primer for the general and academic reader interested in developing a richer understanding of the structural conditions of migrant construction work, the book draws together key studies on migrant construction work in Singapore. The chapters in this volume, contributed by a range of academic experts, spotlight the processes of unequal global development, precarious work, and welfare exclusion that have rendered low-waged labour migrants especially vulnerable to the pandemic. They also highlight migrant men's social identities beyond the sphere of work by attending to their experiences and strategies as members of transnational families and social-cultural communities.

This introductory essay is three-fold. First, the chapter begins by chronicling migrant construction workers' migration trajectories, focusing on the drivers of migration, the role of the migration industry, and their working and living conditions in Singapore. Second, it charts the immediate implications of the pandemic for migrant construction workers and reflects on longer term consequences. Third, the chapter introduces the research articles included in this volume. In order to increase the accessibility of research papers from the perspective of a more general readership, each chapter features a newly written reflection from the authors which provides a concise introduction to the main themes and findings of the paper while tracing connections to migrant construction workers' experiences during the pandemic and its aftermath. Collectively, the chapters reveal how the lives and labour of these men are complexly linked to unequal development, labour brokerage, family separation, and broader structures of exclusion from welfare systems and local communities. By distilling key insights from the collected body of research, the volume will also serve as a useful compendium to inform efforts to review migrant worker policies to improve their welfare in the post-COVID-19 world.

0.1 Migration Trajectories

0.1.1 *Motivations behind migration: Remittances and beyond*

One of the key drivers of migration is simple: the need to make a livelihood. Research has shown that migrant remittances can have a significant impact on poverty alleviation in countries of origin. In 2018, India received the highest amount of remittances in the world (USD 78.61 billion); China was in second place (USD 67.41 billion) [International Organization for Migration, 2020a]; while Bangladesh reportedly received USD 15.56 billion in remittances [International Organization for Migration, 2020b]. Research focusing on Bangladesh has demonstrated a range of positive impacts of remittances in diminishing poverty in remittance-receiving households as opposed to non-remittance receiving households [Kumar, 2019]; increasing food security, mitigating food-related shocks, and improving the quality of diets in remittance-receiving households [Moniruzzaman, 2020]; and building household social resilience by contributing to investments in both human and economic capital [Sikder and Higgins, 2017]. However, the rosy picture painted by the perception of remittances as a panacea to poverty is tempered by an understanding of the financial risks that migrants and their families take in order for members to migrate. Migration is a costly business that often requires families to enter into debt, and the resultant indebtedness may sink migrant households into situations of extreme precarity [Moniruzzaman and Walton-Roberts, 2018]. In some cases, remittances may be meagre and ineffectual in repairing a family economy felled by debt, the loss of personal savings, and capital constraints [Rahman, 2011]. Failed migration, which might happen in up to one in three cases, results in huge financial losses and little community support for the migrant family [Das et al., 2014].

The desire to earn a living is not the only reason why people migrate. It is crucial to look beyond economic rationales to understand the role that myths and images play in influencing people's imaginations of migration [Dannecker, 2013], and also to acknowledge the impact of social and cultural forces on people's migration decisions [Rahman, 2017]. Nitya Rao's [2014] work on Bangladeshi migrants shows that although people migrate because of poverty and family obligations, they also do so because they aspire to metropolitan consumption patterns. It is not the degrading labour conditions that migrants endure which form the locus of attention: as Rao puts it, "the distancing of the worksite invisibilises the degradation associated with such work" [p. 878]. Instead, for migrant men in particular, the generation of wealth from migration allows them to achieve freedom and autonomy through the accumulation of money, the establishment of local businesses, the construction of 'modern' houses, and the increased capacity to marry 'educated' women and observe specific religious practices. The consumption practices of return migrants are thus forces of creativity, expression, and a claim to elite status. Deshingkar et al. [2019, p. 2730] add that men's decision to migrate is also motivated by the desire to find ways to "transgress the spatial and social boundaries that prevent them from improving their socio-economic status". In this light, they found that younger men who had not shown an aptitude for business or education were often encouraged to migrate.

Temporary labour migration is also often not an individual enterprise: precisely because destination countries admit migrant workers as individuals without the accompaniment of family members as a condition for their entry [Baey and Yeoh, 2015], migration is usually a household decision, made in the context of splitting the family across international borders as a concerted livelihood strategy, and has specific gendered impacts [Dannecker, 2005]. Md Mizanur Rahman [2017] adds that, beyond the family, the *bari* — a group of families related by blood, sharing the same courtyard — is another significant but under-regarded unit for meaningful analysis. In Bangladesh, where migration is male-dominated and the migration of women is stigmatised [Bélanger and Rahman, 2013], effects of labour migration on rural communities in Bangladesh include the intensification and hardening of gendered social domains. When men leave the country to become breadwinners, women are expected, more than ever, to carry out the role of homemakers, and come under heightened moral scrutiny as wives are left "alone" with their husbands being away [Rao, 2012].

0.1.2 *The business of migration: Dollars and dalals*

The experiences of aspiring migrants from countries such as Bangladesh and India must be understood in the context of a transnational migration industry that enables the expansion of possibilities for would-be migrants but also profits from driving labour abroad. The COVID-19 crisis disproportionately affected Bangladeshi migrants in the construction work sector [Cai and Lai, 2020], who formed the lion's share of the afflicted cases in Singapore in 2020; Indian migrants constituted the next largest group of affected migrants, with migrants from China, Myanmar, Malaysia, the Philippines, and Thailand making up a handful of the remaining cases.

This section contextualises the migration history of South Asian migrants and examines the way that the labour migration of men into Singapore's construction work sector is inextricable from the rise of the migration industry — the actors who profit from facilitating or constraining migration [Sørensen and Gammeltoft-Hansen, 2012].

The migration of Tamils to Singapore and Malaya is founded in colonial history, where cheap Indian labour comprised a large proportion of lower-paid positions in British Singapore. Despite Singapore's transformation from a colonial port to its current iteration as a global city, the continuity of its dependence on low-paid Indian labour was sustained [Hamid, 2015]. The bulk of Indian migrants in Singapore hail from Tamil Nadu; however, Tamils are generally under-studied in migration scholarship [Hamid and Tutt, 2019], and the focus on Bangladeshi migrants in the chapters included in this book bears this out. For Bangladesh, outward migration began in earnest in the 1970s. The oil price hike created an influx of labour-hungry infrastructural projects in the Gulf and ratcheted up the velocity of temporary migration to these rapidly industrialising economies. Following the Gulf crisis in the 1990s, East and Southeast Asia emerged as new destination regions for migrant labourers from South Asia [Lian and Rahman, 2006]. As demand for labour increased, Bangladesh's government began to formalise labour migration through the creation of government bodies such as the Bureau of Manpower, Employment and Training (BMET). Policy developments like these were concurrent with the popularisation of the *kafala* system, where private citizens or companies in destination countries take on the role of legal sponsors to migrant workers under conditions of highly asymmetrical power relations. Migrant workers' employment contracts and permission to remain in the destination countries are inextricably linked, and in most situations, workers require the sponsor's permission to transfer jobs, terminate employment, and enter or exit the host country. This system "creates and formalises precarity by depriving migrants of full citizenship rights" [Deshingkar et al., 2019, p. 2727].

In the wake of these accelerated flows of migration, private recruiters in countries like Bangladesh entered the picture in the 1980s. Brokers' services are indispensable to potential migrants who want to fulfil particular desires and goals, but they also create and reproduce precarious conditions [Deshingkar et al., 2019]. Recruiters and brokers transformed labour migration from a state-led economic strategy to a transnational business [Rahman, 2012]. Following the entrance of brokers, the cost of migration has shot up. The emergence of dalals — a catch-all term for middlemen, subagents, and informal intermediaries that link aspirant migrants to formal recruiting agencies — added several chains of transaction to the process of leaving the country for work. Compounding this, the practice of visa trading — where Bangladeshi recruitment agencies profit by bidding for sponsorship visas from employers in countries of destination — has become increasingly popular, with the increased costs of these bids transferred to potential migrants [Abrar and Billah, 2017].

A range of informal dalals emerged to fill a vacuum because recruiters located in city centres like Dhaka faced difficulty drawing in potential migrants from the more rural areas. Aspirant migrants were sceptical of the promises of unknown recruiters claiming to be able to send them abroad: Azad [2019, p. 141] explains that potential migrants trusted "neither receipt nor rules" as proffered by an unfamiliar recruiter from a distant metropolis. As trusted community figures whom aspirant migrants feel they can hold accountable should anything go astray during the migration journey, dalals were a necessary connection between aspirant migrants and formal recruiting agencies. Adding multiple layers of financial transactions — frequently conducted through verbal promises rather than written agreements [Siddiqui, 2010] — drove up the cost of migrating abroad. It also allowed recruiting agencies to dodge accountability for excessive charging or other exploitative practices; as Abrar and Billah [2017, p. 155] put it, formal agencies have the "uncanny tendency to conveniently and squarely shift the onus of wrongdoing on the dalals".

Visa trading is another practice which has also made migration expensive for aspirant migrants from Bangladesh. While labour laws in countries of destination may prevent employers from charging migrant workers fees to work, this is bypassed by recruitment agents in origin countries collecting such fees instead, and then passing them on to hiring employers. Recruitment companies in countries of origin also compete for visas by offering kickback fees to companies in countries of destination [Jureidini, 2016]. These costs are invariably transferred to the worker, who essentially has to purchase his job [Kornatowski, 2017]. Aside from incurring exorbitant fees, these practices are accompanied by other issues, such as a lack of clear information about contractual terms or expected work conditions. The process of recruitment and training is also fraught with long wait times, unanticipated financial demands, and harsh training conditions [Baey and Yeoh, 2015].

To fund their journeys, many potential migrants have to raise the necessary capital by borrowing money, selling land, or pawning gold. The choice to enter into debt becomes both an enabling livelihood strategy and a form of entrapment [Platt et al., 2017]. Men's initial years working are often devoted to the repayment of debt rather than the reaping of profit. Baey and Yeoh [2015]'s survey of 205 Bangladeshi migrant workers revealed that the men paid an average sum of SGD 6,612 (USD 4,987) to work in Singapore. Delving deeper into the data, they showed that the costs of migration have increased over the years: workers who arrived in the 1990s paid an average of SGD 4,976 (USD 3,753) for placement fees, whereas workers who arrived after 2011 paid an average of SGD 7,491 (USD 5,650) — a hefty increase. That men have to work an average of 16.5 months before fully repaying their debts means that any disruptions to their income, whether through injury, workplace disputes, or the shortening of their contracts — render them especially vulnerable.

0.1.3 *Working in Singapore: Costly migrations and low-cost labourers*

Prior to the onset of the global pandemic from December 2019, there were 999,000 work permit holders in Singapore, of which 370,100 were migrant workers in the construction, marine shipyard, and process sectors [Ministry of Manpower, 2021a]. While official statistics in terms of the national origins of migrant construction workers in Singapore are not available, it is estimated by local migrant non-governmental organisations (NGOs) that there are around 250,000 South Asian men who work mainly in the construction and marine industries [Harrigan et al., 2017]. In 2016, the Bangladeshi High Commission's labour councillor Ayesha Shelly gauged that there were about 120,000 Bangladeshi migrant workers in Singapore [Ungku and Paul, 2017], which is in line with estimates by local NGO Transient Workers Count Too (TWC2) [Transient Workers

Count Too, 2014]. In the 2019 Bangladeshi Migration Trends report written by the Refugee and Migratory Movements Research Unit, Singapore received 7.12% of Bangladesh's outgoing migrants, ranking fourth in terms of Bangladeshi migrants' destination countries [Siddiqui, 2019].

The cost of migration to Singapore is steep, while in comparison, wages are low for jobs deemed both menial and dangerous. Indian workers are expected to pay about SGD 6,000–7,000 (USD 4,525–5,279) in agent fees; Bangladeshi workers between SGD 8,000–10,000 (USD 6,033–7,542); and Chinese workers between SGD 3,000–7,000 (USD 2,262–5,279) [Datta, 2017]. To put this in perspective, the basic starting monthly salary for migrant workers from India and Bangladesh in Singapore ranges from SGD 400–465 (USD 301–350) [Han, 2018]. In a separate study, Yea and Chok [2018] estimate that Bangladeshi workers are paid between SGD 16–18 per day, which is a rate of pay similar to what they received in the 1990s. As with migration costs, pay rates reflect a level of racial and ethnic stratification among the migrant worker population in Singapore: Chinese workers earn almost double the salary of Bangladeshi and Indian workers (SGD 7 per hour versus SGD 3 and SGD 3.50 per hour respectively), and the wage gap worsens in the case of firms that hire more non-Chinese workers [Chew et al., 2018].

Differential migration costs and pay rates are also consistent with a migration regime that is highly stratified. A hierarchy of visas, pinned to socio-culturally constructed categories of skill and talent, differentiates incoming migrant workers [Yeoh, 2006]. Low-waged contract workers enter at the bottom of the hierarchy, on a visa category known as Work Permits that imposes specific and often onerous conditions and requirements that both employers and employees must meet [Ministry of Manpower, 2021b]. Work Permit holders are expected to meet the Basic-Skilled (R2) requirements by proving that they have achieved the Skills Evaluation Certificate or undertaken the Skills Evaluation Certificate (Knowledge) schemes at one of the many Overseas Testing Centres in origin countries. Their maximum period of employment in Singapore is 14 years, with a provision for a longer maximum period of employment (up to 26 years) if they upgrade their skills in Singapore and become categorised as 'Higher-Skilled' workers. The longer employment period is meant to galvanise employers to hire higher-skilled workers to increase productivity [Baey and Yeoh, 2015]. Each company is limited in terms of the number of Work Permit holders by quota and must pay a levy to Singapore's Ministry of Manpower for each worker hired. The monthly levy for Basic-Skilled workers from non-traditional sources is between SGD 700–950; for Higher-Skilled workers, this is between SGD 300–600. The levy — as a mechanism meant to reduce reliance on cheap foreign labour and channel jobs towards locals — therefore increases the cost of each worker to the employer, and in some instances, its sum can equal or supersede the salary paid to the worker.

In the case of low-waged migrant workers, transience and disposability are key features of Singapore's immigration policy [Rahman, 2017]. South Asian construction workers are expected to form a transient labour force that enters Singapore to work but not stay or integrate into Singaporean society. These migrant men labour under Work Permit conditions that are far more restrictive compared to other visa categories for migrants regarded as more "skilled". For example, those who enter on Employment Passes — which are intended for professional white-collar workers above specified minimum salaries — are allowed to bring their families with them and can apply to become Permanent Residents. Conversely, migrant men on Work Permits are not allowed to bring their family members to Singapore and are prohibited from marrying Singaporean citizens or permanent residents without prior permission from the state [Ministry of Manpower, 2019]. Each Work Permit lasts only up to two years, and every Work Permit holder is subjected to a maximum period of employment. Work Permits are tied to specific employers and occupational sectors, and job mobility is restricted. Realistically, the easiest way a worker can exit a job is by returning to their home country and leaving again, a process that incurs additional costs with no promise of a more suitable employment arrangement in the next contract [Yea and Chok, 2018]. Employers are held legally liable for the workers under their care through the purchase of a security bond and are also able to fire and repatriate workers at will. The constant threat of deportation has had measurable impact on migrant workers' mental health [Harrigan et al., 2017] and effectively divests migrant workers of the ability to exercise their few formal rights, constituting them as "use-and-discard" economic subjects [Bal, 2015]. All of these policy features collude to produce a "low-cost, hyper-productive, docile, and disposable" labouring body in the construction sector [Baey and Yeoh, 2015, p. 12].

0.1.4 *Living at the margins of host society: Needed but not wanted*

The management of transnational labour in Singapore is characterised by a sense of moral distance [Wise, 2013]. By disembedding the moral relationship present in conventional face-to-face employment arrangements, strategies of detachment are prominent in Singapore's construction industry. Work and living conditions in Singapore's construction sector are built around principles of "down-sourcing" risk and responsibility for migrant workers. These are made manifest in strategies such as extended subcontracting chains and the bureaucratic languages of audit culture and euphemism.

Subcontracting is a very common practice in the construction industry that divests the top-of-the-chain contractors from holding responsibility for the migrant workers labouring at the work site. Main contractors often outsource particular portions of a construction project, such as metal casting, piling, or scaffolding: by doing so, uncertainty and risk is "passed down" to an ever-ready pool of labour reliant on punctuated flows of short-term, contractual work for a living [Baey and Yeoh, 2015]. Subcontracting compounds work hazards due to workers' unfamiliarity with the main construction site and a lack of effective coordination across all subcontracted teams working on separate but interdependent tasks [Debrah and Ofori, 2001]. As Wise [2013] writes, "the longer the chain, the less 'human' the workers become to those at the top" [p. 443].

Bureaucratic procedures and public discourse can also serve to alienate migrant men from the rights and benefits due to their status as workers. The state, for example, uses bureaucratic discourse to distance themselves from ethical responsibility for migrant workers [Wise, 2013]. By eliding or manipulating documentation — such as contract substitution, condition papers, and wage manipulation — employers limit migrant workers' bargaining power and create conditions of unfree labour, where workers are unable to leave exploitative situations or seek justice [Yea and Chok, 2018]. Wage theft, where workers receive only a part of their salary because they are underpaid or subject to unlawful deductions, is a common practice in the construction industry; this is compounded by the fact that Singapore does not have a minimum wage law, and extremely low wages are not illegal.

Migrant construction workers' access to public space and community facilities in Singapore can also be contested — the men's presence in the city-state has not been without friction. In 2008, announcements that a former school in the middle-class neighbourhood of Serangoon Gardens was about to be converted into a dormitory housing migrant workers sparked outrage, resulting in a petition against such a decision [Sim and Quek, 2008]. Residents complained that the men would dirty the neighbourhood by littering and spitting, and that they would loiter, become drunk and rowdy, and pose a threat to Singapore citizens. The state eventually built an access road costing SGD 2 million (USD 1.5 million) so that buses transporting the workers from their dormitory to the work site and back would be rerouted in order to minimise any social conflict [Tay, 2009]. While migrant workers may lay claim to informal public spaces as a way to navigate the inequalities they deal with in everyday life [Ye, 2013], the Serangoon Gardens case reveals how locals may act to limit migrants' access to space, particularly in racialised ways that harden into prejudice. As Ong and Yeoh [2012, p. 96] write, cosmopolitan sensibilities, or the lack of, run up against racial stereotypes that "render different groups of people 'in' and 'out' of place in different parts of the city". These stereotypes are rooted in the way that the male migrant body is constituted as a form of technology; it is expected to be a productive machine that performs hard labour and is subject to discipline and surveillance when it transgresses imagined boundaries, even through acts as simple as sharing a train carriage or neighbourhood places [Kathiravelu, 2020].

In terms of living conditions, many migrant construction workers are housed in dormitories that are situated in the outskirts of Singapore or on work sites, reflecting migrant men's marginal status in the city-state (Figure 1). In May 2020, 200,000 of the 725,200 non-domestic Work Permit holders live in the 43 purpose-built dormitories while 95,000 reside in 1,200 factory-converted dormitories [Loong, 2020; Teo, 2020]. The other workers may be living on construction sites and shipyards

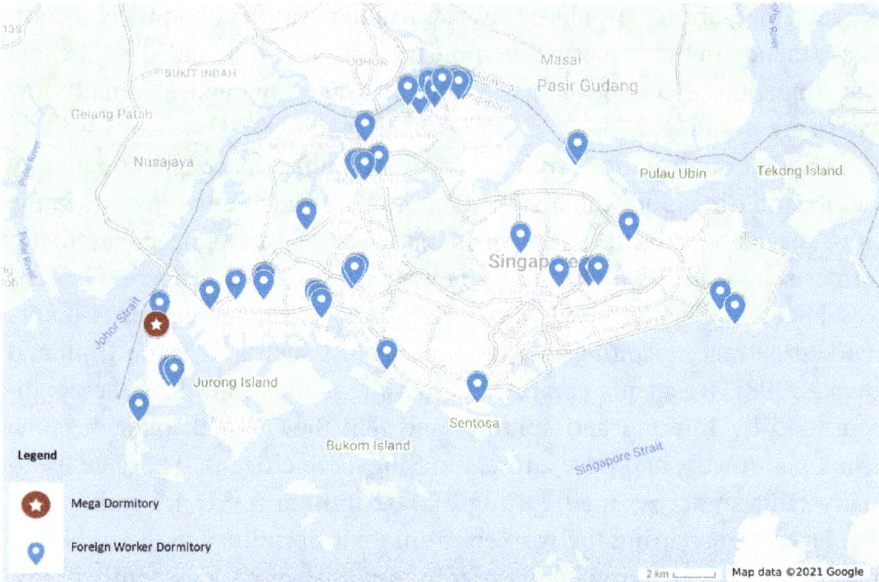

Figure 1 Location of foreign worker dormitories in Singapore.

Source: Created on Google Maps with data from https://www.mom.gov.sg/passes-and-permits/work-permit-for-foreign-worker/housing/foreign-worker-dormitories#/, accessed 17 November 2021

which host temporary housing facilities (20,000), in rented residences (85,000) or elsewhere [ibid.]. The dormitories tend to be crammed, poorly-ventilated, cost-saving affairs, with about 12–20 men to each room on 10 double-deck beds usually no more than one metre apart [Transient Workers Count Too, 2020]. As discussed later, this living arrangement facilitated the wildfire spread of COVID-19 in these dormitories, resulting in clusters of contagion amongst the migrant construction workers.

Under Singapore's temporary migration regime, responsibility for migrant workers' accommodation, medical treatment, and other associated costs of upkeep and maintenance falls on employers. Although the employer is required by law to offer the worker accommodation even in the case of salary or injury disputes, this rarely transpires in reality due to the antagonistic relationship between both parties [Kornatowski, 2017]. Even in cohesive relationships, making employers responsible for the social welfare of their migrant employees has resulted in visible cracks, particularly during extraordinary circumstances such as the pandemic. During widespread lockdowns during the height of COVID-19 to stem the spread of the pandemic, cases of quarantined workers not having their needs met — for example, food delivery — resulted in workers having to flout the law to keep themselves from going hungry [Loong, 2020].

Migrant construction workers hence occupy marginal spaces — physically, structurally, and socially — in Singaporean society. While local NGOs are active in campaigning for their protection and their rights, particularly at the height of COVID-19 — and there is a gradual shift towards the acknowledgement and appreciation of their presence in Singapore — they are structurally disadvantaged by the revolving-door migration policy that enshrines their transience and non-integration. Laws that hold employers responsible for migrant men's welfare and continued legal status in Singapore, as well as the vagaries of the construction industry, also contribute to their precarious status. Additionally, their vulnerability is compounded by the staggering recruitment costs that they are expected to pay in order to secure jobs in Singapore, accumulating into sizeable debts that often take years to pay off. A review of existing literature in 2017 was prescient, noting that migrant workers were likely to be at higher risk than Singaporeans for particular infectious diseases, due to factors such as their socio-economic status, their living conditions, and financial, cultural and language barriers to healthcare access [Sadarangani et al., 2017]. Understanding why and how migrant workers bore the brunt of the contagion at the height of the COVID-19 crisis in Singapore needs to be grounded in an examination of the wider structural conditions and social circumstances that account for their presence in Singapore as "needed but unwanted" men who labour.

0.2 At the Epicentre of the Pandemic Outbreak[1]

As COVID-19 gripped the world in 2020, the closing of borders at the height of the crisis set off a sudden break in the easy back-and-forth churning of low-waged migrant workers across borders. Not only did this

[1] Parts of this section is adapted from Lin and Yeoh [2020].

unanticipated end to transnational mobility undermine what was a highly profitable business for the migration brokerage industry in pre-pandemic times, large numbers of migrant workers who contribute their labour transnationally found themselves stranded on either side of the border. For host nation-states such as Singapore, the 'use-and-discard' logic central to managing temporary migration becomes inoperable, as swift and easy repatriation of 'excess' migrant workers is no longer possible in times of stalled mobility. As major migrant-dependent sectors of the Singapore economy such as the construction industry ground to a halt, migrant bodies — which are not supposed to stay if they are not at labour — can no longer be quickly excised from the host nation-state (even if their "temporary" status suggests otherwise). Now that virus-stricken migrant bodies have become effectively conjoined to the national geobody, the control of virus risk among migrant workers cannot be left simply to the gatekeeping functions of the border.

Infections among migrant workers started with a trickle but built up to five-figure numbers by April 2020 that — for a while — threatened to nullify if not invert Singapore's exemplary record in containing the virus. While it was a foreign domestic worker (infected by her employer, a worker in a health products shop catering to Chinese tourists) who numbered among the first cases of local coronavirus transmission in early February 2020 [Chang and Khalik, 2020], a cluster with five infected Bangladeshi work permit holders linked to the Seletar Aerospace Heights construction sites was confirmed [Ang, 2020a] within days of the first migrant household worker infection. All five migrant construction workers were to eventually recover from the virus, although one of them, Raju Sarkar (referred to as "Case 42" before recovery), had to endure a "painfully long fight against COVID-19" of nearly five months, including two months of struggling for his life on a ventilator and in critical condition [ChannelNewsAsia, 2020].

As Sarkar's life hung in the balance, this early case of migrant worker infection elicited considerable public sympathy and support. In March, his wife gave birth to a baby boy in Bangladesh while he was in intensive care, and a donation drive organised by a social enterprise group collected 33 cartons of items, including diapers, formula milk, and soft toys for the left-behind family. In addition, the government-sponsored Migrant

Worker Centre announced that the centre was "especially pleased to have facilitated a video conference call between the wife and the worker's medical team — in the presence of the husband — a day before her delivery" [Abu Baker, 2020]. As a personalised tale of hard-fought victory over COVID-19's ravages, Case 42 — perhaps because of its singularity at that time — became a showcase featuring the robustness of Singapore's healthcare system in times of pandemic-induced stress, as well as the outpouring of community concern for the virus-stricken migrant worker and his left-behind family.

Notwithstanding the early efflorescence of interest around Case 42, low-waged migrant workers were initially not centre-stage in the response plan to deal with the crisis. Up to the end of March, the main focus of attention in Singapore's battle cry against COVID-19 was trained on stemming the tide of "imported cases" — that is, stopping the wily pathogen at the border — and controlling transmission among the locally resident community through contact tracing, isolation and quarantine measures to resist "new waves of infection… coming from many countries" [Lee, 2020a]. By early April, however, it became increasingly apparent that the virus had been lurking amidst spaces of migrant concentration, and was soon multiplying exponentially by connecting work sites, workers' dormitories, and migrant gathering grounds through rhizomatic, criss-crossing chains of transmission [Wong, 2020a]. All at once, it would seem that the higher risk of contagion is not outside but within the nation-state's well-regulated borders. As attention shifted to the "non-residents" of the nation-state, migrant bodies were prioritised during the rolling out of Singapore's regime of government-sponsored virus-testing and medical surveillance. With extensive testing, COVID-19 was no longer a pathogen of stealth but a highly mobile virus that moved with galvanising speed through the migrant worker population as dormitory after dormitory became gazetted as "isolation areas" in quick succession (Figure 2). Driven by the seemingly unstoppable rise in migrant worker cases, Singapore's COVID-19 statistics soared precipitously from around a hundred in early March to over 45,000 confirmed cases by early July, with "dormitory residents" accounting for over 90 per cent of the cumulative cases (Figure 3).

Risk containment strategies, predicated primarily on epidemiological control, soon bifurcated to target two separate populations — the locally

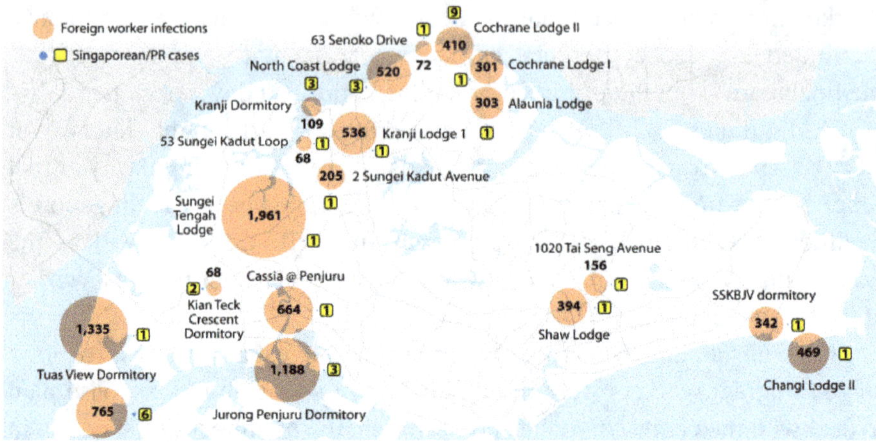

Figure 2 Foreign worker infections and community cases linked to migrant dormitory clusters in May 2020.

Source: ChannelNewsAsia, https://www.channelnewsasia.com/singapore/covid-19-cases-singapore-citizens-pr-dormitory-clusters-linked-932166, accessed 18 November 2021

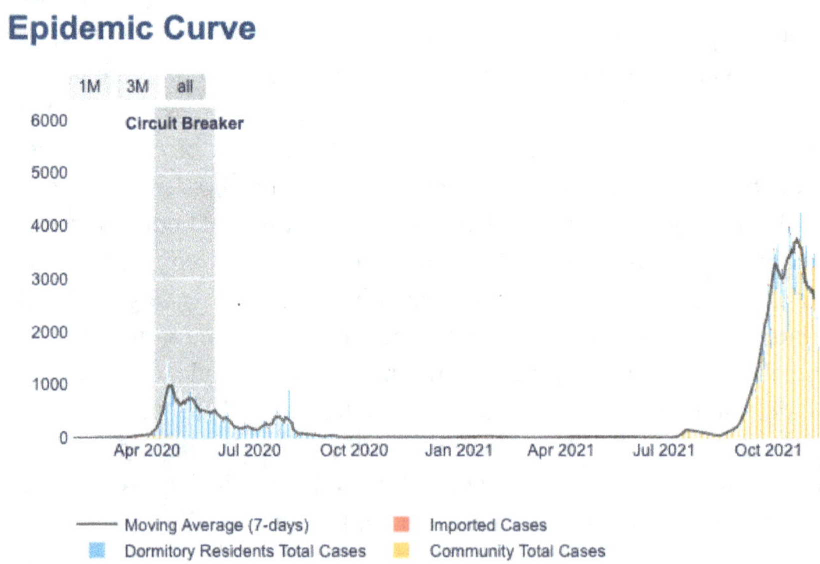

Figure 3 COVID-19 cases in Singapore from January 2020 to 14 November 2021.

Source: Ministry of Health COVID-19 Situation website, https://covidsitrep.moh.gov.sg/, accessed 18 November 2021

resident community and migrant workers (with particular attention to dormitory dwellers). As Lawrence Wong, the Minister co-leading the Multi-Ministry Taskforce on COVID-19, asserts,

> we are dealing with two separate infections — there is one happening in the foreign worker dormitories, where the numbers are rising sharply, and there is another in the general population where the numbers are more stable for now [Wong, 2020b].

By 7 April 2020, the "general population" knuckled down to the new realities of the "circuit breaker" period characterised by work-from-home for most working adults, home-based learning for schoolchildren, closure of most shops and leisure facilities, and prohibitions of social gatherings in both public and private spaces. At the same time, the continuing spike in infection numbers among migrant workers called into place exceptional measures of contagion control for this "separate infection". Despite low susceptibility to illness among an essentially young and healthy population (indeed, the vast majority of infected migrant workers were asymptomatic or had mild symptoms), migrant workers became the target of a slew of containment measures in order to "minimise the risks of spread to the wider community" [Wong 2020a]. Dormitories were essentially locked down to stop in-and-out mobility and prevent cross-infections, while migrant construction workers living outside the dormitories were put on stay-home orders. Immobilising the pathogen living in largely asymptomatic dormitory occupants required the mobilisation of whole-of-government resources, including the military and police force as well as thousands of volunteers, in order to tighten surveillance, enforce mobility control, and provide medical care, food, and welfare services [Han, 2020]. Amidst the escalating battle against COVID-19, it became clear that within the enclosed, tightly packed spaces of the dormitory built in conformity to low-cost principles of high density and shared facilities, the risk of contagion cannot be arrested by simply instituting safe distancing, activity timetabling and "rooming arrangements" [Teo, 2020]. Close to half (47 per cent) of the migrant dormitory population was to eventually become infected with COVID-19 before the end of the year [Ng, 2020a].

Given Singapore's high level of dependence on the migrant workforce for a wide range of "essential services", a "three-prong strategy" in risk containment was devised, not only to separate the infected from the uninfected, but also to ring-fence those needed for essential work by moving them to safeguarded spaces such as vacant public housing flats [Teo, 2020]. It also soon became clear that the epidemiological well-being of the nation-state can only be secured by investing in the urgent construction of community recovery facilities and alternative housing for recovered workers including military camps, exhibition centres, and "floating hotels" so as to "thin out" dormitory spaces [Lim M. Z., 2020].

In pre-pandemic times, migrant worker housing has been unquestioningly relegated to marginal or interstitial spaces so as to be out of the host society's way. The exigencies of the pandemic have paradoxically shown that when migrant housing is inadequately resourced, there are limits to recuperating 'risky' migrant labour through strategies of isolation and separation. Neutralising virus risk through epidemiological control has — at least momentarily — required opening up the possibilities of alternative housing geographies for those who are considered transient but no less essential to national well-being. This was a public health measure that had to be carefully calibrated so as to not distort differential entitlements for citizens and migrants; at one point, 'essential' migrant workers were moved to public housing estates (accessible only to citizens in ordinary times) while their citizen-occupants were moved to hotels further up the accommodation chain to "protect [their] health and well-being" [Lin, 2020].

As the city-state drew up its battle plans against an enemy pathogen within its borders, a hitherto unseen geography of distributed but circumscribed migrant housing and ring-fenced spaces — referred to by unfamiliar acronyms such as PBDs, BRWs, FCDs, CTQs, TOLs, and TLQs[2] — began to gain more visibility. Restoring migrant workers to their ideal state of labour will require fundamental changes to the deployment of migrant labour, necessitating "a whole range of measures covering the worksites, the accommodation and transport of workers, as well as additional precautions taken by the workers themselves" [Wong, 2020a].

---

[2] Purpose-Built Dormitories (PBDs), Blocks of Recovered Workers (BRWs), Factory Converted Dormitories (FCDs), Construction Temporary Quarters (CTQs), Temporary Occupation Licence Quarters (TOLs), and Temporary Living Quarters (TLQs).

For a nation-state that "made a living by connecting itself to the world", it was imperative that Singapore's "international reputation built up over the decades" remained strong in the aftermath of "tectonic shifts" [Lai, 2020, reporting on Prime Minister Lee Hsien Loong's 7 June 2020 broadcast]. In this context, the COVID-19 outbreak among the migrant worker population threw an absolute "curveball" [to use the phrasing of the then Minister for Manpower, quoted in Koh, 2020] that pushed the battlefront for contagion risk management beyond the realm of epidemiological control and into the social-political arena.

Singapore soon found itself exposed to a rash of social-moral critique for being "blindsided" by the turn of events leading to the escalation of COVID-19 cases among the migrant worker population [Han, 2020]. While the government claimed that the virus moved too quickly and "we do not have the luxury of the benefit of hindsight" [Elangovan, 2020, quoting coordinating Minister Lawrence Wong], critics including journalists, commentators, and migrant advocacy groups countered that the government had stumbled in its risk calibration. Kirsten Han [2020], one of the first journalists to offer a commentary, writes "... you can't have foresight for things you refuse to see... There is no way the government did not know of the conditions in which migrant workers live and the risks that they would face during a global pandemic". The migrant rights group TWC2 had earlier (in late March) warned that "it was only a matter of time before Covid-19 would begin to spread in worker dormitories, where conditions are nearly ideal for transmission of infection" [Transient Workers Count Too, 2020]. As the risk of contagion drew the living conditions of migrant workers into the spotlight and made it a "national talking point" [Kok and Jaipragas, 2020], the advocacy group continued to leverage on the unprecedented attention on migrant housing to press for "broader reforms ... and a more ethical relationship with migrant labour" [Gee, 2020]. As the city-state reported the largest number of cases in Southeast Asia at that time (around 55,000 migrant workers had tested positive for the virus by end of August 2020 [Goh, 2021]), international media was quick to pounce on Singapore's rising COVID-19 cases. Commentaries proliferated, reporting on how overcrowding in workers' dormitory made a mockery of social distancing rules while referencing Tommy Koh's (former ambassador to the United Nations) warning that "the dormitories were like a time bomb waiting to explode" [Leung, 2020a; Paul and Geddie, 2020; Ratcliffe, 2020]. Featuring headlines such as "How Singapore Flipped from Virus Hero to Cautionary Tale" [Mokhtar, 2020] and "Once a Model for Coronavirus Response, Lost Control of Its Outbreak" [Leung, 2020b], these reports seemed to frame Singapore's fight against COVID-19 along the lines of hero-to-zero narratives.

At risk of being displaced from its high international standing for contagion control, the litmus test for Singapore to regain its "gold standard" reputation in the fight against COVID-19 lay paradoxically with recuperating the non-resident, migrant population living at close quarters in shared, enclosed spaces. This was not foreseen (or perhaps, not foreseeable) from the start when the response plan was based primarily on safe distancing and contact tracing, strategies that served Singapore well in combating SARS in 2003. As public health expert Jeremy Lim explained, COVID-19 has turned out to be "nothing like SARS" and this has necessitated rewriting "the playbook [while] execut[ing] measures", or in metaphorical terms, "fixing an aeroplane's engine while mid-flight" [quoted in Mokhtar, 2020]. For a nation-state that has been nourished by constant success stories in overcoming the odds, restoring Singapore's reputation in winning the COVID-19 battle, slowly but surely, is all the more crucial. Alongside epidemiologically informed strategies to recuperate 'risky' migrant labour, Prime Minister Lee Hsien Loong [2020b] was quick to assure migrant workers, and their families in source countries, that the Singapore state would assume responsibility for migrant workers' welfare, making sure that that their salaries would be paid and covering their medical care and treatment.

In direct response to criticisms levelled at workers' dormitories, the government announced that new Quick-Build Dormitories (QBDs) in "modular form with a low density" will be rolled out by the end of 2020 (with more in the pipeline) and unused state properties, including former schools and vacant factories, will be fitted out as temporary housing [Phua, 2020]. By the end of June, as a signal that the infection tide was turning among the migrant worker population, the government announced that "70 to 80 per cent of migrant workers staying in dormitories are expected be cleared of COVID-19 by the end of July" [Ang, 2020b]. Out of a total of 26 COVID-19 fatalities at the end of June, only one — a 51-year-old Chinese national who had been working as a foreman for almost 20 years in Singapore — was a migrant worker [Kamil, 2020].

While the majority of workers' dormitories were declared cleared of COVID-19 by August 2020, movement restrictions were not entirely lifted and migrant workers continued to be largely confined to their dormitories and worksites, selectively permitted to venture out to designated recreation centres on their rest days [Goh, 2021]. Particularly for workers confined to isolated dormitories or to their rooms for prolonged periods, this containment strategy inflicted a high mental health burden on the workers in the form of increased symptoms of depression and stress [Saw et al., 2021; Tan and Zhuo, 2020). While mobility curbs were applied to non-work activities, the resumption of work — albeit with a host of safeguards from routine testing, providing dedicated transport to worksites, consolidating workers from the same companies together in the same dormitory blocks, to deploying technology "to ensure tracking and compliance" — was prioritised in order to supply the much needed manpower to restart stalled construction projects in housing and infrastructure [Toh, 2020].

By the end of 2020, as virus case numbers were seemingly in abeyance and with the ramp up of contact tracing and testing capabilities, Singapore announced cautious steps to relax COVID-19 restrictions in the larger community (the so-called Phase 3 of Re-Opening beginning on 28 December 2020) [Chew, 2020]. With the arrival of the vaccine in early 2021 and the successful rollout of the vaccination programme over the course of the next few months, there was fresh hope that the vaccine would prove a major game changer that would allow Singapore to gain momentum in reopening its economy. However, the then Second Minister of Manpower made clear that the risk of re-emergence of Covid-19 among migrant workers was "real and significant" and that relaxing the stringent measures imposed on them would invite "new waves of infection" [quoted in Ng, 2020b]. The Minister went on to reiterate the government's responsibility for the workers' safety and welfare, asserting that "few countries have done as much for their migrant workers as we have. We provided them with the same standard of medical care as Singaporeans enjoy, at no cost to them".[3]

While the journey towards reopening the economy and the nation's borders may appear to be one of fitful stops and starts, it was clear that Singapore had little choice in the matter. As coordinating Minister Lawrence Wong put it, "We are a little red dot fully plugged into the world. Trade and travel are our lifeblood — for us, these are not just good-to-have; they are existential issues" [quoted in Lim M. Z., 2021]. It also became clear that closed borders and stalled mobility severely undermined Singapore's heavy dependence on importing migrant men as low-cost transient labour, as the developing manpower crunch revealed. In May 2021, even as the nation-state entered a period of "Heightened Alert" and increased cautionary measures against the highly infectious Delta variant (such as lengthening quarantine from 14 to 21 days for travellers from high risk countries including South Asian countries, the main source countries of migrant workers), the construction and built environment sector appealed to the government for a "balanced approach … to allow the recruitment and inflow of foreign manpower" [Lim J., 2021]. In making its case, the industry pointed to the increased incidence of workplace safety breaches as the already reduced workforce was stretched to maximum capacity, heightened competition for a shrinking pool of migrant workers within the nation's borders, and disruptions and delays in "public infrastructure projects such as hospitals, MRT and schools and industrial developments which are vital to the nation's economy and people's lives" [quoted in Lim J., 2021]. Despite the imminent loss of their jobs in Singapore, many migrant workers were anxious to return home to their families experiencing the throes of the pandemic, and only a proportion chose to, or were able to, return to re-join the workforce in Singapore [Lim J., 2021]. As a result, the foreign workforce in the construction,

[3]A resurgence of infections among those living in Westlite Jalan Tukang, a newly built foreign worker dormitory, once again reminded the public that the treatment of foreign workers did not appear to have improved a year after. Workers complained about poor living conditions, poor food quality, lack of medical attention and poor isolation measures. The situation culminated in a mass protest on 13 October 2021 where riot police had to be called in [Devaraj, 2021].

marine and process sectors declined from 370,100 in December 2019 to 311,000 in December 2020 [Ministry of Manpower, 2021a].

From mid-2021, with the emergence of a series of community COVID-19 clusters (despite vaccination rates reaching 85 per cent of the population by November 2021 [Pazos and Adeline, 2021]), attention shifted to combating virus spread within the community even as Singapore moved towards treating the disease as endemic. Unlike the previous year when the migrant worker population accounted for around 90 per cent of the COVID-19 cases, the figures were now reversed with the larger proportion of cases occurring within the local community (Figure 3). In September 2021, more than 16 months after movement curbs were first imposed on the migrant dormitory population, a pilot scheme was launched that allowed up to 500 fully vaccinated dormitory occupants to visit pre-identified locations such as Little India, a pre-pandemic weekend enclave popular with South Asian migrant workers, for up to six hours each week [Kok, 2021]. The regulations were further relaxed from December where 3,000 vaccinated dormitory-dwelling workers will be allowed to visit any location in Singapore per day for up to 8 hours [Chew, 2021]. Nonetheless, despite the high vaccination rates across the dormitory (98 per cent) and the community, migrant workers continue to be treated as a separate population subject to far more stringent and prolonged curbs on their mobility and non-work activities compared to local residents. Pandemic times have further reinforced the view that low-waged migrant men are expected to labour but not linger in Singapore society.

Whether Singapore's approach to the control and recuperation of migrant workers during the COVID-19 pandemic has longer term effects for the nation-state's relationship to migrant labour remains an open question. We conclude this section with three sets of suggestions in paving a more sustainable way forward for temporary migration.[4]

0.2.1 *Longer stays, less churn*

Temporary migration is based on time-limited visas and short work contracts with few (if any) legal pathways towards permanent residence. The

[4]These suggestions are adapted from Yeoh [2020].

closing of borders at the height of the crisis put a stop to the easy back-and-forth churning of migrant workers across borders. Particularly in a post-COVID-19 context where a reduced volume of labour migration can be anticipated, offering visas and contracts of longer duration, coupled with skills acquisition opportunities, as well as clearer employer responsibility for home leave and repatriation, may be a viable step forward. Longer stays without the uncertainty of contract termination obviate recurring brokerage fees for the individual migrant and are also conducive to skills acquisition and improved labour productivity. Reduced mobility in post-COVID-19 times can mean less unproductive churning and more productive migrants.

0.2.2 *Incorporating migrants into national safety nets*

The COVID-19 pandemic has made it patently evident recruitment as well as the repatriation of migrant workers speedily and cheaply can no longer be taken for granted. Neither would it be possible to effectively contain the spread of disease by segregating migrant workers from host society. This opens a window of opportunity to reframe transient labour not only within the economic logic of use-and-discard, but also as an integral part of national labour supply to be safeguarded for more sustainable growth and development. Incorporating migrant workers into national safety nets that provide healthcare and income protection will not only have a positive effect on migrant welfare but could be a means of future-proofing the economy against the crippling effects of pandemics and other global crises. Sustainable and effective social protection programmes are a "prerequisite for countries to embark on an inclusive recovery post-COVID-19" and the migrant workforce should be incorporated into these plans [Organization for Economic Co-operation and Development, 2020].

0.2.3 *Integrating migrants as a safeguard against xenophobia*

While racism against migrants is certainly not new, the pandemic has unleashed what the UN Secretary General has described as a "tsunami of hate and xenophobia" across the globe. [International Organization for Migration, 2020c]. In this light, it is all the more important to revisit the commonly held premise that temporary migration provides an "antidote" to excessive nationalist fears of migrants as it allows for a highly controlled form of entry and exit into nation-states that can be calibrated in accordance with industry needs and the degree of social tolerance [Collins and Bayliss, 2020]. As the pandemic reveals, in a time of stalled mobility, it is precisely temporary migrants who become easy targets for vilification and blame. This is exacerbated not only because these migrants have little (if not negative) social capital to claim a place in society, but also their presence — often taking the form of highly visible migrant enclaves and gathering grounds — can no longer be quickly excised from host society (as their "temporary" status suggests). Going forward, the pressing need is to create opportunities for building social cohesion that includes migrants in everyday interaction with citizens rather than fall back on current measures of separation and containment. A more resilient social fabric that can withstand crisis will take efforts on multiple fronts. Investment in inclusive social resilience can take the form of building social ties of interdependence among migrants and citizens, reducing workplace inequalities that produce fixed social hierarchies and perpetuate racially-tinted stereotypes, countering racialising discourse with active promotion of a sense of common humanity, and innovative urban design and provision of common community facilities to avoid sharply segregated migrant communities.

0.3 Overview of the Book

To give more concrete context to the arguments raised in this chapter, the first section of this volume, "A Regime of Temporary Migration", begins by examining the socio-legal status of migrant construction workers in Singapore and the ways they are imagined and treated by the government, the private industry, and local citizenry. It focuses on how the legal and political frameworks that govern the presence of migrant workers contribute to their continued sequestration from the citizen body. The section opens with a chapter by Brenda Yeoh and her colleagues about the politics of (im)mobility in Singapore. It discusses how migrant men are fixed into place through recruitment procedures, heightened processes of surveillance in dormitories, and the tight organisation of their schedules. The following chapter by Jaclyn Neo then draws back to look at the legal system that separates migrant workers from the citizen body, showing how our current laws cast migrant men as undesirable for inclusion in Singapore's society. The third chapter focuses on Little India. Shona Loong shows how migrant men are transformed into security threats in the way that the Little India district is constructed, surveilled, and policed. Finally, Charanpal S. Bal discusses how migrant men's "deportability" not only enables a "use-and-discard" model to construction labour in Singapore, but also how it might serve as the basis for challenges to the system.

The second section of this volume, "Work Conditions and Health Concerns", focuses attention on the processes of the work itself, revealing the toll that heavy construction labour takes on the body, the difficulties workers face in seeking adequate healthcare, and the varying forms of precarity and unfreedom that shape migrant men's journeys through the construction industry. The first chapter by Mohan J. Dutta looks at how migrant men themselves understand workplace risks and injuries, foregrounding experiences of food insecurity, lack of sleep, and unsafe transportation. Following that, Grace Baey and Brenda Yeoh look at how construction work is made precarious through the compounded risks and vulnerabilities as experienced throughout men's migration journeys, from pre-migration indebtedness to workplace vulnerabilities. The third and final chapter in this section by Jia Wei Ang and colleagues looks at how migrant workers have been inadequately informed about their insurance benefits and access to healthcare, thus creating heightened psychological distress.

The third section of this book, "Social Connections, Personal Lives", delves deeper into migrant workers' social lives, their participation in Singapore's urban landscape as they cultivate their own sense of belonging to communities in Singapore, and their connections to families back home. It opens with a chapter by Tim Bunnell and Laavanya Kathiravelu, which examines South Asian migrant men's perspectives on Singapore's "liveability", revealing that friendship and sociality is crucial to their quality of life. Following this, Arul Chib and

Rajiv G. Aricat affirm the importance of mobile phones in migrant workers' lives, showing how mobile phones allow migrant men to embrace cultural hybridity, remain connected to friends and family, and engage in learning. The third chapter by Junjia Ye focuses on how migrant men express and understand their masculinity in a male-dominated industry; for example, in the gifts that they select to bring home for their fathers and wives when they are on leave from work in Singapore. The final chapter then returns to Bangladeshi migrants' homes: Mohammad Jalal Uddin Sikder and Vaughan Higgins look at how remittances sent by overseas workers are re-invested into the household and contribute to social resilience.

Each chapter in the first three sections of the volume is accompanied by short reflections from the authors that not only summarise the findings, but also provide updates on the research context in view of the recent situation. More importantly, the authors make critical connections of COVID-19 to the particular facet of migrant work and/or previous findings, and consider the implications for as well as impacts of COVID-19 on these migrant workers in Singapore. The authors are unanimous in highlighting the increased precarity of these workers during a pandemic and emphasise the urgent areas for change in order for migration to be a sustainable strategy for both receiving and sending countries.

The final section of this volume, "A Migrant's Eye View", features illustrations by Joy Ho accompanying a poem, "The Death of Wishes", penned by Md. Sharif Uddin. The migrant who works as a supervisor in the construction and tunneling sector had written the poem in Bengali while he was quarantined in his dormitory. By spotlighting the migrant's inner voice, the poem and illustrations provide a fitting conclusion to the volume in shedding light on the experiences and feelings of one group of migrants during this pandemic.

References

Abrar, C. R. and Billah, M. M. (2017). *Challenges of labour recruitment for overseas employment*, ed. Rajan, S. I., "South Asia Migration Report 2017: Recruitment, Remittances and Reintegration" (Routledge, London) pp. 147–163.

Abu Baker, J. (2020, 31 March). COVID-19: Wife of critically ill Bangladeshi man in Singapore gives birth to baby boy, *ChannelNewsAsia*. Retrieved from https://www.channelnewsasia.com/singapore/covid-19-singapore-bangladesh-worker-critical-icu-baby-boy-1326201

Ang, H. M. (2020a, 19 February). Construction at Seletar Aerospace Heights halted since first COVID-19 case reported, *ChannelNewsAsia*. Retrieved from https://www.channelnewsasia.com/news/singapore/covid19-coronavirus-construction-seletar-aerospace-heights-halt-12449426

Ang, H. M. (2020b, 1 June). 70% to 80% of migrant workers in dormitories expected to be COVID-19 free by end-July: Lawrence Wong, *Channel News Asia*. Retrieved from https://www.channelnewsasia.com/news/singapore/covid-19-migrant-workers-cleared-end-july-12870264

Azad, A. (2019). Recruitment of migrant workers in Bangladesh: Elements of human trafficking for labor exploitation, *Journal of Human Trafficking*, Vol. 5, No. 2, pp. 130–150. DOI: 10.1080/23322705.2017.1422091

Baey, G. and Yeoh, B. S. A. (2015). Migration and precarious work: Negotiating debt, employment, and livelihood strategies amongst Bangladeshi migrant men working in Singapore's construction industry, *Migrating out of Poverty Working Paper No. 26*, Available at http://migratingoutofpoverty.dfid.gov.uk/files/file.php?name=wp26-baey-yeoh-2015-migration-and-precarious-work.pdf&site=354

Bal, C. S. (2015). Production politics and migrant labour advocacy in Singapore, *Journal of Contemporary Asia*, Vol. 45, No. 2, pp. 219–242. DOI: 10.1080/00472336.2014.960880

Bélanger, D. and Rahman, M. (2013). Migrating against all the odds: International labour migration of Bangladeshi women, *Current Sociology*, Vol. 61, No. 3, pp. 356–373. DOI: 10.1177/0011392113484453

Cai, W. and Lai, K. K. R. (2020, 28 April). Packed with migrant workers, dormitories fuel coronavirus in Singapore, *The New York Times*. Retrieved from https://www.nytimes.com/interactive/2020/04/28/world/asia/coronavirus-singapore-migrants.html

Chang, A. L. and Khalik, S. (2020, 6 February). Coronavirus: S'pore reports first cases of local transmission; 4 out of 6 new cases did not travel to China, *The Straits Times*. Retrieved from https://www.straitstimes.com/singapore/coronavirus-spore-reports-first-cases-of-local-transmission-4-out-of-6-new-cases-did-not

ChannelNewsAsia. (2020, 28 June). 'A new man': Bangladeshi who was critically ill with COVID-19 discharged from hospital after nearly 5 months,

ChannelNewsAsia. Retrieved from https://www.channelnewsasia.com/news/singapore/covid-19-case-42-bangladeshi-worker-discharged-singapore-12877772

Chew, H. M. (2020, 27 December). Singapore to start Phase 3 of COVID-19 reopening on Dec 28, *ChannelNewsAsia.* Retrieved from https://www.channelnewsasia.com/singapore/phase-3-covid-19-singapore-reopening-dec-28-pm-lee-478461

Chew, H. M. (2021, 15 November). COVID-19 restrictions for migrant workers in dormitories to be further eased, more can make community visits, *ChannelNewsAsia*. Retrieved from https://www.channelnewsasia.com/singapore/covid-19-migrant-workers-community-visits-recreation-centres-2314641

Chew, B. M., Chew, Y. W. and Tai, K. Z. (2018). Ethnic discrimination amongst migrant workers: Evidence from the construction industry in Singapore, *Final Year Project*, Nanyang Technological University. Available at https://dr.ntu.edu.sg//handle/10356/73871

Collins, F. L. and Bayliss, T. (2020). The good migrant: Everyday nationalism and temporary migration management on New Zealand dairy farms, *Political Geography*, Vol. 80. DOI: 10.1016/j.polgeo.2020.102193

Dannecker, P. (2005). Transnational migration and the transformation of gender relations: The case of bangladeshi labour migrants, *Current Sociology*, Vol. 53, No. 4, pp. 655–674. DOI: 10.1177/0011392105052720

Dannecker, P. (2013). Rationalities and images underlying labour migration from Bangladesh to Malaysia, *International Migration*, Vol. 51, No. 1, pp. 40–60. DOI: 10.1111/j.1468-2435.2009.00547.x

Das, N., de Janvry, A., Mahmood, S. and Sadoulet, E. (2014). Migration as a risky enterprise: A diagnostic for Bangladesh, *CUDARE Working Papers,* University of California. Available at https://escholarship.org/uc/item/6574658k

Datta, S. (2017). Bangladeshi Muslim construction workers in Singapore: A study in the process of migration and employment, *Islam Realitas: Journal of Islamic & Social Studies*, Vol. 1, No. 2, pp. 117–127. DOI: 10.30983/islam_realitas.v1i2.47

Debrah, Y. A. and Ofori, G. (2001). Subcontracting, foreign workers and job safety in the Singapore construction industry, *Asia Pacific Business Review*, Vol. 8, No. 1, 145–166. DOI: 10.1080/713999129

Deshingkar, P., Abrar, C. R., Sultana, M. T., Haque, K. N. H. and Reza, M. S. (2019). Producing ideal Bangladeshi migrants for precarious construction work in Qatar, *Journal of Ethnic and Migration Studies*, Vol. 45, No. 14, pp. 2723–2738. DOI: 10.1080/1369183X.2018.1528104

Devaraj, S. (2021, 21 October). Disorder in roll-out of Covid-19 protocols among factors that led to delays at Jalan Tukang dormitory: MWC chairman, *The Straits Times*. Retrieved from https://www.straitstimes.com/singapore/housing/some-disorder-in-rollout-of-covid-19-testing-and-isolation-protocols-at-jalan

Elangovan, N. (2020, 9 April). Covid-19: Record 287 new cases in S'pore, with 202 infections linked to dorms with foreign workers who had visited Mustafa Centre, *Today Online*. Retrieved from https://www.todayonline.com/singapore/covid-19-record-287-new-cases-spore-219-infections-linked-dorms-foreign-workers-who-had-visited

Gee, J. (2020, 11 June). Let's get real: Singapore still needs migrant workers. the spotlight on their work and living conditions offers a chance to reform other related practices, *The Straits Times*. Retrieved from https://www.straitstimes.com/opinion/more-than-dormitory-space-a-chance-for-reform

Goh, T. (2021, 30 August). Migrant workers under lockdown in S'pore had higher symptoms of depression and stress: Yale–NUS study, *The Straits Times*. Retrieved from https://www.straitstimes.com/singapore/health/migrant-workers-under-lockdown-here-had-higher-symptoms-of-depression-and-stress

Hamid, W. (2015). Feelings of home amongst Tamil migrant workers in Singapore's Little India, *Pacific Affairs*, Vol. 88, No. 1, pp. 5–25. DOI: 10.550

Hamid, W. and Tutt, D. (2019). "Thrown away like a banana leaf": Precarity of labour and precarity of place for Tamil migrant construction workers in Singapore, *Construction Management and Economics*, Vol. 37, No. 9, pp. 513–536. DOI: 10.1080/01446193.2019.1595075

Han, K. (2018, 25 February). Singapore's migrant workers struggle to get paid, *CNN*. Retrieved from https://www.cnn.com/2018/02/24/asia/singapore-migrant-workers-intl/index.html

Han, K. (2020, 16 April). Singapore's new Covid-19 cases reveal the country's two very different realities, *The Washington Post*. Retrieved from https://www.washingtonpost.com/opinions/2020/04/16/singapores-new-covid-19-cases-reveal-countrys-two-very-different-realities/

Harrigan, N. M., Koh, C. Y. and Amirrudin, A. (2017). Threat of deportation as proximal social determinant of mental health amongst migrant workers,

Journal of Immigrant and Minority Health, Vol. 19, No. 3, pp. 511–522. DOI: 10.1007/s10903-016-0532-x

International Organization for Migration. (2020a). *World Migration Report 2020*, United Nations. Retrieved from https://publications.iom.int/system/files/pdf/wmr_2020.pdf

International Organization for Migration. (2020b). *Migration, Family Remittances, Assets and Skills Categories in Bangladesh*, United Nations. Retrieved from https://publications.iom.int/books/migration-family-remittances-assets-and-skills-categories-bangladesh

International Organization for Migration. (2020c). *Combatting xenophobia is key to an effective COVID-19 recovery*, United Nations. Retrieved from https://www.iom.int/news/combatting-xenophobia-key-effective-covid-19-recovery

Jureidini, R. (2016). Ways forward in recruitment of 'low-skilled' migrant workers in the Asia-Arab states corridor*: ILO white paper*, International Labour Organization. Retrieved from https://www.ilo.org/wcmsp5/groups/public/---arabstates/---ro-beirut/documents/publication/wcms_519913.pdf

Kamil, A. (2020, 1 June). 51-year-old Chinese national is first migrant worker in Singapore to die from Covid-19, *Today*. Retrieved from https://www.todayonline.com/singapore/51-year-old-chinese-national-spores-24th-covid-19-death-3-new-clusters-identified

Kathiravelu, L. (2020). *Bodies that don't matter but labor that does: The low-wage male migrant in Singapore and Dubai*, eds. Boero, N. B and Mason, K, "The Oxford Handbook of the Sociology of Body and Embodiment," (Oxford University Press) pp. 345–360.

Koh, W. T. (2020, 5 July). GE2020 not about individual, residents know COVID-19 a curveball': Manpower Minister Josephine Teo, *Yahoo News Singapore*. Retrieved from https://sg.news.yahoo.com/amphtml/ge-2020-not-about-ndividual-residents-know-covid-19-a-curveball-manpower-minister-josephine-teo-005942474.html

Kok, X. and Jaipragas, B. (2020, 14 April). Coronavirus: Singapore migrant worker dormitories still hot topic as Covid-19 cases rise, *South China Morning Post*. Retrieved from https://www.scmp.com/week-asia/health-environment/article/3079675/coronavirus-singapore-migrant-worker-dormitories-still

Kok, Y. (2021, 9 September). Up to 500 vaccinated migrant workers in S'pore allowed into community each week as part of pilot programme, *The Straits Times*. Retrieved from https://www.straitstimes.com/singapore/health/

up-to-500-vaccinated-migrant-workers-allowed-to-visit-community-each-week-as-part

Kornatowksi, G. (2017). Caught up in policy gaps: Distressed communities of South-Asian migrant workers in Little India, Singapore, *Community Development Journal*, Vol. 52, No. 1, pp. 92–106. DOI: 10.1093/cdj/bsw051

Kumar, B. (2019). The impact of international remittances on poverty alleviation in Bangladesh, *Remittances Review*, Vol. 4, No. 1, pp. 67–86.

Lai, L. (2020, 7 June). Covid-19 will remain a problem for a long time yet, everyone has to adjust the way we live, work and play: PM Lee, *The Straits Times*. Retrieved from https://www.straitstimes.com/politics/covid-19-will-remain-a-problem-for-a-long-time-yet-everyone-has-to-adjust-the-way-we-live

Lee, H. L. (2020a, 12 March). PM Lee Hsien Loong's remarks in English, Chinese and Malay, as well as translated into Tamil, on the Coronavirus disease 2019 (COVID-19) situation in Singapore, delivered on 12 March 2020, *Prime Minister's Office Singapore*. Retrieved from https://www.pmo.gov.sg/Newsroom/PM-Lee-remarks-COVID-19-Outbreak-12-Mar-2020

Lee, H. L. (2020b, 10 April). PM Lee Hsien Loong's remarks in English, Chinese and Malay on the Coronavirus disease 2019 (COVID-19) situation in Singapore, delivered on 10 April 2020, *Prime Minister's Office Singapore*. Retrieved from https://www.pmo.gov.sg/Newsroom/PM-Lee-Hsien-Loong-on-the-COVID-19-situation-in-Singapore-on-10-April-2020

Leung, H. (2020a, 20 April). Why Singapore, once a model for Coronavirus response, lost control of its outbreak, *Time*, April 20. Retrieved from https://time.com/5824039/singapore-outbreak-migrant-workers/

Leung, H. (2020b, 29 April). Singapore was a Coronavirus success story — until an outbreak showed how vulnerable workers can fall through the cracks, *Time*. Retrieved from https://time.com/5825261/singapore-coronavirus-migrant-workers-inequality/

Lian, K. F. and Rahman, M. M. (2006). International labour recruitment: Channelling Bangladeshi labour to East and South-East Asia, *Asian Pacific Population Journal*, Vol. 21, No. pp. 85–107.

Lim, J. (2021, 17 May). Allow foreign workers into S'pore in safe and controlled manner, say construction firms, *The Straits Times*. Retrieved from https://www.straitstimes.com/business/economy/construction-industry-makes-appeal-to-allow-foreign-workers-into-singapore-in-safe

Lim, M. Z. (2020, 12 April). Coronavirus: 2 floating accommodation at Tanjong Pagar Terminal to house foreign workers, *The Straits Times*. Retrieved from https://www.straitstimes.com/singapore/coronavirus-2-floating-accommodation-at-tanjong-pagar-terminal-to-house-foreign-workers

Lim, M. Z. (2021, 11 May). 1,200 travellers daily at Changi in March, but number of new workers still insufficient: Lawrence Wong, *The Straits Times.* Retrieved from https://www.straitstimes.com/singapore/politics/1200-travellers-daily-at-changi-airport-in-march-but-workers-still-insufficient

Lin, C. (2020, 20 April). COVID-19: Residents in Taman Jurong moved to hotels as migrant workers relocate onto vacant units, *ChannelNewsAsia*, [Video]. Retrieved from https://www.channelnewsasia.com/news/singapore/covid-19-residents-in-taman-jurong-moved-to-hotels-as-migrant-12660062

Lin, W. and Yeoh, B. S. A. (2020). Pathological (Im)mobilities: managing risk in a time of pandemics, *Mobilities,* Vol. 16, No. 1, pp. 96–112. DOI: 10.1080/17450101.2020.1862454

Loong, S. (2020, 5 May). Who is responsible for Singapore's migrant workers, and why does it matter?, *Academia.Sg*. Retrieved from https://www.academia.sg/academic-views/who-is-responsible-for-singapores-migrant-workers-and-why-does-it-matter/

Ministry of Manpower. (2019, 3 May). *Work Permit conditions*. Retrieved from http://www.mom.gov.sg/passes-and-permits/work-permit-for-foreign-worker/sector-specific-rules/work-permit-conditions

Ministry of Manpower. (2021a). *Foreign Workforce numbers.* Retrieved from https://www.mom.gov.sg/documents-and-publications/foreign-workforce-numbers

Ministry of Manpower. (2021b, 12 January). *Construction sector: Work Permit requirements*. Retrieved from https://www.mom.gov.sg/passes-and-permits/work-permit-for-foreign-worker/sector-specific-rules/construction-sector-requirements

Mokhtar, F. (2020, 22 April). How Singapore flipped from virus hero to cautionary tale, *Bloomberg*. Retrieved from https://www.bloomberg.com/news/articles/2020-04-21/how-singapore-flipped-from-virus-hero-to-cautionary-tale

Moniruzzaman, M. (2020). The Impact of remittances on household food security: Evidence from a survey in Bangladesh, *Migration and Development*, pp. 1–20. DOI: 10.1080/21632324.2020.1787097

Moniruzzaman, M. and Walton-Roberts, M. (2018). Migration, debt and resource backwash: How sustainable is Bangladesh-Gulf circular migration?, *Migration and Development*, Vol. 7, No. 1, pp. 85–103. DOI: 10.1080/21632324.2017.1358799

Ng, C. (2020a, 30 April). Coronavirus: Fake news used to stir up unhappiness in dorms, says Shanmugam, *The Straits Times*. Retrieved from https://www.straitstimes.com/singapore/shanmugam-fake-news-used-to-stir-up-unhappiness-in-dorms

Ng, C. (2020b, 20 December). Calls to ease restrictions on migrant workers amid S'pore's Phase 3 miss larger issues: Tan See Leng, *The Straits Times*. Retrieved from https://www.straitstimes.com/singapore/calls-for-easing-of-restrictions-on-migrant-workers-miss-larger-issues-tan-see-leng

Organization for Economic Co-operation and Development (OECD) (2020, 20 May). Supporting livelihoods during the COVID-19 crisis: Closing the gaps in safety nets. Retrieved from https://read.oecd-ilibrary.org/view/?ref=132_132985-hrr3dbjimj&title=Supportinglivelihoods-during-the-COVID-19_crisis%20oe.cd/il/30z.

Ong, F. C. M. and Yeoh, B. S. A. (2012). *The place of migrant workers in Singapore: between state multiracialism and everyday (un)cosmopolitanisms*, eds. Lai, A. E., Collins, F. L. and Yeoh, B. S. A., "Migration and Diversity in Asian Contexts," (ISEAS-Yusof Ishak Institute) pp. 83–106.

Paul, R. and Geddie, J. (2020, 6 April). Migrant workers fear massive Singapore dormitory lockdown is Coronavirus time bomb, *Reuters*. Retrieved from https://www.reuters.com/article/us-health-coronavirus-singapore-migrants/migrant-workers-fear-massive-singapore-dormitory-lockdown-is-coronavirus-time-bomb-idUSKBN21O138

Pazos, R. and Adeline, S. (2021). Tracking Singapore's Covid-19 vaccination progress [Last updated November 15]. Retrieved from https://www.straitstimes.com/multimedia/graphics/2021/06/singapore-covid-vaccination-tracker/index.html?shell

Phua, R. (2020, 1 June). COVID-19: Singapore to build new dormitories with improved living standards for migrant workers, *ChannelNewsAsia*. Retrieved from https://www.channelnewsasia.com/news/singapore/covid-19-singapore-new-dormitories-foreign-workers-conditions-12792538

Platt, M., Baey, G., Yeoh, B. S. A., Khoo, C. Y. and Lam, T. (2017). Debt, precarity and gender: Male and female temporary labour migrants in Singapore, *Journal of Ethnic and Migration Studies*, Vol. 43, No. 1, pp. 119–136. DOI: 10.1080/1369183X.2016.1218756

Ratcliffe, R. (2020, 17 April). Singapore's cramped migrant worker dorms hide Covid-19 surge risk, *The Guardian*. Retrieved from https://www.theguardian.com/world/2020/apr/17/singapores-cramped-migrant-worker-dorms-hide-covid-19-surge-risk

Rahman, M. M. (2011). Emigration and the family economy: Bangladeshi labor migration to Saudi Arabia, *Asian and Pacific Migration Journal*, Vol. 20, No. 3–4, pp. 389–411. DOI: 10.1177/011719681102000307

Rahman, M. M. (2012). Bangladeshi labour migration to the Gulf states: Patterns of recruitment and processes, *Canadian Journal of Development Studies*, Vol. 33, No. 2, pp. 214–230. DOI: 10.1080/02255189.2012.689612

Rahman, M. M. (2017). *Bangladeshi Migration to Singapore: A Process-Oriented Approach* (Springer, Singapore).

Rao, N. (2012). Breadwinners and homemakers: migration and changing conjugal expectations in rural Bangladesh, *The Journal of Development Studies*, Vol. 48, No. 1, pp. 26–40. DOI: 10.1080/00220388.2011.629648

Rao, N. (2014). Migration, mobility and changing power relations: Aspirations and praxis of Bangladeshi migrants, *Gender, Place & Culture*, Vol. 21, No. 7, pp. 872–887. DOI: 10.1080/0966369X.2013.810600

Sadarangani, S. P., Lim, P. L. and Vasoo, S. (2017). Infectious diseases and migrant worker health in Singapore: A receiving country's perspective, *Journal of Travel Medicine*, Vol. 24, No. 4. DOI: 10.1093/jtm/tax014

Saw, Y. E., Tan, E. Y., Buvanaswari, P., Doshi, K. and Liu, J. C. (2021). Mental health of international migrant workers amidst large-scale dormitory outbreaks of COVID-19: A population survey in Singapore, *Journal of Migration and Health*, Vol. 4. DOI:10.1016/j.jmh.2021.100062

Siddiqui, T. (2010). Recruitment cost in Bangladesh: Challenges of governing migration in the countries of origin, *Working Paper Series No. 25*, Refugee and Migratory Movements Research Unit. Available at http://www.rmmru.org/newsite/wp-content/uploads/2013/07/workingpaper25.pdf

Siddiqui, T. (2019). Labour migration from Bangladesh 2019: Achievements and challenges, *Migration Trends Reports*, Refugee and Migratory Movements Research Unit. Available at: http://www.rmmru.org/newsite/wp-content/uploads/2021/01/Trends-Report-2019.pdf

Sikder, M. J. U. and Higgins, V. (2017). Remittances and social resilience of migrant households in rural Bangladesh, *Migration and Development*, Vol. 6, No. 2 pp. 253–275. DOI: 10.1080/21632324.2016.1142752

Sim, M. and Quek, C. (2008, 7 September). Dorm not near but problems 'next door', *The Straits Times*. Retrieved from https://www.asiaone.com/News/AsiaOne%2BNews/Singapore/Story/A1Story20080906-86231.html

Sørensen, N. N. and Gammeltoft-Hansen, T. eds. (2012). *The Migration Industry and The Commercialization of International Migration*. (Routledge).

Tan, T. M. and Zhuo, T. (2020, 6 Aug). Steps to ease movement curbs, boost well-being of migrant workers in the works: MOM, *The Straits Times*. Retrieved from https://www.straitstimes.com/singapore/steps-to-ease-movement-curbs-boost-well-being

Tay, D. (2009, 7 December). Serangoon dorm opens, fuss-free, *AsiaOne*. Retrieved from https://www.asiaone.com/News/AsiaOne+News/Singapore/Story/A1Story20091207-184340.html

Teo, J. (2020, 4 May). Ministerial Statement by Mrs Josephine Teo, Minister for Manpower, 4 May 2020, *Ministry of Manpower*. Retrieved from https://www.mom.gov.sg/newsroom/parliament-questions-and-replies/2020/0504-ministerial-statement-by-mrs-josephine-teo-minister-for-manpower-4-may-2020

Toh, T. W. (2020, 6 August). Majority of foreign workers back to work by end-August but Covid-19 cases to fluctuate in next two weeks, *The Straits Times*. Retrieved from https://www.straitstimes.com/singapore/coronavirus-majority-of-foreign-workers-back-to-work-by-end-august-but-cases-to-fluctuate

Transient Workers Count Too. (2014, 2 November). Singapore second most popular destination for Bangladeshi workers in 2013, *TWC2*. Retrieved from https://twc2.org.sg/2014/11/02/singapore-second-most-popular-destination-for-bangladeshi-workers-in-2013/

Transient Workers Count Too. (2020, 3 April). Covid-19: The risks from packing them in, *TWC2*. Retrieved from http://twc2.org.sg/2020/04/03/covid-19-the-risks-from-packing-them-in/

Ungku, F. and Paul, R. (2017, 20 June). Singaporean dream sours for some Bangladeshi workers as they go home with big debts, *Reuters*. Retrieved from https://www.reuters.com/article/us-singapore-migrants-jobs-idUSKBN19A320

Wise, A. (2013). Pyramid subcontracting and moral detachment: Down-sourcing risk and responsibility in the management of transnational labour in Asia, *The Economic and Labour Relations Review*, Vol. 24, No. 3, pp. 433–455. DOI: 10.1177/1035304613498027

Wong, L. (2020a, 4 May). Ministerial Statement by Mr Lawrence Wong, Co-Chair of the Multi-Ministry Taskforce on COVID-19, on 'Second Update on Whole-of-Government Response to COVID-19', *SG Press Centre*. Retrieved from https://www.sgpc.gov.sg/sgpcmedia/media_releases/mnd/speech/S-20200504-1/attachment/Delivered%20Ministerial% 20Statement%20by%20Mr%20Lawrence%20Wong%20on%204%20May%202020%20final.pdf

Wong, L. (2020b, 9 April). Remarks by Minister Lawrence Wong, Co-Chair of the Multi-Ministry Taskforce on COVID-19, at Press Conference on COVID-19 at National Press Centre on 9 April 2020, *SG Press Centre*. Retrieved from https://www.sgpc.gov.sg/sgpcmedia/media_releases/mnd/speech/S-20200409-1/attachment/Remarks%20by%20Minister%20Lawrence%20Wong%20at%209%20Apr%20Press%20Conference%20on%20COVID-19%20final.pdf

Ye, J. (2013). *Migrant landscapes: A spatial analysis of male South Asian male migrants in Singapore*, eds. Ho, E. L.-E., Woon, C. Y. and Ramdas, K., "Changing Landscapes of Singapore: Old Tensions, New Discoveries," (NUS Press) pp. 142–157.

Yea, S. and Chok, S. (2018). Unfreedom unbound: Developing a cumulative approach to understanding unfree labour in Singapore, *Work, Employment and Society*, Vol. 32, No. 5, pp. 925–941. DOI: 10.1177/0950017017738956

Yeoh, B. S. A. (2006). Bifurcated labour: The unequal incorporation of transmigrants in Singapore, *Tijdschrift Voor Economische En Sociale Geografie*, Vol. 97, No. 1, pp. 26–37. DOI: 10.1111/j.1467-9663.2006.00493.x

Yeoh, B. S. A. (2020). Temporary migration regimes and their sustainability in times of COVID-19, *International Organization for Migration (IOM)*, Geneva. Retrieved from https://publications.iom.int/books/covid-19-and-transformation-migration-and-mobility-globally-temporary-migration-regimes-and

Section I

A Regime of Temporary Migration

Chapter 1a

Migrant Workers and the Politics of (Im)Mobility*

Brenda S. A. Yeoh

Asia Research Institute
National University of Singapore

Grace Baey

Independent scholar

Maria Platt

Australia-Indonesia Centre
Monash University

Kellynn Wee

Asia Research Institute
National University of Singapore

The typical image of a migrant construction worker in Singapore is that of a male foreign labourer strapped by a harness, immobilised in precarious positions atop a half-completed high-rise building. In this 2017 article, we

---

* Reflections on Yeoh, B. S. A., Baey, G., Platt, M. and Wee, K. (2017). Bangladeshi construction workers and the politics of (im)mobility in Singapore, *City*, Vol. 21, No. 5, pp. 641–649. DOI:10.1080/13604813.2017.1374786.

use this as a starting point for examining the migration trajectories and employment conditions of Bangladeshi construction workers in Singapore, and to explore the politics of (im)mobility in the city-state's labour migration regime.

We showed how these workers are bound to a cycle of indebtedness and transience governed by short-term contracts, with few opportunities of upward mobility and many barriers against integration into host society. Housed in migrant dormitories, they are socially and spatially segregated from the local population. As low-waged workers performing 3D (dirty, dangerous, and demeaning) work, they wrestle with movement restrictions, job immobility, and constant surveillance. The city-state's migration regime sets socio-legal exclusions that ensure their temporary status, and as a consequence, they inhabit the city as transient subjects expected to labour but not stay. While foreigners such as permanent residents and skilled professionals are granted a range of benefits and privileges, low-waged migrant workers are considered temporary, and are excluded from social safety nets and pathways towards longer-term residency.

Amid the COVID-19 crisis, a different set of images associated with migrant workers circulated in online and news media. Photos of migrant dormitories appeared in news articles and media reports that covered the rise of contagion in these accommodations, which drew public alarm. Singapore's initial success in mitigating the spread of the virus faltered as clusters of infections broke out in dormitories, which commonly house male migrant workers in the construction and shipyard industries, mostly from South Asia. The outbreak prompted immediate containment measures that placed migrant workers under extended quarantine, in which they were prohibited from leaving their accommodation and frequenting public places including migrant enclaves such as Little India.

While intended to control the outbreak, the response measures further immobilised the workers — many who were confined to the dormitories suffered from prolonged isolation, faced mental health issues, and worried over the uncertainty of their jobs and their support for their families. The pandemic response had 'bifurcated' into separate approaches for the local community and for the migrant workers, especially those residing in dormitories [Lin and Yeoh, 2021; Ye, 2021]. Dormitory residents were subjected to regulations and surveillance that further restricted their movements. For some workers, living in the dormitory felt like 'being in jail' [Elangovan, 2021]. As COVID-19 measures eased with a fall in cases within the local community, the restrictions on migrant workers' movements continued, prompting questions about prolonged containment and long-term consequences.

The manner in which migrant dormitories became the epicentre of the COVID-19 pandemic in Singapore does not just signal the limitations of Singapore's pandemic response, or the need for better dormitory management and housing standards. It is also a stark reminder of the downside of a migration regime that compounds low-wage migrant workers' vulnerability as a segregated population and as disposable labour. The arguments we raised in 2017 continue to hold salience for the present in a world upended by a global health crisis that renders both migrants and citizens vulnerable. The outbreak in migrant dormitories is a cautionary tale of the potential consequences of a migration regime that differentially excludes migrant workers, placing them at the margins of society where they are governed by a different set of regulations that would be unacceptable if applied to the local population. Drawing lessons from the COVID-19 pandemic to effect progressive change in migration policy and governance will not only safeguard the city-state against future pandemics, but will go some way in creating a more inclusive society respectful of all those who labour to build its past, present, and future.

References

Elangovan, N. (2021, 29 March). The Big Read: A year after the first COVID-19 outbreak in dorms, how has life changed for foreign workers? *CNA*. Retrieved from https://www.channelnewsasia.com/news/singapore/the-big-read-covid-19-outbreak-dormitories-foreign-workers-14504974

Lin, W. and Yeoh, B. S. A. (2021). Pathological (im)mobilities: Managing risk in a time of pandemics, *Mobilities*, Vo. 16, No. 1, pp. 96–112. DOI: 10.1080/17450101.2020.1862454

Ye, J. (2021). Ordering diversity: Co-producing the pandemic and the migrant in Singapore during COVID-19, *Antipode*, Vol. 53, No. 6, pp. 1895–1920. DOI: 10.1111/anti.12740

Chapter 1b

Bangladeshi Construction Workers and the Politics of (Im)Mobility in Singapore*

Brenda S. A. Yeoh, Grace Baey, Maria Platt and Kellynn Wee

The most iconic image of the foreign construction worker in Singapore's popular imagination is a figure perilously secured by safety harnesses atop a half completed high-rise building. However, we argue that an understanding of the labour process involved in fashioning the migrant worker is predicated on a more expansive understanding of the politics of (im) mobility. In other words, the labour process is not simply secured in the workplace of the construction site but is linked to the politics of mobility and immobility across different spaces in the host nation-state and beyond. Drawing on a mixed-methods study of Bangladeshi construction workers in Singapore, we discuss three interrelated themes: (a) the time-structuring mechanisms of the migration regime; (b) spaces of enclavement, exception, and enclosure; and (c) the governing of time discipline.

Keywords: migrant construction workers, mobilities, temporality, materiality, enclave, transnational labour migration, global cities

---

*This article was originally published in *City*, Vol. 21, No. 5, pp. 641–649. DOI:10.1080/13604813.2017.1374786.

Introduction

In the last half-century, Singapore has undergone rapid infrastructure development in its attempts to position itself as a global city (Goh 2001). As part of Singapore's self-proclaimed rise from 'third world to first', construction projects have become a ubiquitous part of the skyline. Given this context, the image of the foreign construction worker as perilously immobilised in safety harnesses atop a half-completed high-rise building resonates in Singapore's popular imagination — so much so that this image was immortalised through an advertising campaign jointly helmed by Coca-Cola and the Singapore Kindness Movement. Commercials featured 'Coke-drones' which delivered thank-you notes from the Singapore public, tied to cans of Coke, to express gratitude to men who are otherwise rendered invisible (and immobile) by their work aloft partially built skyscrapers.

As a site of mega-construction, Singapore relies heavily upon a foreign labour force to ensure the rapid development of projects. To this end, more than a third of Singapore's total workforce consists of non-citizens, the bulk of whom are low-waged transient workers employed in the construction, marine, manufacturing, and paid domestic sectors (Ministry of Manpower 2016). In the construction industry alone, 65.6 per cent of employees (totalling 326,700) are non-citizens, and Bangladeshis are thought to make up around a third of Singapore's construction workers.

In this paper, we argue that (im)mobilising these workers in the construction of the city goes beyond place-specific sites. Instead, we aim to show that, while construction is usually associated with the materialities of place, the labour process is not simply secured in the workplace but is linked to the politics of mobility and immobility across different spaces: a politics that both reflects but also reorders the exclusionary dynamics of urban citizenship. Mobility is a concept that ranges across different scales: from micro-mobilities at specific sites, to mobilities across the spaces of the national geobody, and movements beyond the nation-state in the form of transnational labour migration. Yet, mobility need not be aligned across scales: the transnationally mobile low-skilled worker may experience conditions of intermittent or protracted immobility at the workplace, giving rise to what Yeoh and Huang (2010) call the 'mobile-but-not-free' worker. Following a brief review of the literature on the politics of (im)mobility and methodology, we draw on cases of Bangladeshi construction workers in Singapore to discuss three interrelated themes: (a) the time-structuring mechanisms of the migration regime in ensuring transient workers; (b) spaces of enclavement, exception, and enclosure; and (c) the governing of time to create productive workers. In conclusion, we contend that training our analytical lenses on construction labour is foundational to unpacking a labour migration regime predicated on regulating the mobility of low-cost workers from less-developed economies in a high-paced industry geared to producing the ever-changing built form of the city. In turn, the spaces of construction — which includes not just worksites but also workers' dormitories, social spaces, and transit routes — provide material testimony to the unequal incorporation of labouring bodies into globalising cities.

The Labour Process and the Politics of (Im)Mobility

The 'mobility turn' views mobility as the 'central fact' of postmodern life (Cresswell 2010, 551), with the politics of mobility coming to the fore in discussions regarding the concept. Historically, while studies of migration, transport, tourism, and time have examined movement, the 'mobilities' approach brings together various forms of movement across scales and disciplines (Cresswell 2006). The 'mobilities' paradigm thus focuses scholars' analytical lens on the fact of movement rather than taking movement as a given, or emphasising space and time at the expense of movement (Cresswell 2010). Scholars recognise that mobility is a resource that hinges upon unequal power relations and hence is differentially accessed. As such, 'there are new places and technologies that enhance the mobility of some peoples and places *even as they also* heighten the immobility of others' (Hannam, Sheller, and Urry 2006, 3). While there is a temptation to replace 'a world of fixities' with the notion of a mobile world (Cresswell 2010, 29), mobility and immobility have a relationship of dialectic *relationality*. As Adey (2006, 87) writes: 'mobilities rely upon moorings, or … immobilities, in order to move, and, vice-versa, relative immobilities and fixities may generate mobilities in order to support their relatively immobile character'. Consequently, any discussion of the politics of mobility must also take into account 'the politics of obduracy, fixity and friction' (Cresswell 2010, 29).

While much of the literature focuses on spatial governance, the experience of temporality for migrant workers on time-bound contracts is equally salient when discussing construction work in Asia. Griffiths, Rogers, and Anderson (2013) write that themes of temporality and migration within existing literature have tended to cluster around two poles. The first pole foregrounds how states govern through temporal frameworks such as visas, censuses, and contracts. States nationalise times, set tempos and schedules for bureaucratic procedures, and create conditions in which migrants have a fraught experience of time. Time, Thompson (1967, 61) writes, becomes a measure whereby 'those who are employed experience a distinction between their employer's time and their "own" time', and becomes a resource for employers who aim to maximise the use of their employees' labour.

The second pole mentioned by Griffiths, Rogers, and Anderson (2013) centralises migrant subjectivity, circling around themes of how time influences feelings of inclusion, exclusion, belonging, and uncertainty. The experience of *waiting*, an experience inherent to the processes and governance of migration and mobilities, has been theorised as 'actively produced, embodied, experienced, politicised and resisted across a range of migrant spaces ... waiting [is] a distinct spatial and temporal dimension of stasis for migrants, as a dynamic effect of international geographies and a lived facet of social structures' (Conlon 2011, 353). Bastia and McGrath (2011) challenge the notion of time being used only in a disciplinary sense. Instead, they emphasise that it is often migrants' aspirations for the future that allow them to tolerate exploitative and humiliating conditions of work, while also giving rise to strategies that help resist and resolve these conditions.

While many typologies of temporalities have been suggested (see e.g. Cwerner 2001), Griffiths, Rogers, and Anderson's (2013) and Cresswell's (2010) conceptualisations work across spatial and temporal mobilities by harnessing ideas of *tempo, synchronicity, flow, velocity*, and *rhythm*, notions that suggest a simultaneous experience of movement and of time. By focusing on Bangladeshi construction workers in Singapore, we add to this literature by showing that, while construction workers' temporalities and mobilities are governed and produced across scales ranging from the body to the geobody, there are ways in which workers are also able to navigate the temporal and spatial scaffolding that structures life and labour.

Methods

Our mixed-methods study used bilingual questionnaires (*n* = 205) and semi-structured interviews (*n* = 30). Between January and May 2014, the quantitative survey was conducted at 11 key sites spread across Singapore. Sampling sites included areas where Bangladeshi migrant workers tended to congregate at weekends (i.e. Farrer Park MRT [Mass Rapid Transit] station [within the Little India enclave] and Boon Lay MRT station), migrant worker dormitories, a restaurant along Rowell Road in Little India where a migrant worker organisation runs a free meal programme, a safety training school for workers, as well as areas close to major construction sites.

Survey respondents were recruited through a mix of stratified and snowball sampling techniques, taking into account the workers' type of visa (i.e. Work Permit, S Pass, or Special Pass holder[1]); marital status (and number of dependents); and type of employer (i.e. labour supply company, subcontractor, or main contractor). The survey identified important trends that were pursued in follow-up interviews with a sub-sample of 30 respondents. Interviews were usually conducted in pairs, with one person leading the conversation and another taking notes. Each interview lasted approximately between one and one-and-a-half hours.

Our overall sample of 205 respondents consisted of 149 Work Permit holders (72.7 per cent), 52 Special Pass holders (25.4 per cent), and four S Pass holders (two per cent; see Figure 1).[2] The majority (56.1 per cent) of the workers were employed by subcontracting firms, 30.2 per cent by a

[1] Special Passes are issued by the Ministry of Manpower to foreign workers who are undergoing salary/employment disputes and/or medical treatment stemming from workplace injuries. These processes allow workers to stay legally in Singapore whilst their cases are being processed and investigated by the Ministry. The majority of them are not allowed to work, except for those who have applied to be on the Temporary Job Scheme.

[2] These percentages do not correspond to actual proportions within the migrant worker population in Singapore, where the numbers of Special Pass holders are much smaller. The decision to recruit more Special Pass holders stemmed from the need to have a sizable population within the sample for data comparison with respondents on other visa passes, given that the focus of our study was on issues of debt and precarity.

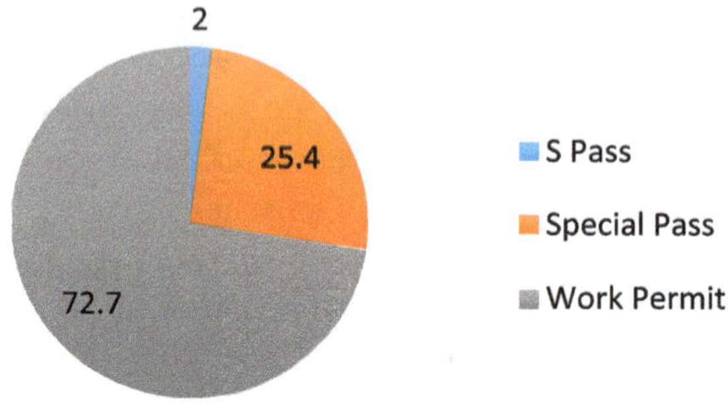

Figure 1 Type of visa (n = 205).

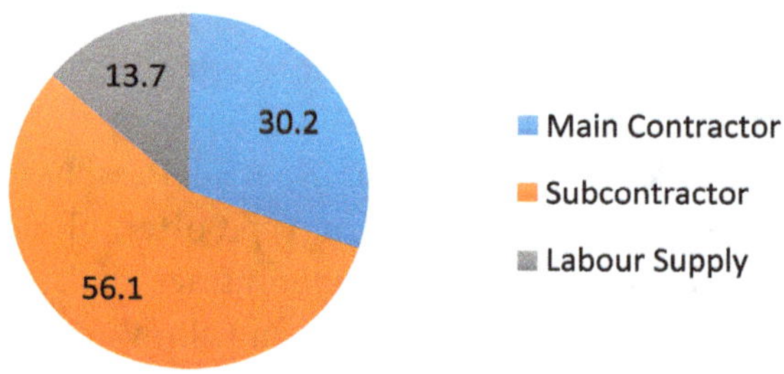

Figure 2 Type of employer (n = 205).

main contractor, and 13.7 per cent with 'labour-only' subcontractors (Figure 2). Less than half (43.4 per cent) of the workers were on their first overseas migration stint (i.e. working with their first employer), whilst 56.6 per cent had either worked for at least two employers in Singapore or had prior overseas work experience in other countries. All were male, as only men of particular nationalities may be recruited as foreign construction workers in Singapore. The majority were young men, the largest group being aged between 26 and 30 years (35.1 per cent), followed by those aged between 23 and 25 years (21.5 per cent) (Figure 3). Just under half (46.3 per cent) had higher secondary education, while the next largest group (29.8 per cent) had secondary education (Figure 4). The majority were single (59 per cent) and among those who were married 31.2 per cent had at least one child.

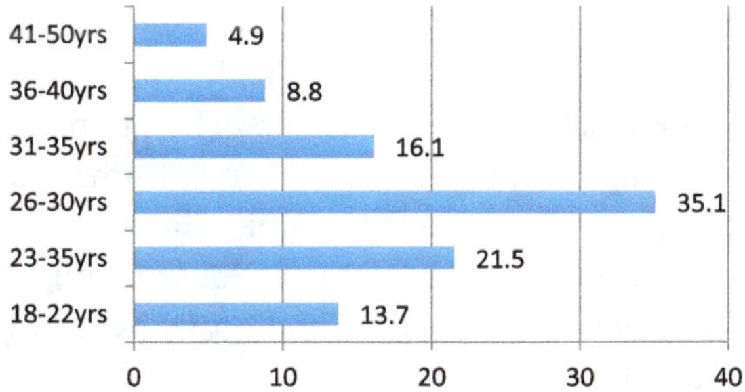

Figure 3 Age (n = 205).

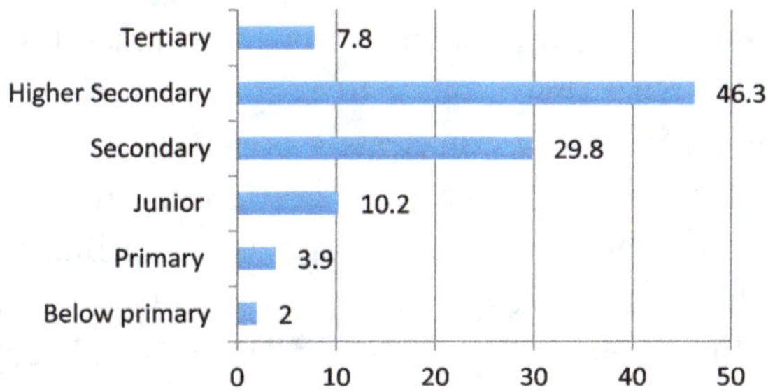

Figure 4 Highest level of education (n = 205).

Time-Structuring Migration to Ensure Transient Workers

Recruited under Singapore's temporary contract labour migration regime, Bangladeshi nationals are required to leave their families behind and enter the country as Work Permit holders with little or no opportunity of gaining formal citizenship. Work Permit holders are subjected to a host of stringent policy and bio-policing measures designed to facilitate the cheap extraction of their labour, which ensure that they remain a transient (and disposable) workforce that can be repatriated in periods of economic downturn (Yeoh 2006). Under the Work Permit system, workers are issued with one- or two-year renewable contracts tied to a specific employer and occupational sector.

As a regime of power, temporary contract migration draws on revolving-door policies and individualising strategies in order to secure the geobody of the nation-state against outsiders who are perceived as likely to become a social burden. Built-in transience is further compounded by the migration industry's role in moving people across nation-states, where business is predicated on increasing transnational mobility (i.e. constant bidirectional movement between home and host), as seen in the account of Kamal (26 years old).

Kamal made the decision to stop his studies in university after a year, as he felt that 'the best way is to go abroad and earn some money'. In his words, 'if I can get into a good company, I can earn [a lot of] money and get a better life'. In this sense, Kamal's aspirations to become a modern subject are very much aligned with Singapore's quest to become a global city. Ironically, these aspirations for the city are intricately bound up with the architectural styles and symbols that its buildings create (Goh 2001) — buildings that individuals such as Kamal help to construct. To facilitate Kamal's first migration stint, he paid an unexpectedly high placement fee of S$6540, as 'the price of the Singapore dollar went up' when he had already signed up at a training centre. After a year was up, his first employer did not renew his contract, and Kamal returned to Bangladesh. He then secured his second contract through a friend working in a Singapore company, but 'to join the company, you must [pay] S$2000. He paid to the boss.' Again, his contract was not renewed with the second employer, and he had to go through an agent in Bangladesh to find a third employer — this time paying S$4200. While his original plan was to work in Singapore for five or at most seven years before returning to Bangladesh to start a business, he found his timeline receding: after working in Singapore for six years, he had to admit that 'I don't think I've saved up enough to start a business in Bangladesh. So I am planning to work for two or three more years to save up and then go back'.

In other words, short contracts characteristic of the construction industry, coupled with the uncertainty of contract renewals, fashion transnational mobility into a form of prolonged back-and-forth migration of the ever-transient, forever-unmoored figure. Migration governance through time-structuring mechanisms has the effect of speeding up transnational mobilities over considerable space, and this further feeds into a burgeoning industry where 'constant churn' makes for a profitable business from recurrent placement fees. The ability of migrants to make long-term plans thus sits at odds with timeframes that structure the construction industry, which are predicated on notions of efficiency and productivity. The emphasis on the timely completion of projects results in distinct time pressures for workers (Dutta 2017), both on the job and in a broader temporal sense.

Constraining Spatial Mobilities in the Host Nation-State to Produce Compliant Workers

While generally confined to worksites during weekdays, low-skilled migrant workers feature most visibly in the Singapore landscape in the form of strongly ethnicised 'weekend enclaves'. Migrant workers congregate temporarily in places such as Little India. Such gatherings are often viewed negatively or with unease by Singaporeans who consider them a form of 'intrusion' into 'their own backyards'. Unease has translated in requests for authorities to step up security measures in these places; the installation of steel barricades around public housing blocks to keep foreign workers out; and petitions to protest the construction of a foreign worker dormitory, regarded as a 'disamenity', in the middle-class housing area of Serangoon Gardens. The state eventually compromised by relocating the entrance of the dormitory to another street and housing mainly Malaysian and Chinese workers (male and female) from the manufacturing and service industries instead of foreign workers from the construction sector (who are male and mainly of South Asian origin). This prompted the observation that while the 'Serangoon Gardens saga' is as much a class issue as it is a racial one, a 'veiled racism' is clearly at work in shaping the spatial politics of exclusion in the city. These voices reflect a 'use-and-discard' sentiment among the general population who want foreign workers to do the work that citizens shun, but at the same time wish that these workers could be erased from the landscape (Ong and Yeoh 2013, 94).

The tensions around 'weekend enclaves' are symptomatic of the contradictions between the need for a large low-waged, low-skilled migrant population that is supposed to be transient, on the one hand, and the fear of the malaise associated with 'migrant concentrations' that appear overwhelmingly visible, palpable, and permanent, on the other hand. The tensions around these spatial politics were further heightened in the aftermath of the 'Little India riot' of December 2013,[3] which led the area to be singled out as a space of exception whereby a ban on alcohol sales and increased police surveillance were put in place.

Simultaneous to the emergence of enclaves and spaces of exception, spaces of enclosure such as mega-dormitories — also built by construction labour — have begun to proliferate. Globalising cities that draw their vitality from showcasing a constant multiplying of megaprojects (Yeoh 2005) also spawn other sorts of mega- and micro-spaces on the underside of the city. In response to the huge influx of construction workers in recent years, workers' dormitories have taken on massive proportions. A recent dormitory, for example, was built to house up to 16,800 men with 'integrated facilities' including a minimart, beer garden and food-court, cinema and cricket field. These spaces are built at peripheral sites as a containment measure to keep the migrant worker population as far as possible away from the Little India enclave. Such containment strategies are predicated not just on control but also on care. One newly built mega-dormitory included not just banking and remittance services, but also had a Migrant Workers' Centre desk at its premises to provide workers an avenue to share grievances. While these facilities are generally appreciated by the residents, they also have the effect of immobilising workers within sequestered spaces away from co-ethnic enclaves and Singapore society more generally, particularly when compounded by long working hours during weekdays and the option of lucrative over-time pay during weekends. This was attested to by workers such as Moinol (34 years old), who said that 'all [they] do in the dormitory is sleeping', adding that

[3] On 8 December 2013, an altercation in Little India involving foreign workers broke out after a male Indian national (a construction worker) died after being hit by a bus ferrying workers back to their dormitories. Angry groups of passers-by attacked the bus and emergency vehicles. Some 300 migrant workers were involved in the incident lasting two hours. This was subsequently described as a 'riot' in mainstream media as well as in government statements. A Committee of Inquiry (COI) identified three factors contributing to the 'riot' — misunderstandings about the accident and response; the culture and psychology of the crowd; and alcohol and intoxication among the Indian workers.

> 'there [is] actually, for entertain[ment], we have playground ... we can play ... and, TV ... the canteen have TV but, no satellite channels, only Singapore local channels [laughs] ... [but] we don't have a lot of time also ... because we have to do work ... from 7.30 [a.m.] to sometimes 7.30, sometimes 8.30, sometimes 10.30 [p.m.]'

Conjoined to strategies of care are those of control and surveillance in fashioning the compliant subject. Dormitories adopt a stringent security regime, numerous surveillance measures having been put in place, including the use of closed-circuit television (CCTV) cameras. A visit to one mega-dormitory revealed that around 400 CCTV cameras had been installed, enabling criss-crossing visuals that maximised the visibility of the migrant body. This dormitory also had two demarcated living quarters, each housing 8400 workers. The dormitory employs a biometric system whereby access is granted upon fingerprint scanning, barring workers living in one area from entering the other. Demarcated living zones are in place as a response to the 'Little India riot' and to ensure that any incident can be quickly contained.

In sum, anxieties over migrant 'hotspots' in the host nation-state have created a 'fear of diversity', triggering processes of 'enclavement' and new forms of 'enclosure'. These strategies of spatial control in constraining mobility and fashioning compliance out of unruly migrant subjects are not only dependent on discipline and surveillance, but are also inextricably conjoined to notions of pastoral care. Beneath the glitzy overlay of high modernity, megadevelopment and 21st-century urbanity valorised by aspiring global cities, we find, on the underside, the gritty realities of segregation, surveillance, and control threaded into the lives, labour, and spaces of the men who have built these cities.

Governing Time and Mobility at the Worksite to Create Productive Workers

As observed by Griffiths, Rogers, and Anderson (2013), under industrial capitalism, controlling temporality is an important structuring device in governing migrant workers; and, at the same time, the chronic temporal uncertainty that underlies the experience of waiting is also inherent to the processes and governance of migration and mobilities. Over time, the time disciplines and controlled micro-mobilities expected at the construction site work to fashion productive workers with a sense of the value of time. Prodded by his wife to 'change [his] fate' by venturing to work in Singapore as opposed to 'just passing the days' in Bangladesh, Sumon (38 years old) — after working in Singapore for three-and-a-half years — declared that he felt that he has 'learned in Singapore that "time is money" and that it is possible to excel'. He in fact became critical of 'people in Bangladesh [who] should make more productive use of their time, as opposed to chatting at tea stalls', and spoke favourably of 'some parents [who] send their children to work abroad as a way of learning discipline — to know what it's like to have to work hard to earn money'. Learning to plan long term and anticipating the need to endure hardship in order to achieve future goals is also integral to creating the productive worker with the ability to defer current wants for future gains, as seen in many cases. For example, Mizan (23 years old) desired to be 'his own boss back home', and had envisaged plans to utilise the skills that he picked up in Singapore to set up a construction business.

The disciplining effects of time structuring on work processes, however, may also have unanticipated consequences. Following in the footsteps of an uncle who had made a success out of his migration experience in Singapore, Mizan submitted himself to a demanding time discipline: 'My company sub-con, so main company always push, push go faster, go faster. Then supervisor also push ah, go fast, this one go fast.' Compounded by the long 14-hour working days and the fact that he had not received proper training and had just been told to shadow a Burmese worker and pick up whatever he could, Mizan fell from a five-metre height whilst working on a flyover and broke both arms. While he had felt the strain of the long hours at work, he had adopted a 'waiting-it-out' approach to the long work hours and submitted to job immobility: 'Yah I feel tired. [But my uncle say] ok you one year, two years, can change [employer]. So I think two years, I can change.' He reckoned that his accident was due to the long hours of work, but felt that he was not in a position to negotiate. '[Boss says] Sunday you want off, ok Saturday you also no come ... You know, [if the boss] say, no working [then] you go back better. So he sends [you back to] Bangladesh, so problem right?' When asked how he felt about the delay in processing his work injury compensation claim, he replied, 'If I crying, then think will be faster? No. So I don't cry.'

Like Mizan, Anwar (38 years old) is another worker-in-limbo on a Special Pass and is hence able neither to work or to return home. He fell at the worksite, an accident he attributed to the fact that he was depressed and distracted at work, as his father had passed away while he was in Singapore. As he had only worked for his employer for two months, the company did not allow him to go back to Bangladesh despite repeated pleas. His company also kept back a 'deposit' of two months' salary (S$3000), leaving him with insufficient funds to pay for his own air ticket home. He said, 'I accept, but my mind not accept. So I'm working, then working, then some mistake, and then accident.' For Anwar, 'waiting' as a suspended time in limbo was initially experienced as an unproductive, immobilised, and restless period, but his frustrations soon gave way to a more productive time of rethinking his life trajectory. He began to use the time to call his family members and to plan his future — either to take up an opportunity to work in Australia at a restaurant, or to start a business with family help back in Bangladesh. 'Waiting' is hence not just a form of immobility characterised by deferment, but may be rendered as a creative time of planning, reconnection, and dreaming different pathways forwards. In a city that moves and morphs at the speed of construction, individuals — whether those who live in or construct the city — are constantly adjusting the temporality of their lives, plans, and strategies, sometimes in tandem with, but at other times in ways that disrupt or slow down, construction time (see also Nguyen, this issue).

Conclusion

In this paper, we have drawn on a case study of Bangladeshi construction workers in Singapore to show that mobility ranges across different scales, sometimes in ways that are misaligned or contradictory (Yeoh and Huang 2010). Indeed, the labour process on which construction work is predicated is not simply secured in the workplace of the construction site, but deeply imbricated in the time–space disciplining of mobility, not just in the host nation-state but also across transnational space. In other words, construction as a process which draws workers to the global city, also contains them.

Construction is hence a powerful force that controls the speed with which material forms of the city come into being, often in tandem with the city's globalising vision and future-facing plans. At the same time, this process is also structurally conjoined to the availability of an external supply of low-cost construction labour, whose presence in the city in turn generates equally low-cost micro-construction to accommodate a foreign workforce in spaces away from the aspirational city. As the city's skyline is visibly transformed by the mega-development race to compete in superlative structures, construction works in much less visible ways as a labour-making and unmaking process, foregrounded on the control of human mobility in, out, and across the city.

Funding

This work has been funded by the Department for International Development (DFID), United Kingdom (UK), through the Migrating out of Poverty Research Programme Consortium; however, the views expressed do not necessarily reflect the UK government's official policies.

References

Adey, P. 2006. "If Mobility is Everything Then it is Nothing: Towards a Relational Politics of (Im)Mobilities." *Mobilities* 1 (1): 75–94.

Bastia, T., and Siobhan McGrath. 2011. "Temporality, Migration and Unfree Labour: Migrant Garment Workers (Working Paper No. 6, July 2011)." Centre for the Study of Political Economy. https://tanjabas tia.files.wordpress.com/2013/06/bastia-mcgrath-2011-unfree-labour-wp.pdf.

Conlon, D. 2011. "Waiting: Feminist Perspectives on the Spacings/Timings of Migrant (Im)Mobility." *Gender, Place, & Culture: A Journal of Feminist Geography* 18 (3): 353–360.

Cresswell, T. 2006. *On the Move: Mobility in the Modern Western world.* New York: Routledge.

Cresswell, T. 2010. "Towards a Politics of Mobility." *Environment and Planning D: Society and Space* 28: 17–31.

Cwerner, S. 2001. "The Times of Migration." *Journal of Ethnic and Migration Studies* 27 (1): 7–36.

Dutta, M. J. 2017. "Migration and Health in the Construction Industry: Culturally Centering Voices of Bangladeshi Workers in Singapore." *International Journal of Environmental Research and Public Health* 14 (2): 132. http://www.mdpi.com/1660-4601/14/2/132.

Goh, R. 2001. "Ideologies of 'Upgrading' in Singapore Public Housing: Post-Modern Style, Globalisation and Class Construction in the Built Environment." *Urban Studies* 38 (9): 1589–1604.

Griffiths, M., A. Rogers, and B. Anderson. 2013. "Migration, Time and Temporalities: Review and Prospect (COMPAS Research Resources Paper, March 2013)." Centre of Migration, Policy & Society. https://www.compas.ox.ac.uk/fileadmin/files/Publications/Research_Resources/Citizenship/Report_-_Migrati on_Time_and_Temporalities_FINAL.pdf.

Hannam, K., M. Sheller, and J. Urry. 2006. "Editorial: Mobilities, Immobilities and Moorings." *Mobilities* 1 (1): 1–22.

Ministry of Manpower. 2016. "Foreign Workforce Numbers." http://www.mom.gov.sg/documents-and-publications/foreign-workforce-numbers.

Ong, F. C. M., and B. S. A. Yeoh. 2013. "The Place of Migrant Workers in Singapore: Between State Multiracialism and Everyday (Un)Cosmopolitanisms." In *Migration and Diversity in Asian Contexts*, edited by A. E. Lai, F. L. Collins and B. S. A. Yeoh, 83–106. Singapore: Institute of Southeast Asian Studies.

Thompson, E. P. 1967. "Time, Work-Discipline and Industrial Capitalism." *Past and Present* 38: 56–97.

Yeoh, B. S. A. 2005. "The Global Cultural City? Spatial Imagineering and Politics in the (Multi)Cultural Marketplaces of South-East Asia." *Urban Studies* 42 (5/6): 945–958.

Yeoh, B. S. A. 2006. "Bifurcated Labour: The Unequal Incorporation of Transmigrants in Singapore." *Tijds-chrift voor economische en sociale geografie* 97 (1): 26–37.

Yeoh, B. S. A., and S. Huang. 2010. "Transnational Domestic Workers and the Negotiation of Mobility and Work Practices in Singapore's Home-Spaces." *Mobilities* 5 (2): 219–236.

Brenda S.A Yeoh is a professor (Provost's Chair) in the Department of Geography and Research Leader of the Asian Migration Cluster at the Asia Research Institute, National University of Singapore. Email: geoysa@nus.edu.sg

Grace Baey is an independent scholar. She was formerly a research associate at the Asia Research Institute, National University of Singapore. Email: gracebaey@gmail.com

Maria Platt is a cluster coordinator at the Australia — Indonesia Centre, Monash University. Email: maria.platt@monash.edu

Kellynn Wee is a research assistant at the Asia Research Institute, National University of Singapore. Email: kellynn.wee@nus.edu.sg

Chapter 2a

Legal Protection and Migrant Rights: The COVID-19 Outbreak in Singapore*

Jaclyn L. Neo

Faculty of Law
National University of Singapore

It has been half a decade since this article was published. Its central critique remains valid, which is that any legal framework premised upon the ability to sequester a massive migrant worker population from the general population, and thereby insulate the latter from any discriminatory impact of such a legal framework, is not viable in the long run. The backdrop for that critique was the Little India riots in 2013 [Chin and Chia, 2013], which gave the occasion for some soul-searching about the treatment of migrant workers, even if one could not directly make a connection between the riots and their labour conditions. As I argued in this article, the legal framework, which is typical of a guest-worker programme, sees migrant workers as temporary labour that can be returned to origin countries in the event of an economic downturn. Thus, there is an underlying

*Reflections on Neo, J. L. (2015). Riots and rights: Law and exclusion in Singapore's migrant worker regime, *Asian J. Law Soc.*, Vol. 2, No. 1, pp. 137–168. DOI:10.1017/als.2015.1. © Cambridge University Press and KoGuan Law School, Shanghai Jiao Tong University.

assumption that by admitting foreign workers on short-term jobs and legalising their stay with contract-bound work permits, a receiving state could reap the benefits of migrant labour without necessarily having to bear social responsibilities towards these workers.

If anything, recent events arising from the COVID-19 outbreak in Singapore have vindicated this argument, revealing the need for a more compassionate approach towards migrant workers in the global city. The 'circuit breakers,' which refer to Singapore's series of safety and social distancing measures [Baker, 2020] may not be explicitly linked to the massive outbreak within migrant workers' dormitories. However, the rapid spread of infections in those dormitories clearly put a strain on Singapore's public health resources. The knock-on effects are clear — the rise in dormitory cases could make it harder to meet the needs of other non-dormitory cases. At the same time, the reporting of cases distinguishes 'community cases' from 'non-community cases,' using a language of distinction that separates 'us' and 'them.' This line between the local population and the migrant worker population cannot be viable, or even desirable, in the long run. My argument remains — the interests of the local population and those of migrant workers are not mutually exclusive or neatly differentiated. They are intertwined in many ways, and this underscores the need for a more inclusive and integrationist approach that recognises migrants' rights to protection. The pandemic has shown that we are only as strong as our most vulnerable groups, including migrant workers. It also calls attention to the gendered ways contract migrant workers are differentially admitted into Singaporean society [Huang and Yeoh, 2003]. Male migrant workers in the construction industry, for example, face labour conditions and needs that may be distinct from that of other foreign workers, such as female domestic workers. The different ways migrants are incorporated into Singapore are important considerations in recognising the legal rights and protection of foreign workers.

There have been some positive developments since this article was written. In my article, I referred to the judicial conceptualisation of migrant workers as important subject of legal protection. This has continued to resonate in the jurisprudence of the Singapore courts. In state discourse, the presence of migrant workers has been increasingly acknowledged. More recently, in his 2020 May Day speech, Prime

Minister Lee Hsien Loong mentioned migrant workers as having made important contributions to Singapore, stating: "This is why we care for our migrant workers, who have done much for us, as we care for Singaporeans. This is why we have taken unprecedented steps to draw upon our reserves, in order to forestall retrenchments and support the low income" [Government of Singapore, 2020]. Such legal-political recognition is important, and needs to be further realised in ensuring stronger labour protection for migrant workers as Singapore develops towards a more equitable society for all.

References

Baker, J. A. (2020, 2 June). Singapore's circuit breaker and beyond: Timeline of the COVID-19 reality. *CNA*. Retrieved from channelnewsasia.com/news/singapore/covid-19-circuit-breaker-chronicles-charting-evolution-12779048

Chin, N. C. and Chia, A. (2013, 8 December). Little India riot, 18 injured, 27 arrested. *Today Online*. Retrieved from https://www.todayonline.com/singapore/riot-breaks-out-little-india

Government of Singapore. (2020, 30 April). PM Lee's May Day 2020 message: COVID-19's impact on Singapore's workers, economy and the road ahead. *Gov.sg*. Retrieved from https://www.gov.sg/article/pm-lee-may-day-message-2020

Huang, S. and Yeoh, B. S. A. (2003). The difference gender makes: State policy and contract migrant workers in Singapore, *Asian and Pacific Migration Journal*, Vol. 12, Nos. 1–2, pp. 75–97. DOI: 10.1177/011719680301200104

Chapter 2b

Riots and Rights: Law and Exclusion in Singapore's Migrant Worker Regime*

Jaclyn L. Neo†

Assistant Professor of Law, National University of Singapore

This article examines the legal framework regulating unskilled and low-skilled migrant workers in Singapore. It argues that the current legal framework discriminates against these migrant workers and conceptualizes them as undesirable for inclusion in the wider society. This, it is contended, is premised on the assumption that migrant workers could be sequestered from the local population to some extent. This article provides some challenges to this assumption, highlighting instead some of the broader social and political consequences of this exclusionary legal framework. Consequently, it is argued that a more inclusive and integrationist approach is needed, and some positive developments are highlighted.

---

*This article was originally published in *Asian J. Law Soc.*, Vol. 2, No. 1, pp. 137–168. DOI:10.1017/als.2015.1.

†LLB (Hon.) (NUS), LLM (Yale), JSD (Yale), Assistant Professor of Law at the National University of Singapore. I would like to thank Juay Wei Tian for her valuable research assistance. Correspondence to Jaclyn L. Neo, National University of Singapore, Faculty of Law, 469G Bukit Timah Road, Singapore 259776. E-mail address: jaclyn.neo@nus.edu.sg.

Keywords: immigration, migrant rights, discrimination, social exclusion, integration

1. Introduction

It was a crowded Sunday night just like any other. Migrant workers, mostly of Indian and Bangladeshi origin, congregated in Singapore's Little India district, mingled among themselves on their only day off for the week. But, on December 8, 2013, the unexpected happened. A "riot" of about 200 people broke out after a private bus accidentally ran over and killed a migrant worker. The incident incensed the crowd, which started to attack first responders as well as subsequent police cars and emergency vehicles. The riot made world news, not because it was particularly serious — indeed, there were no fatalities and only limited property damage — but because it was a rare incident of public disorder in highly regulated and typically well-ordered Singapore.

The Singapore government's response to, what is now known as, the "Little India riot" was characteristically swift and efficient. Those involved in the riot were dealt with in three ways. First, there were 28 migrant workers who, accused of active involvement, were charged for rioting.[1] They allegedly committed acts of violence, damaged property, defied police orders, and/or incited others.[2] Second, those with "less egregious" roles (such as obstructing the police during the incident and defying police orders to disperse) were given "stern police warnings," had their work passes cancelled, and were repatriated.[3] According to the Singapore government, those who received such police warnings were considered "undesirable immigrants" and therefore could be repatriated immediately. They would also be prohibited from entering into Singapore again. In the third category were about 200 workers who were present at

[1] Hussain (2013).

[2] Forty-five persons were initially arrested but eight were released from police custody after it was found that they were not involved in the riot and two released on bail pending further investigations. Although the remaining 35 suspects were charged initially, these charges were withdrawn against seven suspects after further review, *ibid*.

[3] Neo (2013); cf. Ismail (2013).

the scene but said to have played "relatively passive" roles (i.e. they did not participate in the riot and generally obeyed police orders). They were merely cautioned and allowed to remain in Singapore.[4]

In the wake of the riot, questions arose as to its possible social causes, and particularly whether it was related to the treatment of migrant workers in Singapore. Three viewpoints can be identified. First, there were those who drew a causal link between claimed systemic abuses and discrimination that migrant workers faced in Singapore and the riot. This was predominantly the position taken in international news channels. The BBC claimed that the riots, together with an earlier strike by foreign-labour bus drivers, "shone a spotlight on the low wages paid to some migrant workers and the conditions in which some live."[5] *The Daily Beast* argued that, for the many migrants constructing Singapore's "glittering highrises, life can amount to indentured servitude."[6] Consequently, *The Guardian* pointed out that the riot is "likely to fuel concerns about discontent among low-paid foreign workers."[7]

A second line of response to the riot noted that many migrant workers in Singapore were subject to exploitative conditions, but refrained from making causal links between that and the riot. This was the response largely taken by local non-governmental organizations (NGOs), which nonetheless took the opportunity to highlight the exploitative conditions that some migrant workers experience in Singapore.[8] One of the main civil society organizations (CSOs) advocating for migrant workers' rights, Transient Workers Count Too or TWC2, issued a statement asking for restraint and noting that "riots are complex events, often triggered by some minor dispute."[9] TWC2 did however also point out that "the threshold for tipping into anti-social acts is lower" when a group or community "harbors an underlying grievance."[10] In this regard, TWC2 used the incident to highlight its position that migrant worker communities have

[4] Hussain (2013).
[5] BBC (2013).
[6] Han (2013). See also *The New York Times* (2013).
[7] *The Guardian* (2013).
[8] See e.g. Heng (2014); Saad (2014); Shen & Armstrong (2013); Lee (2014).
[9] Heng (2014).
[10] *Ibid.*

experienced substantial "employment unfairness for a long time" which includes not receiving correct salaries or sometimes any salary at all, while others have seen their friends injured at work but denied proper medical treatment by their employers, or seen their friends unjustly and illegally repatriated without receiving full salaries or injury compensation.[11] TWC2 stopped short of saying that these festering grievances played a part in the violence, but nonetheless urged the government to take the opportunity to pay more attention to these grievances.[12]

A third type of response denied any causal link or correlation between the riots and the general conditions experienced by migrant workers. This was put forward by the Singapore government, which quickly and firmly dismissed claims of "widespread abuse." Acting Minister for Manpower Tan Chuan-Jin emphasized in Parliament that it would be "wrong to make negative generalizations about the foreign workforce from this incident," including those pertaining to the "chronic and poor treatment of these workers."[13] Prime Minister Lee also insisted that the riot was "spontaneous" and "localized," and that there was "no reason to believe that the riot in Little India was due to unhappiness among foreign workers here."[14] Instead, Lee suggested that there were signs that alcohol was a factor in igniting the violence.

The government's assessment of the incident, namely that it was localized, alcoholrelated, and unconnected to the working and living experiences of migrant workers, is clearly reflected in the government's immediate response to the incident. Not only did it ban alcohol sale and consumption in public in the Little India area immediately after the incident,[15] but Parliament also passed a new law giving the police enhanced investigative as well as stop-and-search powers within the designated zone. This new Public Order (Additional Temporary Measures) Act[16] continues a general prohibition against the sale, supply, and consumption of alcohol

[11] *Ibid.*
[12] *Ibid.*
[13] Toh (2014).
[14] Chan (2013).
[15] Heng (2013).
[16] Act 12 of 2014.

within the area, and is valid for up to one year.[17] The insistence that the riot was a law-and-order issue, rather than a migrant worker's rights issue, is further reflected in the terms of reference for the Committee of Inquiry appointed to investigate the incident.[18] Although the terms include establishing "the factors and circumstances that led to the riot," the bulk of the terms of reference address law enforcement issues. Thus, the Committee was asked to establish how the riot unfolded and how the response forces managed the incident, to consider whether current measures to manage such incidents in areas where foreign workers congregate such as Little India are adequate, and to recommend any further measures to improve their management and reduce the risk of such incidents.[19]

This law-and-order response to the incident was perhaps to be expected in the social, legal, and political context of highly regulated Singapore. However, an approach that treats this as simply a rare incident of public disorder risks overlooking important social issues that the incident surfaced. Instead, as the second type of response emphasizes, the incident presents an opportunity to examine potentially exclusionary aspects of the current regulatory regime that shape the relationship between unskilled and low-skilled migrant workers and the general Singaporean society. Furthermore, the incident shows that it is necessary to investigate the adverse long-term consequences of the corresponding social and emotional disconnect between the local population and its migrant worker population. There are currently almost one million work permit holders in Singapore: 80% of these are male workers who work primarily in the construction industry whereas the remaining 20% are domestic workers.[20] Putting this in perspective, this means that about 18% of people living in Singapore are work permit holders. The law that regulates their admission and stay in Singapore however permanently

[17] See Ministry of Home Affairs (2014a); Lim (2014); *Channel News Asia* (2014).

[18] Ministry of Home Affairs (2013). The appointment was done pursuant to the Inquiries Act (Cap. 139A), s.9.

[19] *Ibid.*; see also Ministry of Home Affairs (2014b).

[20] As at June 2014, for instance, there were 980,800 work permit holders in Singapore, of which 218,300 were foreign domestic workers. The rest were non-domestic workers with the construction industry making up the highest number at 321,200 workers. See Ministry of Manpower (2014b).

excludes them from being incorporated into Singaporean society. The expanded size of this group of workers poses increasing challenge for Singapore's legal regime, in particular undermining the underlying assumption that the rights and interests of the migrant worker population are and could be sequestered from those of the local population.

This article examines the exclusionary aspects of the legal regime governing unskilled and low-skilled workers, and argues that there are broader implications for the law's conceptualization of the migrant worker as being undesirable for inclusion in the wider society. The article is structured as follows. Part 2 examines the regulatory framework in Singapore for unskilled and low-skilled migrant workers, and highlights the discriminatory aspects of the law. Part 3 challenges the assumption underlying the law, which is that the migrant workers could somehow be sequestered from those of the general population. The social and political consequences arising from this discriminatory regulatory framework are also highlighted. Part 4 provides arguments for a more inclusive and integrationist approach towards migrant workers. Part 5 highlights some positive developments in recognizing the migrant worker as a subject worthy of protection beyond a mere economic actor.

2. Exclusion and the Regulatory Framework

Migrant workers are today recognized as a vulnerable group, with vulnerability understood here as "a social condition of powerlessness ascribed to individuals with certain characteristics that are perceived to deviate from those ascribed to the prevailing definitions of a national."[21] There are several factors for this. First, as non-nationals, they are usually excluded from the political processes which produce decisions that directly affect them.[22] Second, their unfamiliarity with the host state, whether due to language or cultural differences, or due to their lack of knowledge about the legal system and administration, may create conditions of apprehension, anxiety, or even fear. Third, migrants are also more likely to suffer from stereotypes, prejudices, racism, xenophobia, ignorance, and discrimination.[23] Such

[21] Bustamante (2002), p. 340.

[22] Pécoud & Guchteneire (2006), p. 244.

[23] *Ibid.*

cultural elements assign derogatory ideas to immigrants, which tend to justify power differentials between nationals and non-nationals or immigrants.[24] Fourth, with specific regards to low or unskilled workers, their vulnerabilities are exacerbated by the type of economic activity that they are engaged in, which tends to command little respect.[25]

Regulatory frameworks that do not purposefully address these vulnerabilities tend to accentuate them significantly. This could be said of Singapore's work permit regime, which tends to discriminate against migrant workers and lead to their social exclusion. It does so by constructing the migrant worker as being undesirable for inclusion in the broader society. The following sections discuss these laws.

2.1 *Work permit regime: Singapore's guest worker programme*

In 2012, a proposal was mooted as to whether Singapore should house its migrant workers at nearby offshore islands, instead of on the main island in proximity to the general population. The Minister for National Development said in a parliamentary speech that this was a possibility as long as it does not cause "too much inconvenience to [the foreign workers] or to Singaporeans."[26] An assumption underlies this proposal that, apart from considerations of convenience, it is unproblematic to physically segregate migrant workers. Under Singapore's stratified visa scheme for foreigners working here, unskilled and low-skilled migrant workers are employed under the work permit regime. This is different from the "employment pass scheme," which is available to professionals and mid-skilled workers.[27] The dividing line between a work permit and an employment pass is defined

---

[24] Bustamante (2002), p. 339.

[25] Pécoud & Guchteneire (2006): "Many foreign workers work in so-called 'three-D' jobs (dirty, degrading, and dangerous), and are over-represented in marginally viable and sometimes semi-legal sectors such as seasonal agricultural work, domestic services, and the sex-industry, in which the protection of workers is underdeveloped."

[26] Singapore Parliamentary Reports (2013), col. 30; see also Ramesh (2013).

[27] Professionals earning above a certain income bracket would be able to hold an employment pass (EP), while midskilled workers earning a slightly lower salary would be given an S Pass. See Ministry of Manpower (2014a) and Ministry of Manpower (2014d).

by the nature of work, the workers' qualifications, and salary to be earned. Hence, unskilled or low-skilled migrant workers earning low wages are generally governed under the work permit regime. Work permit holders also typically come from developing countries. Besides Malaysia, other common source countries are People's Republic of China, India, Sri Lanka, Bangladesh, Thailand, Myanmar, and the Philippines.[28]

The work permit regime is essentially a temporary foreign worker programme, much like the guest worker programmes implemented in many Western European states during the postwar boom. These temporary worker programmes typically entail state control of recruitment, mobility, and working conditions.[29] Workers are admitted on a temporary basis to fulfil labour shortages in the host country. There is generally an assumption that temporary worker programmes such as these deliver benefits that are immediate, concentrated, and measurable, while their costs could be deferred, dispersed, and would in any case be difficult to quantify.[30]

Singapore's work permit regime gives businesses and individuals the opportunity to access and utilize cheap foreign manpower.[31] This disproportionately improves the economy's competitiveness. As Eng points out, a host country does not have to pay the high costs of bringing up and educating migrant workers but reaps the productive output of the migrants' prime

[28] Until the 1970s, workers from West Malaysia dominated the initial flow of migration. However, in the 1970s, when Malaysia embraced an export-oriented industrialization strategy and restricted the flow of Malaysian workers into Singapore to address its own labour shortages, the Singapore government started permitting the recruitment of migrant workers from "non-traditional" (i.e. non-Malaysian) countries such as India, Bangladesh, Sri Lanka, Indonesia, and Thailand, so as to widen the pool of migrant workers. See Kaur (2007), para. 30. Today, according to the ICA, the common source countries generally fall into one of these three source country/territory groupings: North Asian Sources (NAS) (i.e. Hong Kong, Macau, South Korea, and Taiwan); Non-Traditional Sources (NTS) (i.e. India, Sri Lanka, Thailand, and Bangladesh); and the Republic of the Union of Myanmar and Philippines, and People's Republic of China (PRC): Ministry of Manpower (2014e).

[29] Castles (1986), p. 762.

[30] See discussion generally in Martin (2006).

[31] E.g. Singapore Parliamentary Reports (2007), cols. 929–31. The Minister for Manpower, Dr Ng Eng Hen, explained: "The ability of our companies to access foreign manpower is a comparative advantage."

working years.[32] Like other guest worker programmes, Singapore's work permit regime envisages the workers to be transient. Their recruitment, mobility, and working conditions are heavily regulated to ensure this transiency. The foreign workers enter the country with specific employment often obtained through recruitment agencies. Once in Singapore, their economic mobility is strictly curtailed by regulations tying them to one employer. Any changes in employment are made difficult by the requirement that they require the consent of the current employer. Work permit holders in Singapore are also subject to a myriad of conditions that restrict their ability to freely associate with the local population.

These restrictive regulations construe these migrant workers as mere economic actors, whose other human attributes could be suspended for the duration of their economic engagement in Singapore. This further presumes that their interests and welfare are separable from those of the rest of the population. The legal regulations therefore serve to segregate and exclude them, not only politically, but also physically and socially. As mentioned, there are currently almost one million work permit holders in Singapore, which translates into about 18% of the total population. This is a large percentage of the population to be subject to a regulatory regime that does not sufficiently protect their rights and interests. As the recent events show, it is not viable or desirable to continue to conceptualize the migrant worker as having separable interests from those of the rest of the population. I will discuss this further in the next part. The rest of this section addresses the aspects of the regulatory regime that adversely impact on the rights and welfare of migrant workers, resulting in their social insecurity and exclusion.

2.2 *Insecurity of employment*

> When we look at the migrant workers' issue, we are not looking at it from the perspective of human rights. We are looking at it on a *need basis*.... Like it or not, we need to sustain and grow an economy that is able to generate an annual per capita [Gross Domestic Product] of US$35,000. At the end of the day, whatever factors would be able to help

[32] Eng (1982), p. 196.

> us to sustain the growth of the economy for the benefit of our country-men, for the benefit of our country; we will definitely go for it.

This quote from an interview with Yeo Guat Kwang, parliamentarian and then co-chairman of the Migrant Workers Centre,[33] reflects the deep developmentalist philosophy underlying Singapore's immigration policies.[34] This philosophy sees the employment of foreign labour as necessary to the continued success of the local economy and designs policies according to how best to promote economic success with minimal impact on the local society. Migrant workers impart flexibility to the labour market and the economy: in a tightening labour market, their quick importation relieves the pressure on wages while, in a recession, their quick repatriation could reduce the impact on local labour.[35] What is often regarded as objectionable about this developmentalist philosophy is that the worker is conceptualized as an economic actor, and little else. This tends to result in laws and policies that are economically expedient, but does not sufficiently take into account their discriminatory and exploitative impact. Indeed, several key elements in the work permit scheme legally ensure that migrant workers remain transient. In doing so, however, the work permit scheme also economically and socially excludes migrant workers from mingling with the local population, and makes it difficult for them to integrate into the Singapore society.

Indeed, a developmentalist mindset underlies the single-employer rule that is key to the work permit scheme.[36] Under the current regulations, unskilled or low-skilled migrant workers can only enter the country with a specific job offer from a stated employer in place, and an in-principle approval obtained by the intended employer.[37] Workers are not allowed to

---

[33] The Migrant Workers Centre is a bipartite initiative of the National Trades Union Congress (NTUC) and the Singapore National Employers' Federation (SNEF).

[34] Interview with China Labour Bulletin (19 May 2010), quoted in Chan (2011), emphasis added.

[35] Eng (1982), p. 196.

[36] The starting point of the regulatory framework is s.5 of the EFMA, which prohibits the employment of any foreign employee without a valid work pass and prohibits the employment of a foreign employee "otherwise than in accordance with the conditions of the foreign employee's work pass." See also Employment of Foreign Manpower Act, s.12.

[37] See Ministry of Manpower (2014e).

work for other employers when they initially arrive and they can only change jobs if their existing employer consents to the change, which he can unilaterally withhold without reason.[38] This seriously restricts their economic mobility.[39] Furthermore, employers can unilaterally cancel work permits which entails repatriation to the respective home countries.[40] The law provides some safeguards in terms of obligating the employers to pay all salaries and compensation before repatriation[41] but this is not always done. For instance, in a 2013 survey, researchers at the Singapore Management University (SMU) found that 65% of injured and salary-claim workers surveyed reported having been threatened by their employers with premature repatriation.[42] There have also been reports of employers' repatriating workers in order to avoid paying them their salary arrears.[43]

The government's common justification for this single-employer scheme is that it ensures that employers bear the primary responsibility of ensuring that migrant workers are gainfully employed and provided for.[44] The right to repatriate migrant workers is furthermore characterized as an

---

[38] Employment of Foreign Manpower (Work Passes) Regulations 2012 (S569/2012), Fourth Schedule, Part IV, reg. 1: "The employer shall control and supervise the foreign employee. Except as provided in paragraphs 6 to 12 of Part V, the foreign employee shall be under the employer's direct employment." See the same at Part VI, reg. 1: "The foreign employee shall work only for the employer specified and in the occupation and sector specified in the work permit." See also the criticisms at Transient Workers Count Too (2013b); Tan (2013a).

[39] *Channel News Asia* (2013).

[40] Employment of Foreign Manpower (Work Passes) Regulations 2012 (S569/2012), Fourth Schedule, Part III, regs. 12, 13.

[41] Employment of Foreign Manpower (Work Passes) Regulations 2012 (S569/2012), Fourth Schedule, Part I, reg. 23.

[42] Transient Workers Count Too (2013a); in fact, preliminary findings from a study of workplace injuries and illhealth in 2011 reveal that slightly more than half of total costs fall on workers themselves, when quantified into dollar terms. Transient Workers Count Too (2013c).

[43] Lin (2011).

[44] In response to a question on freelance employment of foreign workers, Mr Gan Kim Yong said that: "[A]s we allow a foreign worker to come into Singapore, we would require an employer to be responsible for the stay and the work of that foreign worker. In the event that this particular foreign worker gets into difficulty, we would need to be able to hold a certain employer accountable and responsible for the well-being of this foreign worker. It will be very difficult for us to open the gate and allow foreign workers to come in without an employer to be responsible for them." Singapore Parliamentary Reports (2010,) col. 1660.

economic necessity that could be beneficial to the migrant workers, since it is "better" for them to return to their home country rather than be without work in Singapore. While these laws may make sense from a regulatory perspective, they have the effect of restricting the economic mobility and thereby autonomy of these migrant workers. This renders them vulnerable to exploitation. Workers who are fearful of being repatriated would be less willing to make complaints against their employers. Unscrupulous employers may also use their right to unilaterally cancel a worker's work permit to threaten workers and suppress their discontent against onerous working and living conditions.[45] New migrant workers are most vulnerable to such exploitative practices because they would have incurred debts to recruitment agencies or private debtors to secure their jobs in Singapore and are especially anxious to keep working to pay back these debts.[46] This is a common reality. For example, TWC2 estimates that a majority of Bangladeshi workers in the construction industry have to work for at least 17.5 months to earn enough to pay off their placement fees.[47] Consequently, even though the employer is legally required to ensure that the employee has "acceptable accommodation," poor living conditions remains an area of significant concern in Singapore. Many workers live in dormitories, some of which are overcrowded and even unsanitary.[48] Others are housed in private flats that are often crammed beyond the legal and humanely acceptable limits.[49]

---

[45] Tan (2013a); Transient Workers Count Too (2014).

[46] Section 21 of the Employment Agencies Act currently penalizes the employment agencies that charge a sum greater than the prescribed fee (i.e. a maximum of two months). However, this does not cover fees charged by employment agencies overseas (i.e. at the home countries). Fees for foreign domestic workers are generally between $1,500 and $2,500 whereas non-domestic migrant workers (such as those in the construction or shipyard industry) would typically pay $8,000 to $10,000. See Transient Workers Count Too (2010). See also Singapore Parliamentary Reports (2012) (especially speech by NMP Tan Su Shan).

[47] Gee (2012).

[48] For example, two dormitories were fined in 2011 for "using space that was not approved for accommodation purposes" and which was overcrowded and had poor ventilation. Asia One (2011); see also Chan (2011); Singapore Parliamentary Reports (2012) (especially speech by MP Christopher de Souza).

[49] For example, the Ministry of Manpower was alerted to two condominium units where about 50 workers were found crammed into them. Rotting food, soiled clothes, and bags

In addition, there are other regulations which, when combined with the single-employer scheme, indirectly encourage excessive employer control over migrant workers and possibly engender an unhealthy chattel mindset. Employers are required to pay a foreign worker levy for each worker[50] and to furnish a $5,000 security bond for each worker.[51] This security bond serves to ensure that employers comply with their obligations to the worker, such as paying salaries on time or bearing the costs of repatriating the worker after employment ceases. Failure to comply would lead to forfeiture of the security bond. The security bond could be said to protect the workers, but its impact is likely to be limited. For instance, not all of the security bond could be accessed to repay workers if employers fail to pay salaries.[52] Furthermore, even in Singapore where there is a high degree of rule of law, the effectiveness of the current regime still relies on the migrant workers' being willing to report the employers for any transgression that would trigger forfeiture. As mentioned, migrant workers do not always find it in their interests to do so, as they might lose their jobs. Consequently, only extremely serious violations would be reported, while grievances accumulate in the meantime.

While these aspects of the regulatory regime are justified on developmentalist grounds and are meant to be economically expedient, there are good reasons to suggest that they are economically counter-productive in the long run. When workers are subject to such employment restrictions, their economic capacity and productivity are kept suppressed, along with their ability to contribute to the Singaporean economy. This is because employers have little incentive to train workers with a view to upgrading their skills. Workers also do not receive salary increments that could incentivize them to increase their productivity. Migrant workers

---

were strewn on the grimy floors of the units where the men slept shoulder to shoulder on the floor or on wooden boards along the corridors outside the apartments. According to Urban Redevelopment Authority guidelines, rented residential properties can house a maximum of eight people, regardless of size. *The Straits Times* (2014).

[50]This is authorized by s.11 of the Employment of Foreign Manpower Act. See also Ministry of Manpower (2014c).

[51]The security bond applies to all foreign nationals with the exception of Malaysian citizens. Ministry of Manpower (2014g): Employment of Foreign Manpower (Work Passes) Regulations 2012 (S569/2012), ss. 12, 13.

[52]Au (2014).

themselves are effectively discouraged by the system to build long-term working relationships. This results in a high turnover of migrant workers in Singapore, which makes it necessary for employers to keep training new workers.[53]

Furthermore, workers who have been in Singapore for an extensive period of time and gained experience and skills are generally unable to become long-term residents of Singapore. They can do so only if they are able to obtain a different employment visa. The next level of work visa would be the S Pass. Work permit holders could qualify for the S Pass if they obtain a technical certificate for skills considered important to key economic sectors in Singapore *and* earn a minimum fixed monthly salary of $2,200. Again, the conceptualization of the workers as transient would tend to discourage employers from providing them with extensive training that could allow them to qualify for the S Pass. This, and the workers' deep reliance on the employers to continue working and staying in Singapore, tends to undermine their bargaining power, keeping their wages depressed. As such, the number of work permit holders who would be able to apply for an S Pass is likely to be negligible.[54]

2.3 *Restricting social integration*

The current regulatory scheme restricts migrant workers' right to family reunion as well as their capacity to form meaningful relationships. First,

[53] Chia (2014); see also Building &; Construction Authority (1992), p. 23: "The large, mostly unskilled and transient pool of foreign workers is a contributing factor to low productivity .... Whatever skills acquired are therefore lost and retraining is required." Interestingly, the construction industry has the lowest productivity rate in Singapore. See also recent governmental efforts to raise productivity where exceptionally, second-phase employment is allowed for work permit holders in the construction sector with effect from June 1, 2015.

[54] There are no publicized statistics on how many work permit holders have been able to obtain work visas that would allow them a path to residency. However, at a panel for my course on Law, Migration, and Citizenship, a representative from the Ministry of Manpower acknowledged that applicants are likely to be extremely few. Immigration Panel, National University of Singapore, Faculty of Law, on February 17, 2014. The only exception was when the legal criteria for S Passes were revised for the service industry, leading to 7,800 work permit holders being upgraded to skilled status in 2013. *The Straits Times* (2013).

work permit holders, unlike holders of employment passes, are not eligible to sponsor dependants. This means that they are not able to bring their families with them when they come to work in Singapore. This reiterates the idea that they are transient workers, as they are expected to stay in Singapore only to work for a limited period of time, after which they are expected to leave the country to rejoin their families or to form new ones, but not in Singapore.

Second, the socially exclusionary character of the work permit regime is reinforced by the restriction of work permit holders to marry a Singapore citizen or a permanent resident only with prior approval of the Ministry of Manpower's Controller of Work Passes (Controller).[55] Marriage to either would entitle the work pass holder to obtain a dependents pass which could eventually grant them the right to stay in Singapore permanently. Work permit holders who marry but fail to obtain prior approval could have their work permit revoked and be barred from returning to Singapore. According to media reports, this condition has caused some hardship for work permit holder and Singaporeans/PR couples who have not been able to obtain approval to marry.[56] The decision to grant such a permission to marry is determined by reference to the economic contribution of the applicants and the ability of the applicants to look after themselves and their family without becoming a burden to the society or state. The stated rationale behind this marriage restriction policy is to prevent large numbers of low-skilled or semi-skilled workers from taking root in Singapore.[57]

Third, another condition of the work permit is that the foreign employee "shall not be involved in any illegal, immoral, or undesirable activities, including breaking up families in Singapore."[58] Female foreign work permit holders, who are mostly domestic workers, are subject to a further condition: they are prohibited from becoming pregnant or delivering any child in Singapore during and after the validity period of her work permit. This is unless she was already married to a Singapore citizen or

---

[55] Employment of Foreign Manpower Act, s.3; see also Yeoh (2006), pp. 26, 29, 36.
[56] Ng (2012).
[57] *The New Paper* (2012).
[58] Employment of Foreign Manpower (Work Passes) Regulations 2012 (S569/2012), Fourth Schedule, Part VI, reg. 8.

permanent resident with the prior approval of the Controller.[59] If a work permit holder becomes pregnant, her permit would be cancelled and she would be sent back to her home country. This is notwithstanding that the father of the child may be Singaporean, thus rendering the child eligible for Singapore citizenship by birth (if the child is born in Singapore) or by descent (if the child is born overseas).

Lastly, the time spent by work permit holders in Singapore does not count towards fulfilling the residency requirements for permanent residency. This denies work permit holders a direct path to citizenship. A migrant worker on a work permit could spend five, ten, or even 20 years in Singapore, but would not be eligible to apply for residency and could be asked to leave the country at any time (i.e. when his/her work permit is cancelled, with or without cause). In contrast, employment pass holders are able to apply for permanent residency after a certain length of time, which would in turn qualify them for a path to citizenship.

These legal conditions attached to the work permit regime makes it difficult for migrant workers to set roots in Singapore, keeping them transient. It also tends to signal to the general population that migrant workers are generally unsuitable and undesirable for inclusion into the Singapore society.[60] This reflects the assumption that allowing low- or semi-skilled workers to stay in Singapore would place a burden on Singapore's national resources. For instance, in justifying the marriage approval scheme, the Ministry of Manpower relies on the need to protect the economic and social security of Singaporeans:

> … we have to control the population size of Singapore. … So imagine if every other ex-workpermit holder were to marry a Singaporean, we would not be able to manage our social services and social system. … Even though we want to increase our population size, we have to ensure that those who want to live and have families in Singapore can look after themselves, their children and their families. That is the basic premise that we all must understand. … Singaporeans do have human rights to be able to look after ourselves and manage our limited resources and to

[59] *Ibid.*, reg. 7.

[60] Tan (2009), p. 117.

> ensure that those legitimate Singaporeans would be well looked after and would not exact too much of our social system.[61]

The contrasting of the rights of Singaporeans against those of the migrant workers risks setting up a relationship of antagonism between the two, with possibly negative consequences for peaceful coexistence and integration. It also establishes a false choice for Singaporeans, as it suggests that migrant workers' rights and interests are inconsistent with theirs. That is of course not the case. On the contrary, not only do migrant workers contribute to Singapore's economic gains, but they also contribute to the wellbeing of Singaporeans, when they are able to form meaningful relationships with them. The most common example is foreign domestic workers who work for certain families for a long time and become an integral part of the family. Other migrant workers could also have the opportunity to form meaningful relationships. A purely economic calculus fails to take into account the emotional and relational benefits that could arise from such relationships. It does not give due weight to the migrant worker who wants to marry his pregnant girlfriend or a pregnant foreign domestic worker who wants to give birth and raise her child born to a Singaporean.

Comparing Singapore's work permit regime to guest worker programmes in Western European countries, one might posit that these restrictions are perhaps the most crucial in ensuring that admitted migrant workers remain transient. As Philip Martins has observed, one crucial reason guest workers programmes fail is that some migrants settle in destination countries and unemployment among the migrant population increases over time. He points out that this has led to the aphorism that "there is nothing more permanent than temporary workers."[62] However, Martins points out, in relation to the guest worker programme in (then) West Germany, it is the assumption that migrants without families would not settle that contributed to the lack of plans or resources directed at ensuring their integration.[63]

---

[61] Singapore Parliamentary Reports (2004), col. 665.

[62] Martin (2006).

[63] *Ibid.*, p. 14.

2.4 *Insecurity of residence*

As mentioned, regardless of how long the work permit holder has lived in Singapore, he/she has no path to long-term residency or citizenship. This results in a lack of security of residence for them. In addition to that, their insecurity is increased by the fact that they may be expelled any time without recourse or due process. The ambit and practical effects of the state's right to expel immigrants takes us back to the aftermath of the Little India riots. More than 50 migrant workers were repatriated after the riots even though their involvement was found to be "less egregious."[64] The legal basis for this is the Immigration Act. Pursuant to section 8(3)(k) of the Immigration Act,[65] these workers were designated by the Minister as an "undesirable immigrant," which rendered them as "prohibited immigrants" under section 8(1) of the Act with immediate effect.[66] This gave the Controller of Immigration the power to cancel their visit passes under Regulation 17 of the Immigration Regulations.[67] Without valid visit passes, these migrant workers became liable to be removed under the Immigration Act.

In justifying the repatriation orders, the government asserted that "foreigners do not have an inherent legal right to work and stay in Singapore." Instead, they can only do so "with the permission of the State." The state asserts the right to expel foreigners who "flout our rules" as this is necessary to "maintain the safety and security" of Singapore.[68] Migrant workers

[64] Neo Chai Chin (2013); cf. Saifulbahri Ismail (2013).

[65] Cap 133, Rev. Ed. 2008; s.8(3)(k) reads: "The following persons are members of the prohibited classes: ... any person who, in consequence of information received from any source or from any government through official or diplomatic channels, is considered by the Minister to be an undesirable immigrant."

[66] *Ibid.*; s.8(1) reads: "Any person, not being a citizen of Singapore, who is a member of any of the prohibited classes as defined in subsection (3) or who, in the opinion of the Controller, is a member of any of the prohibited classes, is a prohibited immigrant."

[67] S259/1972, Rev. Ed. 1998. Regulation 17 states: "If the Controller is satisfied that the holder of pass issued under regulation 9, 10, 11,12,13,14 or 16 is prohibited immigrant, or has failed to comply with the conditions specified in the pass or the purposes for which the pass was issued, or that his presence in Singapore is undesirable or would be prejudicial to public security in Singapore, he shall cancel the pass."

[68] Singapore Parliamentary Reports (2014).

advocates however criticize the lack of a right to appeal against those repatriation orders. According to MARUAH, a human rights NGO, this subordinates due process to expedience.[69] It denies those subject to repatriation orders access to justice, as they are not able to challenge any mistaken allegations or erroneous decisions.

Singapore justifies the right to expel workers as part of its sovereign power and secondarily on the basis of prior consent. Thus, the government has stated that "one of the conditions under which foreign nationals are allowed the privilege to come here to work is that they can be repatriated if, for example, the Minister assesses them to be security threats."[70] With regard to the Little India riot, the government asserts that firm and quick action was necessary to avoid additional security risks, and that it was in the interest of Singaporeans that decisions on repatriation could be expeditiously made by the Minister for Home Affairs. In defending expeditious repatriations, the Ministry of Law sketched out the following scenario, which it asserts would create additional "costs" to Singaporeans:

> If a court process had been necessary before they are repatriated, they could have stayed on in Singapore for a considerable period. They could have been given bail and be free to walk around Singapore, including Little India. And if they had not been given bail, they could be in our jails for a very long time, waiting for deportation. If the rules are such that transgressors can stay on in Singapore to fight their repatriation orders, then at least some among them will be less deterred from transgressing. Some may also go underground. These are not theoretical possibilities. The example of other countries shows that these are altogether likely and the repatriation process can take years. In some countries, repatriation is almost impossible.[71]

On the whole, the emphasis that quick repatriation is beneficial for Singaporeans reflects the underlying developmentalist philosophy on immigration — one that discounts the human rights aspects of migration. Expulsion is a powerful tool for the state to exercise disciplinary powers

---

[69] Mathi (2013); see also MARUAH (2013).

[70] Randhawa (2013).

[71] *Ibid.*

over migrant workers.[72] They would be less likely to challenge existing legal norms that keep them economically and socially depressed.[73]

3. Social and Political Consequences of the Segregationist Policy

The regulatory framework has contributed to segregation between the migrant worker population and the local population. This has contributed to an undue sense of hostility among the local population against migrant workers. "The migrant worker" has thus become a scapegoat for discontent against the government. In this regard, the immigration issue has also been politicized to the detriment of the migrant workers. The following section elaborates on these.

3.1 *Prejudice and the lack of social interaction*

In 2008, a government proposal to locate a migrant workers' dormitory in an upper-middleclass neighbourhood was met with strong opposition by residents.[74] In arguing against the proposal, residents cited fears of an increase in crime, worries that the migrant workers would "seduce" their domestic workers, and even that the dormitory would cause their real estate to devalue.[75] These worries reflect a prejudice among some Singaporeans that migrant workers are more prone to criminal and immoral activities. Indeed, there is no evidence to show that the crime

---

[72] Such disciplinary powers over non-citizens extend even to those who are "permanent" residents. In the 1988 case of *Siah Mooi Guat*, the Singapore courts affirmed that the government has broad powers to declare a permanent resident who had lived in Singapore for decades, owned real estate in Singapore, was gainfully employed, and was generally a law-abiding citizen an undesirable immigrant under the Immigration Act. *Re Siah Mooi Guat* [1988] 2 SLR(R) 165.

[73] *Ibid.*

[74] Tan (2008): some 1,600 residents signed the petition.

[75] *Ibid.*; to pacify them, the government relocated the entrance to the dormitory and built a new road leading up to the dormitory, thereby diverting it away from the estate. It also assigned the dormitory space to male and female workers from the manufacturing and service industries rather than the construction sector.

rates among migrant workers are higher than those among the non-migrant population. In fact, statistics released by the government at that time showed that foreigners, including construction workers, commit proportionally fewer crimes when compared to Singapore residents.[76] The arrest rate for work permit holders was even the lowest among the various groups of foreigners.[77]

The political elite is also prone to perpetuating the stereotype of the "criminal" migrant worker. Recently, the Minister for National Development, Khaw Boon Wan, caused a controversy when he posted a Facebook update justifying a simulation exercise that employed migrant workers of South Asian origins to role play as rioters. He wrote:

> We have a few foreign workers' dormitories. What if some quarrels erupt, leading to fights or worse? These are possible scenarios, given the concentration of foreign workers in one locality. Little India riot was an extreme case, but minor scale fights could happen locally. To test our response capability, the Police, the Singapore Civil Defence Force (SCDF), the dorms operators and our grassroots organisations organised a simulation exercise recently. It was a useful way to network up the various agencies, and spread preventive messages. Prevention is always better than cure.

Social activists criticized the exercise as racist, as it perpetuates the stereotype of migrant workers as being more prone to disorderly behaviour. As one blogger wrote, "the exercise showed only South Asian-looking men, it doesn't take a very deep reading to get the message: when there are many foreign workers of a certain race in one area, violent clashes are more likely to happen."[78] Khaw's post raises a deeper question as to the perceptibility of the political leadership to the vulnerabilities of

---

[76] Othman (2008); see also Transient Workers Count Too (2011).

[77] *Ibid.*; according to the statistics, the arrest rates per 100,000 population were 435 for Singapore residents and 286 per 100,000 for foreigners. In fact, the arrest rate for work permit holders alone was even lower, at 227 per 100,000 (1,644 were arrested). Singapore residents made up 73% of the total population at that time and foreigners 27%.

[78] Han (2014).

the migrant worker to discrimination and social exclusion, and the consequences of such exclusionary perspectives.

Contrary to the stereotype, there is good reason why migrant workers are likely to be more careful not to fall foul of the law. As has been observed, migrant workers often pay significant costs to come to Singapore for employment. Having incurred debts and left their families behind, they are less likely to want to jeopardize their job or immigration status by committing crimes. Many have the singular aim of earning money to support their families back home and for their own financial security in the future. Taking part in illegal activities and committing crime run counter to their financial interests.[79]

One might also posit that the prejudice against migrant workers is partially class-based. Migrant workers on work permits generally perform manual labour in jobs that Singaporeans tend to avoid. As Martin Ruhs points out, one common adverse consequence of temporary foreign worker programmes is the emergence of "immigrant sectors" in the economy, namely sectors that primarily or exclusively employ migrant workers.[80] These immigrant sectors cover what is often perceived as "undesirable work" that the local workforce is assumed to not want to take up any more by virtue of their higher levels of education and/or affluence.[81] This seems to hold true in Singapore, too. Work permit holders are concentrated in the construction, marine, manufacturing, and domestic work sectors.[82]

---

[79] Transient Workers Count Too (2011).

[80] He identifies four other common adverse consequences: the vulnerability of migrant workers towards various forms of exploitation in recruitment and employment, the tendency of temporary foreign worker programmes to become longer in duration and bigger in size than initially envisaged, native workers' opposition against the introduction or expansion of a temporary foreign worker programme, and the emergence of illegal foreign workers who, together with native employers, circumvent the programme. Ruhs (2002).

[81] *Ibid.*, p. 19; as Ruhs explains, the emergence of immigration sectors is reinforced by the restriction of the employment of foreign workers to certain sectors and/or occupations of the host economy. This has led, or at least contributed, to the desertion of these sectors/ occupations by native workers, thus giving rise to (or at least exacerbating) the (further) segmentation of the labour market and the emergence of immigrant sectors.

[82] For the latest statistics on work permit holders, see Ministry of Manpower (2014b).

Immigrant sectors tend to suffer from depressed wages and poorer working conditions relative to the rest of the economy because they employ workers who have very little bargaining power. This perpetuates the undesirability of these sectors in the eyes of the local workforce, thereby perpetuating the unfavourable conditions experienced by migrant workers in these sectors. Ruhs identifies another related problem which is that "immigrant sectors may lead, or at least contribute, to social exclusions and marginalisation of the foreign workers employed in these sectors."[83] These workers are seen as being at the lowest of the socio-economic class, and may be subject to intolerant and xenophobic sentiments among the local population.[84]

The tendency towards intolerance and xenophobia may be exacerbated by the legal and social segregation that a regulatory regime engenders. Singapore's regulations envisage migrant workers to be transient and signal to the host population that they are unsuitable for long-term inclusion. Consequently, they are perceived as being in the country on sufferance, and would otherwise be unwelcome if not for the fact that they provide needed cheap labour. This is further reinforced by aspects of the regulatory regime that effectively require work permit holders to suspend and suppress their social needs. For instance, by restricting migrant workers from marrying Singaporean citizens or residents without prior permission, the law signals to the local population that they are socially inferior, or even that they are predatory — that is, migrant workers would target local residents in order to obtain long-term or even permanent immigration status.

One new regulation that provides recognition of migrant workers as social actors in Singapore concerns weekly rest days for foreign domestic workers. Prior to January 2013, there was no law requiring employers to give foreign domestic workers a weekly day off. This made it legally possible for foreign domestic workers to work for years without a periodic rest day. A new regulation, introduced in 2012, required a compulsory weekly rest day. The Minister of State for Manpower acknowledged that a weekly rest day was an internationally recognized labour right and that, in addition

[83] Ruhs (2002), p. 22.

[84] *Ibid.*

to allowing the domestic worker some physical rest, it also provides her with "an emotional and mental break from work."[85] This recognition of the social needs of the foreign domestic worker, however, remains limited by two features of the new law. First, the law only applies to foreign domestic workers whose work permits were issued or renewed after January 1, 2013. Those whose work permits predate January 1, 2013, still do not have a legal claim to a rest day. Second, the new law provides employers with an "escape" clause; they may obtain the agreement of the foreign domestic worker to work on her rest days and compensate her for those days.[86] The limited application of the law serves the interests of employers.

The regulatory framework's emphasis on the migrant worker as an economic actor, and not as a social actor, creates the perception that migrant workers do not have legitimate claims to social spaces outside of their workplace. This may fuel intolerance and discriminatory treatment when migrant workers do not conform to this expectation. There is an unrealistic expectation that migrant workers are here to work, and nothing more. When their social activities occur in shared public spaces, there are those within the host population that may feel that migrant workers have intruded into "their" exclusive spaces.

This sense of intrusion has increased with the rapid increase of migrant workers living in Singapore. Michael Barr, for instance, notes that, in the past, foreign migrant workers had been largely invisible to Singaporeans who dealt with them only in transactional and incidental encounters such as interacting with one's foreign domestic worker, waiter, boss, or construction workers around one's estate. This invisibility, he notes, is no longer the case.[87] It has become less possible to ignore the presence of almost a million foreign workers.[88] This means that, even though foreign workers still have their enclaves such as Little India (for South Asians), Lucky Plaza (for Filipinos), and Golden Mile Complex (for Thais), they have become more visible and the sense of intrusion has also increased among the local population.

[85] Lim (2012).

[86] Sim (2012).

[87] Barr (2014).

[88] Yeoh & Lin (2012).

3.2 *Politics and politicization*

Discrimination and intolerance against migrant workers affect more than just the migrant workers. There are political consequences, as such intolerant sentiments could be politicized. Ruhs points out that, when temporary foreign worker programmes lead to prolongation or increases in the number of workers that were initially unanticipated — what he calls bloating — this may also lead to the perception that the government has "lost control" over the size of the migrant worker population, inviting an immigration backlash.[89] Indeed, in Singapore, the Little India riot reinforced a perception among the local population that the government has permitted a seemingly uncontrolled inflow of foreign workers. This backlash is liable to be politicized and could adversely affect all foreign workers in the country and reduce or even eliminate the benefits of the migrant worker programme to the host country.[90]

Immigration became particularly politicized in Singapore's most recent general elections in 2012, with the result that the government has started to restrict immigration, including making it more difficult and expensive to employ migrant workers on work permits.[91] The backlash stemmed from the increase in migrant workers, who became a scapegoat for an overwhelmed public transportation system, overcrowded public spaces, and depressing low-end pay.[92] Opposition parties capitalized on rising discontent with the high rates of immigration, which the local population blames for raising the costs of living.[93] The main opposition party, the Workers' Party, sought to present a more moderate perspective by repeatedly emphasizing that it is not anti-immigration but that their proposal was for Singapore to reduce its reliance on a foreign workforce, and for a more moderate pace of immigration.[94] This pace of immigration, it argues, should be accompanied by a similar or higher rate of development and maintenance of public infrastructure, like public transport networks,

---

[89] Ruhs (2002), pp. 27, 32.

[90] *Ibid.*, p. 32.

[91] Chun (2014).

[92] Head (2013); Chun & Venkat (2013).

[93] Lim (2011); *The Japan Times* (2013); see also Adam (2013).

[94] Mokhtar (2014).

hospitals, and schools.[95] That may be so but, in arguing that Singapore should reduce its reliance on a foreign workforce and highlighting the overcrowding of public infrastructure, it inevitably holds out the migrant worker as the scapegoat for public discontent with the government. Indeed, the opposition did profit from the anti-immigrant sentiment that galvanized the electorate against the government in the last general elections.

Politicization of immigration is a common contributor to rising political conservatism.[96] Where immigration places significant stress upon a society's social and economic structure, it becomes easy for politicians to exploit fears and prejudices among the local population, especially where there is little contact and integration between locals and migrants.

For instance, problems associated with the presence of more than two million migrants of Turkish descent became a key political issue in (then) West Germany in the 1980s.[97] Antiimmigration politicians (often barely veiling their racism) found it easy to blame foreign workers for the country's social and economic problems, accusing immigrants of depleting social security, overpopulating schools, and causing housing shortages and social unrest.[98] While it is easy to blame the immigrant, this often merely detracts policy-makers from addressing the real underlying issues. For example, blaming migrant workers for overcrowding belies the fact that no resources were channelled into expanding and improving the public infrastructure to keep pace with population and economic growth. Similarly, in discussing the guest worker programmes in Europe, because permanent immigration was not expected, states refused (or neglected) to take the necessary steps to provide the housing and social amenities needed for orderly settlement.[99] This, Ruhs points out, stems from the attempt of these guest

---

[95] See e.g. The Workers' Party (2013).

[96] In her study of the determinants of the evolution of right-wing extremism in six Western European countries, Knigge finds that rising levels of immigration and public dissatisfaction with the political regime significantly facilitate right-wing extremism. Knigge (1998).

[97] Jacoby (2003), pp. 1590–9.

[98] See Castles (1986), p. 776; as Joppke observes, public debate in Germany often characterized Turkish residents as undesired and difficult. Joppke (1999).

[99] Castles (1986), p. 776.

worker policies to treat workers as purely economic beings, thereby failing to take into account their other human attributes and needs.[100]

4. Arguments for Rights and Integration

There is a tendency for guest worker programmes like that of Singapore's work permit regime to assume that, as long as the workers are kept transient, their rights can be largely ignored and that there is no necessity to integrate them into society. This assumes that the interests and welfare of migrant workers are only minimally economically linked, but not socially connected to that of the host society. In fact, there appears to be an assumption that migrant workers could mostly be sequestered from the local population. In reality, the social interests of the migrant worker and his host are more intertwined than is commonly assumed. Physical sequestration is neither possible nor humane. Not only do migrant workers have a role in the public and social order, but there are also foundational questions about human rights and justice that any society has to address.

4.1 *Social order considerations*

About a year before the Little India riot, on November 26, 2012, Singaporeans were surprised when 171 bus drivers from China who were employed by the Singapore Mass Rapid Transit (SMRT) went on strike, complaining about unequal pay. According to their complaint, Chinese nationals received lower pay than Singaporean and Malaysian drivers in Singapore. They also objected to the living conditions in the workers' dormitories.[101] The incident was extraordinary because labour strikes are extremely rare in Singapore. The last sanctioned labour strike in Singapore was in 1986.[102] Under Singapore laws, trade unions must be registered and can only commence or organize a strike after obtaining the majority of votes from its members.[103] Workers in an

---

[100] *Ibid.*

[101] Neisloss (2013).

[102] Trade unions and strikes are subject to procedural rules stipulated in the Trade Unions Act (Cap. 333, Rev. Ed. 2004) and Trade Disputes Act (Cap. 331, Rev. Ed. 2014).

[103] See Trade Unions Act, s.27(1).

industry considered an "essential service" were subject to more stringent rules. Public transportation is an "essential service" and workers have to give 14 days' notice for any strike. Since the SMRT bus drivers did not provide any notice, their strike was considered illegal.[104]

Twenty-nine of the striking drivers were immediately deported, and four were charged and convicted for instigating an "illegal" strike.[105] This is notwithstanding that some of their grievances were found to be legitimate. SMRT later conceded that dormitory conditions needed improvement. Although it asserted that the unequal pay for Chinese bus drivers was "fair,"[106] it reportedly implemented a new pay scheme after the strike which promises to evaluate and reward all bus drivers on a common set of performance indicators. Efforts were also made to improve communication channels between the company and the bus drivers.[107] Thus, for all intents and purposes, the strike achieved its aims. The bus strikes, like the Little India riot, brought to the fore some of the arguments that migrant worker advocates have been making for some time concerning the discriminatory and potentially exploitative effects of the current regulatory system.

The exclusionary aspects of the legal framework encourage social and economic discrimination against them. Where the law sanctions unequal rights, this often leads to unequal treatment and discrimination in society.[108] Residents including public authorities, employers, teachers, colleagues, and neighbours will be less inclined to treat migrant workers as equals, or give them a fair chance, or the necessary support in the process of integration, if they feel that the immigrant could easily be forced

[104] Essential service workers are subject to the Criminal Law (Temporary Provisions) Act (Cap. 67, Rev. Ed. 1985) and this includes public bus and air transport workers. Essential service workers have to give their employer 14 days' notice of their intention to strike amongst other restrictions. Failure to do so renders the strike illegal. Anyone involved in an illegal strike can be fined up to S$2,000 and/or jailed for up to a year under the Criminal Law (Temporary Provisions) Act.

[105] Neisloss (2013).

[106] *Ibid.*

[107] This includes an annual wage supplement and a year-end annual variable bonus. Tan (2013b).

[108] *Ibid.*, p. 8.

to leave the society again. There is a real risk that they will treat immigrants as second-class residents.[109] This in turn discourages migrant workers from trying to integrate into the host society. In contrast, when immigrants feel that their residence status is secure (even if only semi-permanent), they would have a greater impetus to integrate.[110] As long as they fear that they can be removed from the country at any time, their efforts at integration will be hesitant or half-hearted, and they will continue to orientate their future plans towards their countries of origin.[111] It has been argued that this state of affairs could pose a public order risk for the country should migrant worker discontent reach a tipping point.

Furthermore, the presumption that migrant workers are unsuitable for inclusion in Singaporean society on the basis that they would not be able to provide adequate economic benefits to outweigh the possible social and economic costs to Singapore is a self-reinforcing one. The legal conditions that render their stay transient prevent them from obtaining better economic terms for their work. It is possible that they are kept at a depressed economic capacity precisely because they lack security of residence and other forms of legal protection. This renders them less able to provide greater economic and social benefits to the host society. Indeed, poor legal status has been identified as major factor in marginalization of immigrants within West German society, contributing to ethnic segregation and racism.[112] It is significant that many European countries with large guest worker programmes have reoriented their policies towards integration of immigrants.[113]

4.2 *A human rights perspective*

The human rights framework to migration is a necessary counter to a purely developmentalist approach. A human rights approach emphasizes long-term protection of migrant workers' rights and values their personal

[109] *Ibid.*, p. 7.
[110] Groenendijk (2001), p. 7.
[111] *Ibid.*, p. 7.
[112] Castles (1985), p. 533.
[113] See generally Jacoby (2003).

autonomy and capacities to contribute to economic development. A failure to take a human rights approach has been said to give rise to a perspective of migration in purely economic terms, such that migrant workers may come to be regarded as commodities, rather than as individuals who are equally entitled to the full enjoyment of their human rights.[114]

Guidance can be taken from the International Convention on the Protection of the Rights of All Migrant Workers and Members of their Families (ICMW), which is the most comprehensive treaty specifically addressing the human rights of migrant workers.[115] The ICMW emphatically extends basic rights to migrants and fills in some gaps for migrant protection. It builds upon universal human rights guaranteed under existing human rights instruments, namely the International Covenant on Civil and Political Rights (ICCPR), the International Covenant on Economic, Social and Cultural Rights (ICESCR), the International Convention on the Elimination of All Forms of Racial Discrimination (ICERD), the Convention on the Elimination of all forms of Discrimination against Women (CEDAW), and the Convention Against Torture (CAT), and articulates them in ways which take into account the particular situation of migrant workers and their families. While Singapore is not party to the ICMW, the treaty nonetheless has normative valence and its provisions could serve as guidance on improving the rights and welfare of migrant workers.

Besides the ICMW, migrant workers are also protected under the eight International Labour Organization ("ILO") core conventions (against forced labour and child labour, and for freedom of association, and non-discrimination). The ILO's position is that all labour standards apply to migrant workers in the workplace, regardless of their status. In addition to these conventions, the ILO Multilateral Framework on Labour Migration provides a non-binding but persuasive rights-based framework to labour migration with the objectives of promoting international co-operation, governance of migration, protection of migrant workers, and strengthening migration–development linkages.

[114] International Labour Organization (2006), p. 4.

[115] 1990 International Convention on the Protection of the Rights of All Migrant Workers and Members of Their Families ("ICMW"), at Article 2.

Several of the restrictive provisions of Singapore's regulatory regime for unskilled or low-skilled workers would fall short of the ICMW's injunction for equality of treatment for migrant workers. For example, Article 54 of the convention guarantees migrant workers equality of treatment with nationals of the state of employment in respect of protection against dismissal, unemployment benefits, access to public work schemes intended to combat unemployment, and access to alternative employment in the event of loss of work or termination of other remunerated activity. Singapore's key legislation protecting the rights of employees is the Employment Act. While it applies to migrant workers, it excludes those involved in domestic work. Foreign domestic workers are thus not protected under the Employment Act. Furthermore, even though the Employment Act provides safeguards with respect to termination of employment, this has not provided effective protection for (non-domestic) migrant workers who are liable to have their work permit cancelled at any time by their employers. Under the work permit regime, termination of employment results in the immediate termination of the work permit, in which case the migrant worker must leave Singapore within seven days.[116] This contrasts with the Employment Act, which prescribes longer termination notices for workers who have worked for more than two years, and covers work permit holders, which require payment of salary in lieu of notice.[117]

Another area in which Singapore's current regulatory framework does not meet the standards prescribed under the ICMW relates to family reunion. While the ICMW stops short of guaranteeing all migrant workers the right to family reunion, it does advocate states to:

> ... take measures that they deem appropriate and that fall within their competence to facilitate the reunification of migrant workers with their spouses or persons who have with the migrant worker a relationship that, according to applicable law, produces effects equivalent to marriage, as well as with their minor dependent unmarried children.[118]

[116] Ministry of Manpower (2014f).

[117] See Employment Act, ss. 10, 11.

[118] See Article 44 of the ICMW.

This suggests that there could be restrictions on family reunion but not a blanket prohibition, which is the case in Singapore. Another aspect of Singapore's work permit regime that falls short of the international law standards is the lack of due process rights for migrant workers who face deportation. The ICMW does not prohibit expulsions in individual cases, but guarantees a process for appeal against any executive or administrative decision unless a judicial authority has reached a final decision.[119] Similarly, under clause 33 of ILO Recommendation 151 and Article 9 of Convention 143, migrant workers are entitled to the right of appeal regarding any expulsion orders. These are some aspects of the law that are not only socially exclusionary, but that are also in need of reform to be consistent with international standards.[120]

4.3 *Justice and equality*

Besides social order and human rights considerations, there are more foundational criticisms against guest worker programmes like Singapore's work permit regime. Social theorists and philosophers have argued that guest worker programmes are fundamentally unjust and unequal because they require workers to give up crucially important rights. Guest workers are admitted to free citizens from hard and unpleasant work, but are denied the right to be treated as equal human beings and potential citizens. Michael Walzer characterizes this condition as akin to a family with live-in servants, which he considers to resemble tyranny.[121] According to Walzer, it is politically unjust to lock guest or transient workers into an inferior position, in which the state exercises a pervasive and frightening power that shapes their lives and regulates their every move, keeping them

[119] Article 22(4) of the ICMW states: "Except where a final decision is pronounced by a judicial authority, the person concerned shall have the right to submit the reason he or she should not be expelled and to have his or her case reviewed by the competent authority, unless compelling reasons of national security require otherwise. Pending such review, the person concerned shall have the right to seek a stay of the decision of expulsion."

[120] It must be noted that the ICMW is limited by its commitment to the norms and structures of sovereign statehood; see Bosniak (1991).

[121] Walzer (1983), p. 52.

disenfranchised and docile through the continuous threat of deportation.[122] He thus argues that admitted immigrants must be set on the road to citizenship. In other words, they ought to be able to regard themselves as potential or future participants in politics, and be possessed of basic civil liberties.[123] Indeed, he argues, the principle of political justice requires that the processes of self-determination be open and equally open to all those men and women who live within the state's territory, work in the local economy, and are subject to local law.[124]

Admittedly, not everyone agrees with this position. Anna Stilz observes that many who support guest worker programmes usually dismiss the moral challenge of restricted rights with two arguments: one from consent and one from benefit.[125] First, they point out that guest workers voluntarily contract to work and willingly accepted whatever rights restrictions they may be subject to.[126] Second, advocates usually emphasize that guest worker programmes are of great benefit to the workers who would otherwise end up working for much lower wages in their home countries or would simply remain unemployed.[127] On these bases, advocates argue that it is better to retain guest worker programmes than to abolish or modify them.

Indeed, an argument proffered against providing guest workers more benefits is the potential trade-off involved. According to Martin Ruhs and Philip Martin, requiring countries to offer low-skilled migrant workers more rights may lead to a decrease in the demand for the number of workers. They point out that countries with large numbers of low-skilled migrant workers offer them relatively few rights, while smaller numbers of migrants are typically associated with more rights. This shows a trade-off between numbers and rights, whereby there is an inverse relationship between the number and rights of migrants employed in low-skilled jobs in high-income countries.[128] According to Ruhs and Martin, more rights

---

[122] *Ibid.*, p. 59.

[123] *Ibid.*, p. 60.

[124] *Ibid.*

[125] See generally discussion in Stilz (2010), pp. 296–7.

[126] *Ibid.*

[127] *Ibid.*

[128] Ruhs & Martin (2008), p. 251.

for migrants typically results in higher costs, which reduces the employer's demand for low-skilled labour.[129] Thus, they posit that guest worker programmes typically entail a choice between offering a generous package of rights and benefits to a very small number of workers or a more restricted package to a larger number.[130]

There may well be a trade-off between numbers and rights, but refusing to grant immigrants a path to residency and citizenship has been argued to be fundamentally unjust and indeed inconsistent with liberal democratic ideals.[131] This is especially where guest workers have stayed for a sufficiently long period of time and thereby formed social ties in the host society. Joseph Carens, for example, argues that the formation of such social ties gives migrants a moral claim to full membership there. On Carens's view, it may be permissible to ask short-term residents to waive some rights (like the right to welfare benefits, to vote and run for office, or to be protected against deportation). But the longer their stay, the stronger their claim to membership becomes. As such, once someone has resided in a country for a sufficiently long period, say five years or more, he ought to be granted full citizenship.[132]

While Singapore does not purport to be a liberal democracy, it may be subjected to certain reasonable standards. Even for advocates of the guest worker programme like Stilz, Singapore's work permit regime falls short of what would be considered just and acceptable. For Stilz, who argues that guest worker programmes could be partially defensible, there are nevertheless some baseline conditions that have to be met. She identifies three of them: first, that it must not restrict basic rights of personhood; second, that contracts that waive membership rights may be unconscionable under certain conditions, such as when the migrant's basic needs or membership in his home state are compromised; third, that restricted rights must not render workers exposed to the arbitrary power of employers and others in the receiving society.[133] Singapore's current regulatory

---

[129] *Ibid.*

[130] Stilz (2010), p. 296.

[131] See e.g. Kymlicka (2001), p. 359; Walzer (1983).

[132] Carens (2008), p. 422.

[133] Stilz (2010), pp. 296–7.

regime falls short on this account. For instance, the condition that work permit holders need permission to marry a Singapore citizen or a permanent resident clearly restricts a basic right of personhood, which is the freedom to marry. Furthermore, as discussed in the previous section, the condition tying the migrant worker to a single employer renders them vulnerable to the arbitrary power of employers and others in Singapore.

5. Recognizing the Migrant Worker as a Subject of Protection

It has been observed generally that migrant workers can best contribute to economic and social development in host countries (as well as source countries) when they enjoy decent working conditions, and when their fundamental human and labour rights are respected.[134] Indeed, there is now an increasing realization among the Singaporean leadership that socioeconomic gains and the protection of migrant rights are intertwined. While these fall short of integration, recent legal developments show improvements towards greater recognition for the rights and welfare of migrant workers. This is reflected in recent revisions to the law to better establish the rights of migrant workers and subject employers who fail in their duties to greater penalties. It has also been reflected in judicial cases arising from violations of migrant workers' rights. These reflect a shift in the law, giving migrant workers greater recognition as worthy subjects of the law.

5.1 *Employment of Foreign Manpower Act (EFMA) Amendments*

The 2012 amendments to the EFMA are the most significant to date. Interestingly, the stated objectives of the amendments intertwined the interests of the local population with that of migrant workers. The Ministry of Manpower expressly stated that the amendments were aimed at bolstering their efforts at creating a "sustainable and inclusive growth

[134] Wickramasekara (2008), p. 1248.

and ensure Singaporeans remain at the core of our workforce" and to "stem the worst abuses against foreign workers."[135] Part of the argument is that stricter regulations and heavier penalties are required to ensure that employers pay for the true costs of hiring foreign workers and to create level playing fields for law-abiding employers. Among the 2012 amendments are provisions that do better protect the rights of migrant workers. For instance, it creates new offences, which include criminalizing the collection of employment kickbacks from foreign workers[136] and illegally recovering employment costs from foreign workers.[137] There was also a proposal to require employers to send in-principle approval letters to work permit holders in their native languages before they depart for Singapore.[138] This presumably helps workers to be informed of their actual employment terms and to reduce their reliance on and exploitation by unscrupulous middlemen.[139] Furthermore, the new regulations make it clear that employers are responsible for and would bear the costs of the upkeep and maintenance of the migrant worker awaiting resolution of statutory claims for salary arrears under the Employment Act, or work injury compensation under the Work Injury Compensation Act.[140] This includes the provision of food and medical treatment. The employer is also responsible for ensuring that the worker has acceptable accommodation in Singapore.

These revisions follow a general regulatory trend towards clarifying and expanding employers' responsibilities towards migrant workers. Although the revised regime improves the rights and working conditions of migrant workers, it has been criticized for not going far enough in protecting their rights. For instance, it maintains the starting point that migrant workers should be tied to a single employer. Consequently, the

---

[135] Ministry of Manpower (2013).

[136] Employment of Foreign Manpower Act, s.22A(1).

[137] Employment of Foreign Manpower Act, s.25(4).

[138] Ministry of Manpower (2013).

[139] Singapore Parliamentary Reports (2012) (especially speech by Mr Tan Chuan-Jin, Acting Minister for Manpower and Senior Minister of State for National Development).

[140] Employment of Foreign Manpower (Work Passes) Regulations 2012, at Fourth Schedule, Part III, reg. 16.

expansion of employers' responsibilities and the imposition of stricter laws and penalties merely mitigate the conditions for exploitative conduct, but do not address the root of the problem. Indeed, the prioritization of the Singaporean workforce and its economy means that any advances on the rights of migrant workers remain subject to these interests, including the competing interests of employers. Thus, for instance, it has been pointed out that the employers generally oppose the single-employer regime because it would render them vulnerable to poaching by competitors. This, it is argued, would lead to the undesirable situation whereby an employer may incur costs in training the worker but loses him to a competitor.[141]

Nonetheless, the express interlinking of protecting migrant workers' rights with that of the Singaporean workforce also signifies a positive shift. Migrant workers are no longer regarded as mere tools of production with no relation to the general population, but recognized as having rights, the violation of which affects the economy and the workforce. It has been observed elsewhere that the weakness and exploitation of the migrant workers in the labour market is harmful not only to them, but also often to local workers and unions.[142]

5.2 *Judicial pronouncements*

Another notable development took the form of a 2012 High Court case where the court made important judicial pronouncements endorsing (to some extent) a rights approach to immigration in Singapore. In the 2012 case of *Lee Chiang Theng v. Public Prosecutor* ([2012] 1 SLR 751 (High Court), at para. 1), Justice V.K. Rajah signalled a clear judicial endorsement of migrant workers as worthy subjects of protection under the law. On the facts, the case is not exactly uncommon. An errant employer was charged under the EFMA for failing to provide acceptable

---

[141] This of course begs the question of why the employer could not offer better terms of employment in order to retain the worker. After all, this is a business risk that the employer faces with non-migrant workers.

[142] Castles (1986), p. 762.

accommodation for his foreign workers,[143] for failing to pay them salaries on time,[144] and for employing foreign workers without valid work permits.[145] Justice Rajah opened his judgment with this hard-hitting passage:

> Some employers view the recruitment of unskilled workers as a purely commercial enterprise bereft of any serious responsibilities for these workers' well-being. *This is altogether wrong*. Foreign workers are unquestionably not chattel like slaves of less enlightened times. Like any other employees, they have *basic rights that must be strictly respected*.[146]

This judicially underscores that migrant workers are juridical subjects with basic rights worthy to be protected. In emphasizing the need to protect migrant workers from exploitation, Justice V.K. Rajah laid down certain important principles concerning the meaning of employment. He noted that "[a] contract of employment with any employee, regardless of his origins, has at its core the creation of a sense of financial security, identity and self-worth."[147] In addition, Justice Rajah noted how the current regulatory scheme makes migrant workers especially vulnerable. This in turn makes it even more important for the law to ensure that employers

---

[143] Employment of Foreign Manpower Act, s.22(1)(a) read with s.20. Section 22(1)(a) prescribes: "Any person who (a) being an employer, a foreign employee or a self-employed foreigner to whom a work pass applies or had applied, contravenes any condition (other than a regulatory condition) of the work pass or in-principle approval of the application for the work pass; shall be guilty of an offence and shall be liable on conviction (i) in the case of an offence under paragraph (a), (b) or (c), to a fine not exceeding $10,000 or to imprisonment for a term not exceeding 12 months or to both." Section 20 is a general provision ascribing responsibility for offences by corporate bodies to its officers.

[144] *Ibid.*

[145] These are non-regulatory conditions set out in Employment of Foreign Manpower (Work Passes) Regulations 2012 (S569/2012), Fourth Schedule, Part III, s.5(1) read with s.20 of the EFMA.

[146] *Lee Chiang Theng v. Public Prosecutor* [2012] 1 SLR 751 (High Court), at para. 1 (emphasis added) (hereafter, "*Lee Chiang Theng*").

[147] *Ibid.*, at para. 1.

are strictly liable for failing to comply with their obligations towards migrant workers. Thus, Justice Rajah stated:

> Unskilled foreign workers, in particular, cannot ordinarily seek alternative employment, often have difficulties communicating, are reliant on their employers for appropriate accommodation, have no financial safety net and are therefore especially vulnerable. They are, in a nutshell, entirely dependent on their employers for both their financial security and welfare. A cavalier failure by an employer to appreciate the serious responsibilities concerning these workers' welfare can have profoundly unpleasant consequences.[148]

As Justice Rajah opined, an employer's obligations are non-delegable. Dereliction of duties, which causes harm or abuse to workers, would therefore attract custodial sentences.

This is a very significant judgment. It recognizes the vulnerabilities of the migrant worker, which in turn justifies providing them with more protection. Furthermore, in affirming their basic rights, and emphasizing their status as a contract-maker and an employee, the court treats them as dignified subjects of the law.

5.3 *Civil society and changing employers' mindset*

This increasing recognition that migrant workers' rights need to be better protected is largely a result of persistent and effective civil society mobilization in Singapore in the past two decades. As Koh and Soon observes, there has been an evolution in Singapore's civil societyto-state relationship over the years. In the 1980s, especially, government was seen as highly resistant to civil society. This has changed since the mid-1990s when the government started to demonstrate greater openness to citizen activism and civil society campaigns.[149] In fact, during this time, the government encouraged civil society and "active citizens" to take ownership of community issues and to use their resources to address them. It was

[148] *Ibid.*, at para. 1.

[149] Koh & Soon (2013), p. 93.

also during this time that the government started consulting with civil society and stakeholders.[150] Migrant workers advocacy groups were among the more active and prominent actors in this liberalizing climate. The key organizations involved in migrant workers issues in Singapore are TWC2 and the Humanitarian Organization for Migrant Economics (HOME), both of which have played key roles in advocating for labour reforms benefiting migrant workers. For instance, the two organizations have been integral in pressuring the government to impose a legal requirement for a weekly rest day for foreign domestic workers. They have also been active in educating migrant workers and helping them enforce their rights against errant employers.

The slow evolution towards greater protection of migrant workers is further reflected in the changing attitudes of employers. Generally speaking, employers have an interest in maintaining structural conditions that would continue the availability of low-cost immigrant labour, and thereby perpetuate the conditions which render them vulnerable as subjects of human rights.[151] Since employers have a higher status in the political and economic power structure of the country, the government often faces a dilemma in trying to balance the human rights and welfare of migrant workers, and to safeguard the interests of the employers. This is because employers tend to be voters, whereas migrant workers are not.[152] This is not to say that there is necessarily collusion between the government and the employers and, indeed, evidence suggests otherwise. But, as in other immigration states, the protection of migrant workers' rights in Singapore is necessarily complicated by this power structure. Changing the attitudes of employers is therefore a key strategy in immigration reform. There is some evidence that employers are more aware of the interconnectedness of their economic interests with the welfare of their workers.

---

[150] *Ibid.*, p. 94.

[151] Bustamante (2002), p. 351.

[152] Note that Ruhs and Chang argue that it is fundamentally problematic to ask states to protect the rights of foreigners, since it devalues the meaning and content of citizenship, and can be a source of costs which policy-makers and citizens cannot realistically be expected to assume. Ruhs & Chang (2004), p. 95.

6. Conclusion

In a recent survey commissioned by the Ministry of Manpower (MOM) and the Migrant Workers Centre, it was found that more than 90% of foreign migrant workers said they were satisfied, or very satisfied, to work in Singapore.[153] About 92% said that they hoped to continue working here even after their current employment scheme.[154] Of the 930 surveyed, only 2.3% said they were dissatisfied or very dissatisfied.[155] These preliminary findings were released to show that the root cause of the December 8 riot in Little India was not foreign workers' systemic dissatisfaction with employment and living conditions here. That may well be the case. But, as this article tried to demonstrate, the key lesson from the Little India riot was that it shows that a neat delineation between the interests of the local population and the interests of the migrant worker population is simply not possible. The two interests are intertwined, economically and socially. Fostering migrant workers' harmonious integration in receiving societies is a condition for social cohesion, peace, and democracy.[156] Indeed, good practices in high-immigration countries not only involve improving their living and working conditions, but also include integration policies, which place emphasis on finding ways to overcome cultural differences in a pluralistic society through — *inter alia* — the extensive provision of language teaching.[157] Other good practices would include providing migrant workers with access to services as well as having strong political will to investigate and prosecute charges of exploitation.

While not directly causally linked, the Little India riot has raised serious questions about the viability and desirability of the current work permit scheme which socially excludes and economically discriminates against a significant proportion of the population. To regard work permit holders as transient and therefore neglect to attempt to integrate them into Singaporean society could be a risky policy to continue. While it is politically expedient to emphasize the interests of the local population over

---

[153] Salleh (2014).

[154] *Ibid.*

[155] *Ibid.*

[156] Pécoud & Guchteneire (2006), p. 245.

[157] International Labour Organization (2006), p. 11.

those of migrant workers, the truth of the matter is that these are not neatly differentiated interests, but are intertwined in many ways. The developmentalist assumptions underlying the current immigration regime may not best serve the country's economic and social interests in the long run.

References

Adam, Shamim (2013) "Singapore Protest Exposes Voter Worries about Immigration," *Bloomberg*, 18 February, online <http://www.bloomberg.com/news/2013–02–16/singaporeans-protest-planto-increase-population-by-immigration.html> (last accessed 20 November 2014).

Asia One (2011) "Two Dorm Operators Fined for Poor Living Conditions," 23 May, online <http://news.asiaone.com/News/AsiaOne+News/Singapore/Story/A1Story20110523–280286.html> (last accessed 11 November 2014).

Au, Alex (2014) "Salary Non-Payment a Big Issue for Migrant Workers," *The Straits Times*, 25 August, online <http://www.straitstimes.com/premium/forum-letters/story/salary-non-payment-big-issue-migrant-workers-20140825> (last accessed 20 November 2014).

Barr, Michael (2014) "Singapore's Impotent Immigration Policy," *Asia Sentinel*, 2 April, online <http://www.asiasentinel.com/society/singapore-impotent-immigration-policy/> (last accessed 20 November 2014).

BBC (2013) "Singapore to Deport 53 Foreign Workers," 18 December, online <http://www.bbc.com/news/world-asia-25426243> (last accessed 11 November 2014).

Bosniak, Linda S. (1991) "Human Rights, State Sovereignty and the Protection of Undocumented Migrants under the International Migrant Workers Convention." 25(4) *International Migration Review* 737–70.

Building & Construction Authority (1992) "Raising Singapore's Construction Productivity," online <http://www.bca.gov.sg/publications/BuildabilitySeries/others/rscp_intr2.PDF> (last accessed 20 November 2014).

Bustamante, Jorge A. (2002) "Immigrants' Vulnerability as Subjects of Human Rights." 36(2) *International Migration Review* 333–54.

Carens, Joseph (2008) "Live-In Domestics, Seasonal Workers, and Others Hard to Locate on the Map of Democracy." 16(4) *Journal of Political Philosophy* 419–45.

Castles, Stephen (1985) "The Guests Who Stayed: The Debate on 'Foreigners Policy' in the German Federal Republic." 19 *International Migration Review* 517–34.

Castles, Stephen (1986) "The Guest-Worker in Western Europe: Obituary." 20 *International Migration Review* 761–78.

Chan, Aris (2011) "Hired on Sufferance: China's Migrant Workers in Singapore," *China Labor Bulletin*, February, online <http://www.clb.org.hk/en/files/File/research_reports/Singapore.pdf> (last accessed 20 November 2014).

Chan, Fiona (2013) "No Evidence that Unhappiness among Foreign Workers Led to Little India Riot: PM Lee," *The Straits Times*, 14 December, online <http://www.straitstimes.com/breaking-news/singapore/story/no-evidence-unhappiness-among-foreign-workers-led-little-india-riot-pm> (last accessed 11 November 2014).

Channel News Asia (2013) "Migrant Workers' Centre Urges Flexibility in Change of Employer Policy," *Channel News Asia*, 19 January, online <http://www.channelnewsasia.com/news/migrant-workers–centre-urges-flexibility-in-change-of-employer-policy/560504.html>> (last accessed 20 November 2014).

Channel News Asia (2014) "Public Order (Additional Temporary Measures) Act to Come into Force April 1," *Channel News Asia*, 31 March, online <http://www.straitstimes.com/breaking-news/singapore/story/little-india-riot-complete-ban-alcohol-race-course-road-area-coming-we> (last accessed 11 November 2014).

Chia, Yan Min (2014) "Push to Raise Skills, Productivity in Construction Sector," *The Straits Times*, 31 October, online <http://www.straitstimes.com/news/singapore/more-singapore-stories/story/push-raise-skills-productivity-construction-sector-20141> (last accessed 20 November 2011).

Chun, Han Wong (2014) "Singapore to Delay Infrastructure Work to Limit Influx of Foreigners," *The Wall Street Journal*, 29 May, online <http://blogs.wsj.com/indonesiarealtime/2014/05/29/singapore-to-delay-infrastructure-work-to-limit-influx-of-foreigners/> (last accessed 17 November 2014).

Chun, Han Wong, & P.R. Venkat (2013) "Singapore Tightens Curbs on Foreign Labor," *Wall Street Journal*, 25 February, online <http://online.wsj.com/news/articles/SB10001424127887323384604578325940594344014> (last accessed 20 November 2014).

Eng, Fong Pang (1982) *Education, Manpower and Development in Singapore*, Singapore: NUS Press. Gee, John (2012) "Worst Off for Working? Kickbacks, Intermediary Fees, and Migrant Construction Workers in Singapore," *Transient Workers Count Too*, 12 August, online <http://twc2.org.sg/2012/08/12/worse-off-for-working-kickbacks-intermediary-fees-and-migrant-construction-workers-in-singapore/> (last accessed 20 November 2014).

Groenendijk, Kees (2001) "Long Term Immigrants and the Council of Europe," in Elspeth Guild, P. Paul, & E. Minderhoud, eds., *Security of Residence and Expulsion: Protection of Aliens in Europe*, The Hague: Kluwer Law International, 7–22.

Guardian, The (2013) "Singapore Shocked by Worst Riots in Decades, as Migrant Workers Vent Anger," 8 December, online <http://www.theguardian.com/world/2013/dec/09/singapore-riots-decades-migrant-workers> (last accessed 11 November 2014).

Han, Kirsten (2013) "Singapore's Exploited Immigrant Workers," *The Daily Beast*, 8 November, online <http://www.thedailybeast.com/articles/2013/11/08/singapore-s-exploited-immigrant-workers.html> (last accessed 11 November 2014).

Han, Kirsten (2014) "COMMENT: Public Disorder Exercise in Singapore Raises Tough, Uncomfortable Questions," *Yahoo! News Singapore*, 12 November, online <https://sg.news.yahoo.com/blogs/singaporescene/comment-public-disorder-exercise-in-singapore-raises-071227334.html> (last accessed 22 November 2014).

Head, Jonathan (2013) "Singapore's Mid-Life Crisis as Citizens Find their Voice," *BBC News*, 21 October, online <http://www.bbc.com/news/world-asia-24540080> (last accessed 20 November 2014).

Heng, Janice (2013) "Little India Riot: Complete Ban on Alcohol in Race Course Road Area this Coming Weekend," *The Straits Times*, 9 December, online <http://www.straitstimes.com/breaking-news/singapore/story/little-india-riot-complete-ban-alcohol-race-course-road-area-coming-we> (last accessed 11 November 2014).

Heng, Russell (2014) "Little India Riot: Learning the Right Lessons from this Episode," *Transient Workers Count Too*, 10 December, online <http://twc2.org.sg/2013/12/10/little-india-riot-learning-the-right-lessons-from-this-episode> (last accessed 11 November 2014).

Hussain, Amir (2013) "28 Charged as Police Complete Riot Probe," *Today Online*, 18 December, online <http://www.todayonline.com/singapore/28-charged-police-complete-riot-probe?singlepage=true> (last accessed 10 November 2014.

International Convention on the Protection of the Rights of All Migrant Workers and Members of their Families (1990), 18 December, A/RES/45/158, online <http://www.refworld.org/docid/3ae6b3980.html> (last accessed 16 December 2014).

International Labour Organization (2006) "ILO Multilateral Framework on Labour Migration; and UNOCHR, Migration and Development: A Rights Based Approach," online <http://www2.ohchr.org/english/bodies/cmw/docs/HLMigration/MigrationDevelopmentHC%27spaper.pdf> (last accessed 20 November 2014).

Ismail, Saifulbahri (2013) "Workfair Singapore Seeks Clarification on Riot Deportations," *Today Online*, 25 December, online <http://www.todayonline.com/singapore/workfair-singapore-seeks-clarification-riot-deportations#inside> (last accessed 10 November 2014).

Jacoby, Nicole (2003) "America's De Facto Guest Workers: Lessons from Germany's Gastarbeiter for U.S. Immigration Reform." 27(4) *Fordham International Law Journal* 1569–662.

Japan Times, The (2013) "Singapore's PAP Loses By-Election to Workers' Party," 28 January, online <http://www.japantimes.co.jp/news/2013/01/28/asia-pacific/singapores-pap-loses-by-election-to-workers-party/#.U7v-17E7nyU> (last accessed 20 November 2014).

Joppke, Christian (1999) *Immigration and the Nation-State: The United States, Germany, and Great Britain*, Oxford: Oxford University Press.

Kaur, Amarjit (2007) "International Labour Migration in Southeast Asia: Governance of Migration and Women Domestic Workers." 15 *Intersections: Gender and Sexuality in Asia and the Pacific*, online <http://intersections.anu.edu.au/issue15/kaur.htm> (last accessed 10 November 2014).

Knigge, Pia (1998) "The Ecological Correlates of Right-Wing Extremism in Western Europe." 34 *European Journal of Political Research* 249.

Koh, Gillian, & Debbie Soon (2013) "The Future of Singapore's Civil Society," *Social Space* 92 online <http://lkyspp.nus.edu.sg/ips/wp-content/uploads/sites/2/2013/04/SocialSpace2012-GillianKoh-DebbieSoon.pdf> (last accessed 12 November 2014.

Kymlicka, Will (2001) *Contemporary Political Philosophy: An Introduction*, Oxford: Oxford University Press.

Lee, Amanda (2014) "Little India Riot Wasn't Just about Alcohol: MARUAH," *Today Online*, 12 March, online <http://www.todayonline.com/singapore/little-india-riot-wasnt-just-about-alcohol-maruah> (last accessed 11 November 2014.

Lim, Karen (2012) "Maids to Get Weekly Rest Days," *Asia One*, 5 March, online <http://news.asiaone.com/News/Latest+News/Singapore/Story/A1Story20120305–331728.html> (last accessed 12 November 2014).

Lim, Philip (2011) "Opposition Taps Anti-Immigrant Sentiment in Singapore," *AFP News*, 1 May, online <https://sg.news.yahoo.com/opposition-taps-anti-immigrant-sentiment-singapore-023446455.html> (last accessed 20 November 2014).

Lim, Yan Liang (2014) "New Public Order Law to Take Effect in Little India from Tuesday," *The Straits Times*, 31 March, online <http://www.straitstimes.com/breaking-news/singapore/story/new-public-order-law-take-effect-little-india-tuesday-20140331> (last accessed 11 November 2014).

Lin, Wenjian (2011) "MOM Warns 2 Repatriation Companies," *Straits Times*, 15 December.

Martin, Philip (2006) "Managing Labor Migration: Temporary Worker Programmes for the 21st Century," *International Symposium on International Migration and Development*, Doc. No. UN/ POP/MIG/SYMP/2006/07, 21 June, online <http://www.un.org/esa/population/migration/turin/Symposium_Turin_files/P07_Martin.pdf> (last accessed 11 November 2014).

MARUAH (2013) "MARUAH Reply to Ministry of Law on Repatriations," 23 December, online <http://maruah.org/2013/12/23/maruah-reply-to-ministry-of-law-on-repatriations/> (last accessed 20 November 2014).

Mathi, Braema (2013) "Due Process Should Not Be Subordinated to Expediency," *Today Online*, 20 December, online <http://www.todayonline.com/voices/due-process-should-not-be-subordinated-expediency> (last accessed 20 November 2014).

Ministry of Home Affairs (2013) "Press Release: Appointment of a Committee of Inquiry into Little India Riot on 8 December 2013," 13 December, online <http://www.mha.gov.sg/news_details.aspx?nid=MzA1OA%3D%3D-smkPXK7bzI4%3D> (last accessed 15 November 2014).

Ministry of Home Affairs (2014a) "Press Release: Public Order (Additional Temporary Measures) Bill," 20 January, online <http://www.mha.gov.sg/news_details.aspx?nid=MzA4NA%3D%3D-yK9x8BI1X9I%3D> (last accessed 11 November 2014).

Ministry of Home Affairs (2014b) "Report of the Committee of Inquiry into the Little India Riot on 8 December 2013," 27 June, online <http://www.mha.gov.sg/Data/Files/file/Little%20India%20Riot%20COI%20report%20-%202014–06–27.pdf> (last accessed 14 November 2014).

Ministry of Manpower (2013) "Executive Summary of the Amendments to the Employment of Foreign Manpower Act (EFMA)," online <http://www.mom.

gov.sg/Documents/foreign-manpower/EFMA/EFMA-Executive-summary.pdf> (last accessed 14 November 2014).

Ministry of Manpower (2014a) "Employment Pass — Before You Apply," online <http://www.mom.gov.sg/foreign-manpower/passes-visas/employment-pass/before-you-apply/Pages/default.aspx> (last accessed 15 November 2014).

Ministry of Manpower (2014b) "Foreign Workforce Numbers," 25 September, online <http://www.mom.gov.sg/statistics-publications/others/statistics/Pages/ForeignWorkforceNumbers.aspx> (last accessed 14 November 2014).

Ministry of Manpower (2014c) "Guidelines for Employers of Foreign Works: How to Calculate Your Quota and Levy Bill," 19 August, online <http://www.mom.gov.sg/Documents/services-forms/passes/Guide_on_Comp_of_Company_Quota_Balance.pdf> (last accessed 12 December 2014).

Ministry of Manpower (2014d) "S Pass — Before You Apply," 27 October, online <http://www.mom.gov.sg/foreign-manpower/passes-visas/s-pass/before-you-apply/Pages/default.aspx> (last accessed 15 November 2014).

Ministry of Manpower (2014e) "Work Permit — Before You Apply," 20 November, online <http://www.mom.gov.sg/foreign-manpower/passes-visas/work-permit-fw/before-you-apply/Pages/over-view.aspx> (last accessed 20 November 2014).

Ministry of Manpower (2014f) "Work Permit (Foreign Worker) — Cancellation & Renewal," 14 April, online <http://www.mom.gov.sg/foreign-manpower/passes-visas/work-permit-fw/cancelation-renewal/Pages/pass-cancellation.aspx> (last accessed 19 December 2014).

Ministry of Manpower (2014g) "Work Permit (Foreign Worker) — Security Bond," 20 October, online <http://mom.gov.sg/foreign-manpower/passes-visas/work-permit-fw/before-you-apply/Pages/security-bond.aspx> (last accessed 20 November 2014).

Mokhtar, Maryam (2014) "PAP and WP Argue over Immigration Issue," *The Straits Times*, 2 June, online <http://news.asiaone.com/news/singapore/pap-and-wp-argue-over-immigration-issue> (last accessed 20 November 2014).

Neisloss, Liz (2013) "Chinese Bus Drivers Sentenced after Going on Strike in Singapore," Cable News Network, 26 February, online <http://edition.cnn.com/2013/02/25/world/asia/singapore-bus-drivers> (last accessed 12 November 2014).

Neo, Chai Chin (2013) "Little India Riot: Four More Workers Deported," *Today Online*, 21 December, online <http://www.todayonline.com/singapore/

little-india-riot-four-more-workers-deported?singlepage=true> (last accessed 10 November 2014).

New Paper, The (2012) "85 per cent Get Okay to Marry S'poreans," 13 March, online <http://news.asiaone.com/News/Latest+News/Singapore/Story/A1Story20120312–333024.html> (last accessed 12 November 2014).

New York Times, The (2013) "Singapore's Angry Migrant Workers," 27 December, online <http://www.nytimes.com/2013/12/28/opinion/singapores-angry-migrant-workers.html?_r=0> (last accessed 11 November 2014).

Ng, Esther (2012) "Not Easy to Marry a Work Permit Holder," *The New Paper*, 7 November, online <http://news.asiaone.com/News/Latest%2BNews/Singapore/Story/A1Story20121105–381617.html> (last accessed 10 November 2014).

Othman, Zul (2008) "Unjustified Fears," *Today*, 15 September.

Pécoud, Antoine, & Paul de Guchteneire (2006) "Migration, Human Rights, and the United Nations: An Investigation into the Obstacles to the UN Convention on Migrant Workers' Rights." 24(2) *Windsor YB Access Just* 241–66.

Ramesh, S. (2013) "S'pore Open to Idea of Housing Foreign Workers at Offshore Islands: Khaw," *Channel News Asia*, 8 April, online <http://www.channelnewsasia.com/news/singapore/s-pore-open-to-housing/631856.html> (last accessed 15 November 2014).

Randhawa, Praveen (2013) "Ministry of Law's Statement on the Repatriation of Foreign Workers," 23 December, online <http://www.mlaw.gov.sg/news/replies/statement-on-the-repatriation-of-foreign-workers.html> (last accessed 20 November 2014).

Ruhs, Martin (2002) "Temporary Foreign Worker Programmes: Policies, Adverse Consequences, and the Need to Make Them Work." *Centre for Comparative Immigration Studies*, Working Paper No. 56, online <https://www.compas.ox.ac.uk/fileadmin/files/Publications/Reports/Temporary%20foreign%20worker%20%20%20%20programmes.pdf> (last accessed 12 November 2014).

Ruhs, Martin, & Ha-Joon Chang (2004) "The Ethics of Labor Immigration Policy." 58 *International Organization* 69–102.

Ruhs, Martin, & Philip Martin (2008) "Numbers vs Rights: Trade-Offs and Guest Worker Programmes." 42(1) *International Migration Review* 249–65.

Saad, Imelda (2014) "More Can Be Done to Address Foreign Workers' Social, Emotional Needs: NGOs," *Channel News Asia*, 20 January, online <http://www.channelnewsasia.com/news/singapore/more-can-be-done-to/959986.html> (last accessed 11 November 2014).

Salleh, Mohamad, & Nur Asyiqin (2014) "Little India Riot: MOM Survey Shows Foreign Worker Satisfaction Levels Remain High," *The Straits Times*, 7 July, online <http://www.straitstimes.com/the-big-story/little-india-riot-two-months/story/little-india-riot-mom-survey-shows-foreign-worker-s> (last accessed 12 November 2014).

Shen, Rujan, & Rachel Armstrong (2013) "Rare Singapore Riot Forces Soul Searching over Foreign Workers," *Reuters*, 10 December, online <http://www.reuters.com/article/2013/12/10/us-singapore-riots-workers-idUSBRE9B908G20131210> (last accessed 11 November 2014).

Sim, Fann (2012) "Foreign Domestic Workers to Get Mandatory Weekly Off Day," *Yahoo! News*, 5 March, online <https://sg.news.yahoo.com/blogs/singaporescene/foreign-domestic-workersmandatory-weekly-off-day-124140875.html> (last accessed 12 November 2014).

Singapore Parliamentary Reports (2004) *Marriage Restriction Policy*, 21 September, vol. 78, col. 665.

Singapore Parliamentary Reports (2007) *Employment of Foreign Workers (Amendment) Bill*, 22 May, vol. 83, cols. 929–31.

Singapore Parliamentary Reports (2010) *S-Pass and Work Permit Approvals*, 23 November, vol. 87, col. 1660.

Singapore Parliamentary Reports (2012) *Employment of Foreign Manpower (Amendment) Bill*, 11 September, vol. 89.

Singapore Parliamentary Reports (2013) *Oral Answer by Ministry of National Development on Having Offshore Islands to House Foreign Workers*, 8 April, vol. 90, col. 30.

Singapore Parliamentary Reports (2014) *Ministerial Statement on the Little India Riot by Mr Teo Chee Hean, Deputy Prime Minister, Coordinating Minister for National Security and Minister for Home Affairs*, 20 January, vol. 91.

Stilz, Anna (2010) "Guestworkers and Second-Class Citizenship." 29 *Policy and Society* 295–307.

Straits Times, The (2013) "7,800 Work Permit Holders to Be Granted Skilled Status," 14 March, online <http://www.singapolitics.sg/news/7800-work-permit-holders-be-granted-skilled-status> (last accessed 12 November 2014).

Straits Times, The (2014) "50 Workers Found Crammed into Two Condo Units," 20 November, online <http://www.straitstimes.com/news/singapore/more-singapore-stories/story/50-workers-found-crammed-two-condo-units-20141120> (last accessed 20 November 2014).

Tan, Amelia (2013a) "Let Foreign Workers Change Employers," Asia One, 13 February, online <http://news.asiaone.com/print/News/AsiaOne%2B

News/Business/Story/A1Story20130209–401235.html> (last accessed 20 November 2014).

Tan, Dawn Wei (2008) "The 'Them and Us' Divide," *The Straits Times*, 12 October.

Tan, Eugene K.B. (2009) "Managing Female Foreign Domestic Workers in Singapore: Economic Pragmatism, Coercive Legal Regulation, or Human Rights?" 43(1) *Israel Law Review* 99–125.

Tan, Jeanette (2013b) "Former SMRT Bus Driver: Why We Went on Strike (Part 1)," *Yahoo! News*, 5 April, online <https://sg.news.yahoo.com/former-smrt-bus-driver–why-we-went-on-strike–part1–135100687.html> (last accessed 12 November 2014).

The Workers' Party (2013) "Punggol East By-Election Rally Speech by Candidate Lee Li Lian," 23 January, online <http://wp.sg/category/speech-2/> (last accessed 20 November 2014).

Toh, Yong Chuan (2014) "No Basis to Say there Is Widespread Abuse of Foreign Workers: Tan Chuan-Jin," *The Straits Times*, 20 January, online <http://www.straitstimes.com/breaking-news/singapore/story/no-basis-say-there-widespread-abuse-foreign-workers-tan-chuan-jin-2014> (last accessed 11 November 2014).

Transient Workers Count Too (2010) "Policy Paper: Singapore's Employment Agencies Act and Rules," online <http://twc2.org.sg/wp-content/uploads/2013/09/Employment-Agencies-Act-Review1.pdf> (last accessed 20 November 2014).

Transient Workers Count Too (2011) "Fact Sheet: Work Permit Holders Have Lowest Crime Rate of Three Categories," 1 September, online <http://twc2.org.sg/2011/09/01/fact-sheet-work-permit-holders-have-lowest-crime-rate-of-three-categories/> (last accessed 20 November 2014).

Transient Workers Count Too (2013a) "65 Percent of Injured and Salary Claim Workers Threatened with Premature Repatriation," 9 October, online <http://twc2.org.sg/2013/10/09/65-percent-of-injured-and-salary-claim-workers-threatened-with-premature-repatriation/> (last accessed 20 November 2014).

Transient Workers Count Too (2013b) "Our Stand: Work Permit Holders Should Be Free to Change Employers and Stay Longer," 17 October, online <http://twc2.org.sg/2013/10/17/work-permit-holders-should-be-free-to-change-employers-and-stay-longer> (last accessed 20 November 2014). Transient Workers Count Too (2013c) "Workers Will Bear Over 5 Billion of Costs for Injuries Sustained in 2011," August 1, online <http://twc2.org.sg/2013/08/01/

workers-will-bear-over-5-billion-of-costs-for-injuries-sustained-in-2011/> (last accessed 20 November 2014).

Transient Workers Count Too (2014) "Why the Right to Seek Another Job Is Important," 2 April, online <http://twc2.org.sg/2014/04/02/why-the-right-to-seek-another-job-is-important/> (last accessed 20 November 2014).

Walzer, Michael (1983) *Spheres of Justice: A Defense of Pluralism and Equality*, New York: Basic Books Inc.

Wickramasekara, Piyasiri (2008) "Globalisation, International Labour Migration and the Rights of Migrant Workers." 29(7) *Third World Quarterly* 1247–64.

Yeoh, Brenda (2006) "Bifurcated Labour: The Unequal Incorporation of Transmigrants in Singapore." 97(1) *Tijdschrift voor economische en sociale geografie* 26–37.

Yeoh, Brenda, & Weiqiang Lin (2012) "Rapid Growth in Singapore's Immigrant Population Brings Policy Challenges." *Migration Policy Institute*, 3 April, online <http://www.migrationpolicy.org/article/rapid-growth-singapores-immigrant-population-brings-policy-challenges> (last accessed 20 November 2014).

Chapter 3a

From the 'Little India Riot' to the COVID-19 Pandemic: Migrant Workers and Public Space in Singapore*

Shona Loong

School of Geography and the Environment
University of Oxford

COVID-19 has dramatically altered the manner in which migrant workers experience public space in Singapore. Between early April, with the lock-down of migrant dormitories and the introduction of "circuit breaker" regulations for all, and October 2020, hundreds of thousands of migrant workers have been disallowed from leaving their residences. Even as migrant workers returned to work, a September 2020 survey by Transient Workers Count Too [2020] indicated that only four out of 57 men surveyed (7%) were able to leave the dormitories for leisure. Many areas once frequented by migrant workers, including Little India, remain eerily empty.

Yet COVID-19 is not the first time that the state has restricted migrant workers' use of public space. This article draws on research done in 2014,

* Reflections on Loong, S. (2018). 'This country, law very strong': Securitization beyond the border in the everyday lives of Bangladeshi migrant workers in Singapore,' *Geoforum*, Vol. 90, pp. 11–19. DOI: 10.1016/j.geoforum.2018.01.012. © 2018 Elsevier Ltd.

several months after the 'Little India Riot' resulted in state-enforced alcohol bans and heightened policing [Chin and Chia, 2013; Lee, 2014]. The Bangladeshi migrants who participated in this research were familiar faces that I encountered while volunteering with a local non-governmental organisation (NGO). In the article, I made the following arguments. Firstly, I showed that the state regulates migrant workers' activities in Little India through strategies both spectacular and surprisingly banal. It is clear that the state associates Little India with South Asian migrant bodies that it construes as particularly disorderly and in need of control. The article catalogued various means by which migrant workers encountered state power, including littering regulations, urban infrastructure, and the control of migrant workers' movements at void decks and in open or public spaces.

Secondly, I argued that whereas the state sees migrant workers as troublemakers, migrant workers complied with state policies. Not only did they applaud Singapore's 'law' for being 'strong,' they appropriated these restrictions into their understandings of what it means to be a 'good' migrant, with their eyes trained on providing for a family back home. This brings me to my final point: that migrants' experiences of public space must be understood in relation to their larger migration journeys. I argued that Singapore's migration regime consigned work-permit holders to a state of 'permanent temporariness.' Hence, migrant workers understood state restrictions in relation to the responsibilities they had back home, rather than as a constraint on their lives, as a citizen might.

I do not know when or if Little India will come back to life. However, some lessons from this research hold true. It bears remembering that migrants' experiences of the city are likely to be fundamentally different to how citizens experience it. While doing this research, I asked migrant workers why they gathered in Little India. My interviewees gave two answers: firstly, gathering in public space is crucial for migrant workers who, often indebted, do not have the money to gather in shopping malls or cafes; secondly, in Little India, migrant workers new to Singapore could meet relatives, friends-of-friends, and compatriots who did not stay in the same dormitories. However we reorganise the city in coming years, this should not come at the expense of migrant workers' need for sociability in a foreign place. It also bears remembering that migrant workers' definitions of problems may not align with ours. Many of the migrant workers I interviewed were more worried about their wages than the alcohol ban, which they viewed in a positive light. Similarly, during COVID-19, more invisible problems deserve attention, particularly those that cut at the heart of migrants' reasons for leaving home and their sense of self-worth. Here, I am thinking of migrant workers' inability to remit money home.

Finally, this article was made possible through the trusting relationships I formed with migrant workers through civil society organisations, who themselves are sometimes cast as troublemakers. As I have written elsewhere [Loong, 2020], in a society where migrant workers are denied channels to voice their own concerns, civil society organisations function as crucial intermediaries between migrant workers and the state. A state that takes civil society seriously is not disunited, but strengthened by its capacity to listen.

References

Chin, N. C. and Chia, A. (2013, 8 December). Little India riot, 18 injured, 27 arrested. *Today Online*. Retrieved from https://www.todayonline.com/singapore/riot-breaks-out-little-india

Lee, A. (2014, 30 June). Little India riot: Misunderstanding fuelled riot, says COI. *Today Online*. Retrieved from https://www.todayonline.com/singapore/little-india-riot-misunderstanding-over-accident-and-response-fuelled-riot-says-coi

Loong, S. (2020, 5 May). Who is responsible for Singapore's migrant workers, and why does it matter? *Academia.sg*. Retrieved from https://www.academia.sg/academic-views/who-is-responsible-for-singapores-migrant-workers-and-why-does-it-matter/

Transient Workers Count Too. (2020, 17 September). Research finding: Only a handful of workers have had rest days out from dorms. Retrieved from https://twc2.org.sg/2020/09/17/research-finding-only-a-handful-of-workers-have-had-rest-days-out-from-dorms/

Chapter 3b

'This Country, Law Very Strong': Securitization Beyond the Border in the Everyday Lives of Bangladeshi Migrant Workers in Singapore*

Shona Loong

Department of Geography, National University of Singapore, 1 Arts Link, Kent Ridge, Singapore 117570, Singapore
shonaloong@u.nus.edu.

While work on the securitization of migration has often held borders to be the site at which state power is most keenly felt, this paper draws on static and walking interviews with Bangladeshi male migrant workers in Singapore to understand their everyday experiences of the securitization within state territory. These narratives demonstrate how the Little India district in Singapore has been scripted as an exceptionally problematic space associated with dangerous migrant bodies, within which Bangladeshi migrants encounter state power in a variety of guises, ranging from police patrols to video surveillance technologies. They also reveal how Bangladeshi migrants continually struggle against these state-led scripts of insecurity, even if their sojourn in Singaporean

*This article was originally published in *Geoforum*, Vol. 90, pp. 11–19. DOI: 10.1016/j.geoforum.2018.01.012.

territory is circumscribed by a condition of permanent temporariness. Through this discussion, the securitization of migration is conceptualized as an unfinished project that is often exerted unevenly and paradoxically within state territory. The security-migration nexus should also not only be understood with recourse to bodies deemed "illegal" and "unwanted" — such as asylum-seekers and undocumented migrants — but should also account for temporary labour migrants who have been legally admitted into state territory, whose labour power is central to the host state's economy but who are disallowed from ever belonging within the countries they work in.

Keywords: Securitization, Migrant workers, Singapore Biopolitics, The everyday

1. Introduction: The "Little India Riot"

On 8 December 2013, 33-year-old Indian national Sakthivel Kumaravelu was run over by a bus in Singapore's Little India district, a heritage area historically associated with Singapore's ethnic Indian community, where tens of thousands of Bangladeshi and Indian male migrant workers congregate on Sunday evenings. Kumaravelu's instantaneous death was reported to cause more than 400 of these South Asian men in the vicinity to react violently (COI, 2014). By the next morning, a complete alcohol ban was imposed on Little India. Investigations conducted by a committee convened by the state declared that effective responses to the "riot" must be directed towards "enhanc [ing] the security' of Little India as a "congregation location for foreign workers" (COI, 2014: 64).

These state responses bring together three different spaces. For one, the *precise spot* at which the riot occurred was discursively rescaled to subject the *whole of Little India* to emergency responses. These state-led responses, targeted at "maintain[ing] the safety and security of [Singaporean] society" (Ministry of Home Affairs, 2014) and territory *as a whole* were therefore directed only towards a select portion of state territory associated with South Asian migrant men. In addition, state narratives tend to portray Little India as a homogeneous area utilized by Singapore's South Asian migrant population. This is not the case. The "Little India Riot" occurred in the section of Little India frequented by

Indian workers; the 160,000 Bangladeshi citizens working in Singapore (Aw, 2016) do not see themselves or their compatriots as implicated in the riot, but find themselves subject to state interventions following the incident as they frequent the area. State responses to the Little India Riot therefore brought into sharp relief the ways in which Little India has often been associated with the presence of a putatively monolithic group of disorderly South Asian male migrant bodies. Moreover, interventions into this area are not new, but build on a longer — and quieter — history. Local NGO Transient Workers Count Too has, for one, suggested that migrants have long been managed as threats to state security as they traverse the area through extraordinarily frequent police patrols and littering law enforcement (TWC2, 2012; 2015). While the policing of migrant bodies certainly occurs in other spaces associated with low-wage migrants in Singapore (see Kitiarsa, 2014 on Thai workmen; Yeoh and Huang, 1998 on female domestic workers), I have chosen to focus on Little India because of its recent associations with the "Little India Riot".

Drawing on the narratives of ten Bangladeshi men, this paper traces the ways in which temporary Bangladeshi labour migrants encounter state power as they traverse Little India. It makes two main contributions to a body of literature about the securitization of migration that foregrounds how non-citizen bodies are governed as threats to national security (e.g. Bigo, 2008; Huysmans, 2006). Firstly, by focusing on the act of deportation, literature on the securitization of migration often presupposes a clear split between migrants who belong in state territory, and migrants who do not (usually undocumented migrants and asylum seekers). However, the experiences of Bangladeshi migrants show that securitization works through the bodies of "differentially excluded" migrants that are legally "incorporated into certain areas of society (above all the labour market) but denied access to others (such as welfare systems, citizenship and political participation)" (Castles, 1995, page 294). I argue that although these regular migrants are legally admitted into state territory on temporary work-permits, they continue to be managed as security threats. The securitization of migration must therefore be understood as a strategy imposed *within* the host state's territory, and not just at its borders. Secondly, I contend that the securitization of migration is best understood as a practice woven into the everyday lives of migrant workers (see Mitchell, 1991; Mountz, 2003; Painter, 2006). A focus on the everyday also reveals how migrants do not remain passive in the face of state policies that script them as unruly security threats, but that they are able to skillfully navigate the restrictions imposed on the spaces they inhabit.

This paper begins by reviewing literature on the securitization of migration, noting a turn towards the embodied aspects of security. The following section discusses Foucault and de Certeau as key theorists that have grappled with how power is exercised and negotiated in everyday life. Foucault's work on biopower provides insight into how state securitization strategies are targeted at both individual migrant bodies and a generalized population of migrant workers, while his work on the security *dispositif* allows for an understanding of how state power works through the regulation of migrant workers' mobilities within state territory are regulated. Whereas Foucault allows me to come to grips with the exercise of state power, I draw on de Certeau to show how subjects maneuver within the constraints of state-led securitization strategies to further their own ends. After discussing the static and walking interviews utilized for this study and providing some background information on migrant workers in Singapore, I catalogue Bangladeshi migrants' encounters with state power in Little India. By showing how state securitization strategies are targeted both at migrant workers as a whole (what Foucault terms *biopolitics*) and at individual migrant bodies (or *anatomo-politics*), I argue that the securitization of migration impinges on the mobilities of migrants within state territory, and not just their ability to traverse state borders. In Little India, a space deemed particularly "dangerous" and "disorderly" for its association with migrant bodies, the state works through various proxies (e.g. video cameras, state policemen, auxiliary policemen, and urban architecture) to make its presence felt in the everyday lives of work-permit holders. Thereafter, drawing on de Certeau, I turn to migrants' negotiations of state power by way of spatial practices and spatial stories. Spatial practices refer to how migrants confound state power through their bodies, while spatial stories to refer to how migrants construct their own identities as oppositional to the state's construction of them as security threats and mere laboring bodies. The paper closes by highlighting some wider implications of these findings.

2. Securitizing Migration

Security and migration are "interlinked and immutable" in two ways: "people move because of some threat to security or to improve their security. In doing so, they are often seen as a threat to the security of the receiving population" (Graham, 2000, page 186). A substantial body of work on the securitization of migration has shown how states invoke tropes of fear, unease and threat to legitimize the exclusion and/ or management of migrant bodies (e.g. Guild, 2009). Two interrelated lines of inquiry can be detected here. Firstly, earlier work on the securitization of migration extends the basic premises of securitization theory espoused by the Copenhagen School of security studies (see Buzan et al., 1998; Huysmans, 1998; Wæver, 1995) to reveal how speech-acts are deployed to position migrants as existential threats to the nation-state (e.g. Huysmans, 2006). Authors writing in this mode were keen to push critical security studies beyond its national-scale preoccupation with deconstructing military strategy, towards the consideration of various 'non-traditional' insecurities, including the movement of people across international borders. Didier Bigo (2008), for instance, shows how control of the EU's external borders occurs through laws on terrorism and organized crime once considered the province of internal security, as well as sophisticated databases that compile profiles of people deemed likely to commit a crime (see also Huysmans, 2000). Together, these strategies allow migrants to be governed according to an overarching "governmentality of unease" by which migrant movements are regulated according to the degree of risk they pose to the security of host societies (Bigo, 2008, page 6).

While this set of works deals with security on a transor supranational scale, a second, more recent approach to the securitization of migration deals primarily with individual bodies. Securitization, here, is conceptualized as a "scattered process" enacted in accordance with calculations of risk and probability (Huysmans, 2011, page 377; Müller, 2011), through which migrant bodies are regulated as threats through the continuous unfolding of practices. For instance, Topak (2014) shows how the most extreme effects of the securitization of migration are materialized along the Greece-Turkey borderzone as practices of pushback leave migrants to drown in the Aegean sea (for similar perspective on the US-Mexico border, see Doty, 2011). Another securitization strategy that hinges on the bodies of migrants is biometric risk profiling that breaks the subject up into categories (e.g. 'Arab', 'Muslim', 'woman') associated with varying degrees of risk, in order to determine their admissibility into state territory (Amoore, 2006). This approach to the securitization of migration complements recent shifts in geographies of security. Whereas the concept of security was once the province of critical geopolitics scholars interested in the global geopolitical order (e.g. Dalby, 2003; Ingram and Dodds, 2009; Philo, 2012, page 2) has argued that geographers should attend how security plays into *both* the "seemingly more mundane matters of 'small-s' security" and the "geopolitical machinations" associated with 'big-S' security. Geographers have responded to this call by attending to security as an embodied feeling, rather than a state-led script (e.g. Bondi, 2014). They have also extended their methodological toolkit beyond analyses of official policy papers, to include analyses of popular and literary texts (e.g. Noxolo 2014; Fluri, 2014) and psychogeographic walks (e.g. Paasche and Sidaway, 2010). Still, despite a turn towards studying security as it is embodied, little has been written on how the 'securitized' speak back to state power. Hence, following Staeheli and Nagel (2008), I ask: how might our conception of the security-migration nexus be challenged by drawing insights from migrants' experiences of security?

In addition, studies of the security-migration nexus have often centred on foreign bodies deemed "illegal" and "unwanted"; the "waste [s] of globalization" that must be disposed of by states keen to assert control over their own territory (Bauman, 2004: 58). As a result, borders have emerged as a primary site of analysis. Studies of the US often examine how discourses about 9/11 have been used to legitimize heightened border controls (e.g. Amoore, 2006; Müller, 2004), while similar themes explored in the European context argue that the EU's enlargement and the formation of the Schengen Area have prompted the EU to harden its external boundaries (e.g. Huysmans, 2006; van Houtum, 2010). Conceptualizations of the border as devolved (Coleman, 2009), dispersed (Walters, 2006), and embodied (Amoore and Hall, 2009) continue to be wedded to a notion of security premised on the question of who is expelled from state territory and how. De Genova (2002, page 439) draws attention away from the act of deportation and toward the ways in which a 'palpable sense of deportability' is maintained by states to produce its undocumented migrant workforce as a vulnerable and tractable commodity (see also Walters, 2002; Willen, 2007). De Genova's work on the way in which deportability as a possibility rather than an act is closely aligned with the arguments I am making in this paper. Yet I argue that migrants which are not 'deportable' (given their regularized status) are similarly subject to a condition of insecurity and permanent temporariness. Bailey et al. (2002, page 139) describe permanent temporariness as a state that combines 'the static experience of being temporary' and the 'knowledge that such temporariness is permanent'. Similarly, the Bangladeshi migrants in this paper understood that their work-permits would be valid only for two-years at a time and that they cannot be converted into permanent residency regardless of how long the migrant has resided in Singapore. Just as De Genova argues that deportability imbues everyday life, so too I argue that permanent temporariness becomes present in the everyday life of migrants through their encounters with state power in Little India. Such encounters exert 'a disciplining power' over their bodies that 'helps promote the interests of the state and capital' (Bailey et al., 2002, page 139).

This paper therefore argues that the securitization of migration affects not just irregular migrants, but also regular low-wage migrants whose lives are circumscribed by temporary work-permits. This only becomes clear when examining instances in which migrants encounter state power in their everyday life; as such, the securitization of migration must be understood as a process enacted within state territory, and not at its border alone. The next two sections argue that Foucault's discussion of biopower and security *dispositif* and de Certeau's theorisation of modes of resistance to state power are helpful for understanding this dynamic, after which I apply these concepts to my empirical material.

3. Biopower, Security and the Everyday

Michel Foucault has traced a shift from sovereign power, which deals with subjects over whom the sovereign holds the power of life and death, to biopower, which seeks to "achieve a mastery at the level of life itself" (Macey, 2009, page 187; Foucault, 2007). In Foucault's (2003, page 50) words, we can discern within biopower both the "body-organism-discipline-institution series" (i.e. *anatomo-politics*) and the "population-biological-process-regulatory-mechanism-State [series]" (i.e. *bio-politics*). Through anatomo-politics, individual bodies become sites for normalization and control in two moves. Power is internalized by subjects who modulate their own behavior to conform to societal norms within a 'purified' space (Sibley, 1995). On the flipside of disciplinary power is bio-politics, which seeks to manage the well-being of a massified population according to aggregated measurements of risk. Biopolitics is central to the operation of capitalist society, insofar as the economic well-being of a population is dependent on the state's ability to maximize the productivity of various types of workers within its administrative purview (Rasmussen, 2011). Yet, anatomo-politics and bio-politics are not mutually exclusive: they merely constitute two poles of state governance (Dillon and Lobo-Guerrero, 2008). Anatomo-politics, after all, individualizes subjects to become *part of a mass*, whereas bio-politics aggregates *individualized behavior to the level of populations*.

In the context of transnational migratory flows, it is important to note that biopower does not range over immobile bodies or populations, but over a space of circulation. Migrant bodies are constantly on the move — they move across borders and within state territory — such that migration controls that condition migrants' entry into state territory also condition how they experience spaces within state territory. Foucault's (2007) work on the security *dispositif* is apt for understanding how state power works through a space that can never be entirely closed off from the circulation of various bodies and materialities. Within this space, the same infrastructures — such as roads and thoroughfares — developed to facilitate flows that enhance the well-being of a population (e.g. the movement of trade and commerce through a city) also leave the population vulnerable to the circulation of disease, vagrants, and other 'undesirables'. The security *dispositif* is directed towards managing this tension; it aims not to enclose or forbid, but strives towards "maximizing the good circulation by diminishing the bad" (Foucault, 2007, page 18; Salter, 2013; Usher, 2014) in the interests of how 'how circulation functions within capitalism in relation to production and labour' (Aradau and Blanke, 2010, page 53). Hence, security might be considered a form of biopower that seeks to optimize human life by regulating mobilities and flows. This is not to say that the security *dispositif* is not concerned with territory; rather, security conceives of territory as a heterogeneous space within which subjects are constantly on the move.

Foucault, however, has often been criticized for presenting biopower as an accomplished project that forecloses opportunities for resistance and/or negotiation (Allen, 2003). It is not necessarily true that Foucault sidelines resistance completely. For instance, there exists work on counter-conduct, or means of resistance through which subjects seek to be governed differently, 'by other *conducteurs*… towards other objectives… and through other procedures and methods' rather than rejecting idea of government *in toto* (Foucault, 2007, page 194–5; Death, 2010). Yet in the context of this case, de Certeau's (1984) distinction between 'strategies' and 'tactics' in *The Practice of Everyday Life* provides a particularly helpful means of conceptualizing both the potency of state (bio)power while remaining attentive to how power might be experienced and contested at specific spaces and times. Through strategies, producers of a space fix a delimited space that is protected from perceived threats by a "subject of will and power" that imposes on it from "above" (de Certeau, 1984, page xiv). Foucauldian biopower may thus be construed as a strategy through which a state secures its territory. Yet such strategies are not totalizing in the sense that 'groups or individuals already caught in the nets of 'discipline'' often display 'dispersed, tactical, and makeshift' forms of contestation that make over a space to the purposes of ordinary people (de Certeau, 1984, page xiv; Crang, 2000). These are tactics: embodied, minute, and mundane forms of resistance that are contingent on the specific spaces and times in which they are expressed. By conceptualizing tactics in this way, de Certeau helpfully positions the body and the everyday at the center of his understanding of resistance.

De Certeau uses the practice of walking in the city to illustrate what he means by tactics. This analogy works in three ways. Firstly, walking is a *banal* practice through which pedestrians assert their agency within the routes prescribed by urban planners; likewise, tactics are not forms of extraordinary, grandiose subcultural resistance, but are built into the rhythms of everyday life. Secondly, just as pedestrians use their bodies to move about the city, subjects tactically appropriate strategic designs for their own purposes through the materiality of the body. Thirdly, the improvisational paths that pedestrians chart through the city do little to destabilize the designs of urban planners. Similarly, tactics present themselves only as fleeting, fragmentary refusals of proprietary power. De Certeau's tactics are thus appropriate for understanding how lowwage labour migrants, whose day-to-day lives are constrained by the temporary work visas they hold, exploit fissures in state power to reinscribe their own presence within the Singapore nation-city-state.

Yea (2016) has previously used de Certeau to understand the "weapons of the weak" (Scott, 1985, 1990) deployed by trafficked women in Korea. Her analysis attends to the micro-scale dynamics of the *gijich'on* club, suggesting that each space (e.g. stage, tables, booths, VIP rooms) offers varying possibilities for women to heighten their own ability to cope, and that these small resistances can ultimately allow women to extricate themselves from the club completely. Her account therefore subverts imaginations of trafficking victims as passive, hopelessly incarcerated victims. Similarly, this paper draws attention to a range of spaces within Little India (e.g. open spaces, residential blocks, bedspaces) to show how the state-led strategies aimed at managing the circulation of migrants through Little India are enforced and resisted through a "patchwork" (Zedner, 2009) of spaces. Migrants' ability to make over public spaces for their own purposes have been studied previously, both in Singapore (e.g. Yeoh and Huang, 1998) and elsewhere (e.g. Harney, 2013; Law, 2001; Noussia and Lyons, 2009; Park, 2015). I wish to show that migrants demonstrate a similar ability in the face of the nexus between security and migration.

4. Methodology

This study is based on the experiences of ten low-wage male Bangladeshi migrants in Singapore that I met and befriended through my involvement with a migrant rights NGO in Singapore that has now continued for more than three years. The men were aged between 24 and 35 years old, had made between one to three migration trips to Singapore, and had spent between 4 and 11 years in Singapore altogether. They had all entered Singapore on work-permits that allowed them to work for a specific company within either the construction and shipyard industries. At the time of the interview, however, these men were all holding a Special Pass instead of a work-permit. A Special Pass is granted to workers who have made a claim for a work-accident and/ or for salary arrears to legalize their stay in Singapore until the claims process is complete. During this time, they are barred from legal employment; many therefore rely on NGOs for meals and advice on how to navigate the claims system. The differences between migrant workers on work-permits and those with Special Passes have been explored in aspects of mental health (Harrigan and Koh, 2016), masculinity (Ye, 2014), and housing (TWC2, 2013). Yet, for the purposes of this study, I found it worthwhile to work with Special Pass holders for two reasons. Firstly, it is difficult to access migrant workers who are currently employed. They stay almost exclusively in housing provided by their employers, in purpose-built dormitories far from the centre of Singapore or on construction sites themselves. These migrant workers are also likely to have only between one to four days off each month. Secondly, I felt it important to build up trust between myself and my interviewees; something which I could do only with the out-of-work migrant workers I was assisting as a volunteer. I sought to minimize the power imbalance between volunteer and beneficiary by recruiting only participants who were comfortable with me and who consented to participating in the study. In my view, this study's small sample size (n = 10) is a worthwhile tradeoff for the in-depth narratives I could procure with my participants. To circumvent biases that may result from this small sample, my findings are supplemented with references to media and NGO reports. Moreover, my long-term involvement with Bangladeshi migrants also allowed me to see my participants' narratives in relation to hundreds of conversations I have had with migrant workers and other volunteers.

Static and walking interviews were conducted with all participants between August and September 2014, with the exception of one, who opted out of a walking interview. Static interviews that lasted between 60 and 90 min were geared towards understanding individuals' migration journeys, migration goals, and perceptions of Singapore in general. In contrast, walking interviews hoped to elicit in-depth narratives about specific sites (Brown and Durrheim, 2009; Evans and Jones, 2011). These off-the-record mobile interviews lasted up to three hours, during which I asked my participants to lead me to places in Little India that were important to them, while offering suggestions as I deemed fit. Immediately after each walkabout, handwritten notes were consolidated into detailed fieldnotes that sought to record participants' personal experiences with the specific features of each site, the routes we took, and changes in their bodily comportment as we moved. In this paper, quotes from these fieldnotes have been denoted with the term 'Author's notes'. Pseudonyms are used throughout.

5. Singapore's Securitized Migration Regime

Singapore's migration regime allots differential rights to migrants depending on the varying degrees of threat they are presumed to pose to the nation-state (Yeoh, 2006). The ten Bangladeshi migrant workers interviewed for this study are part of a population of 993,900 work-permit holders in Singapore (MOM, 2015) who occupy the bottom rung of this regime.[1] Unlike the skilled expatriate professionals that enter Singapore on an Employment Pass, work-permit holders are consigned to a state of permanent temporariness: they are prohibited from applying from permanent residence or citizenship, must renew their workpermits every two years at the discretion of a single employer, and are subject to deportability through Singapore's Immigration Act, which allows the state to deport migrants "in the interests of public security" (AGC, 2012). A logic of "differential exclusion" (Castles, 1995) is clearly at work here: work-permit holders are readily incorporated into Singapore's economy insofar as they perform work considered demeaning by locals, but are also excluded from the rest of Singapore's populace insofar as all routes to citizenship and political participation are closed to them. This situation is compounded by the hefty placement fees that low-wage migrants pay to middlemen to acquire a job in Singapore (Baey and Yeoh, 2015). All my participants paid upwards of SGD 8000 (approximately USD 5600) for their first trip to Singapore — often taking loans from relatives or banks — knowing that it would take approximately two years' work in Singapore to break-even. These debts make migration a risky and precarious venture from the outset. Migrants often manage this risk by actively complying to

[1] Official statistics that group work-permit holders according to nationality are unavailable.

state regulations in order to gain favour with employers and thus prolong their stay in Singapore (Bal, 2013). Paradoxically, even as the state scripts lowwage migrants as threats to the nation-state, work-permit holders themselves are cornered into passivity and obedience as their livelihoods become over-determined by the power of the state. These tropes of threat, danger and insecurity are conjoined not only with the bodies of low-wage labour migrants, but also with the spaces within state territory these migrants are presumed to congregate, such as Little India. With Foucault and de Certeau in mind, it is to migrants' experiences of state power in this space that I now turn.

5.1 *Encountering securitization: bio-politics*

On Sunday evenings, an estimated 100,000 Bangladeshi and Indian migrants gather in Little India (COI, 2014). Little India comprises myriad sites central to the lives of Bangladeshi migrants: these include Bangladeshi banks for sending remittances, commercial spaces for buying groceries and telephone cards, and open spaces where migrants socialize and seek out *hundi* (informal remittance) agents. Although migrants from different districts in Bangladesh have their own gathering points, Lembu Road Open Space — known as the 'Minimart' — is unanimously acknowledged as the largest and most important of these open spaces (see Fig. 1). Crucially, Bangladeshi migrants are not the only occupants of Little India. Indian migrants frequent the area as well, but gather in almost entirely

Figure 1 The Minimart on a weekday morning (left) and a Sunday night (right).

Source: author's own.

separate sites. Indeed, although the state uses the name 'Little India' to refer to a contiguous area associated with *all* South Asian migrant men, Bangladeshi migrants use 'Little India' specifically to refer to the portion of this area where Indian men congregate. Bangladeshi migrants, on the other hand, refer collectively to the spaces they claim on Sunday nights as 'Serangoon'. In addition, Little India is also a popular tourist destination and houses the residents of several public housing blocks (Chang, 2000). Given the "coevalness" of heterogeneous uses and groups of people within this area, Little India can be read as a "throwntogether" space in which the "negotiation of intersecting trajectories… is forced upon us" (Massey, 2005, page 154). Securitization is one form of such negotiation, through which exertions of state biopower within Little India produce Bangladeshi migrants as a distinct population (*bio-politics*) and as individual, disciplined bodies (*anatomo-politics*) governed according to principles of differential exclusion.

State power (re)produces Bangladeshi migrant workers as a massified population in two main ways. All my participants attested to a heightened police presence in Little India's streets and open spaces. To them, police in the area invariably appear at the 'Minimart' at least once in the morning and once in the evening, ostensibly to check if migrants have valid immigration papers. Faruk, a 29-year old construction worker who has spent eleven years in Singapore, stated that there are three places in Singapore with heightened policing: "Little India, Serangoon, Geylang." Notably, the three areas he mentions are associated primarily with low-wage migrant men — Indian, Bangladeshi, and Chinese men respectively — rather than a more generalized population of migrants. Following Herbert's (2008) argument that the police embody state power by imposing a public order ordained by the state on the dynamics of everyday situations, the heightened police presence in Little India might be read as a biopolitical strategy that positions migrants within a larger population of work-permit holders, whose sojourn on state territory is permanently temporary.

Besides police patrols, state power is also manifest in cues in Little India's urban landscape. Like most public housing in Singapore, public housing in the area contains ground-floor open spaces ('void decks') accessible to residents and non-residents. However, unlike elsewhere in

Singapore, these void decks feature large signs that proclaim a maximum fine of S$1000 for drinking and eating and several fences that cut across the space, making it difficult for large groups to congregate (see Fig. 2). These modifications of the built environment are supplemented by the presence of auxiliary police personnel who enforce the aforementioned fines, reprimand loiterers, and break up migrant gatherings. Unlike state policemen concerned with visas and immigration papers, who are responsible for the security of state territory as a whole, auxiliary police responsible only for these void decks often ask migrants to relocate themselves to areas beyond their purview (see Paasche et al., 2014). This strategy of displacement is facilitated by large signs that designate each open space within Little India with a unique name (see Fig. 3). These signs, like the

Figure 2 Fences and signs under a public housing block in Little India.

Source: author's own.

Figure 3 Signs that name open spaces in Little India.

Source: author's own.

fences that fragment Little India's void decks, are not erected elsewhere in Singapore. Well aware of these dynamics, Bangladeshi men pass through these void decks as a short cut, but do not gather or linger there. Unlike residents of public housing in the area, migrants are encouraged to see sheltered void decks as transit-spaces that disallow lingering and attachment. Conversely, migrants are encouraged to dwell in open-air spaces sanctioned by the state, where they come under the gaze of state policemen.

Together, state policemen and auxiliary policemen work to securitize Little India as a space associated with a distinct population of lowwage migrant men. Here, in line with Foucault's security *dispositif*, the securitization of migration operates by regulating migrant mobilities between public and quasi-public spaces; through "circuits that isolate particular individuals/populations without rendering them immobile" (Salter, 2013, page 16). This approach to securitization can also be read with recourse to Foucault's formulation of racism. Foucault (2003) argues that racism is central to biopolitics insofar as it demarcates the boundaries of the population that comes under the state's administrative purview. To him, racism distinguishes worthy from unworthy life, hence legitimizing the exclusion of others to maintain the purity and health of a 'worthy' population (Crampton, 2007; Dillon and Neil, 2008; Macey, 2009; Rasmussen, 2011). However, while Foucauldian racism posits an unambiguous split between worthy and unworthy lives, the differential exclusion of migrants reveals how racism may operate according to shades of life, rather than a sharp distinction between life and death. While Bangladeshi work-permit holders are clearly partitioned from Singapore citizens according to the state's migration regime, they are not strictly unwelcome within state territory. Rather, their lives — which 'matter' (Zylinska, 2004) primarily as an inexpensive supply of labour that allows Singapore to pursue capital accumulation — are biopolitically governed *such that* migrants conform to these aims. Bangladeshi migrants are not — as in the case of refugees and asylum-seekers — "left to die" at state borders (Topak, 2014, page 830); instead, they encounter the state in its numerous guises as they travel in and through a range of public and quasi-public spaces.

5.2 *Encountering securitization: anatomo-politics*

Just as state strategies produce Bangladeshi migrants as an aggregated, differentially excluded population, they also work to circumscribe Little India as an "embodied securityscape" within which the "micro-gestures, sensitivities and micro-changes" of bodies become targets of securitization (Noxolo, 2014, page 295) through strategies of normalization and control (*anatomo-politics*). Although the subjection of bodies has been implicit in preceding discussions, this section turns more resolutely towards the body as a site for exertions of state power through (1) the governance of bodily comportment and (2) technologies of self-regulation.

The most blatant means by which migrant bodies are regulated is the heightened enforcement of littering regulations in Little India. Although littering is criminalized throughout Singapore, within Little India's void decks and open spaces South Asian migrant men receive fines for littering with a troubling frequency, even when they are sitting next to the objects they are accused of leaving behind (TWC2, 2012; 2015). Fines, which range from S$150 to S$400, can take a heavy financial toll on migrants who are already in a state of indebtedness and who are responsible for remitting money regularly. Sandir, a 32-yearold shipyard worker, pointed out the spot where he once received a fine for littering as we stood in the 'Minimart' together.

> [Sandir] tells me that 'everywhere eat', there will be fines. He himself was fined $150 in 2008 for littering. He was chewing on a betel nut (*paan*), and spat out the leaves, throwing it on the ground. He then heard a Malay plainclothes policeman behind him saying, '*bhai* [brother], why you throw that leaf?' The policeman then took his permit for his details, and issued him a 'receipt' that stated why he was fined and what to do. The policeman also warned him not to protest, or the fine would increase to $200 or $300… [He tells me] 'I think about the fine, I very crazy. $150 a lot of money.'
>
> Author's notes

The enforcement of littering laws reveals how the bodily comportment of migrants is subject to state power. Even practices as banal as sitting next to a Coke can that one has finished drinking or spitting into a roadsite drain (see TWC2, 2015) are opportunities for the state to demonstrate its power over individual migrant bodies. Moreover, as Sandir's narrative shows, these expressions of state power are amplified by the hyper-precarious subject position that temporary migrants occupy, to produce a "layering of insecurities" in which the financial toll of fines is aggravated by a migration regime that locks migrants into a state of indebtedness to agents and overdependence on employers (Lewis et al., 2015, page 593). Conversely, many of my participants had engaged in informal, ad-hoc work, but told me that they rarely feared being caught for working illegally. This is to say that migrant men are far more likely to be accused of flouting the law in their leisure time. In this sense, migrant encounters with the state are once again conditioned by differential exclusion: migrants are left alone while engaging in economically productive activities, whereas migrant-bodies-at-leisure are compelled to comport themselves to the trope of the 'good, docile Other' (Abdullah, 2005).

Self-regulation, then, is an important facet of anatomo-politics. Perhaps the most blatant way in which individual migrant bodies are compelled to internalize state power is through video surveillance. Closed-circuit television (CCTV) cameras operated by either the state police or commercial establishments are inescapable in Little India's open-air spaces and car parks. The gaze that these cameras cast over open spaces is enhanced by the scrupulous pruning of trees in the area and the provision of adequate night-time street lighting (Tan, 2015). Bangladeshi migrants themselves are well aware of these CCTVs. I asked Safiqul, a 25-year-old shipyard worker, about these cameras as we stood in the 'Minimart' together:

> He gestures around, trying to count: 'I think one… two… three… four?' but eventually gives up and tells me that there are a lot of 'police cameras' around. He believes that the police watch the cameras, reiterating what he said before: that 'Singapore's police and [private] security [companies] same, both very strong.
>
> Author's notes

Safiqul's sentiments are significant for several reasons. Firstly, like many other migrants, he is convinced that CCTVs are ubiquitous in Little India. Secondly, Safiqul believes that the CCTVs are being watched. Not all my participants shared this belief: Sandir, for example, stated that "police see or not, I don't know... but I scared. People scared." Still, even though Sandir cannot tell whether these cameras are watched, the possibility that they might be causes him to regulate his behavior to avoid arousing suspicion. The person behind the camera is irrelevant to migrants' belief that CCTVs serve a panoptic function within Little India; in response, migrants reign in their own behavior to comply with the norms projected by a putatively omnipresent and omnipotent Singaporean state. Overall, through video surveillance, state power is not just exerted over an aggregated population, but also diffused through individual bodies (see Koskela, 2000). The securitization of migrant is not just about securing state borders; it is, in this case, about state power producing migrants as both a distinct population (*bio-politics*) and as individual, disciplined bodies (*anatomo-politics*).

5.3 *Negotiating securitization: working with(in) biopower*

Inasmuch as state biopower intrudes into the everyday life and spaces of Bangladeshi migrants, the everyday is a realm in which state power is negotiated, rather than passively reproduced. A survey of the spatial stories and spatial practices deployed by migrants reveals these frayed ends. I use 'spatial practices' to refer specifically to the ways in which migrants elude and confound state power through the materiality and (im)mobility of their bodies. Just as de Certeau's (1984) pedestrians utilize their bodies to confound the strategic designs of urban planners, so too do migrants trace "corporeal choreographies" (Noxolo, 2014) that allow them to contest state securitization in their everyday routines. In contrast, 'spatial stories' refer to the ways in which migrants 'story' their own, idealized collective identities against tropes of a messy and corrupt Bangladeshi state, the 'lawless' migrant, and their past (pre-migration) selves. In so doing, migrants insist that they are neither the passive subjects nor the security threats that the Singaporean state makes them out to be. Here, I catalogue two spatial practices and three spatial stories used by migrants. This list is not meant to be exhaustive, but to gesture towards how the securitization of migration can be considered an incomplete process that is contested by migrants themselves.

The first of these spatial practices is *evasion*. Migrants evade state power by choosing to gather and linger in spaces that seem invisible to it (see also Bailey et al., 2002). Jamail, a 32-year-old shipyard worker began to rent a bedspace in Little India after he was put out-of-work by a workplace accident. Unsurprisingly, Jamail's room is cramped and uncomfortable: most out-of-work migrants who choose to stay in Little India must put up with rooms shared by eight to twenty men on bunk beds, all of whom share a single bathroom. Yet, Jamail chooses to spend his free time here:

> "Here, I no *jalan-jalan lah* [Singlish: to walk around]. I stay room inside, see movie, like that *lah*. Because [staying outdoors] wastes time… police talking, suddenly police want to check… They talking [about] the work-permit, giving the work-permit.

Jamail, in other words, confines himself to private spaces to avoid encounters with the police, who pester him for his immigration papers and question him for loitering in open spaces. Even though the bedspace that Jamail — and other migrants — rents is likely to be illegal (see Wong, 2010), he feels that his leisure time is less likely to be disrupted if he remains there, instead of in open spaces sanctioned for migrant gatherings. His choice to remain indoors can be read as a tactical maneuver that Jamail skillfully charts between various spaces in Little India, over which state power is exerted unevenly and paradoxically.

Next, migrants also deploy tactics of *occupancy*. Even as migrants restrict their gatherings to open-spaces regulated by police patrols and video surveillance, crowds allow migrants to confound state power. It was common for my participants to suggest that the sheer number of migrants who gather on Sunday evenings render everyday practices of securitization futile. Sandir, for instance, estimates that thirty to forty thousand people gather here on these nights, so much so that "many people, police cannot control". There is the sense that the police simply cannot check everyone's papers or look out for minor offences because overwhelming crowds render individual migrant bodies invisible. While de Certeau's (1984) walker traverses the city alone, on Sunday evenings it is the impermanent "constitution of confused, massified bodies" that confounds state intelligibilities (Woodward, 2014, page 28), as opposed to the stable populations carved out by Foucauldian biopower (see also Noussia and Lyons, 2009).

Besides these two spatial practices, I encountered three spatial stories through which migrants 'story' their collective identities against a range of imagined Others to assert themselves as legitimate users of Little India. These stories have to do with (1) the 'law', (2) the 'good' migrant, and (3) the migrant self.

All my participants applauded Singapore's 'law' for being 'strong'. The 'law' — a word invoked by all ten — refers to the state's ability to impose order over its populace, comprising the ability of police to apprehend criminals effectively and the enforcement of anti-littering laws. Participants' praise for Singapore's 'law' is frequently juxtaposed against experiences with bribery, corruption and disorderliness in Dhaka and/or Bangladesh. For instance:

> "Dhaka good. But same? No. Singapore very nice. Because Singapore law also very good. I like this Singapore law"
>
> Nadir

> "I see-see Singapore very nice. Good country... So many people have, also no fighting, no anything. Bangladesh, many people have, fight a lot. Singapore law very high. Very strong. CC camera have, many people have also cannot fighting, after catch already police."
>
> Safiqul

> "Singapore, actually, discipline very good. But my country, discipline no good. Law also no good. All time fighting-fighting, police also no good."
>
> Abbas

Moreover, participants frequently compared their experiences with parliamentary elections (or 'politics') in both countries to emphasize this, telling me that they have seen several general elections in Singapore that have gone peacefully because of Singapore's 'law'. While the policing of Little India and Singapore's democratic procedures may be considered quite disparate expressions of state power, these processes were often woven into an narrative that emphasized Singapore's orderliness vis-à-vis

Bangladesh. It is telling that Tarif, a 31-year-old construction worker, first responded to Little India Riot by thinking that "this [is] like Bangladesh". Tarif is quick to reprimand the perpetrators of the incident, telling me that fighting is "no use" in a context where the state is bound to clamp down on violence swiftly and effectively. These expressions of respect for Singapore's 'law' are means by which migrants fold together disparate encounters with the state power to present themselves as people with a deep respect for orderliness. They therefore reject state-led imaginings of themselves as dangerous, lawless individuals.

Secondly, migrants see state power as enabling the circulation of "good" migrant bodies in Little India. Many Bangladeshi migrants portray Little India as a space in which the threat of being robbed or cheated by *other migrants* renders them insecure. For this reason, Jamail is exceedingly positive about the potential of the police to guarantee his safety in the area. He states that with the police around, "people no noisy, no crazy, free can talking, can walking." Sandir is similarly positive about alcohol restrictions imposed after the riot:

> He tells me that 'cannot drink outside is good, very good.' He is very adamant about this. 'Some people, they very stupid… [when they] drink, people take everything, wallet, handphone.
>
> Author's notes

There is a moralized hierarchy invoked in these statements: impositions of state power on Little India provide a sense of freedom and security for migrants who do not pose a threat to other migrants; conversely, participants imply that state power rightfully constrains the circulations of migrants who take advantage of their compatriots. In so doing, self-styled "good" migrants insist that the population of lowwage migrants carved out by the state do not pose a uniform threat to state security. In addition, migrants perceive that these state securitization strategies enable everyone — not just themselves — to navigate Little India safely. Many Bangladeshi migrants express amazement that women in Singapore can freely navigate public spaces without the threat of sexual harassment, as compared to the restricted spatialities of women in a predominantly Muslim context back home. For instance:

> Jamail is surprised at how girls in Singapore wear 'so short thing'… He couches this in terms of the law and freedom (for women): 'Like this can do, because Singapore is very good. Law is very good. Law very strong, cannot touch anybody.
>
> Author's notes

To them, women are free to move about and dress as they please in Singapore *because* of the blatant intrusion of state power (the 'law') into public spaces. This impression evinces highly gendered sentiments that state interventions in Little India *make possible* the unimpeded circulation of people — migrant and non-migrant, male and female — so long as they do not pose a threat to the state or to one another. While day-today migrant mobilities are managed with a view of diminishing the threat that migrants pose to society, migrants see exertions of state power as means whereby 'good' migrants are positioned as legitimate users of Little India.

Finally, besides juxtaposing themselves against other putatively threatening migrant bodies, Bangladeshi men rework securitization strategies into narratives of self-improvement. During his second migration trip (out of three), Sandir began to drink to cope with the stress of being unable to repay debts. Drinking, however, soon became expensive and unfulfilling:

> "He tells me that he drank everyday for three months, but soon realized that 'drink also, cannot earn the money. This drink cannot give anything, happiness, joy. [After realizing this], I never drink… If no drink, save money."
>
> Author's notes

Instead of understanding alcohol restrictions as a means of imposing security on Little India, Sandir interprets these restrictions as a form of positive discipline that *enables* himself to be a "good" migrant focused on remitting money, fulfilling familial responsibilities and attaining migration goals. Crucially, a condition of permanent temporariness continues to underlie Sandir's insistence on performing the role of a 'good', responsible migrant. Sandir knows that there is no hope of staying in Singapore in the long term; hence, he would therefore rather focus on securing a good future for himself in Bangladesh by way of maximizing remittances during his sojourn in Singapore. Although such spatial stories are a weak form of resistance that does not aim at overthrowing the structural constraints that migrant workers face in Singapore, they are 'not without longer term, transformative potential' directed towards bettering one's life in the long run (Yea, 2016, page 969).

In sum, the securitization of migration must be conceptualized as an everyday process exerted within state territory that is continually contested by migrants themselves, who deploy spatial practices and spatial stories. Spatial practices pertain to the stubborn insistence of the migrant body in the face of attempts to manage migrant mobilities in Little India, whereas spatial stories foreground the stubborn insistence of meanings that migrants ascribe to encounters with state power. Still, two caveats are in order. Firstly, while migrants are hardly passive subjects, the tactical trajectories that migrants trace remain "arts of the weak" that manipulate state designs without seeking to overthrow them (de Certeau, 1984, page 37). Secondly, these tactics must be distinguished from "acts of citizenship" through which "subjects constitute themselves as citizens... to whom the right to have rights is due" (Isin, 2008, page 18). Given the condition of transience imposed on workpermit holders, Bangladeshi migrants never presumed that their stay in Singapore could ever have been permanent; rather, they were interested in working within impositions of state power to further goals directed towards a life back home. Differential exclusion rears its head at every point.

6. Conclusion: Securitization Beyond the Border

Although Coleman (2007, page 57, 69) argues for conceptualizing immigration enforcement as "much more complicated than the straightforward enforcement of an either/or territoriality at the edges of the state", his work remains centered on deportation as a form of "border enforcement from afar" premised on a divide between inclusion/exclusion and legal/illegal. More broadly, a fixation on the dichotomous logic of borders runs throughout studies of the securitization of migration, even as borders are increasingly understood to be spatially diffuse. In contrast, I argue that temporary labour migrants in Singapore who are legally admitted into state territory are nonetheless scripted as threats to the security of the host nation-state. Foucault's understanding of biopower and the security *dispositif* are helpful analytics for understanding how securitization works within the state's interior. Instead of curtailing migrant mobilities altogether, the state governs temporary labour migrants through several proxies (policemen, video surveillance, urban architecture) that operate between a range of spaces in Little India. In so doing, the state positions migrant bodies as insecure, even as they are begrudgingly tolerated for the labour power they contribute to the Singapore state's goals of capital accumulation and urban development. As such, the logic of differential exclusion that undergirds Singapore's migration regime also comes to bear on migrants' everyday experiences of public space.

In addition, by drawing on migrants' experiences of security (following Staeheli and Nagel, 2008), this paper argues that securitization is a contested process. Labour migrants grapple with state power in two registers: by choreographing their movements through Little India in ways that elude state power and by reinterpreting state securitization strategies as means of furthering their own migration goals. Various authors (e.g. Katz, 2001; Sparke, 2008) have pointed out that global, macro-scale processes can be met by varying degrees of contestation ranging between subtle and overt. In the case of Bangladeshi migrant workers in Singapore, the forms of resistance they can engender are limited by a predetermined condition of permanent temporariness, but they do aim at some form of transformation within the life of an individual, even if the structures that constrain these individuals remain obdurate.

Acknowledgements

I am grateful to Dr. Woon Chih Yuan for supervising the project on which this paper was based. Two anonymous reviewers provided helpful comments on this draft. All errors remain my own.

References

Abdullah, N., 2005. Foreign bodies at work: good, docile and Other-*ed*. Asian J. Soc. Sci. 33 (2), 223–245.

AGC, 2012, Immigration Act (Chapter 133) Attorney General's Chambers, <http://statutes.agc.gov.sg/aol/search/display/view.w3p;orderBy=date-rev, loadTime;page=0;query=Id%3A3bbbd706-b0f5-4069-893fbd6b2b035ca8; rec=0>.

Allen, J., 2003. Lost Geographies of Power. Blackwell Publishing, Oxford.

Amoore, L., 2006. Biometric borders: governing mobilities in the war on terror. Political Geogr. 25 (3), 336–351.

Amoore, L., Hall, A., 2009. Taking people apart: digitized dissection and the body at the border. Environ. Plann. D: Soc. Space 27 (3), 444–464.

Aradau, C., Blanke, T., 2010. Governing circulation: a critique of the biopolitics of security. In: de Larrinaga, M., Doucet, M.G., (Eds.), Security and Global Governmentality: Globalization, Governance and the State, Routledge, Abingdon, pp. 44–58.

Aw, C.W., 2016. Bangladeshis 'mostly peace-loving'. The Straits Times, 21 Jan.

Baey, G., Yeoh, B.S.A., 2015. Migration and precarious work: negotiating debt, employment, and livelihood strategies amongst Bangladeshi migrant men working in Singapore's construction industry, Working Paper 26, Migrating Out of Poverty, University of Sussex, <http://migratingoutofpoverty.dfid.gov.uk/files/file.php?name=wp26-baey-yeoh-2015-migration-and-precarious-work.pdf&site=354>.

Bailey, A.J., Wright, R., Mountz, A., Miyares, I.M., 2002. (Re)producing Salvadoran transnational geographies. Ann. Assoc. Am. Geogr. 92 (1), 125–144.

Bal, C.S., 2013. The Politics of Obedience: Bangladeshi Construction Workers and the Migrant Labour Regime in Singapore. PhD thesis. Asia Research Centre, Murdoch University, Perth.

Bauman, Z., 2004. Wasted Lives: Modernity and Its Outcasts. Polity Press, Cambridge and Malden.

Bigo, D., 2008. Globalized (in)security: the field and the ban-opticon. In: Bigo, D, Tsoukala, A., Terror, (Eds.), Insecurity and Liberty: Illiberal Practices of Liberal Regimes After 9/11. Routledge, Abingdon, pp 5–49.

Bondi, L., 2014. Feeling insecure: a personal account in a psychoanalytic voice. Soc. Cultural Geogr. 15 (3), 332–350.

Brown, L., Durrheim, K., 2009. Different kinds of knowing: generating qualitative data through mobile interviewing. Qualitative Inquiry 15 (5), 911–930.

Buzan, B., Wæver, O., Wilde, J., 1998. Security: A New Framework for Analysis. Lynne Rienner Publisher, Boulder.

Castles, S., 1995. How nation-states respond to immigration and ethnic diversity. J. Ethnic Migration Stud. 21 (3), 293–308.

Chang, T.C., 2000. Singapore's Little India: a tourist attraction as a contested landscape. Urban Stud. 37(2) 343–366.

COI 2014 Report of the Committee of Inquiry into the Little India Riot on 8 December 2013 Committee of Inquiry into the Little India Riot, <http://www.mha.gov.sg/Data/Files/file/Little%20India%20Riot%20COI%20report%20-%202014-06-27.pdf>.

Coleman, M., 2007. Immigration geopolitics beyond the Mexico-US border. Antipode 39 (1), 54–76.

Coleman, M., 2009. What counts as the politics and practice of security, and where? Devolution and immigrant insecurity after 9/11. Ann. Assoc. Am. Geogr. 99 (5), 904–913.

Crampton, J.W., 2007. Maps, race and Foucault: eugenics and territorialization following World War I. In: Elden, S., Crampton, J., (Eds.), Space, Power, Knowledge: Foucault and Geography, Ashgate, Aldershot, pp. 223–244.

Crang, M., 2000. Relics, places and unwritten geographies in the work of Michel de Certeau (1925–86). Routledge, London and New York, pp. 136–153.

Dalby, S., 2003. Calling 911: geopolitics, security and America's new war. Geopolitics 8 (3), 61–86.

De Certeau, M., 1984. The Practice of Everyday Life. University of California Press, Berkeley.

De Genova, N.P., 2002. Migrant "illegality" and deportability in everyday life. Annu. Rev. Anthropol. 31, 419–447.

Death, C., 2010. Counter-conducts: a Foucauldian analytics of protest. Soc. Movement Stud. 9 (3), 235–251.

Dillon, M., Lobo-Guerrero, L., 2008. Biopolitics of security in the 21st century: an introduction. Rev. Int. Stud. 34 (2), 265–292.

Dillon, M., Neal, A.W., 2008. Introduction. In: Dillon, M., Neal, A.W., (Eds.), Foucault on Politics, Security and War, Palgrave Macmillan, New York, pp 1–20.

Doty, R.L., 2011. Bare life: border-crossing deaths and spaces of moral alibi. Environ. Plann. D: Soc. Space 29, 599–612.

Evans, J., Jones, P., 2011. The walking interview: methodology, mobility and place. Appl. Geogr. 31 (2), 849–858.

Fluri, J.L., 2014. States of (in)security: corporeal geographies and the elsewhere war. Environ. Plann. D: Soc. Space 32 (5), 795–814.

Foucault, M., 2003. Society Must Be Defended. Picador, New York.

Foucault, M., 2007. Security, Territory, Population: Lectures at the Collège de France 1977–1978. Palgrave Macmillan, Basingstoke.

Graham, D.T., 2000. The people paradox: human movements and human security in a globalising world. Routledge, London and New York, pp. 186–216.

Guild, E., 2009. Security and Migration in the 21st Century. Polity Press, Cambridge.

Harney, N., 2013. Precarity, affect, and problem solving with mobile phones by asylum seekers, refugees and migrants in Naples, Italy. J. Refugee Stud. 26 (4), 541–557.

Harrigan, N., Koh, C.Y., 2016. Vital yet vulnerable: emotional health of South Asian migrant workers in Singapore, Lien Centre for Social Innovation, Social Insight Research Series.

Herbert, S., 2008. Coercion, territoriality, legitimacy: the police and the modern state. In: Cox, K.R., Low, M., Robinson, J, (Eds.), The SAGE Handbook of Political Geography, SAGE Publications, London, pp. 169–183.

Huysmans, J., 1998. Security! What do you mean? From concept to thick signifier. Eur. J. Int. Relations 4 (2), 226–255.

Huysmans, J., 2000. The European Union and the securitization of migration. J. Common Market Stud. 38 (5), 751–777.

Huysmans, J., 2006. The Politics of Insecurity: Fear, Migration and Asylum in the EU. Routledge, New York and Abingdon.

Huysmans, J., 2011. What's in an act? On security speech acts and little security nothings. Security Dialogue 42 (4–5), 371–383.

Ingram, A., Dodds, K. (Eds.), 2009. Spaces of Security and Insecurity: Geographies of the War on Terror. Ashgate, Aldershot.

Isin, E.F., 2008. Theorizing acts of citizenship. In: Isin, E.F., Nielsen, G.M., (Eds.), Acts of Citizenship, Zed, London, pp. 15–43.

Katz, C., 2001. On the grounds of globalization: a topography for feminist political engagement. Signs: J. Wom. Cult. Soc. 26 (4), 1213–1234.

Koskela, H., 2000. 'The gaze without eyes': video-surveillance and the changing nature of urban space. Prog. Hum. Geogr. 24 (2), 243–265.

Kitiarsa, P., 2014. The 'Bare Life' of Thai Migrant Workmen in Singapore. Silkworm Books, Chiang Mai.

Law, L., 2001. Home cooking: Filipino women and geographies of the senses in Hong Kong. Ecumene 8 (3), 264–283.

Lewis, H., Dwyer, P., Hodkinson, S., Waite, L., 2015. Hyper-precarious lives: migrants, work and forced labour in the Global North. Prog. Hum. Geogr. 39 (5), 580–600.

Macey, D., 2009. Rethinking biopolitics, race and power in the wake of Foucault. Theory, Culture Soc. 26 (6), 186–205.

Massey, D., 2005. For Space. SAGE Publications, London.

MHA, 2014, Ministerial Statement on the Little India Riot Ministry of Home Affairs, 20 Jan, <https://www.youtube.com/watch?v=kX5Mfn52k1U>.

Mitchell, T., 1991. The limits of the state: beyond statist approaches and their critics. Am. Political Sci. Rev. 85 (1), 77–96.

MOM, 2015, Foreign Workforce Numbers Ministry of Manpower, 17 Sep, <http://www.mom.gov.sg/documents-and-publications/foreign-workforce-numbers>.

Mountz, A., 2003. Human smuggling, the transnational imaginary, and everyday geographies of the nation-state. Antipode 35 (3), 622–644.

Müller, B.J., 2004. (Dis)qualified bodies: securitization, citizenship and 'identity management'. Citizsh. Stud. 8 (3), 279–294.

Müller, B.J., 2011. Risking it all at the biometric border: mobility, limits and the persistence of securitization. Geopolitics 16 (1), 91–106.

Noussia, A., Lyons, M., 2009. Inhabiting spaces of liminality: migrants in Omonia, Athens. J. Ethnic Migration Stud. 35 (4), 601–624.

Noxolo, P., 2014. Towards an embodied securityscape: brian Chikwava's Harare North and the asylum seeking body as site of articulation. Soc. Cultural Geogr. 15 (3), 291–312.

Paasche, T.F., Sidaway, J.D., 2010. Transecting security and space in Maputo. Environ. Plann. A 42, 1555–1576.

Paasche, T.F., Yarwood, R., Sidaway, J.D., 2014. Territorial tactics: the significance of private policing strategies in Cape Town. Urban Stud. 51 (8), 1559–1575.

Painter, J., 2006. Prosaic geographies of stateness. Political Geogr. 25 (7), 752–774.

Park, D., 2015. Bangladeshi fruit vendors in the streets of Paris: vulnerable asylum seekers or self-imposed victims of exploitation? In: Waite, L., Craig, G., Lewis, H., Skrivankova, K. (Eds.), Vulnerability, Exploitation and Migrants: Insecure Work in a Global Economy. Palgrave Macmillan, London, pp. 129–142.

Philo, C., 2012. Security of geography/geography of security. Trans. Inst. Br. Geographers 37 (1), 1–7.

Rasmussen, K.S., 2011. Foucault's genealogy of racism. Theory, Culture Soc. 28 (5), 34–51.

Salter, M., 2013. To make move and let stop: mobility and the assemblage of circulation. Mobilities 8 (1), 7–19.

Scott, J., 1985. Weapons of the Weak: Everyday Forms of Peasant Resistance. Yale University Press, New Haven.

Scott, J., 1990. Domination and the Arts of Resistance: Hidden Transcripts. Yale University Press, New Haven.

Sibley, D., 1995. Geographies of Exclusion. Routledge, London and New York.

Sparke, M., 2008. Political geography — political geographies of globalization III: resistance. Prog. Hum. Geogr. 32 (3), 423–440.

Staeheli, L.A., Nagel, C.R., 2008. Rethinking security: perspectives from Arab-American and British Arab activists. Antipode 40 (5), 780–801.

Tan, C.C., 2015. Gathering Spaces for Migrant Workers in Little India: A Study on the Spatialisation of Control. Masters thesis. Department of Architecture, National University of Singapore.

Topak, Ö.E., 2014. The biopolitical border in practice: surveillance and death at the Greece-Turkey borderzones. Environ. Plann. D: Soc. Space 32, 815–1533.

TWC2, 2012.NUS students witness cleansing operation against foreign workers, Transient Workers Count Too, 6 Nov, <http://twc2.org.sg/2012/11/06/nus-students-witness-cleansing-operation-against-foreign-workers/>.

TWC2, 2013. Migrant worker housing: a survey of men in TWC2's Cuff Road Project, Transient Workers Count Too, <http://twc2.org.sg/wp-content/uploads/2013/09/Housing_conditions_report_v6-9.pdf>.

TWC2, 2015. Caught spitting and a life may be ruined, Transient Workers Count Too, 20 Jun, <http://twc2.org.sg/2015/06/20/caught-spitting-and-a-life-may-be-ruined/>.

Usher, M., 2014. Veins of concrete, cities of flow: reasserting the centrality of circulation in Foucault's analytics of government. Mobilities 9 (4), 550–569.

Van Houtum, H., 2010. Human blacklisting: the global apartheid of the EU's external border regime. Environ. Plann. D: Soc. Space 28, 957–976.

Wæver O, 1995, Securitisation and desecuritisation. In: Lipschutz, R.D., (Ed.), On Security, Columbia University Press, New York, pp. 46–87.

Walters, W., 2002. Deportation, expulsion, and the international police of aliens. Citizsh. Stud. 6 (3), 265–292.

Walters, W., 2006. Border/control. Eur. J. Soc. Theory 9 (2), 187–203.

Willen, S.S., 2007. Toward a critical phenomenology of "illegality": state power, criminalization, and abjectivity among undocumented migrant workers in Tel Aviv, Israel. Int. Migration 45 (3), 8–38.

Wong T, 2010, "Crackdown on illegal dorms in Little India" The Straits Times, 25 Aug.

Woodward, K., 2014. Affect, state theory, and the politics of confusion. Political Geogr. 41, 21–31.

Ye, J., 2014. Migrant masculinities: Bangladeshi men in Singapore's labour force. Gender, Place & Culture 21 (8), 1012–1028.

Yea, S., 2016. Everyday spaces of human trafficking: (in)visibility and agency among trafficked women in U.S. military-oriented clubs in South Korea. Ann. Assoc. Am. Geogr. 106 (4), 957–973.

Yeoh, B., 2006. Bifurcated labour: the unequal incorporation of transmigrants in Singapore. Tijdschrift voor Economische en Sociale Geografie 97 (1), 26–37.

Yeoh, B.S., Huang, S., 1998. Negotiating public space: strategies and styles of migrant female domestic workers in Singapore. Urban Stud. 35 (3), 583–602.

Zedner, L., 2009. Security. Routledge, Oxford.

Zylinska, J., 2004. The universal acts: Judith Butler and the biopolitics of immigration. Cultural Stud. 18 (4), 523–537.

Chapter 4a

Dealing with Deportability in a Pandemic-hit Labour Migration Regime*

Charanpal S. Bal

Department of Political Science and International Relations
The University of Western Australia

Low-wage migrant workers in Singapore are deportable — employment laws allow employers to unilaterally terminate work permits and repatriate workers on short notice. Employers have been commonly found to forcefully repatriate migrant workers as a means of settling employment disputes. In tandem with other political and economic factors, the deportability of migrant workers presents obstacles to accessing the few employment rights that they have. However, such arrangements have been challenged through the work of civil society actors [Koh *et al.*, 2017]. The escalation of individual employment disputes has seen migrant workers seek help from independent non-governmental organisations (NGOs) that have played a critical role in advocating for the reform of employment and migrant labour laws [Bal, 2015].

---

*Reflections on Bal, C. S. (2015). Dealing with deportability: Deportation laws and the political personhood of temporary migrant workers in Singapore, *Asian J. Law Soc.*, Vol. 2, No. 2, pp. 267–284. DOI: 10.1017/als.2015.17. © Cambridge University Press and KoGuan Law School, Shanghai Jiao Tong University.

This pressure has led the government to make limited reforms but these serve to displace worker grievances rather than improving their wellbeing. The government-controlled National Trades Union Congress (NTUC) subsequently formed the Migrant Workers' Centre (MWC) and the Centre for Domestic Employees (CDE) to provide support for migrant workers in need without independent advocacy. In contrast to independent NGOs, the MWC and CDE work towards socialising workers to avoid conflict and disputes with their employers. While their work helps individual workers in resolving employment disputes quickly, they do not tackle the deeper structural issues that disempower these workers.

The COVID-19 pandemic has affected low-wage migrant workers in difficult, but also contradictory ways. Despite warning signs, migrant worker dormitories were an early blind spot in the government's otherwise effective pandemic response. The subsequent lockdowns on these dormitories have left large proportions of migrant workers confined to their rooms for months without work and pay, compounding the pre-existing problem of recruitment debt [Elangovan, 2021].

However, these distressing conditions have temporarily made migrant workers less disposable. Government pandemic protocols and the shortage of flights have made it cumbersome and expensive for employers to repatriate migrant workers. While the government attempts to mitigate the economic slides by expanding construction projects, new migrant workers cannot be recruited from abroad. The consequent labour crunch has led to a temporary alignment of interests between contractors, policymakers, and migrant workers. In April 2020, the Ministry of Manpower (MOM), in coordination with the Singapore Business Federation (SBF) and the Singapore Contractors Association Limited (SCAL), introduced a temporary scheme that significantly relaxes rules that require migrant workers to be repatriated before changing jobs. Under these new provisions, it is possible for a migrant worker to change jobs, without their employer's approval whilst remaining in Singapore [Lai, 2020]. Later, however, while the scheme retained job transfers within their business sectors, it discontinued from March 2021 the arrangement of transfers across sectors, due to the low demand for these transfers [Ministry of Manpower, 2021].

While positive, these changes are not permanent and will sunset in February 2021. While it is too early to decipher how a 'new normal' will look like, the opening of borders will inevitably quell the appetites of contractors and businesses to rehire existing workers. New hires from abroad provide greater opportunities for kickbacks which are often used to subsidize business costs. Current platforms that seek to connect employers to existing workers, such as SCAL's Construction Manpower Exchange[1] and SBF's Manpower Connect,[2] appear to be temporary fixes rather than designed to be long-term solutions. More concrete and meaningful steps need to be taken to reduce the debt burden on migrant workers and to prevent employers from benefitting from kickbacks through high recruitment fees. The Singapore state certainly has the capacity for this. What is now needed is a society that will no longer accept the systematic maltreatment of our low-wage migrant workers.

References

Bal, C. S. (2015). Production politics and migrant labour advocacy in Singapore, *Journal of Contemporary Asia*, Vol. 45, No. 2, pp. 219–242. DOI: 10.1080/00472336.2014.960880

Elangovan, N. (2021, 29 March). The Big Read: A year after the first COVID-19 outbreak in dorms, how has life changed for foreign workers? *CNA*. Retrieved from https://www.channelnewsasia.com/news/singapore/the-big-read-covid-19-outbreak-dormitories-foreign-workers-14504974

Koh, C. Y., Wee, K., Goh, C. and Yeoh, B. S. A. (2017). Cultural mediation through vernacularization: Framing rights claims through the day-off campaign for migrant domestic workers in Singapore, *International Migration*, Vol. 55, No. 3, pp. 89–104. DOI: 10.1111/imig.12332

Lai, L. (2020, 1 April). Coronavirus: MOM to allow foreign worker transfers between sectors to help firms with manpower needs. *The Straits Times*. Retrieved from https://www.straitstimes.com/singapore/coronavirus-mom-to-allow-foreign-worker-transfers-between-sectors-to-help-firms-with

Ministry of Manpower. (2021, 28 May). Helping businesses on manpower issues. Retrieved from https://www.mom.gov.sg/covid-19/helping-businesses-on-manpower-issues

[1] https://www.scmx.com.sg/

[2] https://www.sbf.org.sg/media-centre/manpowerconnect

Chapter 4b

Dealing with Deportability: Deportation Laws and the Political Personhood of Temporary Migrant Workers in Singapore*

Charanpal S. Bal[†]

Visiting Lecturer, Faculty of Social and Political Science, Parahyangan Catholic University, Bandung, and Associate, Asia Research Centre, Murdoch University, Western Australia.

By severely constraining the political personhood of temporary migrant workers, states' use of deportation laws seeks to curb agitation among

*This article was originally published in *Asian J. Law Soc.*, Vol. 2, No. 2, pp. 267–284. DOI: 10.1017/als.2015.17. © Cambridge University Press and KoGuan Law School, Shanghai Jiao Tong University.

[†]Charan Bal is a Visiting Lecturer at the Faculty of Social and Political Science in the Parahyangan Catholic University, Bandung. He completed his PhD in Politics at Murdoch University's Asia Research Centre in November 2013. He researches on migrant labour politics in Asia. The author would like to thank Lynette Chua, Daniel Goh, Garry Rodan, and Jane Hutchison for the support and constructive suggestions they have made in the research and writing of this paper. Thanks also go to the two anonymous reviewers for their constructive suggestions and comments. The usual disclaimers apply. Correspondence to No. 10, Jalan Hegarsari III, Hegarmanah, Bandung 40141, Indonesia. E-mail address: charanpal.s.bal@gmail.com.

these workers. Despite this, various episodes of unrest have been witnessed in both liberal and illiberal regimes across Asia. Drawing on a case study of Bangladeshi migrant construction workers in Singapore, this paper examines the development of migrant labour politics as deportation laws, and their enforcement, construct these workers as "use-and-discard" economic subjects. Data for the paper are drawn from multi-level sources — government, industry, media, and non-governmental organization (NGO) reports; interviews with key actors; and a participant observation stint in a construction firm — collected between 2010 and 2014. The paper argues that, rather than solely constraining, deportability serves as a constituent of certain forms of tactical worker contestations in the workplace. Specifically, under different workplace conditions, deportability can translate into differing forms of worker tactics, ranging from accommodation to confrontation and desertion. The outcomes of these strategies, in turn, have significant repercussions for the ways in which civil society groups and state-actors, respectively, challenge and reconfigure the political personhood of temporary migrant workers.

Keywords: temporary migrant workers, deportation, political personhood, migrant labour politics, Singapore

1. Introduction

Deportation laws are a key feature of guest-worker regimes around the world. They are a crucial part of a legal order enacted by labour-receiving states to ensure that migrant workers remain temporary and disposable despite constituting a permanent feature of these economies. Temporary migrants are only permitted to remain within recipient societies as long as they are economically required, as states afford employers the freedom to terminate their employment regardless of the legally sanctioned length-of-work tenure. The personhood of temporary migrant workers is, thus, constructed by states, through deportation laws, as disposable economic subjects with few or no political rights.

The existing literature on migrant labour politics accordingly indicates that such a legal order enforced by states undermines or even negates the political personhood of temporary migrant workers. Deportation laws may preclude workers from certain rights available to citizens and residents (such as rights to political representation) or may obstruct then from accessing the few rights that they may be afforded by states (such as economic rights).[1] It is also argued that the undermining of their political personhood through deportation laws impedes struggles for the protection and promotion of migrants' economic and political interests.[2] Yet, at the same time, various episodes of migrant labour unrest have been witnessed in many recipient countries with both relatively open and illiberal political systems. Such episodes of unrest have resulted in not only the use of deportations to quell unrest, but also significant reforms to employment and immigration laws. These observations suggest that it is necessary to look beyond the constraining effects of deportation laws and to examine how these laws constitute and engender the contextual nature of struggles for migrant worker rights.

Using the case of Bangladeshi temporary migrant workers in Singapore's construction industry, this article investigates how deportation laws and their application influence the nature of contestations over the political personhood of these workers. I focus on how the deportable status of these workers as well as threats and practices of deportation influence the formation of tactics used to address worker grievances in the workplace. In contrast to existing perspectives, I take deportability as a constituent, rather than simply an impediment, to prevalent forms of workplace politics. Consequently, I argue that different forms of workplace politics — ranging from accommodation to confrontation and desertion — influence how well civil society groups are able to contest state constructions of migrant workers as disposable economic subjects. I further argue that minor policy reforms, resulting from migrant labour unrest and civil society pressure, emphasize individual over collective political rights in order to administratively depoliticize tensions between migrant workers and employers over working conditions.

The following section clarifies the concept of deportability and examines the way it shapes both the personhood and politics of temporary migrant workers. Section 2 describes the methods and data used for the analysis while Section 3 provides an overview of deportation laws and

[1] Castells (1975); Sassen-Koob (1981); Arnold & Hewison (2006).

[2] Castles & Kosack (1973); Binford (2009).

practices in Singapore. In Section 4, I highlight key aspects of the construction workplace in Singapore as the context within migrant workers experience vulnerability to deportation as well as discontent with working conditions. Sections 5 and 6 explicitly deal with the micro-politics of production. Section 5 demonstrates how factors relating to production geography and employer strategies allow workers to mitigate their vulnerability to deportation whilst simultaneously trying to improve their working conditions on an informal and individualized basis. Section 6 examines how this form of tactical accommodation breaks down and escalates into disputes, confrontation, forced deportation, and, eventually, worker desertion. Finally, Section 7 examines the link between worker desertion and civil society efforts in contesting migrant labour laws, particularly those relating to the deportability of migrant workers. The penultimate section also draws out the broader implications of authorities making limited expansions to the political personhood of these workers.

2. Deportability, Political Personhood, and Migrant Labour Politics

Deportability is related to but distinct from actual practices of deportation. This article deals with both these aspects. While the forced deportation of migrant workers by government authorities and employers often serves to regulate labour supply or stymie labour agitation within host societies, it is the deportable legal status of these temporary migrants that renders their labour power a "distinctly disposable commodity."[3] At the same time, deportation laws intersect with a host of related factors — deprivation of citizenship rights, occupational immobility, inability to access trade union movements, and high recruitment debt — to make guest workers both tractable and vulnerable, allowing state authorities and employers greater leeway in politically controlling the migrant workforce.

In this sense, deportation laws render temporary migrant workers as "use-and-discard"[4] or disposable economic subjects rather than political

[3] de Genova (2005), p. 8; Liow (2011), p. 14.
[4] Yeoh (2006), p. 32

persons who are "bearer[s] or rights … [who] can hold values, make choices."[5] On paper at least, states tend to afford these migrants a limited range of economic rights. In Singapore, for instance, temporary migrant workers have the right to prompt payment of wages, overtime and rest-day pay rates, pro-rated annual leave, severance payments in lieu of notice, and work-injury compensation. In Malaysia, they are even entitled to the same minimum wage as citizens. Many states also allow workers to lodge formal claims and complaints in order to have these economic rights enforced. These limited rights only allow workers to politically participate as individual complainants within state-sanctioned bureaucratic spaces rather than as autonomous and collective political actors.

At the same time, the deportable status of these workers as well as state/employer practices of forced removal inhibits or precludes them from accessing these few rights that they have been afforded. Their vulnerability to forced deportation at the whims of authorities and employers means that they face significant obstacles in enforcing these economic rights as individual complainants. In other words, their deportability and deportation practices mean that the few rights that they have on paper do not often get enforced in practice. Furthermore, the limited rights that they have do not sufficiently address the various issues that they face in host societies such as low wages, debt bondage, and arbitrary termination of employment. In this sense, deportation laws undermine the political personhood of temporary migrant workers by effectively disallowing them from any form of meaningful political participation of contestation within host societies.

The literature on migrant labour politics accordingly argues that these laws impede struggles for the protection and promotion of migrants' economic and political interests.[6] As a consequence, particular segments of capital are able to benefit from "cheap" and easily controllable workers who are unlikely to resist exploitation and abuse. Based on a study of contract Mexican farm labour in Canada, Binford points out that, while discontent at working conditions among migrant workers exist, it

[5]Taylor (1985), p. 97.

[6]Castles & Kosack, *supra* note 2; Castells, *supra* note 1; Sassen-Koob, *supra* note 1; Arnold & Hewison, *supra* note 1; Binford, *supra* note 2.

develops "under … severe structural constraints" and the potential for collective resistance tends to impeded by possible and actual practices of forced deportation of suspected "ringleaders" of wildcat strikes.[7] In short, the literature argues that deportation laws ensure that migrant workers struggles are politically constrained because they have few formal rights to influence the institutions that subordinate them. Deportation laws, therefore, represent a form of structural coercion that limits or impedes the spaces that migrant workers have to resist or contest the exploitation and abuse that they face at work.

In spite of such laws, protests, strikes, and riots by migrant workers have been witnessed in many labour-importing countries across Asia such as Hong Kong, Singapore, Malaysia, and several Gulf states.[8] It is of note that such unrest has been reported in both countries with relatively open (Hong Kong) political systems which offer guest workers relatively more political freedoms as well as in countries with illiberal or autocratic political systems (Singapore, Malaysia, and the Gulf states) whose states tend to severely inhibit any form of collective mobilization. While authorities in these states have shown a willingness to use forced deportation to quell unrest, they have also made modest but significant political concessions to migrant workers by way of reforms to migrant labour laws. Authorities in Dubai, for instance, moved to legalize strike action insofar as they are confined within individual labour camps.[9] In the wake of migrant labour unrest and civil society pressure during the Global Financial Crisis (GFC) in 2008/09, authorities in Singapore opened up further avenues for individual claims and complaints by illegalizing kickbacks and instituting compulsory no-work pay.[10]

Such developments indicate that deportation laws may do more than simply impede struggles for migrant labour rights. Using the Singapore case, I examine how deportability and deportation laws both constrain and engender certain forms of political contestations. Specifically, I focus on the micro-politics of production as the site where workers deal with their

[7] Binford, *ibid.*, pp. 512–17.

[8] Hsia (2009); Buckley (2013); Bal (2015).

[9] Buckley, *ibid.*

[10] Bal, *supra* note 8.

consequent vulnerability by resorting to a range of tactics from accommodation to confrontation and desertion. The manner in which these worker tactics play out, in turn, have significant repercussions for the extent to which civil society groups are able to contest state constructions of temporary migrant workers as disposable economic subjects. Finally, the small-scale reforms to migrant labour laws are examined for how they mitigate the deportability of guest workers by expanding the scope for individualized administrative complaints in order to depoliticize existing workplace tensions.

3. Data and Methods

Data for this paper were drawn from a number of multi-level sources between 2010 and 2014. Between October 2010 and May 2012, I conducted in-depth interviews with 45 Bangladeshi migrant workers who were working or had worked in Singapore as semi- or unskilled construction workers on work permits. These interviews covered a total of 103 work stints which focused on the production arrangements within construction sites and the employment experiences of these workers. At the time of the respective interviews, 22 respondents were currently employed in Singapore while ten of them were shelter residents seeking non-governmental organization (NGO) assistance for employment disputes with their employers. The other 13 respondents were return migrants who had previously worked in Singapore and were interviewed whilst they were in between jobs in Bangladesh. Despite their vulnerable position, my respondents spoke freely about their working conditions and episodes of conflict and tension at work that they thought were significant. The return migrants felt little fear of repercussions while those currently employed felt secure in their own tactics of dealing with deportability (see Section 3). The workers engaged in employment disputes, on the other hand, were even more eager to speak out against the treatment they received at the hands of their bosses and supervisors.

I also conducted a four-month participation observation stint at a local construction firm where I worked as steel fitter on pedestrian bridges, bus shelters, and walkways. While I was not deportable nor was I straddled with the debt that my co-workers had, the stint allowed me to directly observe how managerial control strategies were applied and manifested on a day-to-day basis. Together with the interview data, the data drawn from these observations were used to detail worker tactics in dealing with their deportability. Additionally, I collected 50 case-file documents from a local migrant worker NGO called the Humanitarian Organization for Migration Economics (HOME). These case files document the cases of legal assistance provided to workers from 2007 to 2011. Together with the interview data, these case files document how worker grievances turn into instances of confrontation and disputes. Both these sources also provided a fairly detailed documentation of practices of forced deportation and workers' efforts in escape and evasion. A number of secondary sources such as media, government, construction industry, and NGO reports were also used. Finally, targeted interviews were conducted with key informants such as contractors in Singapore and NGO staff and volunteers in order to fill particular gaps in the data.

4. Deportation Laws and Forced Deportation in Singapore

The deportability of contract migrant workers in Singapore can be traced back to 1977 when immigration laws were enacted to make it an offence for non-resident employees to remain in the country upon the expiry of their work passes.[11] In 1989, the criminalization of "overstaying" was intensified when the government introduced mandatory caning for work-permit holders who overstay their visas by more than 90 days.[12] The enactment of the Employment of Foreign Manpower Act (EFMA) in 1991, which currently regulates the terms and conditions of the employment of semi- and unskilled guest workers, gave employers free rein to unilaterally terminate the work permits (and effectively, the employment) of migrant workers under their charge.[13]

The enactment of EFMA by the government came about as construction contractors took to abandoning their guest workers mid-tenure in

[11] No Author (1977).

[12] No Author (1989)

[13] Government of Singapore (1991).

order to dodge rising foreign-worker levy rates imposed by the government from 1987. Guest-worker levies were introduced across several industries (construction, shipbuilding, and manufacturing) in 1987 as a pricing mechanism to force employers to adopt more capital-intensive production methods. Construction contractors, being largely small and medium-sized enterprises, did not have the means to invest in new machines and production techniques. They took to levy dodging, either by abandoning their migrant workers during business slumps or illegally employing these abandoned workers who had overstayed their visas. The government subsequently responded by incarcerating and deporting "overstayers" and prosecuting employers. At the height of this, in 1989 alone, these "overstayers" made up 17% of the total prison population and cost S$9.4 million a year to feed and clothe.[14] Until 1991, it was the state that had to bear the cost of incarcerating and deporting migrant workers who had been left destitute by levy-dodging contactors.

With the enactment of EFMA that year, the legal responsibility of repatriating guest workers was put on to individual employers. The Act required all employers to put up an S$5,000 bond with the Labour Ministry for every temporary migrant worker hired which would only be discharged upon the effective repatriation of the respective worker. A combination of immigration and labour laws ensure that responsibility of repatriating unwanted guest workers became the legal responsibility of the employer. Effectively, these laws endow employers the legal powers to terminate the employment of and deport guest workers under their employ at any given time.

In recent years, the state itself has used deportation to manage outbreaks of migrant labour unrest such as the SMRT Corporation bus drivers' strike in 2012 and the Little India riot in 2013. In both cases, only key figures involved in the disturbances were prosecuted and incarcerated. Most of the alleged participants were only subject to preliminary investigations and forcefully deported without trial. However, these were exceptional incidents as, long before this, employers have commonly taken advantage of deportation laws to forcefully repatriate their migrant workers. It is common for employers to terminate the employment of their

[14] Pereira (1989).

workers and forcefully repatriate them when faced with real or anticipated worker insubordination or economic downturn.

A key aspect of these "everyday" practices of deportation is the use of repatriation companies. Repatriation companies in Singapore specialize in the repatriation of work-permit holders. They are not legally required to have a special license to operate. In 2005, there were between five and ten such companies in Singapore.[15] These companies, known to most migrant workers simply as "gangsters," escort workers from the dormitory or work-site and hold them in custody at their premises until they are ready to be deported. The period of time workers are held at these premises can vary from a few hours to over a week. During this time, workers are confined and typically not allowed to leave and are physically and psychologically intimidated into accepting repatriation. Once the workers' relevant documents have been prepared by the employer, the repatriation company escorts these workers to the airport where they are sent through the immigration gates. These companies are also hired to track down missing workers.[16]

While many of their activities contravene the Penal Code in Singapore — such as wrongful confinement or wrongful restraint — the police do not consider this a criminal offence.[17] According to local NGOs, the police see migrant workers as "social problems and potential immigration offenders" and are "happy that repatriation companies can perform this function" of forceful repatriation for them.[18] While the Singapore Police Force have not publicly responded to these claims, the Ministry of Manpower did conduct one round of inspections on two repatriation companies in November 2011 and found no legal violations.[19] In the same press release, the ministry reiterated that it would not tolerate the use of wrongful restraint and the forceful repatriation of workers with outstanding salary or work-injury claims. First-hand accounts from activists, however, suggest that violations occur on a fairly regular basis.[20]

[15] Sim (2005).
[16] HOME & TWC2 (2010); Lim (2011).
[17] Basu (2009); HOME & TWC2, *ibid.*, p. 8.
[18] Lim, *supra* note 16.
[19] Ministry of Manpower Singapore (2011).
[20] Wham (2011).

All the workers I spoke to (both during interviews and at the participant observation stint) were acutely aware of their deportable legal status and were aware that their employers could forcefully deport them at any time. Many demonstrated a clear understanding of their legal vulnerability as a result of the deportation laws they were subject to. Yet they were not unduly concerned by this, as they felt that their respective employers would not do so. It did not appear as if this was due to some inherent trust they had in their respective employers or even a display of machismo. All workers who were currently employed during the interviews and participant observation voiced serious grievances over working conditions. They were also, to varying extents depending on tenure, worried about servicing their recruitment debts (between S$2,000 and S$10,000) and providing for their families back home. In order to understand this seemingly contradictory disposition, I examine production-related factors within the workplace which intersect with migrant worker deportability.

5. The Production Process in the Construction Industry in Singapore

The construction industry in Singapore does not only refer to the construction of buildings. It includes a broad range of activities such as: the building, alteration, maintenance, and removal/demolition of fixed structures such as roads, bridges, railways, harbours, cableways, canals, pipelines, tunnels, and viaducts; electrical, water, gas, and telecommunications installation and maintenance; drainage and plumbing workers; and land reclamation, among many others. Due to the varied and diverse nature of the industry, work arrangements are largely heterogeneous. Workers may be deployed to work in large enclosed construction sites or small non-automated workshops. They may be deployed in small autonomous detachments (usually under the charge of a supervisor or foreman) to various open sites around the island or within the premises of clients when doing maintenance work. The duration of each deployment can vary greatly, depending on the nature of the company's work and the size of the construction project. Many contractors have operations on more than one site and may often redeploy or cross-deploy workers based on their overall labour needs.

Despite these variations, there is a degree of consistency within the industry regarding the manner in which work is commanded, delegated, and co-ordinated at various worksites. The industry is highly labour-intensive and relatively un-automated. A very significant proportion of it (96%) comprises small and medium-sized firms.[21] Such firms do not have the ability or resources to utilize sophisticated and complex bureaucratic controls to command and coordinate work. Managerial procedures cannot always be easily routinized or institutionalized into systematic administrative structures.

As a result of this, employer strategies of labour control in the industry tend to be largely direct, ad hoc, hierarchical, and highly personalized. As and when projects get awarded, contractors and/or project managers personally delegate tasks to supervisors and foremen who command, instruct, guide, and assist workers at the designated point of production. The hierarchical command and co-ordination of work are based on the positional and personal authority that bosses and supervisors have over their charges. While there are no formalized means for workers to challenge or negotiate supervisory commands, these commands are constantly negotiated on a highly informal and personal basis. The autonomy/informality of supervision as well as the geographically dispersed nature of production plays a crucial role in influencing how deportable workers formulate tactics to deal with the workplace grievances that they face whilst addressing their sense of vulnerability.

6. Tactical Accommodation as Protection from Deportation

The interviews and participation observation revealed overwhelming worker grievances over working conditions, particularly low and stagnant wages, legal and illegal wage deductions made by employers, having to pay kickbacks indirectly to employers for employment and contract renewal, as well as the physically demanding and "dirty" nature of their work. In short, these workers felt that their existing employment

---

[21] Construction Industry Development Board Singapore (2000).

arrangements required too much physical effort while leaving them with little or no monetary reward to realize their migration objectives. Despite this, at work, workers tend to obey orders based on the personal authority of bosses or other work superiors such as managers and supervisors. These workers were explicitly aware that they had few formal rights and, therefore, lacked the "power" to openly challenge their employers on work conditions. Through their experiences at the worksite and their interactions with other migrant workers, they learn that there is little they can do to directly change the terms of their employment. Workers regard themselves has "power no have," primarily because of their deportable legal status — "can send back." They see others with resident rights (Singapore citizens or permanent residents) as people who have more "power" because they do higher-status work ("service" or "business" as opposed to menial wage work) and are not deportable.

At the same time, these workers feel that the success of their migration objectives necessarily depends on having a "good relationship" with people who "have power" with their bosses and work superiors being the most immediate manifestation. Hence, every worker I interviewed seemed keen to meet or exceed the expectations of their work superiors in terms of the proficiency and timeliness of their work, especially in the first six to nine months of employment. Workers consciously present themselves to work superiors as men who "can do" (willing to work), "can follow" (obedient to orders), and who are "working understand" (competent and proficient). Having established their individual competence and obedience to work superiors, they make informal requests for wage increments, preferential deployments, and contract renewals. At the same time, they take advantage of periods of non-supervised production to engage in forms of "everyday resistances" such as informal output restriction in order to minimize or moderate the amount of energy they put into their work.

Here, I emphasize the tactical aspect of worker obedience. Following de Certeau,[22] Sargeson understands "tactics" as the way in which less powerful groups use systems of knowledge and practices in ways not intended by their makers "with a view to subversion or carving out a space

[22] de Certeau (1984).

which they can manoeuvre in."[23] Workers deliver a façade of obedient and competent work whilst engaging in covert "everyday resistances" for two reasons — to siphon better rewards (wages, tenure, deployments) from work superiors and to avoid open conflict with them. My data show that workers tend to be less successful in accomplishing the former, as they have little political leverage in gaining better terms of work, even informally. However, such forms of tactical accommodation do prove to be particularly useful in preventing employers from using deportation threats and forceful deportation against them. While workers were aware that they could be "send back" or threatened with deportation, they did not believe their employers would do so, at least if they avoided "fighting" with their work superiors. It was their tactical performance of obedience rather than fear that gave them this sense of security.

The vulnerability and tractability of migrant workers as a result of deportation laws are, by themselves, insufficient to explain the prevalence of tactical accommodation among Bangladeshi construction workers. The key aspect of tactical accommodation is that it represents a conscious attempt by these workers as a kind of protection from deportation whilst attempting to renegotiate the terms of work. Workplace politics tend to take this form because of way the deportability of migrant workers intersects with production-related factors — such as the geography of production and specific managerial strategies — in Singapore's construction industry.

The geography of production in this industry includes frequent incidences of small-scale and fairly autonomously supervised work deployments based on the division of labour of construction work and the prevalence of subcontracting. In such instances, points of production are often geographically dispersed as workers are deployed to work in small groups of two to seven. It is important note that points of production in construction are often multiple and often direct supervision is punctuated rather than constant. These production arrangements allow individual workers greater autonomy to regulate the pace and intensity of their efforts. Workers may choose to work faster and exceed the expectations of work superiors to prove their competence; they may choose to step up their efforts during cooler parts of the day while slacking off during the

[23] Sargeson (2001), p. 54.

mid-day hours while unsupervised. Periodic supervision allows them to work slowly and consistently with short regular breaks. Workers are often able to renegotiate deadlines as long as they demonstrate progress in their work and provide justifications that their lack of progress was hampered by factors beyond their control, such as that materials provided were not of the correct specifications, the physical terrain prevented tasks from being completed in a routine manner, machine malfunction, etc. Based on the interviews as well as my own experiences on the job, these come across as common and plausible given that many construction firms (mostly small and medium-sized enterprises) are run quite chaotically. One interviewee even told me that, during a particular work stint, he spent most of his night shifts napping in large iron pipes because supervision was so lax and work was so poorly co-ordinated.[24] Furthermore, supervisors, who often come from the rank-and-file and share the same grievances as workers, actively collaborate with them to moderate the pace and intensity of work. The point here is that the dispersed nature of production and relatively autonomous supervisory arrangements allow workers the opportunity to redress grievances over working conditions while steering clear of confrontation with their employers.

In terms of managerial strategies, a clear distinction needs to be made between employers' use of deportation threats to direct and command work activities and their use of such threats to counteract worker dissent or resistance. The labour migration literature almost exclusively focuses on the latter.[25] There is little doubt that this is true in the present context as employers here attempt to suppress worker insubordination with threats, blacklisting, forced deportation, and various forms of physical and mental abuse. However, within the workplace, deportation threats or other forms of direct coercion are not the primary means by which employers make migrant workers perform work tasks. This is not due to employers' incapability or reluctance to do so. Rather, this comes about because workers are constantly pre-empting deportation threats through the aforementioned tactics of accommodation. This effectively allows employers to utilize the obedience orientation of workers to direct work with less effort and complication.

---

[24] Interview, 26 April 2012.

[25] Sassen (1988); Mitchell (1996); Arnold & Hewison, *supra* note 1; Binford *supra* note 2.

Deportation threats and forced deportation are used strategically across the industry in order to prevent or pre-empt worker agitation or insubordination. In an interview with a former manager of a construction firm, the respondent outlined how the company dealt with "problem" workers. First, the worker will be given a simple order by a work superior to "get in line." If the worker does not comply with this order, the managing director will approach the worker for "counselling." At this point, the manager will attempt to find out what problems the worker is facing. During "counselling," the manager makes an attempt to persuade the worker to do as he is told — "we will tell the worker that he is here to make money for his family, and if he wants to continue doing this, he must know how to follow orders." It is only when persuasion fails that the manager rings up a repatriation company in order to forcibly deport the "problem" worker — "if they don't want to listen, then they can go back to where they came from."[26] In short, deportation threats and forced deportation are not used indiscriminately by employers to set their workers to work; they are used strategically when obedience is not forthcoming from individual workers.

These production-related factors — the often dispersed geography of production, autonomous supervisory arrangements, and the strategic use of direct coercion — serve as an outlet of sorts in releasing tensions between workers and employers over working conditions. As workers experience a sense of vulnerability due to their deportable status within a fairly autonomous work regime, opportunities for confrontation and agitation are foreclosed while opportunities for tactical accommodation are opened up. While deportability inhibits workers from overtly confronting managerial control, it also makes it necessary for them to tactically produce a façade of obedience in order to protect their migration objectives.

7. The Compulsions of Confrontation and Desertion

While workers consciously avoid confrontation with employers in order to protect themselves from forced deportation, under certain workplace

[26] Interview, 10 January 2012.

conditions, confrontation becomes necessary. This tends to happen when working conditions deteriorate to the point that workers are unable to effectively exercise tactical accommodation and disputes become inevitable. Employer–worker relations tend to deteriorate in times of economic crisis or downturn, rising cost pressures for contractors, or mismanaged work injuries. Under such circumstances, migrant workers are unable to exercise tactical accommodation and are drawn into disputes over unpaid wages, increased wage theft, intensified work regimes, underdeployment (no work, no pay), and work-injury compensation. Within these disputes, workers are compelled to confront their employers and demand redress. Such confrontations invariably unleash the coercive power of employers who respond with deportation threats, physical and verbal abuse, and, finally, forced deportation. It is particularly instructive that employers use these forms of coercion specifically as a means to resolve workplace disputes rather than to set their workers to work.

Construction contractors, a majority of which are small and medium-sized enterprises operating within a highly competitive industry, have been faced with rising cost pressures due to the unrelenting rise in foreign-worker levy rates (payable to the government) and dormitory rates (to house their migrant workers). Contractors have responded to these cost pressures by attempting to transfer some of these costs onto their workers in the form of wage deductions and stagnating or depressing basic wage rates as well as attempting to intensify work regimes to achieve greater productivity from workers. As supervision at work becomes more intense and wage deductions prove to be overbearing, most workers see little point in pursuing tactical accommodation. Their immediate objectives of migration — servicing debt and sending money home to their families — are immediately threatened when their monthly earnings are undercut by increasing wage deductions. On top of that, many workers have to contend with physical tiredness and fatigue as the intensifying of work regimes leave them little leeway in engaging in "everyday resistances."

During economic downturn or crisis, migrant workers are not deployed or are sparsely deployed to work over long periods of time. This is often because their employers do not have sufficient jobs or because projects have been delayed or cancelled. Many contractors (particularly labour-supply firms) have little qualms about bringing in surplus labour as they able to profit from kickbacks via recruitment fees that workers pay. During the GFC between 2008 and 2009, local NGO HOME recorded about 440 complaints of underdeployment out of 1,047 total complaints between April 2008 and March 2009. In contrast, before the GFC, earlier records revealed an almost negligible number of similar cases. Underdeployment proves to be a major problem for affected workers, since, being daily rated, they are not paid at all when not deployed to work. NGO case-file reports also reveal that, when not deployed and not earning anything, workers are still subject to various wage deductions mandated by the company such as for rent, food, and utilities. These deductions are carried over to months when workers are deployed. This leaves affected workers with negligible or no earnings for several months in a row. Under such circumstances, tactical obedience becomes unfeasible.

Under Singapore's work-injury compensation laws, all workers injured in the course of work are entitled to a range of compensatory benefits which are ultimately provided for by compulsory insurance policies that employers have to take up for their employees. Despite this, a number of contractors are often keen to conceal work injuries for a range of reasons — reporting the injury might lead to further investigations into the company's safety practices, employers are concerned about increases in insurance premiums, the insurance policy has lapsed, they are concerned about having to house and feed an unproductive worker, or they simply believe the injury is not serious or the worker is faking injury. NGO reports and interview data also reveal that employers also prevent workers from lodging claims of their own by not providing workers with suitable medical attention, colluding with company doctors, and confiscating the medical certificates of workers. Threats are also made to other workers who have personally witnessed these work accidents. Under these circumstances, workers are unable to engage in tactical obedience as they feel that their right to access workinjury compensation is undermined or doing so would expose them to more physical pain.

When such disputes arise, workers are unable to engage in tactical accommodation. Constant and intrusive supervision closes off spaces for workers to informally renegotiate the terms of work, heightening existing tensions over wage theft and harsh work regimes. Workers are also unable to use such tactics when they are not deployed to work, as there are barely any terms of work to speak of when there is no work, or pay. An injured worker who is ordered to return to work or deprived of medical care feels that his physical wellbeing is at stake and cannot tactically accommodate such orders. Furthermore, these workers have no alternative recourse in the midst of such disputes — contractor firms do not have formal complaints mechanisms, collective bargaining platforms are inaccessible to these workers, and they face major obstacles in individually accessing labour justice at the Labour Ministry, not least because of their deportable status.

Workers in such situations, which are neither routine nor exceptional, feel compelled to confront their bosses with their grievances. This is in spite of their ordinarily conservative orientation in avoiding open conflicts with work superiors. Workers usually often make initial pleas to their bosses to make improvements to work regimes. These pleas are almost always ignored or dismissed. Workers then go on to make more firm demands, often verbally but also in writing to bosses or managers. One respondent, Shahin, for instance, demanded that salary deductions for "security deposits" and utility bills be repealed and refunded back to him when he requested an audience with his managing director.[27] Kamrul and his eight coworkers, who were paid below statutory rates for overtime and rest-day work, asked their employer to restore these rates to the statutory level and to back-pay them for previous months' work.[28] In another case, about 100 Bangladeshi workers got a local "friend" to help them write a letter of demand, signed by all 100 workers, to management after going unpaid for three months. After outlining the problems faced by their families in Bangladesh, the letter demanded that all owing wages be paid "within [a] short time" and wages, in future, were to be paid punctually on the tenth day of every month. Their employer ignored these demands and the workers subsequently approached HOME for legal assistance.[29] Workers, usually out of frustration, sometimes combine these demands

[27] Interview, 25 December 2011.

[28] HOME case report, 17 August 2009.

[29] HOME case report, 12 July 2010.

with overt demonstrations of disobedience at work such as work stoppages and truancy.

Aside from one specific documented case, worker confrontation and disobedience inevitably unleash the coercive power of employers who respond with deportation threats, physical intimidation, and finally forced deportation. It is worth emphasizing that these employer strategies are primarily used to resolve workplace disputes (such as those mentioned) rather than to ordinarily direct work activities. Al Amin's demands for proper medical attention and work-injury compensation were met with an ultimatum from his production manager, who told him, "Amin, do you want to go back to Bangladesh or do you want to stay in Singapore to work and earn money for your family? If you want to stay then you must go back to work!"[30] Masud's employer threatened to "throw" him back to Bangladesh "like rubbish."[31] When deportation threats are made, workers are told not only that they will be instantly deported if they do not follow orders, but that they will also be blacklisted and never be allowed back into Singapore.

When other methods of coercing recalcitrant workers back in line fail, employers attempt to forcefully deport them. Employers cannot simply terminate the employment of migrant workers — they are held legally responsible by the Labour Ministry for repatriating workers who have been terminated or have ended their terms. Employers may terminate a worker's work permit at any time but they are legally required to repatriate the worker within seven days of this termination or the S$5,000 bond with the ministry may not be refunded. Employers, therefore, call in repatriation companies to take "problem" workers into custody from their dormitories or worksites awaiting repatriation. Physical and verbal intimidation is often used on workers who refuse to comply. Shahid, for instance, had his medical certificates confiscated and found himself locked up in a room on his company's premises for days while being subject to constant verbal threats by his employer.[32] Mohamed Asadullah was abducted by men from a repatriation company right outside the Ministry of Manpower building

[30] Interview, 28 December 2011.

[31] HOME case report, 11 October 2010.

[32] Interview, 29 December 2011.

after lodging a complaint for unlawful wage deductions.[33] Hashim had his mobile phone seized from him and was subjected to physical and verbal threats whilst locked away at the premises of a repatriation company.[34]

In fear and desperation, workers desert their employers; they discreetly move away from the worksite or dormitory to another place — their friends' dormitories or the streets of the Little India district where Bangladeshi workers usually congregate — where their employers can neither control nor reach them. Some workers pre-empt forced deportation by deserting even before they are intimidated or threatened. Other workers, like Muqbul, are tipped off by their co-workers or even supervisors when the repatriation staff is on their way to take the worker into custody.[35] Some workers manage to escape while being escorted from their dormitories by the repatriation company. Some workers who fail to escape until they are escorted to the airport either refuse to go through immigration gates or refuse to board the flight after clearing immigration. Some workers who are unable to escape from repatriation companies ring up the police for assistance but are often told to comply and be repatriated. Some manage to contact NGO helpdesks to request assistance. In such cases, NGO staff would go directly to these repatriation companies to negotiate the release of workers. Should negotiations fail, NGO staff would go to the airport to assist workers in refusing to enter immigration gates. Often, this leads to confrontations between activists and repatriation staff. The former often secure the release of workers in "custody" by signing an "indemnity" with the repatriation company bearing responsibility for the employer's security bond should the worker go "missing." However, there is little evidence to show that such "indemnities" have ever been legally enforced by repatriation companies or employers. It is likely that such "indemnities" are used by repatriation companies to placate their clients when activist successfully obstruct forceful repatriation. Nonetheless, these indemnities have proved useful for NGOs in getting workers released from the custody of repatriation companies.

[33] Transient Workers Count Too (2011).

[34] Interview, 28 December 2011.

[35] Interview, 28 December 2011.

8. Contentious Politics, Mitigating Deportability

Deserting workers either stay on to find work in Singapore as overstayers or they seek out other social actors — the police, their recruitment agents, friends, relatives, lawyers, NGOs — to assist them with their predicament. Here, I focus exclusively on the latter. In such circumstances, they get very limited assistance from those mentioned — the police often tell them to return to their employers, their agents refuse to reimburse their recruitment fees, their friends and relatives might provide them with a place to stay, some meals, and an "illegal" day job but little else in terms of addressing their continued deportability, lawyers will only assist those with work-injury compensation issues. Through contacts provided by friends or lawyers, many deserting workers find their way to migrant worker NGOs like HOME and TWC2. These NGOs assist workers with their daily needs — HOME has two worker shelters while TWC2 runs a soup kitchen in Little India that is open for lunch and dinner several times a week. More significantly, NGOs provide legal assistance to workers and use these cases of assistance to advocate for the reform of migrant labour laws. In both cases, the deportability of migrant workers is somewhat mitigated.

Case workers and volunteers at these NGOs translate worker grievances over work injuries, underdeployment, and wage theft into formal complaints at the Labour Ministry. By querying workers on their grievances, case workers attempt to find out which particular labour laws or regulations have been breached by employers. They then proceed to assist the worker to lodge relevant claims to the ministry such as work-injury claims, salary claims, and complaints regarding the infringement of EFMA regulations. In all cases, once the formal claim is registered with the ministry, workers are given the legal right to remain in the country until the resolution of their cases through "special passes" — a visa renewable on a weekly or fortnightly basis. These "special passes" are given out to workers based on their new (but still temporary) legal status as claimants (for wages or work-injury compensation) or state witnesses (for employer violations of EFMA). The temporary stay can range from any between several weeks (salary disputes) to over one year (work-injury cases, EFMA cases). State witnesses for EFMA cases are usually allowed to sign on with a ministry-sponsored Temporary Job Scheme (TJS) where they may look for temporary (six-month) legal jobs which can be made permanent subject to a number of the ministry's conditions.

While immediate legal assistance in this form mitigates the deportability of individual workers, these cases provide NGOs with the impetus to lobby the ministry for reforms to deportation laws. Since 2009, NGOs have demanded that repatriation companies be outlawed and prosecuted for wrongful confinement and forced repatriation of migrant workers. They have also called for the Labour Ministry to repeal all work-permit regulations (under EFMA) that give employers the unilateral right to cancel the work permit of workers as well as the liberalization of the current Change-of-Employer (COE) regulations to allow existing migrant workers to change employers without having to be repatriated. While these NGOs were unable to mobilize migrant workers or public opinion to their cause, they drew on a mass of case work that they had amassed over several years which documented how employers used repatriation companies to resolve workplace disputes in a way which violated statutory standards.

Of the few formal rights they have, temporary migrant workers are allowed to lodge complaints regarding wage disputes, work injuries, and illegal deployments at the ministry. However, their deportable status poses an obstacle that inhibits them from accessing these rights. NGO direct services come in the form of legal assistance in lodging claims in the face of deportation threats and interventions into everyday practices of deportation. These allow workers to access these rights by mitigating their vulnerability to deportation and forestalling their actual deportation. Furthermore, by lobbying the ministry to reform labour laws, NGOs put pressure on the state to broaden migrant worker rights and revise the latter's status as discardable political subjects.

The GFC spill-out of 2008/09 proved to be a shot in the arm for NGO advocacy. During this period, thousands of migrant workers (mostly Chinese and Bangladeshis) from the construction and shipbuilding industry deserted their workplaces after confrontations over unpaid wages, underdeployment, and alleged employer kickbacks resulted in deportation threats from employers. Large groups of workers approached NGOs for assistance while others staged a sit-in outside the Ministry of Manpower building in Havelock Road demanding redress. The ministry initially called for the immediate deportation of all underdeployed workers. However, as the spill-out intensified as more groups of workers deserted, the ministry decided to grant affected workers a one-month grace to source for alternative employment within the same stipulated industry. This one-off concession gave NGOs the drive to lobby the ministry further to grant conditional COEs to all migrant workers engaged in employment disputes with their employers so that they would not have to be deported. Closed-door advocacy to ministry officials was intensified following the GFC spill-out while NGOs used existing documentation of forced repatriation cases to inform the US Department of State Trafficking in Persons Report and Singapore's first Universal Periodic Review by the UN Human Rights Council.

Since then, the ministry has moved to create additional employment offences such as the illegalization of kickbacks for employment and compulsory no-work pay. They have also revised the existing COE regulations to allow workers whose tenure has expired to seek new jobs in the country without being repatriated. NGOs have criticized the latter for being insufficient to protect migrant workers from forced deportation and employer abuse. Nonetheless, the expansion of the COE system is particularly significant. Under the old COE system, workers were only (if ever) granted a COE under very strict conditions — the most significant one being that their existing employer had to agree to it. Workers who have their employment prematurely terminated by their employer, often due to employment disputes, would, thus, have to return to their countries of origin and fork out another huge sum of money in order to secure a new job in Singapore. Under the revised COE framework, employer consent is not required. Workers may be granted COEs, at the ministry's discretion, once they complete their current term of employment or, in cases of underdeployment, where employers do not have sufficient jobs to sustain their migrant workforce. Under such circumstances, workers do not need to return to their countries of origin in order to secure a contract with a new employer. While the new regulations could have negative implications for worker empowerment in the workplace, they significantly temper the ease with which these workers can be used and discarded.

At the same time, it is equally important to note that the tweaking of labour laws does not necessarily constitute a concession to the welfare of migrant workers. Rather, this is a form of "technocratic problem solving" where existing tensions between employers and migrant workers over working conditions can be managed through administrative means.[36] State-sponsored administrative channels for contestation are being broadened in order for migrant workers to politically participate as individual complainants rather than as an independently mobilized collective entity. The additional employment offences and a revised COE framework will allow disputes to be managed through the administrative channels of the ministry rather than through spontaneous collective action (as witnessed during the GFC) or independent NGO advocacy. In this sense, mitigating migrant worker deportability through minor reforms provides for a depoliticized resolution to workplace disputes without actually addressing the core tensions in the workplace which give rise to these disputes.

9. Conclusion

State deportation laws render temporary migrant workers as "use-and-discard" economic subjects with few formal rights. While these laws severely undermine the political personhood of migrant workers, the deportable status of these workers may contribute towards civil society efforts to contest state constructions of these workers as disposable economic subjects. This article has stressed the importance of the micro-politics of the workplace as the site through which issues of deportability and practices of deportation shape migrant worker agency. Articulated together with a range of political-economic factors, deportability engenders a range of worker tactics to deal with existing workplace grievances. Responses such as tactical accommodation and confrontation/desertion come about under different workplace conditions depending on how migrant worker deportability intersects with production-related factors, such as production geography and employer control strategies, that govern the terms of work.

---

[36] Rodan & Jayasuria (2007).

These different tactics, in turn, have varied implications for the shape of migrant labour politics in the country in terms of broader civil society pressures to reform migrant labour laws. Certain outcomes of workplace conflicts, particularly confrontation and desertion rather than tactical accommodation, allow civil society groups to contest state constructions of temporary migrant workers as disposable persons without political rights. Civil society pressure, in turn, leads to state responses in revising the legal status of these workers. While deportation laws inhibit migrant workers from accessing the few formal rights they are endowed with, the reforms introduced by the Manpower Ministry encourage workers to make contestations as individual complainants within the state's bureaucratic mechanisms rather than as collectively mobilized actors or through independent NGO advocacy. The state's belated but limited expansion of migrant worker political personhood as individualized complainants through the mitigation of deportability, therefore, serves to depoliticize enduring worker grievances over working conditions.

References

Arnold, Dennis, & Kevin Hewison (2006) "Exploitation in Global Supply Chains: Burmese Migrant Workers in Mae Sot, Thailand," in K. Hewison & K. Young, eds., *Transnational Migration and Work in Asia*, London and New York: Routledge, 165–90.

Bal, Charanpal S. (2015) "Production Politics and Migrant Labour Advocacy in Singapore." 45 *Journal of Contemporary Asia* 219–42.

Basu, Radha (2009) "Holding Area Is a Room in the Office: Close Tabs Kept on Workers in Case They Try to Run Off," *The Straits Times*, 31 January.

Binford, Leigh (2009) "From Fields of Power to Fields of Sweat: The Dual Process of Constructing Temporary Migrant Labour in Mexico and Canada." 30 *Third World Quarterly* 503–17.

Buckley, Michelle (2013) "Locating Neoliberalism in Dubai: Migrant Workers and Class Struggle in the Autocratic City." 45 *Antipode* 256–74.

Castells, Manuel (1975) "Immigrant Workers and Class Struggles in Advanced Capitalism: The Western European Experience." 5 *Politics and Society* 33–66.

Castles, Stephen, & Godula Kosack (1973) *Immigrant Workers and Class Structure in Western Europe*, London: Oxford University Press.

Construction Industry Development Board Singapore (2000) *Census of the Construction Industry 2000*, Construction Economics and Resources Unit, Construction Industry Development Board, Singapore.

de Certeau, Michel (1984) *The Practice of Everyday Life*, translated by Steven Rendall, Berkley: University of California Press.

de Genova, Nicholas P. (2005) *Working the Boundaries: Race, Space and "Illegality" in Mexican Chicago*, Durham and London: Duke University Press.

Government of Singapore (1991) "Employment of Foreign Manpower Act (Chapter 91A), Amended 9 November 2012, Attorney-General's Chambers," online <http://statutes.agc.gov.sg/aol/search/display/view.w3p;page=0;query=DocId%3Ad07a73ca-043a-4531-8132-357598e0a9ab%20%20Status%3Ainforce%20Depth%3A0;rec=0> (last accessed 15 July 2013).

Hsia, Hsiao-Chuan (2009) "The Making of a Transnational Grassroots Migrant Movement." 41 *Critical Asian Studies* 113–41.

Humanitarian Organization of Migration Economics (HOME) and Transient Workers Count Too (TWC2) (2010) *Justice Delayed, Justice Denied: The Experiences of Migrant Workers in Singapore*, Singapore: HOME and TWC2.

Lim, Philip (2011) "Migrant Workers Hunted Down in Singapore," *The Jakarta Globe*, 3 August. Liow, Eugene Dili (2011) "The Neoliberal-Developmental State: Singapore as Case-Study." 38 *Critical Sociology* 1–24.

Ministry of Manpower Singapore (2011) "Joint Proactive Enforcement Inspections on Repatriation Companies," Press Release, 14 November.

Mitchell, Don (1996) *The Lie of the Land: Migrant Workers and the California Landscape*, Minneapolis: University of Minnesota Press.

No Author (1977) "Employment Passes for These Alien Workers," *The Straits Times*, 28 December.

No Author (1989) "Boon Heng: Govt Considering 'Final Amnesty' Appeal," *The Straits Times*, 11 July.

Pereira, Brandan (1989) "470 Illegal Thai Workers Sent Back in Past 72 Hours," *The Straits Times*, 18 March.

Rodan, Garry, & Kanishka Jayasuria (2007) "The Technocratic Politics of Administrative Participation: Case Studies of Singapore and Vietnam." 14 *Democratization* 795–815.

Sargeson, Sally (2001) "Assembling Class in a Chinese Joint Venture Factory," in J. Hutchison & A. Brown, eds., *Organising Labour in Globalising Asia*, London: Routledge.

Sassen, Saskia (1988) *The Mobility of Labor and Capital: A Study in International Investment and Labor Flow*, Cambridge and New York: Cambridge University Press.

Sassen-Koob, Saskia (1981) "Towards a Conceptualization of Immigrant Labor." 29 *Social Problems* 65–85.

Sim, Chi Yin (2005) "They're Runaway 'Bounty Hunters'," *The New Paper*, 26 November.

Taylor, Charles (1985) *Philosophical Papers: Volume 1, Human Agency and Language*, Cambridge: Cambridge University Press.

Transient Workers Count Too (2011) "Twice Abducted by Repatriation Agents, Asadullah Goes Home Poorer than when He Arrived," online <http://twc2.org.sg/2011/12/31/twice-abducted-by-repatriation-agents-asadullah-goes-home-poorer-than-when-he-arrived/> (last accessed 5 February 2015).

Wham, Jolovan (2011) "Repatriation Companies — Manpower Minister's Response Belittles the Efforts of Migrant Workers," online <http://www.theonlinecitizen.com/2011/11/repartriation-companies-manpower-ministers-response-belittles-the-efforts-of-migrant-workers/> (last accessed 26 June 2015).

Yeoh, Brenda (2006) "Bifurcated Labour: The Unequal Incorporation of Transmigrants in Singapore." 97 *Tijdschrift voor Economische en Sociale Geografie* 26–37.

Section II

Work Conditions and Health Concerns

Chapter 5a

Health, Safety and Well-being: Listening to the Voices of Migrant Workers in a Pandemic*

Mohan J. Dutta

Center for Culture-centered Approach to Research and Evaluation
Massey University

Singapore's infrastructural development as a global 'smart' city is built on the backs of migrant workers, whose jobs put them at greater risk of workplace fatalities, injuries, and other threats to their health and well-being. This 2017 paper is based on the culture-centered approach (CCA) as a means of articulating the narratives of workplace conditions, injuries, and health risks, from the voices of Bangladeshi migrant workers in Singapore. In this paper, I discussed how this approach had co-created voice infrastructures for low-wage migrant workers in Singapore, in which advisory groups of workers collectively identified key challenges to workplace health and safety, and possible solutions. The narratives of the migrant

---

*Reflections on Dutta, M. J. (2017). Migration and health in the construction industry: Culturally centering voices of Bangladeshi workers in Singapore, *Int. J. Environ. Res. Public Health*, Vol. 14, No. 2, 132. DOI: 10.3390/ijerph14020132.

workers include construction site injuries, living conditions such as food insecurity, lack of sleep, and transportation, as well as issues like communication barriers, misunderstandings, and workplace incivility.

Amidst the COVID-19 outbreak in migrant worker dormitories, advisory group members mobilised to identify the key challenges, and constructed a conceptual framework for advocacy to address these challenges. Drawing from the voices of the workers, our research team, involving community researchers and academics at the Center for Culture-centered Approach to Research and Evaluation (CARE), conducted digital ethnography, accompanied by in-depth interviews and a multi-pronged survey with migrant workers. The advisory group was also involved in producing the interview protocol and survey instrument, which focused on the key challenges of poor housing infrastructure, food insecurity, poor sanitation conditions, and the absence of communicative resources. Emergent themes from the fieldwork were shared with the advisory group, resulting in a co-constructive process of sense-making. In addition, our academic team has been doing ongoing translation work with low-wage migrant workers and their interactions with civil society organisations and journalists, further building narrative registers. The findings were used to produce white papers, with specific policy recommendations for building health infrastructures for the well-being of low-wage migrant workers.

The 2017 article shows how voice infrastructures for migrant workers are important for understanding their workplace conditions, health, and safety. A similar insight can be drawn from the case of the COVID-19 outbreak in migrant worker dormitories. Overcrowded and unsanitary dormitory conditions led to a rapid spread of infections among migrant workers [Ratcliffe, 2020]. Migrant workers had to endure months of prolonged quarantine and movement restrictions both inside and outside the dormitories [Paulo and Grosse, 2021]. As I argued in another paper, these conditions are linked to the state's 'smart city' model of governance, an offshoot of which is the silencing of migrant worker voices and the repression of worker collectivisation [Dutta, 2021]. Yet, the dormitory outbreaks have shown how discourses on migrant health should involve creating infrastructures for migrant worker voices and collectivisation. The participant narratives, for example, highlight the ways in which the COVID-19 outbreak in migrant worker dormitories would have been prevented with decent housing infrastructure that addressed the fundamental rights to health and well-being of workers.

References

Dutta, M. J. (2021). Singapore's extreme neoliberalism and the COVID outbreak: Culturally centering voices of low-wage migrant workers, *American Behavioral Scientist*, Vol. 65, No. 10, pp. 1302–1322. DOI: 10.1177/00027642211000409

Ratcliffe, R. (2020, 23 April). 'We're in a prison': Singapore's migrant workers suffer as COVID-19 surges back. *The Guardian*. https://www.theguardian.com/world/2020/apr/23/singapore-million-migrant-workers-suffer-as-covid-19-surges-back

Paulo, D. A. and Grosse, S. (2021, 25 February). A year since COVID-19, dorm life leaves migrant workers still hoping for better. *CNA*. Retrieved from https://www.channelnewsasia.com/news/cnainsider/year-since-covid-19-dormitory-life-leaves-migrant-workers-hoping-14244702

Chapter 5b

Migration and Health in the Construction Industry: Culturally Centering Voices of Bangladeshi Workers in Singapore*

Mohan J. Dutta

Center for Culture-centered Approach to Research and Evaluation
Department of Communications & New Media
National University of Singapore
Singapore 117416, Singapore
cnmmohan@nus.edu.sg

Academic Editors: Albert P. C. Chan and Wen Yi

Construction workers globally face disproportionate threats to health and wellbeing, constituted by the nature of the work they perform. The workplace fatalities and lost-time injuries experienced by construction workers are significantly greater than in other forms of work. This paper

---

*This article was originally published in *Int. J. Environ. Res. Public Health*, Vol. 14, No. 2, 132. DOI: 10.3390/ijerph14020132.

draws on the culture-centered approach (CCA) to dialogically articulate meanings of workplace risks and injuries, voiced by Bangladeshi migrant construction workers in Singapore. The narratives voiced by the participants suggest an ecological approach to workplace injuries in the construction industries, attending to food insecurity, lack of sleep, transportation, etc. as contextual features of work that shape the risks experienced at work. Moreover, participant voices point to the barriers in communication, lack of understanding, and experiences of incivility as features of work that constitute the ways in which they experience injury risks. The overarching discourses of productivity and efficiency constitute a broader climate of threats to worker safety and health.

Keywords: workplace risks; injury; workplace safety; culture-centered approach; migration; health

1. Introduction

Construction workers globally face disproportionate threats to health and wellbeing, constituted by the nature of the work they perform [1]. The workplace fatalities and lost-time injuries experienced by construction workers are significantly greater than in other forms of work [2]. The productivity-driven and efficiency-based nature of the construction industries place tremendous burden on the health of workers [2,3]. Add to this the large number of migrants that work in the construction industries globally, contributing further to the precarious nature of construction work, marked by limited protections and the lack of access to resources (such as health care, insurance etc.) that are otherwise guaranteed to citizens [4,5]. Essential to cotemporary global patterns of migration and construction work are the exploitative conditions of global labour in the construction industries, often taking advantage of flexible labour-related policies that offer little protection to migrants [6,7]. The low and semi-skilled nature of migrant construction work is accompanied then by the contractual nature of the work in global economic flows, and the productivity-driven pressures that are placed on construction workers.

In the dominant health communication literature on workplace safety and health, the normative idea of workplace safety focuses on promoting individual behavior change in workers through the development of effective messages [8,9]. Salient in this framework is the conceptualization of communication as promotion of individual behavior change, placing emphasis on the safety training of workers [10,11]. Workers are targeted through informative and/or persuasive messages, with the emphasis of health communication therefore in developing effective messaging strategies [12–15]. Safety is conceptualized in terms of specific behaviors that are promoted in the target population of workers, tied to awareness [12,13]. Similarly, studies on workplace safety cultures examine the perceptions held by workers regarding the support in the organizational culture for safety practices, operationalizing cultures of safety as aggregates of individualized perceptions. Missing from this framework of individual behavior change are structures of construction work and the nature of workplaces. The risks situated amidst these structures mostly remain unaccounted for in the dominant body of scholarship on workplace safety and health, with its narrow emphasis on behavior change [15,16].

On a similar note, health communication interventions targeting migrants often take migrant culture as deficit, to be targeted through effective health promotion messages [15–18]. In this framework, culture is conceptualized as a static collection of beliefs and values, mapping immigrant culture in relationship to the host culture, and developing recipes for cultural transformation through communication as persuasion [19–21]. Communication, connected to culture, is culturally tailored in order to adapt to the characteristics of the immigrant community, with the goal of generating culturally sensitive messages that are persuasively effective with the targeted immigrant community. Culturally sensitive messages are based on identifying characteristics of the culture that can be spoken to in order to generate affiliation and persuasive message processing. Missing often from this dominant thread of health communication are the local cultural contexts of immigrant communities [21–23]. In configuring immigrants as passive recipients of health messaging, the agentic capacities of immigrants are erased. Also absent from dominant health communication theorizing are the voices of local communities of immigrants, their lived experiences, and their negotiations of health. Moreover, the individualistic health communication frameworks often fail to take into account the broader political economy of immigrant life [20,24,25].

Migrant workers from Bangladesh working in the construction industry in Singapore form a part of this global flow of labour, negotiating their health amid global structures of flows of capital and labour [25–27]. In this manuscript, I apply the theoretical framework of the culture-centered approach (CCA) to listen to the voices of migrant construction workers in Singapore, focusing on the articulations of health, risk, and safety in the realms of construction work [20,23,25]. The concepts of culture, structure, and agency are offered as conceptual anchors for foregrounding local meanings of risk and safety in construction work. The voices of the workers presented in this manuscript attend to the structures that constitute everyday experiences of construction work, the threats to health and safety as understood by construction workers, and the potential solutions to risks at workplace that are suggested by construction workers. Rather than suggesting behavior change in the form of individual-level solutions that are typically recommended in workplace safety communication interventions, the voices of the participants articulate anchors for structural transformations that attend to the contextual features of construction work.

1.1. *Workplace safety, health and communication*

The dominant approach to workplace safety in the health communication literature conceptualizes health as individualized responsibility, developing workplace safety programs and training interventions directed at promoting safety practices [8,10,20]. The overarching theoretical framework informing workplace safety interventions is driven by the impetus to create effective health promotion messages that would promote healthy behaviors in workplaces. The emphasis is placed on deciphering the appropriate communication strategies that would effectively persuade the audience of workers to practice safe workplace practices. In this backdrop of the dominant framework of workplace safety communication, the culture-centered approach (CCA) offers an entry point for exploring the ways in which local contexts shape the everyday experiences of risks among construction workers, and the lived experiences of workers with these risks [22,23].

1.2. *Culture-centered approach*

Health is constituted in the everyday meanings individuals and communities make of health, embedded within local contexts and in the cultural formations of community life [15–17]. Conceptualizing culture as dynamic, fragmented, and ever-transforming, the CCA foregrounds meanings as entry points for the constructions of health and wellbeing [15,24–26]. The CCA proposes that cultural contexts are anchors for understanding how health risks are understood, how they are made sense of, and the ways in which they are negotiated by community members [27–30]. Based on a dialogic approach to culture and community life, it suggests that the theorizing of health needs to be embedded within sense-making processes of local communities, developing entry points for solutions to health risks that are embedded in the everyday negotiations of structures, resources, and contexts [17].

Meanings of health and health risks are located at the intersections of culture, structure, and agency [27]. Culture is a complex web of shared practices, beliefs, and values that offers the anchor for interpretive frames. Meanings draw upon cultural resources and in turn, shape the ways in which cultural scripts are constructed and reproduced. Structure refers to the material realities that constrain and enable human action, depicting the distribution of resources within social systems [16,17]. Agency reflects the capacity of community members to make sense of structures and to negotiate these structures, drawing on cultural scripts and interpretive frames that are meaningful to them. The intersections of culture, structure, and agency depict the constraints and challenges to health experienced by community members, their sense-making processes in understanding these structures, and their day-to-day practices of negotiating these structures. This article draws from the CCA and co-constructs [25,26] meanings of health with Bangladeshi construction workers, attending to the ways in which these workers make sense of these risks in their everyday lives. Singapore has grown increasing reliant on immigrant labor in the last 15 years, with the number of foreign workers almost doubling between 2000 and 2010 [31,32]. It houses 319,000 laborers working in the construction sector alone in December 2013 [33]. The Singapore government is a major consumer of construction services through public housing development — over 17,000 flats were built in 2011 alone (SDS, 2012). Foreign workers are hired under a Work Permit (WP), which is granted to foreigners who wish to work in Singapore. They must also come from approved countries of origin, which are grouped into 4 categories: (1) *Malaysia*; (2) *North Asian Sources (NAS)*, which comprise Hong Kong, Macau, South Korea, and Taiwan; (3) *Non-Traditional Sources (NTS)*, which comprise India, Sri Lanka, Thailand, Bangladesh, Myanmar, and Philippines; and (4) *People's Republic of China* (Singapore Ministry of Manpower (MOM), 2012). Employers in Singapore are required by law to meet several conditions in hiring foreign workers. One of the conditions is that employers must foot a monthly levy per unskilled worker. With regard to the health and wellbeing of the migrant workers, the Employment of Foreign Manpower Act states that employers must fulfill requisites such as ensuring healthy and safe working conditions, paying for initial medical examinations, bearing the cost of medical treatments when the worker falls sick or is injured, and purchasing and maintaining individual medical insurance (MOM, 2011). The Act also clearly disallows employers from passing on health care costs and other employer financial obligations on to the foreign employees.

2. Materials and Methods

The article draws on 60 ethnographic in-depth interviews (out of a total of 180 interviews, only selecting those in-depth interviews that voiced risks of injury at construction work) conducted with Bangladeshi construction workers in Singapore, part of a broader ongoing culture-centered ethnographic project that was initiated in 2008 and that resulted in an advocacy campaign on worker rights in 2014–2015. The construction workers who participated in the project were selected through the snowball sampling strategy and reflect a variety of subsectors (e.g., residential construction, commercial, public works), and trades (e.g., masonry, ironwork, electrician). The project was approved by the University's Institutional Review Board (IRB) (NUS-IRB Ref 12-392) and informed consent was secured from the participants. The in-depth interviews ranged from 40 min to two hours in length, with an average interview being 55 min in length. The interviews were conducted in Bengali and then translated into English. The in-depth interviews that this paper draws on resulted in 725 pages of single-spaced transcripts. In addition to the in-depth interviews, I conducted participant observations at public spaces where Bangladeshi construction workers hang out, spending time in Little India (space in Singapore where migrant workers gather, especially on their day off on Sundays), attending performances put together by migrant workers, accompanying migrant workers during their visits to run errands, accompanying migrant workers during visits to doctors, and coordinating broader discussions with migrant workers as part of the larger culture-centered project driven toward identifying problems and developing solutions. The narratives shared by the participants in the project point toward the structural contexts of migrant construction work, and the threats to health and safety that are constituted amid these structures. In this article, I will share snippets from these conversations to elucidate the interplays of structure and agency in articulations of migrant worker health, wellbeing and safety within the broader ambits of construction work.

3. Results

The narratives shared by the participants point toward their everyday struggles for negotiating health amid the structures of migrant construction work. The everyday meanings of health are situated amid the local cultural understandings of food, culturally embedded meanings of and approaches to health, and the structures of construction work that shape the distribution of resources. In sharing their experiences with structures, participants point toward the profit-driven framework of the structures that often directly threaten human health and wellbeing. Moreover, participants share their strategies of everyday enactments of agency.

3.1 *Health and workplace injuries*

Health is constituted in the ambits of the everyday risks of doing construction work. For many workers, workplace injuries are salient in their lives in the construction industry. *Abdul* (the names of the participants have been changed to protect their identity) shares, "These injuries are part of our daily life. That you will get hurt while working is something you don't worry about. You know that these things happen." Similarly, shares *Jamal*, "I had an accident while lifting a bag of cement. I was trying to hurry. I know this happens to you if you are working in this industry." The participants point toward the notion of risks to safety as embedded in their day-to-day work, attaching meaning to risk at work in the ambits of the structures of work in the construction industry. As shared by *Kaseem*, "This work, I work on tall buildings, there is risk every day. When I am working at height, there is always the chance of fall. You don't think about that." For *Kaseem*, knowing that his work is by nature risky, constitutes his "not thinking about work." That risk is an everyday part of their lives as workers in the construction industries shapes the everyday negotiations of risk. He further notes, "It's the wish of *Allah*." This culturally-embedded religious narrative of workplace risk is situated in relationship to the structures of work on tall buildings. The structure of construction work constitutes the sense of inevitability that is articulated in a narrative of religiosity. Similarly, *Bashir* shares:

> I know that I have to do this kind of work. It is tough. I know it is difficult and there are risks in the different things I do. If I just worried about how difficult the work is, or what the risks are, I would not be able to do the work. I would be scared, and try to avoid it. But my family needs the money. So I have to do this work. I am making the money and sending home every month. I don't really think about anything else.

This notion of not really thinking about the risks of work is shared by a number of participants. Note in these narratives shared by the participants the ways in which they understand risks to health and safety as part of their everyday lives, pointing to the overarching structural context of deprivation and familial needs within which they voice not really thinking about the risks of work. The cultural articulation of familial ties and family needs as the reason for work shapes the meanings of inevitability the workers construct around workplace risks. For *Abdul*, "I have come here to earn and send money home. I took a big loan, my wife put all her jewellery for mortgage to get loan. So now I just have to do the work. If it is risky, I can't worry about it." *Abdul's* sense of not worrying about the risk ties the structure of construction work with his cultural values of earning money to care for family and send money home.

At the same time, participants share that workplace injuries are life events that can transform their lives and push them into immobility. They share stories of co-workers who have been killed in workplace accidents. *Maqbool* witnessed a co-worker killed in an accident, and shared the following: "It just happened. I was going with my work. And then this sound. He had fallen. When things like this happen, they change everything. I know this can happen to me." Similarly, for *Bashir*, the death of a co-worker drives home the vulnerable conditions of construction work, "I know that this can happen to me as well." This is also shared by *Arnab*, "I have seen a number of these accidents take place in my worksite. Some are life threatening. One time, *Robin*, he was working right in the next station, and then some friends came and said, he has been crushed by the cement mixer. I ran. He was dead by then." Sharing similar experience of having witnessed a co-worker lose a toe, *Bimal* notes, "When you are working in construction, these things can happen. You just know that they can happen." Note here the paradox between the articulation of "not thinking about the risks to health" and "being aware of the vulnerabilities to health constituted amid everyday work." Participants on one hand suggest that they don't really think about workplace injuries, and on the other hand, are well aware of the everydayness of injuries as routinized into their jobs. In participants' stories of workplace deaths and workplace injury-related disabilities, the costs of injuries to them and to their families in Bangladesh emerge strongly. Participants note how injuries at work are significant threats to their health, livelihoods, and economic mobilities of their families.

3.2. *Workplace injuries and health seeking*

For a number of participants in this ethnographic project, workplace injuries present challenges in the realm of seeking treatment, after care, and securing adequate medical leave. Shares *Sobuj*, "When I dropped a plank on my feet, it hurt a lot. The supervisor gave some first aid and then said it will be alright. Then that night, it swelled. I did not know where to go for treatment. The supervisor said it will become better, just give it some time." *Sobuj* did not have access to medical treatment and did not know how to secure access to a health provider. For a number of participants, the supervisor ignored the injury and asked the worker to get back to work. Also participants noted the ways in which the limited access to health information (about health resources and where to locate them) shaped their inability to seek out treatment after an injury.

Ahmed voiced the following narrative, "I broke my toe one day while carrying a load and fell down. I had to be in rest, and could not go to work. Did not get my salary for those days." *Ahmed's* experience of workplace injuries is intertwined with experiences of economic vulnerabilities at work shared in the previous section. Having a workplace injury meant the inability to earn money, which translated into a weakened ability to send money back home to family. He went on to note, "This month, I will have very little to send home. So no matter what, I just let it get better a little and went back [to work]." Even though Ahmed was still experiencing the pain, he noted that being absent from work any longer would mean his family in Bangladesh wouldn't have the resources needed for the coming month. The physical threats to health posed by workplace injuries translate into worries about what would happen to their economic condition and to their ability to return the debt or take care of their families. This means that in spite of their injuries, workers often go back to work just to earn the money needed to support their families. The culturally-situated articulations of familial responsibility shape the ways in which the workers experience workplace injuries.

Although existing policy frameworks dictate that workers qualify for medical leaves when injured, a number of participants discussed the ways in which the doctors the company arranged them to see were reluctant to issue medical certificate as that would mean less money for the company. A number of participants felt that company-assigned doctors often worked in collusion with the company. When asked why they didn't seek other options, they often noted that they were constrained by their company with respect to which doctor they could see, and that they did not have access to adequate information about health resources that would be available to them. In other words, not being aware of the healthcare infrastructure in Singapore, they often did not know where to go to or how to navigate the structure. This point is shared by *Najmool*, "I cut my finger, and went to the company doctor because that's where the boss [boss is a term used by migrant construction workers to refer to individuals in power at the workplace (e.g., crew leader, supervisor, owner of company, contractor)] sent me. The doctor was no good, just gave me a bandage and no MC [referring to medical certificate]. I did not know anyone else. I went back to work the next day, and my finger was still hurting."

3.3. *Efficiency and workplace risk*

The experiences of workplace injuries are constituted in the backdrop of the risks that are built into workplaces in Singapore. Participants share that the risks to their everyday health and safety are often posed by the productivity and efficiency demands experienced in the construction industry. *Sajal* shares, "The nature of construction work itself is risky. Then think about all the time pressure that shapes the work we do. There are volumes that need to be met. Certain number of things that we need to finish by a date. There are project deadlines." The notions of project volume and project deadline emerge consistently in the interviews. For *Nabin*, "Everyone is working hard, and the boss is always pushing. The boss needs to deliver a set of complete jobs by this date. Then the boss pushes everyone to meet that target. So there is that pressure to get the work done." Similarly, notes *Babulal*, who has worked as a supervisor, "Things need to be done efficiently. That means get as much out with as little number of workers and as little time. So there is always a push for the numbers." This pressure of getting the job done efficiently translates into pressures on the job, with workers "rushing through tasks." Notes *Babu*:

> There are many things that need to be finished in a day. So the supervisor is always trying to meet the deadlines. Yelling at the workers to get moving quickly. To get all the things done. And there is no time. So it is easy to miss something. Or to have an accident. Because I am thinking, I need to get this, this, and this done. I have a lot of tension on my mind. I am trying to get all the things done. And that's when I make a mistake.

The point shared by *Babu* suggests that taking care of the assigned tasks in the limited timeframe increases the risks of injury. Worth noting in the narrative is the voicing of risk tied to the errors made amidst the time and productivity pressures at work.

Further elaborating on the discourses of productivity, participants note the ways in which the overarching discourse governing their work is of performance, meeting the targets that have been established. Notes *Rasul*, "These targets are very hard to meet. They are set very high. So you are always pushing, pushing, pushing just to meet the target. Then all you are thinking about is the target." The articulation of targets at high levels that are typically unachievable means that workers focus entirely on meeting these targets. Given the precarious nature of construction work and the uncertainties tied to work, the pressures of performance translate into the risks workers take in getting the job done in a timely fashion, meeting the pre-established deadlines.

3.4. *Food insecurity, fatigue, and workplace safety*

Moreover, participants noted their everyday lives as risks to health and threats to workplace safety. For example, for *Nabin*, to be able to carry out the heavy load of construction work, "the basic food is a must." He shared how construction work is heavy work, and is demanding on the body, and therefore requires the adequate supply of nourishment to the body. To do such work as he did at the construction sites, often lifting heavy weight and carrying the weight for distances, called for him to have enough physical strength, which in turn, he derived from eating adequate food. Yet he noted, "Food is something that is often absent from the lives of Bangladeshi workers. I work long hours, and by the time I get back, the food that is catered is already stale. There are many nights when I don't get to eat anything." The participants discussed the heavy work at construction sites, juxtaposed in the backdrop of the absence of sufficient food from their everyday lives. This for many participants led to injuries in workplaces, producing fatigue on the job. This point was elucidated by *Jahan*, "Without the food, there is no energy left to do the work. I feel tired. And because I am tired, I am going to make some error on the job."

For *Mohsin*, "without the food, also because I skip a meal when the food has gone stale, it affects my health." On a similar note, *Kareem* shares, "The hard work in the construction site goes from 7 in the morning until 8 or 9 in the evening. This is hard work. How can I do the work when I don't have enough food in my body and feel lethargic? I feel very tired and then worry that I am going to fall or have an accident. My stomach is empty." The hard work at construction sites is juxtaposed in the backdrop of the absence of quality food, which in turn results in the feeling of lethargy and the increased likelihood of making errors on the job.

Bangladeshi construction workers in Singapore often live in dormitories, and this shapes the overarching context of inaccess to food. While there are a wide range of dormitories in Singapore, in most of these dormitories, there are no cooking facilities. As a result, most of the workers receive food from catering agencies. There are a range of catering agencies that operate in Singapore, and the extent of regulation of catering agencies varies. Whereas some of the catering agencies are licensed, there are also a number of catering agencies that are not licensed. Workers typically learn about and sign up for catering agencies through middle men, who can be other more senior workers, security and other personnel at the dormitory, or colleagues through workplaces. *Rezan* shares his dependence on the catering companies, "We can't cook our own food in the dormitory. There is no facility to cook own food. So I will have to depend on the catering company. Even though the quality of the food delivered by the catering company is of poor quality, I have no other choice." Many Bangladeshi construction workers share similar problems with the quality of the food delivered by the catering company. This is what *Zoeb* shares, "The problem is with the workers having to get the food from a catering company, and the catering company does not really care about the quality of the food we get. It just gets something to the workers. For most days, I can't just eat the food because it has gone stale." Workers share that the lunch, which they usually eat at work around noon, is usually delivered early in the morning before they take the transport to work, and is cooked the night before. As a result, the cooked food often goes stale. Shares *Bilkis*, "I end up not eating the food many times, just skipping it because it has gone stale."

Participants share stories of stale or unhygienic food that results in sickness. Shares *Gholam*:

> The food is so unhealthy that it can get you sick. There are many times I have had to take a medical certificate (MC) for a leave because I have gotten sick from eating the food. One time, it was stale. I knew it when I ate it. But I was so hungry that I ate it. Later it made me sick." In the narrative shared by *Mustaq*, we hear the experience of unhealthy food that made him sick. Along similar lines, *Saleem* shares, "The food has often gone stale by the time I eat it. It is delivered in the dorm at 5 a.m. in the morning and is cooked the previous night. I eat it only at noon during lunch time and that's when it has already become stale. So many times I just skipped the meal because the food had gone bad.

The story of food that has gone bad is shared by a number of participants. The poor quality of food emerges as a consistent theme in participant narratives of health, situating food within their cultural contexts and depicting the structures of the dormitories and catering companies that limit their access to healthy food.

The sense of food insecurity then is tied to articulations of fatigue. Notes *Mahmood*:

> I have not eaten proper food for many days. You look at this food. It has gone bad. How can you expect workers to eat this food and still carry on with work? I am very tired most of the time. I just don't have the energy, or I am feeling sick from the bad food. This makes me make mistakes at work.

The storying of lack of access to quality food is tied to experiences of poor health and fatigue shared by workers. Moreover, experiences of poor health and fatigue are tied to risks of workplace injuries. The centrality of food in the narratives voiced by the participants reflects the broader cultural constructions of food in Bangladesh. Moreover, given the importance placed on food, having access to culturally appropriate food emerges as a risk for workplace injuries.

3.5. *Lack of sleep and fatigue*

Yet another source of fatigue shared by the participants is the lack of sleep. For a number of participants living in dorms far away from the construction sites where they work translates into having to wake up early in the morning (often between 4:30 a.m. and 5:30 a.m.) to get in the queue for using the bathroom facilities. The sites of work are in many instances between half-hour to 40 min away from the dorms, depending on the traffic. At the end of the day, after completing work, workers often return to their dorms between 8 p.m. and 9:00 p.m. The participants share that the limited rest during the weekdays often results in fatigue at work, which once again increased the chance of injuries. This is what *Alam* had to say:

> I am tired at work, throughout the week. It is just the amount of time it takes to get to work and then to go back to the dorm room. And then in the dorm, it is hard to go to bed early because there are so many people in the room, and everyone is trying to do their own thing. And in the morning, I have to wake up very early so I can use the bathroom.

The long lines to go to the bathroom and get ready in the morning emerge across the interviews. The participants note the ways in which their schedules accompanied by work pressures result in injuries. The notion of feeling tired because of the lack of adequate facilities in the dorm is also voiced by *Sojol*, "The tiredness at work is what causes an accident. When you don't have good sleep the night before and wake up early to make in time for the truck, you are going to be very tired." This notion of feeling fatigue because of the lack of sleep, and resulting in workplace injuries is also shared by *Rehan*, "I don't get more than 6–7 h of sleep each day. After the work, also many times in the heat, I get very tired, and then not enough rest. What to do?"

3.6. *Mistreatment, incivility, and workplace risks*

The narratives shared by the participants often voice uncivil communication directed at the workers, and these experiences of incivility then translate into greater likelihood of errors and injuries at work. For *Boshir*,

"When the boss shouts at me, I make mistakes because I am so worried." Participants share stories of being mistreated at work by the supervisor and this threatens their health by making them vulnerable to accidents at construction sites. *Koreem* shares, "The boss is always shouting. Shouting and calling names. I get nervous, trying to hurry, and that's when I make mistakes on the job." On a similar note, *Sajal* shares, "I try very hard to follow what the boss says, but sometimes I can't understand and the boss gets angry." Not understanding is a theme that is reiterated in a number of interviews, suggesting that the lack of understanding leads to errors on the job. *Nitai* points out, "I can't understand what the supervisor says, and that makes him angry. Then I am feeling the pressure, and end up dropping something or stepping on something."

In these narratives, participants shared the ways in which being mistreated at work makes them vulnerable to making errors. *Chitta* posits, "When someone is shouting and saying things to you, you become absent-minded because you are upset. That's when mistakes happen because you are not fully concentrating on the work." Salient across the participant narratives is the interplay of being mistreated and the risks of workplace injuries, mediated by expressions of feelings of being upset. This is voiced by *Rajib*, "I have injured my hand at work because the boss was shouting at me and asking me to hurry. I could not understand what the boss was saying and so was trying to carry the crates even faster, and twisted my wrist." Not understanding the supervisor is a theme that emerges across the in-depth interviews, with participants noting the pressures on the work that are related to not understanding the supervisor. This point is made by *Biram*, "I don't understand what the boss says because he speaks in a different language, something that is not really English. The more I don't understand, the more he starts shouting. And that makes me anxious, leading to mistakes I make."

Reyaz shares, "The work is very hard, and I try to work hard so the boss will not abuse me. One time, I fell down while trying to hurry. The boss did not even let me rest properly, and I went on with the work." This notion of "trying to hurry" is voiced throughout the interviews, with participants noting that their work is constituted amid demands of workplace efficiency and productivity. Similarly, articulates *Abdul*, "I am very tired with the work. Push my body really hard and the boss is still not happy.

The boss will yell, and call us lazy. And I work hard so the boss will not call me lazy." Errors then are made while "trying to hurry" in "finishing the job." Worth noting here is the context of middle or lower middle class families in Bangladesh from which the workers often come, placing emphasis on civility of workplace interactions. Moreover, a number of the participants shared that they were educated until college, and were not used to the abusive behaviours of supervisors.

3.7. *Health and uncertainty*

Sharing the uncertainties of their jobs, participants suggest that these uncertainties pose risks at work. Noting that the worry about finances is often distracting while on the job, they articulate the ways in which such distractions can cause workplace injuries. *Kabir* voices the following, "I am worried what will happen. How will I pay back all this money? Even at work, I am thinking about this. Sometimes this will take my mind away from work, and that can lead to an accident." This point is also noted by Suman, who notes that "not knowing that I can keep this job, worrying about my family, worrying about the money in debt, I can't focus on what I am doing. One time, I twisted my hand because I was not holding the wrench in the right way. I was worrying." The anxieties related to income and the debt that most Bangladeshi workers have taken to come to Singapore are reiterated throughout the interviews.

The worries around high debts which are often taken to find the job in Singapore translate into mental pressure experienced by workers, which in turn, is articulated as a catalyst for workplace injuries. This is shared by Bashir, "When I worry, and have this pressure on my head, how can I concentrate on the job?" For *Dilbur*, "I paid the agent fees to get this job in Singapore. How can we afford the agent fees? My family is poor. So my family put on mortgage the only thing we have, the land. Now every month, I send money home. If there is delay in payment, then the interest goes up. So if salary does not arrive on time, I worry a lot." The monthly income earned by construction workers such as *Dilbur* goes toward repaying the debt incurred. Delays in salary therefore result in greater levels of stress experienced by Bangladeshi construction workers in Singapore. This translates into being under constant mental pressure to return the money, articulated by the participants as the uncertainties of everyday life of migrant construction work.

The worries about debt are intertwined with worries about work, constituted around the uncertainty of work. Participants point toward the absence of adequate labor protections which leave a great deal of power in the hands of employers. "I am worried about my job, what is going to happen. Is the boss going to send back home? The boss can decide what to do. So I am worried about the job. I have the debt and can't lose the job." The uncertainties of the job translate into power in the hands of employers, with workers often experiencing this power as a source of everyday worries. For *Jamil*, "The job is not guaranteed. Now for example, a lot of workers are not working because the number of projects are less. So the company is going to cut people. I am thinking about that." The sense of worry that *Jamil* experiences is often voiced by participants, sharing the challenges to health, safety, and wellbeing that are embodied in the uncertainties of work in the construction industries in Singapore.

4. Discussion

The narratives shared by the participants note the structural contexts of migrant construction work, situating the stories of workplace risks of injuries amid the broader ecology of migrant construction work. In response to the framework of workplace safety-based health communication interventions that emphasize individual behavior change [5,6], the narratives shared by the participants point toward the ways in which lived experiences with workplace safety are situated amidst the shifting contexts of work, attending to the overarching sociocultural contexts of workplaces as well as spaces of everyday living. Central to the findings of this study is the theorizing of risks of workplace injuries in the realms of spaces of everyday living, connecting workplace injuries to experiences with food, sleep, access to bathroom facilities, and transportation. In other words, workplace injuries are situated within the overarching structures of migrant construction work, attending to aspects of life beyond the work itself. Work, safety, and risks are tied to a plethora of contextual features of lives of migrant construction workers in Singapore, suggesting the interpenetration of contexts. One of the key theoretical contributions of this article therefore is in locating workplace injury in relationship to features of the broader environment of living experienced by migrant construction workers. These findings suggest that current safety strategies focusing on training (aimed at behavior change) may not be effective as long as workers are facing physical, financial, and emotional insecurity, constituted in the structures of the construction industry. Rather, a focus on behaviors needs to be complimented with policies ensuring access to quality food and shelter, organizational practices emphasizing good communication, and a broader culture of respect for migrant construction workers. The articulations of the workers point toward the necessity of a rights-based approach to workplace safety.

Moreover, the voices of the participants note the interplay between articulations of workplace injuries as embedded in the practices of day-to-day work, and their constructions of not really thinking about the risks of injuries at work. The participants share that because they witness and experience workplace injuries, they think of these injuries as parts of their everyday work. Their lived experiences with risks to health and witnessing these risks to health also shape the ways in which the participants situate the workplace risks to health as being beyond their everyday cognitions. Their vulnerabilities to risks of workplace injuries shape the ways in which the migrant construction workers participating in this project come to make sense of their work; in this context, "not thinking about" the risks at work becomes a way for the participants to continue working amid their everyday vulnerabilities to these risks. Therefore, to avoid thought about workplace injuries is a coping mechanism in response to a sense of extreme vulnerability and everyday susceptibility to workplace injuries. A culturally situated narrative of destiny draws upon the sense of inevitability that is tied to the structures of construction work. The culture-structure-agency framework of the CCA offers a lens for interpreting the ways in which cultural stories about fate emerge in enactments of agency (not thinking about risks) and are shaped by structures (risks in construction work).

Also, the participant narratives attend to the role of power in the realm of workplace injuries and health seeking [4,15,16,28]. For instance, the power of the employer in controlling health care resources shapes the experiences of participants with seeking out healthcare after the injury, access medical leave, and secure compensation. Participant narratives noting that the health care providers for treating the injuries are assigned by the companies point to the ways in which the prescription of the medical certificate is constituted amidst power. In these narratives, the doctor treating the injury is aligned with the interests of the company, depicting the ways in which the power in overarching organizing structures of work is tied to the health seeking options available to migrant construction workers in the backdrop of workplace injury. Note here the overarching role of structures in shaping the access to healthcare after workplace injuries [15,24,25,27]. The worries about being economically viable after an injury depict the vulnerabilities of migrant construction work, and also point to the precarious nature of such forms of work.

In voicing the causes of workplace injuries, the Bangladeshi construction workers participating in this project point to the organizing structures that constitute their everyday lives. The structures extend beyond the spaces of work in the construction industry to spaces of everyday life, depicting the features of structures of living that are closely intertwined. Not having access to healthy, safe, and clean food for instance can result in threats to health of migrant construction workers. Workers share the ways in which not having adequate and proper food results in fatigue, which in turn increases the likelihood of injuries in the workplace. The experience with food insecurity is intertwined with experiences of risks at the workplace. The emergence of food as a key element in the discursive space is tied to the centrality of food in Bangladeshi life. On a similar note, the lack of adequate sleep results in fatigue, which in turn results in risks of workplace injury. The lack of sleep in turn is constituted in relationship to the distance of workplaces from spaces of living, transportation, lack of adequate bathroom facilities, and the shared nature of living spaces where many workers sleep in one room. The articulation of risks of workplace injury within the broader ecology of life of migrant construction workers points toward an integrated framework of workplace injuries in construction work that foregrounds arrangements of living that are accessible to construction workers. Articulations of workplace safety cultures are complemented by structural features of living such as food, shelter, and transportation.

Moreover, the participant narratives point to the ways in which workplace productivity and efficiency targets place workers in the construction industry at risk of injury. Noting that the drive to efficiency translates into being rushed on the job, workers share the challenges they experience when rushed on the job, increasing the likelihood of making errors. The anchoring of construction work in narrow productivity targets increases the risks of injury at work. These culture-centered articulations thus call for shifting the overarching narratives of productivity and efficiency that emerge as monolithic narratives driving the nature of work. In the voices of the participants, the overarching framework of productivity as the driving force for work translates into affective experiences of anxiety, which in turn, result in likelihood of errors.

Finally, the participants narrate the role of communication shaping their experiences of work, the risks they experience at work, and the anxieties that are intertwined with these risks. In the voices of the workers, the threats to dignity reflected in experienced "being shouted at" result in experiences of anxiety, which in turn result in errors and corresponding injuries. For a number of participants, language and communication barriers are key challenges that exacerbate the experiences of incivility. Although a number of participants are conversant in English (with a substantive number having a college education), the different accents and linguistic styles used by the supervisor result in miscommunication and/or lack of understanding. In a wide range of narratives, participants share the ways in which they are "shouted at" for not understanding the instructions given by the supervisor. These experiences suggest the importance of developing adequate communication programs for supervisors in construction sites that address issues of incivility, impolite communication, and mistreatment. Moreover, these experiences suggest development of appropriate organizational policies for building cultures of respect for workers. In addition, appropriate policy solutions are needed that offer exit options to workers, addressing the unequal power relations within which they toil.

Challenging a behaviourally driven framework that is focused on developing effective health/risk messages, the voicing of overarching structures of work and everyday living attends to the context of migrant construction work. Contexts shape the ways in which work is experienced, carried out, and negotiated. Moreover, contexts shape the ways in which workplace errors and injuries are understood and experienced. Structures constitute these contexts, working hand-in-hand with cultural narratives and interpretive frameworks that are anchored in culture [3,5,9,17,19,23,30]. Also worth noting are the linkages between the immediate contexts of workplace risks and the broader contexts of familial debt and economic responsibility to family spatially located in Bangladesh. The participants in our culture-centered project contextualize the vulnerabilities of health that flow from Bangladesh to Singapore, and point to the neoliberal global policies that produce precarious conditions that threaten human health and wellbeing.

Adding to a growing body of literature on immigration and health communication grounded in the tenets of the CCA [15,19,24,27,28], this article highlights the role of work as a defining feature of migrant health amid neoliberal flows of labour. Health is constituted in the vulnerabilities of/at work, connected to features of everyday living. Work and life in this sense are porous, flowing from each other, and interconnected in a broader framework of marginalization amid organizing structures of construction work. The precarious nature of construction work with limited to no security on the job renders workers vulnerable, depicting the ways in which power constrains and enables the nature of work, and the constructions of health at work sites. The uncertainties of work, accompanied by the economic uncertainties experienced by the construction workers renders them vulnerable, producing anxieties, difficulties in concentrating on the job, and risks of workplace injuries. The health of migrant construction workers is threatened by the often unprotected working conditions they experience. Particularly salient in this context is the development and implementation of adequate policy frameworks and comprehensive interventions that offer the needed protections to migrant construction workers. Moreover, when workers have access to spaces where they can represent their voices, they can participate in shaping the living and working conditions of their everyday lives. The urban subaltern in the neoliberal city, voices pathways of representation and recognition by challenging structures that constrain subaltern agency, and by interrogating the overarching organizing logics of structures. Future scholarship on immigrant health ought to examine the challenges of communication work that seeks to interrogate the structures and make entry points for listening to subaltern voices, both in worksites as well as in policy spaces that govern work and life of migrant construction workers. One of the limitations of this study is its focus on a small section of migrant construction workers. The in-depth interviews reported for this paper specifically draw from the experiences of Bangladeshi construction workers in Singapore. Future scholarship ought to examine the experiences with construction work among other communities of workers, specifically exploring the similarities and differences in patterns of experiences.

5. Conclusions

The CCA co-creates entry points for inverting the marginalization experienced by contractual migrant workers in the construction industry, and it does so by disrupting the dominant discourses of migrant construction work. For instance, dominant articulations of migrant labour to be strategically managed through efficiency, awareness, and effective management of workplaces [25–28] is shifted into the hands of migrant workers, who point toward the necessity for creating opportunities of articulation that offer contractual migrant workers modes of access to addressing the health threats they experience, and opportunities for meaningfully participating in platforms that enable their articulations to be heard in ways that matter [28–30]. The interplays of culture, structure, and agency depict the ways in which workers enact their agency by drawing on cultural stories, situated amid the structures of construction work. The narratives sharing the role of health service providers who work in collusion with employers to deny medical leave or treatment to workers points toward the need for the development of intervention measures that hold health service providers and employers accountable in addressing the health needs of construction workers. Similarly, the experiences of being mistreated by employers and the effects of such mistreatment on workplace health risks point toward the importance of addressing the stigmatization of work and the cultural codes of inequality that are built into workplace management practices. The articulations of health as dignity point toward the need for developing health communication that is directed at addressing the overarching inequalities in the distribution of power in construction industries in the global North that employ migrant workers, and the ways in which these inequalities play out in relationships between workers and supervisors in construction sites.

Acknowledgments

This project was funded by the Provost's grant to the Center for Culture-Centered Approach to Research and Evaluation (CARE), NUS.

Conflicts of Interest

The author declares no conflict of interest.

References

1. Ringen, K.; Seegal, J.; England, A. Safety and health in the construction industry. *Annu. Rev. Public Health* **1995**, *16*, 165–188. [CrossRef] [PubMed]
2. Yi, W.; Chan, A.P.C. Optimizing work-rest schedule for construction rebar workers in hot and humid environment. *Build. Environ.* **2013**, *61*, 104–113. [CrossRef]
3. Chan, A.P.; Yam, M.C.; Chung, J.W.; Yi, W. Developing a heat stress model for construction workers. *J. Facil. Manag.* **2012**, *10*, 59–74. [CrossRef]
4. Strauss, K.; McGrath, S. Temporary migration, precarious employment and unfree labour relations: Exploring the 'continuum of exploitation' in Canada's Temporary Foreign Worker Program. *Geoforum* **2017**, *78*, 199–208. [CrossRef]
5. Yea, S. The art of not being caught: Temporal strategies for disciplining unfree labour in Singapore's contract migration. *Geoforum* **2017**, *78*, 179–188. [CrossRef]
6. Ahonen, E.Q.; Benavides, F.G.; Benach, J. Immigrant populations, work and health — A systematic literature review. *Scand. J. Work Environ. Health* **2007**, *33*, 96–104. [CrossRef] [PubMed]
7. O'Connor, T.; Loomis, D.; Runyan, C.; dal Santo, J.A.; Schulman, M. Adequacy of health and safety training among young Latino construction workers. *J. Occup. Environ. Med.* **2005**, *47*, 272–277. [CrossRef] [PubMed]

8. Arcury, T.A.; Mills, T.; Marín, A.J.; Summers, P.; Quandt, S.A.; Rushing, J.; Lang, W.; Grzywacz, J.G. Work safety climate and safety practices among immigrant Latino residential construction workers. *Am. J. Ind. Med.* **2012**, *55*, 736–745. [CrossRef] [PubMed]
9. Jasani, P.K.; Joshi, J.B.; Kartha, G.P.; Mehta, H.; Shah, I. A study of knowledge and utilization of safety measures against occupational hazards among constructional workers in Surendranagar city, Gujarat, India. *Int. J. Commun. Med. Public Health* **2016**, *3*, 3055–3058. [CrossRef]
10. Shrestha, P.P.; Menzel, N.N. Hispanic construction workers and assertiveness training. *Work* **2014**, *49*, 517–522. [PubMed]
11. Ricketts, M. Using stories to teach safety: Practical, research-based tips. *Prof. Saf.* **2015**, *60*, 51–57.
12. Shamsi, M.; Pariani, A.; Shams, M.; Soleymani-Nejad, M. Persuasion to use personal protective equipment in constructing subway stations: Application of social marketing. *Inj. Prev.* **2015**. [CrossRef] [PubMed]
13. Dutta, M.J. Decolonizing communication for social change: A Culture-Centered approach. *Commun. Theory* **2015**, *25*, 123–143. [CrossRef]
14. Dutta, M.J. *Neoliberal Health Organizing: Communication, Meaning, Politics*; Routledge: New York, NY, USA, 2015.
15. Dutta, M.J. *Communicating Health: A Culture-Centered Approach*; Polity Press: London, UK, 2008.
16. Dutta, M.J. Poverty, structural barriers and health: A Santali narrative of health communication. *Qual. Health Res.* **2004**, *14*, 1–16.
17. Dutta, M. The unheard voices of Santalis: Communicating about health from the margins of India. *Commun. Theory* **2004**, *14*, 237–263. [CrossRef]
18. Kaur, S.; Tan, N.; Dutta, M.J. Media, migration and politics: The coverage of the Little India Riot in The Straits Times in Singapore. *J. Creat. Commun.* **2016**, *11*, 27–43. [CrossRef]
19. Cohen, D.A.; Scribner, R.A.; Farley, T.A. A structural model of health behavior: A pragmatic approach to explain and influence health behaviors at the population level. *Prev. Med.* **2000**, *30*, 146–154. [CrossRef] [PubMed]
20. Dutta, M.J.; Jamil, R. Health at the margins of migration: Culture-centered co-constructions among Bangladeshi immigrants. *Health Commun.* **2013**, *28*, 170–182. [CrossRef] [PubMed]
21. Dutta, M.J. Cultural context, structural determinants, and global health inequities: The role of communication. *Front. Commun.* **2016**, *1*, 5. [CrossRef]
22. Dutta, M.J. Violence in Gaza: An academic-activist agenda for health communication. *Health Commun.* **2016**, *31*, 1579–1581. [CrossRef] [PubMed]

23. Dutta, M.J.; Basu, A. Health among men in rural Bengal: Exploring meanings through a culture-centered approach. *Qual. Health Res.* **2007**, *17*, 38–48. [CrossRef] [PubMed]
24. Blankenship, K.M.; Friedman, S.R.; Dworkin, S.; Mantell, J.E. Structural interventions: Concepts, challenges and opportunities for research. *J. Urban Health* **2006**, *83*, 59–72. [CrossRef] [PubMed]
25. Holmes, J.; Stubbe, M. *Power and Politeness in the Workplace: A Sociolinguistic Analysis of Talk at Work*; Routledge: Abingdon, UK, 2015.
26. Charmaz, K. Grounded Theory: Objectivist and Constructivist Methods. In *Handbook of Qualitative Research*, 2nd ed.; Denzin, N.K., Lincoln, Y.S., Eds.; Sage Publications: Thousand Oaks, CA, USA, 2000; pp. 509–535.
27. Dutta, M.; Jones, C.; Borron, A.; Anaele, A.; Gao, H.; Kandukuri, S. Voices of Hunger: A culture-centered approach to addressing food insecurity. In *Reducing Health Disparities: Communication Interventions*; Dutta, M., Kreps, G., Eds.; Peter Lang: New York, NY, USA, 2013.
28. Gao, H.; Dutta, M.; Okoror, T. Listening to Chinese immigrant restaurant workers in the Midwest: Application of the culture-centered approach (CCA) to explore perceptions of health and health care. *Health Commun.* **2016**, *31*, 727–737. [CrossRef] [PubMed]
29. Airhihenbuwa, C. *Health and Culture: Beyond the Western Paradigm*; Sage: Thousand Oaks, CA, USA, 1995.
30. Mokros, H.B.; Deetz, S. What counts as real? A constitutive view of communication and the disenfranchised in the context of health. In *Communication and Disenfranchisement: Social Issues and Implications*; Ray, E.B., Ed.; Lawrence Erlbaum: Mahwah, NJ, USA, 1996; pp. 29–44.
31. Key population indicators. In *Census of Population 2010: Advanced Census Release*; Singapore Department of Statistics: Singapore, 2010.
32. Construction and real estate. In *Yearbook of Statistics 2012*; Singapore Department of Statistics: Singapore, 2012.
33. Foreign Workforce Numbers 2014. Available online: http://www.mom.gov.sg/statistics-publications/others/statistics/Pages/ForeignWorkforceNumbers.aspx. (accessed on 1 November 2016).

Chapter 6a

Compounding Precarity in Migrant Worker Trajectories*

Grace Baey

Independent scholar

Brenda S. A. Yeoh

Asia Research Institute
National University of Singapore

In Singapore, the temporary labour migration regime admits foreign workers according to a hierarchy of skills and salaries with corresponding policies that govern their living and working conditions. Low-waged migrant workers admitted on short-term contracts are subjected to regulations that ensure their temporary socio-legal status in the city-state, keeping them disposable and deportable. Precarity is institutionalised in this regime, where migrant workers remain transient and excluded, and where they have to contend with the burden of debts to finance migration, limited options for job mobility, and constrained bargaining power in relation to workplace safety and risks, among others. These processes, occurring at

---

*Reflections on Baey, G. and Yeoh, B. S. A. (2018). 'The lottery of my life': Migration trajectories and the production of precarity among Bangladeshi migrant workers in Singapore's construction industry, *Asian Pac. Migr. J.*, Vol. 27, No. 3, pp. 249–722. DOI: 10.1177/0117196818780087. © 2018 Scalabrini Migration Center.

different points in the migration trajectory, are mediated by state agencies, the migration industry, and labour markets.

In this context, we argued in this article written in 2018 that precarity is cumulative and compounded throughout migrant worker trajectories. In other words, the precarious condition of low-waged migrant workers is produced across a continuum, from their accumulation of debt before migration, to the risks they face as they undergo recruitment and training, and to their compliance under difficult workplace conditions in the destination country.

The spread of COVID-19 has exacerbated the already precarious condition of low-waged migrant workers in Singapore. First, migrant workers are entrenched in a cycle of indebtedness [Platt et al., 2017], which begins with the accumulation of debt in order to pay exorbitant recruitment fees to secure employment in the destination country, and continues as they undergo a series of debt-financed temporary job contracts abroad. In the case of construction workers in Singapore, companies and sub-contractors keep migrant workers on a treadmill of short-term jobs in which they constantly face risk and uncertainty [Platt et al., 2017]. As Singapore responded to the threat of COVID-19 with circuit breakers and social distancing measures, construction companies had to put projects on hold. As a result, thousands of migrant workers in the sector could not work and only received base salary payments, while others were underpaid, or did not receive wages [Kathiravelu, 2020]. The outbreak had also immobilised these workers in their dormitories, preventing them from venturing to weekend migrant enclaves to send remittances. The pandemic interrupted not only the jobs of migrant workers, but also their debt repayment plans and sending financial support to their families back home.

Second, the compounded precarity of migrant workers is also symptomatic of a pandemic-hit migration industry. COVID-19 has disrupted businesses and industries in Singapore, including large-scale projects in the construction sector, which employs thousands of migrant workers, mostly from South Asia. Border closures and international travel restrictions have ruptured the flow of labour at all skill levels in the region [Lin and Yeoh, 2021], causing blockage in recruitment, training, and employment processes underpinning the deployment of migrant labour. Labour shortages in various sectors including construction were keenly felt, as seen by appeals among companies, industry groups, and employers to ease travel restrictions in order to fill jobs and replace workers who have already returned to their home countries. As the migration industry grappled with the impact of COVID-19, migrant workers also faced abrupt changes, loss of livelihood, and further risk and uncertainty.

Third, the impact of COVID-19 on industries in Singapore has also raised concerns of occupational safety and health, as reported incidents such as workplace fatalities, accidents, and injuries have risen. As contractors and sub-contractors face mounting pressure to complete projects with reduced labour supply, workers are at risk of accidents and injuries at worksites, especially if they are made to speed up their work or work longer hours [Yuen and Ng, 2021]. As workers often undertake hefty loans to finance their job placement in Singapore, coupled with the fact that their work permits are tied to a single employer, this imbalance of power may exacerbate safety lapses as workers may not have the bargaining right to voice complaints, for fear of losing their jobs.

The impact of COVID-19 on migrant workers in Singapore adds to the argument we have made in this article about multiple compounding precarity. The pandemic accentuates how precarity continuously pervades migrant worker trajectories. Cycles of indebtedness and the enforced temporariness of contract labour become increasingly detrimental to life and livelihoods particularly under disruptive conditions such as financial crises and global pandemics. This calls for concerted efforts towards better migration policies, in ways that consider the role of sending and receiving states, migration brokers, and employers in the production of migrant precarity, and the changes needed for a more sustainable and ethical approach to migrant labour.

References

Kathiravelu, L. (2020, 11 November). COVID-19 exposes the Singapore migrant worker experience, East Asia Forum. *East Asia Forum.* Retrieved from https://www.eastasiaforum.org/2020/11/11/covid-19-exposes-the-singapore-migrant-worker-experience/

Lin, W. and Yeoh, B. S. A. (2021). Pathological (im)mobilities: Managing risk in a time of pandemics, *Mobilities*, Vol. 16, No. 1, pp. 96–112. DOI: 10.1080/17450101.2020.1862454

Platt, M., Baey, G., Yeoh, B. S. A., Khoo, C. Y. and Lam, T. (2017) Debt, precarity and gender: Male and female temporary labour migrants in Singapore, *Journal of Ethic and. Migration Studies*, Vol. 43, No. 1, pp. 119–136. DOI: 10.1080/1369183X.2016.1218756

Yuen, S. and Ng, K. G. (2021, 17 May). Concern over workplace safety mounts as S'pore firms grapple with COVID-19 pressures. *The Straits Times*. Retrieved from https://www.straitstimes.com/singapore/concern-over-workplace-safety-mounts-as-firms-grapple-with-covid-19-pressures

Chapter 6b

"The Lottery of My Life": Migration Trajectories and the Production of Precarity Among Bangladeshi Migrant Workers in Singapore's Construction Industry*

Grace Baey

Independent Scholar

Brenda S. A. Yeoh

National University of Singapore

Within the scholarship on precarity, low-waged contract-based migrants are recognized as centrally implicated in precarious employment conditions at the bottom of neoliberal capitalist labor markets. Precarity as a socially corrosive condition stems from both the multiple insecurities of the workplace as disposable labor, and a sense of deportability as

*This article was originally published in *Asian Pac. Migr. J.*, Vol. 27, No. 3, pp. 249–722. DOI: 10.1177/0117196818780087.

Corresponding author: Brenda S. A. Yeoh, National University of Singapore, Department of Geography and Asia Research Institute, AS8 #07-01, 10 Kent Ridge Crescent, Singapore 119260, Singapore. Email: geoysa@nus.edu.sg

migrant subjects with marginal socio-legal status in the host society. Our study of Bangladeshi construction workers in Singapore contributes to refining understandings of precarity by approaching labor migration as a cumulative, intensively mediated process, whereby risks and vulnerabilities are compounded across different sites in migrants' trajectories, even as they enact themselves as mobile, aspiring subjects. As a condition-in-the-making, precarity is experienced and compounded, through a continuum beginning in pre-migration indebtedness, multiplying through entanglements with the migration industry, and manifesting in workplace vulnerabilities at destination. It is most finely balanced when predictability and planning yield to arbitrary hope.

Keywords: temporary migration regimes, construction workers, precarity, aspiration, Asia

Introduction

Within the burgeoning literature on precarious employment in the context of neoliberal capitalism, there is growing evidence that low-waged migrants concentrated in sectors such as construction, hospitality and care work — in both developed and developing economies — are particularly vulnerable to exploitation (McDowell et al., 2009; Wills et al., 2009; Anderson, 2010; Banki, 2013; Lewis et al., 2015; Swider, 2015; Khurana, 2017). As "a political-economic regime that has at its center the suppression of labor costs and labor's power," neoliberalism not only accords weak worker protections, but in the case of migrants, also limits access to social citizenship rights (Torres et al., 2013: 145). Conceptual terms like "hyper-precarity" (Lewis et al., 2015) have been coined to highlight the multiple layering of insecurities that migrants face as a result of their marginal socio-legal status and labor market position, while undertaking jobs that are typically low paid, insecure and irregular. Increasingly, scholars have argued for adopting an expansive approach in our understanding of experiences of precarity, looking not just at employment relations and conditions but "their transnational social status, migration strategies, alongside subsequent constraints on citizenship imposed through immigration regimes" (Lewis et al., 2015: 582). Particularly when migrants' rights to residence are tied to their jobs, employment precarity meshes with immigration precarity, rendering migrants vulnerable to unexpected repatriation, should they unwittingly fall out of employment (Banki, 2013). By casting an inexorable shadow of "deportability" onto migrants' sense of self, migrant precarity is continually produced as a state of the mind as migrants attempt to navigate the narrowing spaces hemmed in by the "intractable antagonism between market demands for migrant labor and citizen demands for closure" (Garcés-Mascareñas, 2010: 87). Under these pervasive circumstances of life and labor, migrants themselves become active agents in the construction of precarious subjects, typically undertaking a substantial degree of risk and investment (often through debt and collateral loans) to gain entry into overseas job markets. Precisely because migrant aspirations and livelihoods are folded into these migrant trajectories, the consequences of these compounding precarities are far-reaching in shaping lived experiences and migrant subjectivities (Attanapola, 2013).

In this paper, we draw on a case study of Bangladeshi low-skilled migrant workers in Singapore's construction industry to understand the way precarity is produced in the everyday realities of migrant lives. In December 2017, approximately 70 percent of Singapore's 1.37 million-strong foreign workforce was composed of migrant contract workers on temporary work permits employed in labor intensive sectors such as construction, shipyard, conservancy and landscaping. Of the 965,200 work permit holders, 284,900 (nearly 30 percent) were construction workers.[1] Although a nationality breakdown of migrant construction workers in Singapore is not available, Singapore is ranked third (after Oman and Qatar) in the list of top 10 countries receiving Bangladeshi workers (54,750 deployed in 2014).[2] The number of Bangladeshi workers in Singapore has risen steadily over the last three decades, often in tandem with periods of construction boom (see Baey and Yeoh, 2015 for compiled figures). Bangladeshi migrant workers are usually recruited as basic-skilled workers and tend to occupy the lowest rungs of the wage ladder in the construction industry (Baey and Yeoh, 2015).

[1] http://www.mom.gov.sg/documents-and-publications/foreign-workforce-numbers

[2] http://www.bpb.de/gesellschaft/migration/laenderprofile/216104/international-migration-from-bangladesh

In this study, we examine the different conditions of precarity that underpin men's migration for work in the construction sector by scrutinizing significant junctures in the migration trajectory. Understanding migration as a process intensively mediated by both state institutions and industry (Xiang and Lindquist, 2014) prompts us to give attention not just to one specific site within the trajectory, but to consider conditions of pre-departure training and recruitment at source, as well as workers' employment experiences at destination in understanding migrant precarity. In other words, we seek to uncover the place-based nature of migrant-specific vulnerabilities and how these vulnerabilities accumulate, intersect and converge along migrant trajectories in producing precarious migrant subjects. While much of the literature on precarious work has focused on labor market studies and neoliberal immigration regimes in post-industrialist societies (Sassen, 2001; McDowell et al., 2009; Anderson, 2010), we extend the field of analysis to incorporate the migration industry — comprising transnational networks of training centers and brokers that straddle the "middle space" of migration — as a key site where precariousness is reproduced and enacted. Whereas the concept of brokerage can include an "ensemble of entrepreneurs, firms and services which, chiefly motivated by financial gain, facilitate international mobility, settlement and adaptation, and communication and resource transfers across borders" (Hernandez-Leon, 2013: 1), we focus specifically on the role of recruitment brokers (primarily at source) in facilitating access to construction work in Singapore. Through an analysis of the processes of recruitment, training and entry as mediated by these brokers, we show how migration brokerage becomes complicit in compounding experiences of precarity, particularly for migrants who are compelled to undertake substantial debt to access overseas job opportunities. We add to this body of work on the production of precarity in mediated, low-waged, migrant-dominated employment by demonstrating how modes of governance and the materialities of place across migrant trajectories coalesce to produce precarious subjects. Such an approach to place gives serious attention to the materialities through which precarity is mediated, experienced and folded into everyday lives and senses of self.

Migrant Contract Labor and Compounding Precarity

Although understandings of "precarity" tend to vary (Arnold and Bongiovi, 2013), there is general acknowledgment that precarious work refers to "the *uncertainty, instability*, and *insecurity* of *work* in which *employees bear the risks* of work (as opposed to businesses or the government) and *receive limited social benefits and statutory entitlements*" (Kalleberg and Hewison, 2013: 271, emphasis in the original, quoting Vosko, 2010). In other words, precarious employment is "uncertain, unpredictable and risky from the point of view of the worker" (Branch and Hanley, 2011: 569). Scholars agree that precarity is symptomatic of the socially "corrosive" effects of neo-liberal capitalism (Sennett, 1998), as witnessed in the growing casualization of labor and the weakening of social safety nets, even as global competition and technological development intensify. Specific drivers of the growth of precarious work include: the increasing prevalence of subcontracting and temporary staffing, labor market deregulation, global competition resulting in wage squeezes, the lack of a collective voice in the labor market and declining public sector budgets (Bauder, 2006; Standing, 2011; Coe, 2012). In the context of Asia, Wise (2013) points to the down-sourcing of risk in subcontracting arrangements "whereby firms and governments distance themselves from [negative] consequences" to be borne by flexibilized labor. Elcioglu's (2010: 121) research on temporary staffing agencies (TSAs) in the US interrogates how labor brokers work to exploit and capitalize on existing structural vulnerabilities already produced by the labor market to perpetuate conditions of precariousness for workers. Specifically, TSAs reproduce precariousness through efforts to constrain wellperforming temporary workers from obtaining permanent positions with client firms as a way of extending profit margins. Notwithstanding the essential training and job-matching services they provide workers with, TSAs should not be seen as neutral arbiters in the labor market; rather, they often actively exploit and reproduce contingency for profit through various "market-*making* practices" (Peck and Theodore, 2002 as cited in Elcioglu, 2010: 119).

Precarity also encompasses more than the sphere of work. Rendering the laboring migrant body "flexible" as a normalized state not only redistributes risks in the direction of the worker, but also reproduces notions of flexibility in the workforce as an ideal cultural imaginary emblematic of contemporary life. As Neilson and Rossiter (2006: 10) note,

> [P]recarity leads to an interminable lack of certainty, the condition of being unable to predict one's fate or having some degree of stability on which to construct a life [that] extends beyond the world of work to encompass other aspects of intersubjective life, including housing, debt and the ability to build affective social relations.

In short, the "precariousness of life" reveals itself when people are prevented from anticipating the future to build a social life (Anderson, 2010: 304).

In the context of transnational labor migration, material and symbolic conditions of precarity may lie across borders. Migration undertaken as a household livelihood strategy for income diversification or socio-economic mobility may quickly metamorphosize into a journey of perilous gamble (Deshingkar and Start, 2003). For example, studies of transnational labor in global cities show that migrant workers tend to dominate "bottom-end" positions of the labor market, reflecting the entrenchment of a "new migrant division of labour," particularly in the construction, hospitality, care and cleaning sectors (Sassen, 2001; May et al., 2007; Wills et al., 2009). Apart from their tolerance for low-paid, "3D" (dirty, dangerous and difficult) jobs given perceived wage differentials between host and home countries, it is argued that migrants' lack of access to collective organization, social protection and citizenship entitlements are seen as desirable qualities that make them particularly susceptible to insecure and potentially exploitative employment conditions (Berntsen, 2016). For these reasons, migrant workers represent "the perfect workforce in this evolving global capital-labor and class relations: commodified and exploitable; flexible and expendable" (Walia, 2007 as cited in Kalleberg and Hewison, 2013: 281).

Migrant precarity is also produced by the "political and institutional context" of migration (Waite, 2009: 421). Anderson's (2010) work on immigration policies in the UK reveals how conditions of precariousness are exacerbated for low-waged migrants through the creation of categories of entrant, the molding of employment relations, and the institutionalization of uncertainty. In a similar vein, Garcés-Mascareñas (2010: 87) explains how a sense of insecurity is created among migrants through what she calls the "confine of legality," which ensures that legal migrants are "immobilised in the job market, made dependent on their employers, and defined as purely and exclusively temporary labor." Particularly when workers' rights to residency are tied to their employment contracts, "precarious legal status [may] channel them into precarious employment relations," and vice versa (Strauss and McGrath, 2017: 203; Banki, 2013). In Yea and Chok's (2018: 12) words, when "curtailments on the freedom to exit employment relations and enter new ones is institutionalized ... there are, in fact, causal relations between these different forms of unfreedom."

As thus far discussed, scholars deploying precarity as a conceptual lens have mainly focused on the interacting roles of the state and the market in producing precarious conditions (Siegmann and Schiphorst, 2016: 116). In this vein, migration researchers have argued that increasingly restrictive immigration governance is complicit in "laying a legal foundation for [precarious] employment relations" (Siegmann and Schiphorst, 2016: 118). Beyond the state and the market, there has been less attention on the role of migration brokers and labor market intermediaries in producing conditions of precarity, despite Enright's (2013: 296) observation that formal and informal labor market intermediaries play an active role in facilitating migration, molding employment relations and "reshaping the spatialities of workers' mobility, thus having a dramatic effect both in constraining and enhancing worker agency." Particularly in industries such as construction where the use of brokers for recruitment and subcontracting remains prevalent, it is important to analyze the role of intermediaries in simultaneously facilitating labor market flexibility by down-sourcing risk to migrants, and exploiting these vulnerabilities for profit (Debrah and Ofori, 1997; Enright, 2013). As Reza (2016: 45) explains, mediated or indirect recruitment "through layers of individual recruiters blurs their responsibility toward workers and such employment practices increase the intensity of precariousness by favoring capital against labor." Given the inherent volatility associated with economic ups and downs in the construction sector, businesses cope with the risks of the "boom-bust character" of the industry by using labor supply intermediaries where the risks can be downloaded through the recruitment process onto the workers, thus intensifying precarity (Reid-Musson et al., 2015: 11).

In order to consider the way the state, the market and the migration industry cohere in shaping the conditions of migrant precarity, we follow Lewis et al. (2015: 587, original emphasis) in emphasizing "the importance of complexities, variations, processes, relations, contexts and, above all, *continuums*, in understanding labor experiences." Specifically, a "continuum approach" helps illustrate "how migration trajectories, constrained rights and entitlements, and precarious labour collide to close down alternatives to entering or continuing in often severely exploitative unfree labour" (Lewis et al., 2015: 594). Rather than enumerate multiple forms of migrant precarity, we take into account the operations of state, market and labor market intermediaries in following the migrant across space and time in order to understand the cumulative, compounding, but contingent effects of precarious conditions as they impinge on the migrant's capacity for agency. This perspective is useful in teasing out how different forms of risk and vulnerability assemble at particular sites and junctures of the migration process to compound the 'hyper-precarious' lives of low-waged migrants while not obliterating the migrants' situated agency.

Research Methods

This paper focuses on Bangladeshi male migrant workers recruited under a temporary contract labor migration regime for Singapore's construction industry. Occupying the lowest rungs of the wage spectrum, these workers are required to leave their families behind and enter the country as individual workers with little or no opportunity for long-term residency and formal citizenship. Based on quantitative and qualitative data gathered from questionnaires (n = 205) and life story interviews (n = 33) in 2014, the research examines conditions of pre-departure training and recruitment in Bangladesh, as well as workers' employment experiences in Singapore to analyze different areas of risk and vulnerability that workers face over the course of their migration journeys.

While the lack of statistical data on Bangladeshi construction workers in Singapore obviated the possibility of obtaining a randomized sample, we tried to ensure that the data collected provided a fair representation of the overall population. Fieldwork was thus conducted at 11 sites (including weekend gathering grounds, migrant worker dormitories and in the vicinity of construction sites) across the island to avoid excessive clustering. Stratified snowball sampling methods were also applied to ensure a good mix across variables such as type of visa (Work Permit or Special Pass Holder[3]), type of employer (i.e., whether the company is a main contractor, subcontracting firm, or labor supply company), and marital status, in addition to geographic location. Given space constraints, we refer the reader to our working paper (Baey and Yeoh, 2015) for a detailed overview of the 205 survey respondents. Here, as a background sketch to contextualize subsequent discussion, we provide a profile of respondents who participated in the life story interviews (Table 1).

While the survey provided basic information on the issues the respondents confronted in seeking to migrate and secure employment in Singapore, the interviews (lasting 1–2 hours and conducted at a venue of the respondents' choice) provided deeper insights into the motivations for migration and the migration experience itself, as well as work experiences and encounters in the host society. Interviewees were recruited from survey respondents who expressed willingness to share their life story narratives. Understanding how the migrants experienced and reacted to precarious conditions across the migration journey from their own perspectives is central to this analysis. The interview accounts[4] allow us not only to trace the circumstances under which low-waged labor migration occurs, but also to better understand how the agentic behavior of the migrants interacts with structural conditions in producing different degrees of precarity.

---

[3]Work Permit holders are typically basic-/semi-skilled workers (with no minimum wage) employed in the construction, manufacturing, marine, process or service sector. Special Passes are issued to workers who have employment and/or work injury claims filed with the Ministry of Manpower. The visa legalizes their stay in Singapore while their cases are being processed and investigated.

[4]Interview quotes from respondents have not been edited for language.

Table 1. Profile of interviewees.

Pseudonym	Visa	Age	Marital status and Number of children	Year of first arrival	Number of employers	Type of employer
Rasel	Work Permit	29	Single	2009	3	Subcontractor
Anwar	Special Pass	39	Married, 2 children	2007	4	Main contractor
Kalam	Special Pass	43	Married, 2 children	2012	1	Main contractor
Moinol	Work Permit	34	Married, 1 child	2008	1	Subcontracting
Sajib	Work Permit	27	Married, 1 child	2010	2	Main contractor
Ripon	Special Pass	32	Married, 1 child	2007	2	Labor supply
Omar	Work Permit	32	Married, no children	2011	2	Subcontractor
Mehedi	Work Permit	18	Single	2013	1	Labor supply
Sumon	Work Permit	38	Married, 2 children	2009	2	Subcontractor
Zabed	Special Pass	28	Single	2008	2	Subcontractor
Mostafa	Special Pass	31	Single	2010	1	Main contractor
Saiful	Special Pass	24	Single	2012	1	Labor supply
Javed	Work Permit	34	Single	2000	3	Labor supply
Mamun	Work Permit	23	Single	2013	1	Subcontractor
Mizan	Special Pass	23	Single	2011	1	Subcontractor
Shohel	Special Pass	26	Single	2011	1	Labor supply
Salim	Special Pass	32	Married, no children	2007	4	Subcontractor
Hasan	Special Pass	34	Married, 1 child	2008	2	Subcontractor
Saju	Work Permit	22	Single	2010	1	Subcontractor
Kabir	Work Permit	37	Married, 2 children	2001	4	Subcontractor
Uzzal	Work Permit	46	Married, 2 children	2004	5	Subcontractor
Habib	Work Permit	35	Married, 2 children	1997	4	Subcontractor
Mokter	Work Permit	27	Married, 1 child	2013	1	Main contractor
Rubel	Work Permit	28	Single	2007	1	Subcontractor
Alam	Work Permit	39	Married, 2 children	2007	3	Subcontractor
Arif	Work Permit	38	Married, 1 child	1998	4	Main contractor
Mishkat	Work Permit	30	Married, 1 child	2000	3	Main contractor
Rohan	Work Permit	26	Single	2011	2	Main contractor
Rifat	Work Permit	45	Married, 1 child	1997	1	Subcontractor
Syed	Work Permit	24	Single	2013	1	Subcontractor
Kamal	Work Permit	26	Single	2008	3	Labor supply
Golam	Work Permit	45	Married, 2 children	1998	5	Main contractor
Hussein	Work Permit	23	Single	2013	1	Main contractor

Institutionalizing Precarity: Singapore's Labor Migration Regime

Stratified rights and enforced temporariness

Singapore's managerial migration regime consists of a complex and stratified system of eligibility and benefits that differentiates between highly skilled professionals (under the "Employment Pass" category), mid-skilled workers (under "S Pass") and low-waged contract workers ("Work Permit" holders). Although workers under the Employment and S Pass categories (above particular salary thresholds) are able to bring along their spouses and children, Work Permit holders can only enter the country as individual workers with little or no claims on residency rights or pathways to formal citizenship. Instead, their right to stay is contingent upon one- or two-year contracts that are tied to a specific employer and occupational sector, and these have to be renewed on a regular basis. As low-waged, low-skilled migrants, Bangladeshi construction workers are thus treated as a transient and disposable workforce through a 'use-and-discard' approach, designed to cushion the economy during periods of downturn while allowing businesses the flexibility to respond to fluctuations in demand. Like the internal migrants contracted under mediated employment configurations in China's construction industry discussed by Swider (2015: 49), they are best characterized as "permanently temporary" migrants.

The Ministry of Manpower (MOM) currently imposes maximum periods of employment of 10 and 22 years, respectively, for basic-skilled (R2) and higher-skilled (R1) work permit holders from 'Non-Traditional Source' countries — namely, India, Bangladesh, the Philippines, Thailand and Sri Lanka — and China. According to MOM (2012), this policy is "designed as an administrative control to ensure that [work permit holders] remain transient and do not sink roots in Singapore." Workers employed under the R2 category must possess either a Skills Evaluation Certificate (SEC) or SEC (Knowledge) (SEC(K)) issued by Singapore's Building and Construction Authority (BCA), typically at a designated testing center located in a source country. To be qualified under the R1 category, workers must be registered with the Construction Registration of

Tradesmen (CoreTrade) or Multi-Skilling scheme, and issued with BCA-recognized trade certifications in addition to having four years of construction experience in Singapore. At the same time, the state regulates the inflow of foreign labor by allocating specific "Man-Year Entitlements (MYEs)" — calculated based on the value of a particular contract awarded — for the number of workers companies are eligible to hire on a project-by-project basis. When companies exceed this quota, they have to pay an extra SGD 400 (USD 312) over and above the standard monthly levy rate of SGD 550 (USD 429) for each R2 worker, and SGD 300 (USD 234) for each R1 worker.

At the same time, job mobility is largely restricted for Work Permit Holders as they are not permitted to seek a change of employer apart from those in the construction sector, where written consent from one's current employer is required. Since workers' visas are tied to their employment contracts, they have to be repatriated if their employer chooses to cancel or fails to renew their work permit. In this regard, precarity becomes institutionalized by virtue of state migration policies that enforce the transient status of low-waged migrant workers in Singapore. These policies that enforce transience and disposability are part of what McCormack and Salmenniemi (2016) call a "biopolitics of precarity and the self," where culturally embedding understandings of the low-waged migrant worker as a transgressive figure that unsettles the nation-state are normalized through the regulation and management of labor.

Outsourcing risk in the construction industry

The construction industry in Singapore has traditionally been reliant on subcontractors that provide labor and/or specialized services such as scaffolding, electrical wiring installation and metal casting. It has been argued that construction companies utilize labor subcontracting as a "labor market strategy" to maintain flexibility and cope with uncertainties in demand (Debrah and Ofori, 1997). In particular, its strategic importance

> [lies in the availability of] a 'floating' pool of skilled and unskilled site labor from which required numbers of tradespersons and laborers are engaged from project to project ... sometimes from week to week [...

> while relieving] the main contractor of contractual obligations to the workforce (Debrah and Ofori, 1997: 697).

As a result, risks and uncertainty in the labor market are systematically passed down to workers who are made to be reliant upon a continuous flow of short-term work to ensure income stability.

Since 2005, the state has made it mandatory for foreign construction workers to be trained and tested at source before being eligible for a work permit in Singapore. Through the SEC (K) scheme, prospective migrants must now undertake training in a specialized trade skill, such as metal casting, waterproofing or electrical wiring installation, and pass a standardized skills test administered by the BCA through designated overseas testing centers in order to be formally certified. These policy changes signal a deliberate shift toward hiring skilled laborers in the construction workforce in a concerted effort to increase productivity in the sector. The entrant category of "unskilled" workers was phased out after July 2011, and replaced with tiered categories of "basic skilled" (R2) and "higher skilled" (R1) workers. Stemming from this, employers are incentivized to hire skilled workers through differential levy rates tagged to R1 and R2 categories, where concessions are provided for the former.

Although the move to implement mandatory skills testing at source was intended to ensure the quality of migrants brought in to work in the construction sector, the policy has also had the effect of outsourcing the costs of training beyond Singapore's borders. As a consequence, workers tend to bear the brunt of these extra costs, where it is typical for migrants to have to pay for their own training, job placement fees and travel costs. In the survey, 97.1 percent of respondents ($n = 205$) paid money to an agent or training center in Bangladesh before they left for work in Singapore, where the average total amount paid was BDT 393,275 (USD 4,987). This figure typically includes training and accommodation costs, as well as intermediary fees for job placement services. When we segregated the amount by year of arrival, we found that workers arriving after 2011 paid on average 39 percent more than those who arrived before 2000. To finance these fees, the majority (80.5 percent) had to borrow money from a variety of sources including relatives, household members and the bank. Even among those who did not have to borrow, many migrants either sold material assets, such as land or gold, to obtain the necessary capital.[5] By normalizing short-term, contractual work and making workers bear the brunt of their migration costs, the industry effectively outsources risk to individual migrants, where precarity is embedded and reproduced in current recruitment and employment practices. Migrant subjects are, in this sense, made to embody precarity as subjects upon which precarity is overlaid in multiple forms, ranging from the burden of financial risks to the potential threat of repatriation and uncertainties of familial connections.

Compounding Precarities: Indebtedness and Constraining Mobilities

As earlier discussed, the literature thus far has focused on the production of precarity on an institutional level (Anderson, 2010) and by giving attention to workplace dynamics and employment relations (Yea, 2017). Building on this body of work, we take an expansive approach by analyzing how precarities are cumulative and compounding from the migrants' perspective as they undertake their journeys from source to destination. In so doing, we pay attention to specific sites and junctures of the migration process where precarity is produced and compounded by multiple constraints of indebtedness, workers' marginal socio-legal status and restricted employment rights along what Lewis et al. (2015) have termed as a "continuum of unfreedom." As they argue, notions of unfreedom often imply "the preclusion of exit ... through indebtedness and/or withholding wages, but also because of workers' own perceptions of their responsibilities, obligations or debts which are in turn used as disciplining mechanisms by employers." Even as Bangladeshi migrants undertake conscious decisions to embark on migration as a livelihood strategy, the sheer barriers to entry and investments required to gain access to Singapore's labor market tend to severely limit their options for mobility and bargaining power at the workplace. As a result, workers sometimes chose to endure unsafe and/or

[5] Given the large cost of migration, it is evident that the construction industry in Singapore tends to attract Bangladeshi migrants predominantly from the middle-class stratum of society. The majority (88.4 percent) of the respondents in the study had at least secondary school qualifications.

exploitative employment conditions, rather than risk having their work permits (and visas) revoked. In this vein, an understanding of the multiple processes producing precarity would benefit from a perspective that follows the migrant as the primary subject through different sites, not as a freewheeling individual, but as a mobile, aspiring subject straining to move toward life goals even as precarious conditions accumulate.

In the following sections, we explore how different forms of insecurity intersect and assemble at particular sites and junctures of men's migration trajectories, beginning from raising money to finance the migration at home, waiting to be "trained" at the training center in Bangladesh to employment at the workplace in Singapore. We will also examine instances where some migrants find themselves out of employment as a result of employment breaches or workplace injury. In so doing, we analyze how multiple forms of precarity are produced and compounded at different junctures, even as migrants negotiate everyday life along their migration journeys.

Debt-financing migration at source

Inasmuch as labor migration entails its own set of risks and costs, it also represents a form of risk diversification for migrants and their families (Rosenzweig and Stark, 1989; Attanapola, 2013). For the large majority of Bangladeshi migrants in our survey (80.5 percent), debt was utilized as a strategy and enabling factor to secure one's livelihood options for the future. Stemming from the interviews, the main push factor that led many migrants to explore overseas job opportunities was a perceived lack of viable employment for improving standards of living in Bangladesh. In particular, men's aspirations often took the form of securing higher earnings to build a new house or start a business venture back home (see also Rahman, 2009). For example, 38-year-old Sumon chose to leave his job at his father's business because he saw migration as a step that would be able to "change my fate." Although he was able to make ends meet with his current job, he felt that the business did not offer "a perfect earning source to change my lifestyle [and] my fate." His wife had initially mooted the idea, saying, "Go there [to Singapore]. Many people have been there. Your friend has changed his life, and now it is your turn to change our fate. You will come back, and you will have some money." With this in mind, he borrowed BDT 90,000 (USD 1,097) from several individuals to raise the BDT 270,000 (USD 3,292) needed to finance his migration journey to Singapore.

In the survey, the average amount of money that workers had to borrow was BDT 258,423 (USD 3,278), which accounted for 65.7 percent of their average total placement fee. When asked why so many Bangladeshi men were willing to undertake such substantial loans to finance their migration journeys, 43-year-old Kalam explained that the decision is often made by weighing these initial costs against the longer-term benefits of securing higher earnings from overseas work. In his words:

> Bangla person will think, 'If I go to Singapore, I can earn a lot of money, because I can take a loan, then I return.' ... He will calculate maybe 4 months, 5 months, 3 months, after which I can return all the money I borrowed.... Because the agent fee is typically 4 or 5 lakhs (USD 5,070 or USD 6,341) ... and he has some money-... then he will borrow 2 lakhs (USD 2,437), 3 lakhs (USD 3,814). Then he may also arrange ... to sell or mortgage his land, and sell many things.

Inasmuch as migrant aspirations are commonly projected over the medium- or long-term — as captured by the migrants' own phrases such as the desire to "earn a lot of money," "change my fate," or "develop myself" — the work permit system in Singapore stipulates that workers are only allowed to be issued oneor two-year contracts with no guarantee of renewal. Stemming from the sheer sum of money that workers were compelled to borrow to finance their pre-departure fees, those who managed to fully repay their loans reported taking an average 16.5 months to do so. Furthermore, since employers can arbitrarily cancel workers' permits at any time (following which workers have to be repatriated after outstanding employment claims are settled), the costs and risks involved are indeed far-reaching.

The training center as gateway

Since workers are required to be trained and tested at source under BCA regulations, the training center in Bangladesh often represents the first gateway to securing a work permit in Singapore. Training centers work closely with BCA-appointed overseas testing centers and recruitment agents in Singapore to serve as a one-stop portal by providing an integrated range of services, including skills training and testing, dormitory facilities and job placement, as well as travel logistical arrangements for prospective migrants. Upon enrollment, students are typically required to place an initial deposit (usually 10 percent of their total placement fee) before commencing theory and practical lessons in a specialized trade skill. These courses typically last three to four months, after which students are scheduled to undergo the SEC (K) skills test to be formally certified. Although test slots are obtainable on a monthly basis, they are often limited and highly competitive as availability is contingent upon the MYEs' quota that employers in Singapore are issued with. After successful completion of the test, migrants then await receipt of an In-Principle Approval (IPA) letter issued by MOM, which serves as a temporary visa for them to gain entry into Singapore. Once the IPA is issued, migrants then pay the bulk of remaining fees to recruitment agents or the training center,[6] which, for migrants who arrived in Singapore after 2011, typically ranges from BDT 400,000 to 500,000 (USD 5,070 to 6,341).

Although training centers were set up to facilitate the training and recruitment process for Singapore-bound construction workers, the generally unregulated and commercial nature of the industry has brought about several pitfalls and issues. Through the interviews, we found that men's experiences at the training center were often fraught with mismatched expectations with regard to the ease and speed of securing employment, and, on some occasions, extra financial costs that were largely unanticipated. In the first instance, practices such as the collection of deposits and retention of workers' passports mean that workers are bound to the system upon enrollment. A common issue encountered was the protracted length of time at which workers stayed at the training center to wait for a test slot, resulting in unforeseen delays and extra costs. On a few occasions, workers reported having to stay up to 12 months in view of a large oversupply of students vying for limited test slots. Twenty-three-year-old Mizan

[6] In most cases, the persons behind the training center and the recruitment agents are the same individuals, although some act as sub-agents as well, mediating between the training center and the prospective migrant.

found his experience at the training center mentally pressuring, seeing that only 10 percent of students were successful in bidding for a test slot for every month. He shared that some of his peers eventually chose to drop out due to the lengthy wait, and had to forfeit their enrollment deposits. As he notes, "some people stay nine months or one year [... and sometimes] he stop, [and] he surrender."

At times, workers' placement fees were arbitrarily raised after they had completed both training and testing, with the alleged reason that "the [Singapore] dollar value has increased." For 26-year-old Kamal, the increase was over 37 percent above what he was initially told by his agent. In his words:

> When I first went to the training center, I had a contract for BDT 250,000 (USD 3,170) but there were a lot of people in the training center, and so it took me six months to finish the training. Then after six months, they said BDT 250,000 (USD 3,170) is not enough, we need BDT 400,000 (USD 5,073) ... because the price of the Singapore dollar went up. This price went up, and so you have to pay BDT 400,000 (USD 5,073). I thought okay, I did the training for six months and I passed [the examination]. Whatever money it takes, I eventually have to go to Singapore. I went through the hard work, I paid some money, so what's the point of sitting down? As I have done it, it is better that I go. If I go to Singapore, then I can earn money.

Kamal's experience highlights the vulnerabilities that migrants face by virtue of having to go through the standardized route of the training center to obtain a work permit in Singapore. Having invested a substantial amount of time, money and energy to complete his training, he remained determined to cross this initial hurdle regardless of the extra costs. When asked whether or not he tried to negotiate the increase, he shared that he was just "focused on paying the money and going to Singapore." As he explained,

> Even if I don't go now, I will go after two months ... because the guy from whom I heard about Singapore, this guy was working in a good company. So if I can get into a good company, I can earn the money [back] and get a better life.

The importance of securing a good company was frequently emphasized by workers, because the work permit system in Singapore operates on a sponsorship basis where workers' visas are tied to a sole employer. Despite paying exorbitant amounts of money to access job placement services at the training center, the process remains largely obscure to workers as argued by 28-year-old Zabed: "They only say that they will give good company. Only this. What is good or bad, we were not able to understand it. [The agent would collect the] same amount from all. What is allocated depends on fate." For many Bangladeshi migrants, good employers were generally perceived as those that offered a decent salary, adhered to proper safety procedures and provided adequate rest for their employees. Companies that were main contractors for construction projects (as opposed to subcontractors and labor supply companies) were seen as those most likely to offer these terms. In some instances, workers tried to circumvent the risk by tapping into social networks to approach separate agents to match them with a better company. However, this move often entailed paying a penalty in exchange for retrieving their passports from the training center, as well as additional fees to engage an external agent.

The attrition of bargaining power at the workplace

Stemming from having to invest large sums of money to access mandatory skills training and testing in Bangladesh, workers typically arrive in Singapore with a substantial debt burden. As such, remaining in employment to ensure a regular flow of income is often of chief concern, especially for newly arrived migrants. When asked whether or not they felt able to negotiate employment terms with their employers, many workers cited the fear of early repatriation as the source of their main hesitation. Because Singapore's work permit system prescribes that workers' visas are tied to a single employer, losing one's job effectively means that one would also lose the ability to remain in the country. At this juncture, therefore, concerns of job insecurity become intensified by migrant indebtedness and workers' vulnerability to repatriation. As Kalam explains:

> If a worker says anything, then the employer will be angry. He will say, 'I send you back to Bangladesh if you talking many, many.' Then the

> worker will also be scared. He paid a lot of money to invest in his migration stint. If he says anything, and he gets sent back to Bangladesh, then how?

Indeed, it is not uncommon for employers to exploit workers' vulnerability and use the threat of repatriation as a disciplining mechanism to ensure compliance. In Zabed's view, "the fate of the worker depends on the supervisor. If he reports negatively to the company ... then his renewal will be halted. They will send him back to the country." These practices often translate into feelings of disempowerment among workers who sometimes feel compelled to endure unsafe and/or exploitative workplace conditions, for fear of having their work permits revoked by their employers. In the case of 38-year-old Sumon, he shared that although his employer has consistently failed to pay him proper overtime wages, he felt that he had little bargaining power to negotiate this because he did not wish to be sent home before his contract expired. In a resigned tone, he shared that "we must understand that this is not our country. We can't do a lot of things even if we want to. Like I said, my overtime-hourly pay is SGD 3 (USD 2.30), but according to Singapore government law, [my employer] should pay 1.5 times [the basic rate], which they don't. But if I bargain, they will send me back."

Similarly, Kalam's employer failed to pay him the full amount of overtime wages that were due, seeing that he frequently clocked 24-hour shifts beyond the maximum number of hours allowed. His company supposedly paid his basic wage via electronic transfer, but chose instead to pay his overtime salary in cash so as to evade the law. In Kalam's view, this practice was a deliberate ploy to short-change workers of their wages while masking illegal and exploitative workplace practices. When he decided to confront his employer to demand proper payment, however, the company promptly threatened him with repatriation. In his words: "I shouting, and I say to my employer, 'every month, my overtime salary is SGD 560 (USD 437), and you pay only SGD 160, 145 (USD 125, 113). Why like this? Why?'... Then he say he will send me back."

The erosion of migrant workers' bargaining power at the workplace is hence reinforced by their insecure foothold in the host nation-state. As contract workers brought into the nation-state under a regime of enforced temporariness, they are permanently "out-of-place" (Cresswell, 1996). In Sumon's words, "we must understand that this is not our country," and those who wish to remain have to take it upon themselves to self-discipline and self-censure in order to become compliant subjects.

Risking life and limb at the workplace

Migrants' weak bargaining power has important implications on issues of workplace safety, especially when workers feel compelled to undertake work they deem as risky or unsafe. In Singapore, the construction sector remains the top contributor to workplace fatalities, accounting for 57 percent of all fatalities in 2013 (Workplace Safety and Health (WSH) Institute, 2014). Construction companies preferred to pay fines for safety breaches than "invest substantially more in a safety system that could cost up to 15 percent of their contract's value (*Straits Times*, 2016). Feedback from industry professionals also pointed out that "companies rushing to meet project deadlines amid rising demand for construction activities [and] the tighter labor market contributing to 'over-stretching their workers'" (*TODAY*, 2014) are common underlying factors behind the surge in workplace accidents in the construction industry. Similarly, our interviews with injured workers revealed fatigue stemming from excessive overtime work and tight project deadlines as key contributing factors. At the same time, scholars have argued that the prevalence of subcontracting in the industry tends to result in a "diffusion of responsibility [that] could lead to a decline in house-keeping" (Debrah and Ofori, 1997: 699).

Living and working precariously are recurrent themes in everyday life for the migrant construction worker. Mizan broke both his wrists when he fell from a scaffolding structure while working on a flyover. He was working a daily average of 14 hours including Sundays, and reckoned that the accident happened because he was physically drained from excessive overtime work. He was also not wearing a safety harness when the accident occurred. Although he felt unsafe and frequently overworked, he felt that he had little power to raise these issues with his employer because he was a new worker in the company. In his words:

> My boss will say to me if Sunday you want to take time off, ok, then Saturday you also no need to come. You go back better.... My company 'subcon' [subcontractor], so main company always push, push workers to go faster, go faster. Then supervisor also push ah, saying 'Go fast, this one go fast.... If the safety supervisor sometimes tell me must working properly, my Korean supervisor will talk loudly to the safety supervisor, saying 'Why you talk to my worker? Why you disturb my worker?' ... My supervisor will say: 'Koreans all hardworking, money also a lot. If Singapore 20 years working, Korean 5 years working enough. He say 'I give money, I give salary, so you follow me.' So since I first time coming Singapore, that's why cannot talk loud. I am scared to be sent home. You know if he says, no working, you go back better, then he send me back to Bangladesh, so it is a problem right? Yah, so two years, three years, then we can talk loud.

Employed as a general worker in his company, Mizan also felt that he did not receive proper training to do his work, which involved extending a flyover structure. Having trained in waterproofing, he was told to shadow a Burmese colleague to learn whatever he could. In his view, "99.9 percent [of men work] like this" — that is, they do not utilize the skill they were trained for in Bangladesh. Rather, the experience at the training center was more of a formality and a way of weeding out weak workers, because the process of getting certified was highly competitive and not everyone makes it through. Zabed echoed similar sentiments, saying:

> If you can work after enduring that challenge, then they think you'll also be able to work in Singapore. They want a person who can work hard. A person who can't work hard — what will be the use of them in Singapore?

As Ajslev et al. (2017: 895) observe in the case of Danish construction workers, reconfiguring their bodies and "trading health for money" is a "necessary deal" for those who wish to retain their jobs. Unfortunately, there is a limit on how far workers can push themselves to work relentlessly. In Hasan's case, he injured his back and shoulder from an accident in July 2013, which he said was a result of fatigue and unsafe work practices. Like 23-year-old Mizan, he was pushed to undertake work that he felt uncomfortable to do, which resulted in his injury:

> Boss put pressure on us to do overnight duty during the fasting month. If not, he said he would send me back to Bangladesh the next day. I told him because it's fasting month, it's not possible for me to work beyond 10:00pm ... but he pressured me, saying must do. At last, I had no choice ... I was tired. I was fasting ... and the scaffolding joint was weak. There was also not enough lighting. They gave us safety harness belts, but we complained about the lighting and they said to carry on with the work. The lighting will be provided later, but they didn't [do so].

Stuck in limbo on a special pass

When a workplace accident is reported, MOM issues a Special Pass to injured workers to legalize their stay in Singapore while they undergo medical treatment and wait for their work injury compensation to be processed. Workers who have filed a formal complaint against their employers for employment breaches, such as the non-payment of salaries, are also placed on the same pass to assist the Ministry with investigations. Apart from those eligible for the Temporary Job Scheme, the majority of workers on a Special Pass are prohibited from working on a legal basis. The precarity of their conditions stems not only from the fact that day-to-day survival in Singapore is uncertain and difficult, but the emotional toll exacted during the protracted waiting period, and the sense of shame that their migration bids have run aground, often conspire to isolate them from family and friends back home. As Ye (2014: 1015) observes, the "intersections of precarious work and working-class masculinity" often render migrant men "unable to speak of their suffering" to left-behind family members and kin. Precarity is hence not only an exterior condition that is constitutive of the contemporary life but often experienced as an accumulation of circumstances that chisels away — continually and even relentlessly — at the worker's sense of self and well-being. In other words, as a sense of precarity increasingly takes root in individual lives, it soon becomes a 'structure of feeling' operating across this category of workers and their families.

For example, Kalam who has been awaiting his insurance payout for two- and-a-half years lamented that "*makan* (meaning: eating) also difficult, sleeping also difficult. Everything is difficult, too difficult." When he had no money to pay for his rent, he had to make do with sleeping by the roadside or at a 24-hour café at Mustafa Center. He also shared that it was painful to communicate with his family while being in such dire straits, saying: "Sometimes I talk to my son, and my heart is crying. My eyes water [tears] cannot come, but heart is crying.... Family only give me sympathy, but I say okay, no problem, no need this one." Likewise, 24-year-old Saiful feels that he is unable to tell his parents the full extent of his situation:

> If I tell them everything, then they will suffer a lot. I love them most, and for this reason I have not told them.... I will return home and then tell my mother. If she cries, then I will try to manage her. On the mobile, I cannot manage her.

Depending on the nature of a workers' injury and the complexity of the case, the average duration of the claims process[7] can range from three or four months to over two years. Mizan has been left in a state of limbo since the accident took place two years ago and his parents are anxious for his return to Bangladesh. Nonetheless, he insists on awaiting his insurance payout to settle outstanding loans from his initial placement fee, and use the remaining amount to set up a small business in Bangladesh. Precarious subjects continue to narrate a sense of hope as they contemplate uncertain futures.

This sense of hope — as a means of resisting precarity — is evident even among those in dire circumstances. Faced with limited employment options stemming from permanent injury, workers on the Special Pass often place enormous value on the compensation they hope to receive. In the case of 31-year-old Mostafa, he feels that his livelihood options have been severely diminished and the future remains uncertain. Yet, he pinned

[7] Under the MOM, the Work Injury Compensation Act allows workers to make claims for work-related injuries or diseases without having to file a civil suit under common law. See also Yea (2017).

his hopes that there would be a change of fortunes if the insurance compensation is substantial — in his words:

> I will build my whole life on that money. I do not know the amount but I realized that a huge damage has been done to my physical body. If the sum is large, then I can do something after returning to my country. I will not be able to do heavy work. I cannot work with the cattle or start the machine. Now, I am fully depending on the insurance money. How much I will get is the lottery of my life.

Conclusion

The growing vein of scholarship on migrant workers undertaking low paid, insecure and irregular jobs have shown how experiences of precariousness are inextricably linked to broader patterns of intensifying neoliberalism, labor market deregulation and the flexibilization of labor in post-industrialist societies. Drawing on a case study of Bangladeshi construction workers in Singapore, we have built on this work to show how precarity as a conceptual lens can advance our knowledge of what is generally known as the disadvantaged position of migrant contract workers. We argue that in order to understand migrant precarity more fully, we need to approach migration as a cumulative, intensively mediated process. This approach gives emphasis to the place-based trajectory of migrant-specific vulnerabilities, and how different forms of risk and vulnerabilities accumulate, intersect and converge to render migrants more susceptible to workplace exploitation and, at the same time, even more persevering under precarious conditions. In other words, we argue that precariousness does not just emanate from state policy or the market at the reception end of the migration process, but is a *condition-in-the-making* that has its roots in pre-migration impoverished circumstances, multiplies as migrant subjects become entangled with the migration industry, and is further deepened and made manifest in the workplace at destination. We contribute to the understanding of precarity through incorporating place-specificities and a sense of temporality by treating it as a contingent yet compounding condition, where aspiring migrant subjects are channelled into a tunnel of entrapment where there is little choice but to go forward, even as options get narrower and narrower, and the gap between actual circumstances and original aspirations becomes wider and wider. As a human condition that interweaves life and labor, "precarity, thus, conjures life worlds that are inflected with uncertainty and instability" (Waite, 2009: 416).

In a regime of "mediated employment" (Swider, 2015: 46) where rural men from underdeveloped regions are recruited by labor brokers to work in wealthy global cities, migrant subjects are caught in a liminal state of permanent temporariness, neither strongly embedded in the moral economy of their home villages nor integrated enough into the social worlds at destination to be able to benefit from formal and informal safety nets. Instead, where the state, the migration industry and employers are aligned in outsourcing the bulk of the risk to the individual migrant, the coping mechanism for the migrant subject often turns on approaching migration as a risk-ridden gamble, sustained by the hope that the next throw of the dice would be in their favor. In the words of our interviewees, at each site along the migration journey, even when life and livelihood conditions are at their bleakest, such as when the migrant body has been "destroyed" as a result of severe injury (in Hasan's words), migrants fasten their hopes on what Mostafa calls "the lottery of my life." Precisely because "precarity suggests the potential for exploitation and abuse, but not its certain presence" (Banki, 2013: 450), it is always conjoined to hope, that is, the belief in the prospect that this time, fate will deal one a fair hand. In other words, precarity is at its most finely balanced when "the right to plan one's future with a minimum of security and job certainty" (Ahmad, 2008: 303) has to be replaced by an arbitrary belief that the tide will turn in one's favor. Our paper has tried to "return [migrant] subjects of development to the center of theorizations about them" (Ye, 2014: 1014, quoting Silvey and Lawson, 1999), not as freewheeling human agents but as aspiring subjects acting under conditions not of their own making. By combining attention to the "disappearance of predictability" (Ahmad, 2008: 302) fostered by a neoliberal migration-labor regime, with a bio-cultural perspective that centers the migrant as an agentic subject, we glimpse how site-produced precarities are experienced and compounded, even as migrants enact themselves as aspiring, mobile subjects.

Acknowledgments

Although this work has been funded by UK Aid from the UK government through the Migrating Out of Poverty Research Programme Consortium, the views expressed do not necessarily reflect the UK government's official policies.

Declaration of Conflicting Interests

The authors declare no potential conflicts of interest with respect to the research, authorship, and/or publication of this paper.

Funding

This research was funded by the UK Aid from the UK government through the Migrating out of Poverty Research Programme Consortium.

References

Ahmad AN (2008) Dead men working: Time and space in London's ('illegal') migrant economy. *Work, Employment Society* 22(2): 301–318.

Ajslev JZN, Møller JL, Persson R, et al. (2017) Trading health for money: Agential struggles in the (re)configuration of subjectivity, the body and pain among construction workers. *Work, Employment Society* 31(6): 887–903. DOI:10.1177/09500 17016668141.

Anderson B (2010) Migration, immigration controls, and the fashioning of precarious workers. *Work, Employment Society* 24(2): 300–317.

Arnold D and Bongiovi JR (2013) Precarious, infirmalizing, and flexible work: Transforming concepts and understandings. *American Behavioral Scientist* 57(3): 289–308. Attanapola CT (2013) Back and forth with hopes and fears: Sri Lankan men's narratives on gender and mobility in transnational livelihoods. *Norsk Geografisk Tidsskrift* 67(4): 219–228.

Baey G and Yeoh BSA (2015) Migration and precarious work: Negotiating debt, employment, and livelihood strategies amongst Bangladeshi migrant men working in Singapore's construction industry. In: *Migrating out of Poverty Working Paper 26*. Brighton: University of Sussex. Available at: http://

migratingoutofpoverty.dfid.gov.uk/documents/wp26-baey-yeoh-2015-migration-and-precarious-work.pdf

Banki S (2013) Precarity of place: A complement to the growing precariat literature. *Global Discourse* 3(3–4): 450–463.

Bauder H (2006) *Labour Movement: How Migration Regulates Labour Markets*. Oxford: Oxford University Press.

Berntsen L (2016) Reworking labour practices: On the agency of unorganized mobile migrant construction workers. *Work, Employment and Society* 30(3): 472–488.

Branch EH and Hanley C (2011) Regional convergence in low-wage work and earnings, 1970–2000. *Sociological Perspectives* 54(4): 569–592.

Coe NM (2012) Geographies of production III: Making space for labour. *Progress in Human Geography* 37(2): 271–284.

Cresswell T (1996) *In Place/Out of Place: Geography, Ideology, and Trangression*. Minneapolis: University of Minnesota Press.

Debrah YA and Ofori G (1997) Flexibility, labour subcontracting and HRM in the construction industry in Singapore: Can the system be refined? *The International Journal of Human Resource Management* 8(5): 690–709.

Deshingkar P and Start D (2003) *Seasonal Migration for Livelihoods in India: Coping, Accumulation and Exclusion*. Working Paper 220. London: Overseas Development Institute.

Elcioglu EF (2010) Producing precarity: The temporary staffing agency in the labour market. *Qualitative Sociology* 33: 117–136. DOI 10.1007/s11133-010-9149-x.

Enright B (2013) (Re)considering new agents: A review of labour market intermediaries within labour geography. *Geography Compass* 7(4): 287–299.

Garcés-Mascareñas B (2010) Legal production of illegality in a comparative perspective: The cases of Malaysia and Spain. *Asia Europe Journal* 8(1): 77–89.

Hernandez-Leon R (2013) *The Migration Industry: Brokering Mobility in the Mexico-US Migratory System*. Los Angeles: UCLA International Institute.

Kalleberg AL and Hewison K (2013) Precarious work and the challenge for Asia. *American Behavioral Scientist* 57(3): 271–288.

Khurana S (2017) Resisting labour control and optimizing social ties: Experiences of women construction workers in Delhi. *Work, Employment and Society* 31(6): 921–936.

Lewis HM, Dwyer PJ, Hodkinson S and Waite L (2015) Hyper-precarious lives: Migrants, work and forced labour in the Global North. *Progress in Human Geography* 39(5): 580–600.

May J, Wills J, Datta K, et al. (2007) Keeping London working: Global cities, the British state and London's new migrant division of labour. *Transactions of the Institute of British Geographers* 32(2): 151–167.

McCormack D and Salmenniemi S (2016) The biopolitics of precarity and the self. *European Journal of Cultural Studies* 19(1): 3–15.

McDowell L, Batnitzky A and Dyer S (2009) Precarious work and economic migration: Emerging immigrant divisions of labour in Greater London's Service Sector. *International Journal of Urban and Regional Research* 33(1): 3–25.

Ministry of Manpower (MOM) (2012) Employment of Foreign Manpower Act (Chapter 91A): Employment of Foreign Manpower (Work Passes) Regulations 2012. Available at: http://www.mom.gov.sg/Documents/services-forms/passes/WPSPassConditions.pdf

Neilson B and Rossiter N (2006) From precarity to precariousness and back again Labour, life and unstable networks. *Variant* 25(2): 10–13.

Peck JA and Theodore N (2002) The temporary staffing industry: Growth imperatives and limits of contingency. *Economic Geography* 78(4): 463–493.

Rahman MM (2009) Temporary migration and changing family dynamics: Implications for social development. *Population, Space and Place* 15(2): 161–174.

Reid-Musson E, Buckley M and Anderson B (2015) Building Migrant Precarity: Employment, Citizenship & Skill in Toronto and London's Construction Sectors. Working paper, Urbanization From Below: Precarious Migrant Construction Work in Toronto, Canada and London, UK Project. Available at: http://www.migrant-workersrights.net/en/resources/building-migrant-precarity-employment-citizen-ship-s

Reza S (2016) Hyper-individualized recruitment: Rural-urban labour migration and precarious construction work in Bangladesh. *Migration, Mobility & Displacement* 2(2): 40–61.

Rosenzweig MR and Stark O (1989) Consumption smoothing, migration and marriage: Evidence from rural India. *Journal of Political Economy* 97(4): 905–926.

Sassen S (2001) *The Global City: New York, London, Tokyo*. Princeton: Princeton University Press.

Sennett R (1998) *The Corrosion of Character: The Personal Consequences of Work in the New Capitalism*. London/New York: W. W. Norton.

Siegmann KA and Schiphorst F (2016) Understanding the globalizing precariat: From informal sector to precarious work. *Progress in Development Studies* 16(2): 111–123.

Silvey R and Lawson V (1999) Placing the migrant. *Annals of the Association of American Geographers* 89(1): 121–132.

Standing G (2011) *The Precariat: The New Dangerous Class*. London: Bloomsbury Academic.

Straits Times (2016) Workplace fatality rate set to rise this year. 25 August. Available at: http://www.straitstimes.com/singapore/manpower/workplace-fatality-rate-set-to-rise-this-year

Strauss K and McGrath S (2017) Temporary migration, precarious employment and unfree labour relations: Exploring the 'continuum of exploitation' in Canada's Temporary Foreign Worker Program. *Geoforum* 78(1): 199–208.

Swider S (2015) Building China: Precarious employment among migrant construction workers. *Work, Employment Society* 29(1): 41–59.

TODAY (2014) New rules on construction industry likely after rise in workplace deaths. 18 February. Available at: http://www.todayonline.com/singapore/new-rules-construction-industry-likely-after-rise-workplace-deaths

Torres R, Heyman R, Munoz S, et al. (2013) Building Austin, building justice: Immigrant construction workers, precarious labor regimes and social citizenship. *Geoforum* 45(3): 145–155.

Vosko LF (2010) *Managing the Margins: Gender, Citizenship and the International Regulation of Precarious Employment*. Oxford: Oxford University Press.

Waite L (2009) A place and space for a critical geography of precarity? *Geography Compass* 3(1): 412–433.

Walia H (2007) Increasing precarity: The politics of migrant labor. *Left Turn*. Available at: http://www.leftturn.org/increasing-precarity-politics-migrant-labor

Wills J, May J, Datta K, et al. (2009) London's migrant division of labour. *European Urban and Regional Studies* 16(3): 257–271.

Wise A (2013) Pyramid subcontracting and moral detachment: Down-sourcing risk and responsibility in the management of transnational labour in Asia. *Economic and Labour Relations Review* 24(3): 433–455.

Workplace Safety and Health (WSH) Institute (2014) Workplace Safety and Health Report: National Statistics, January to June 2014. Available at: https://www.wsh-institute.sg/files/wshi/upload/cms/file/Workplace%20Safety%20and%20Health%20Report%202014%20(January%20to%20June).pdf

Xiang B and Lindquist J (2014) Migration infrastructure. *International Migration Review* 48(s1): S122–S148.

Ye J (2014) Migrant masculinities: Bangladeshi men in Singapore's labour force. *Gender, Place & Culture* 21(8): 1012–1028.

Yea S (2017) The art of not being caught: Temporal strategies for disciplining unfree labour in Singapore's contract migration. *Geoforum* 78(1): 179–188.

Yea S and Chok S (2018) Unfreedom unbound: Developing a cumulative approach to understanding unfree labour in Singapore. *Work, Employment and Society*. Epub ahead of print 5 January 2018. DOI:10.1177/0950017017738956.

Chapter 7a

Healthcare for Migrant Workers in Singapore: Insights from the COVID-19 Experience*

Jia Wei Ang

Lee Kong Chian School of Medicine
Nanyang Technological University

Colin Chia

HealthServe Community Clinic

Calvin J. Koh

Division of Gastroenterology and Hepatology
National University Hospital, National University Health System

Brandon W. B. Chua

Department of Pharmacy
KK Women's and Children's Hospital

*Reflections on Ang, J. W., Chia, C., Koh, C. J., Chua, B. W. B., Narayanaswamy, S., Wijaya, L., Chan, L. G., Goh, W. L. and Vasoo, S. (2017). Healthcare-seeking behaviour, barriers and mental health of non-domestic migrant workers in Singapore, *BMJ Glob. Health*. Vol. 2, No. 2, pp. e000213. DOI: 10.1136/bmjgh-2016-000213. © 2021 BMJ Publishing Group Ltd.

Shyamala Narayanaswamy

Department of Pharmacy
Singapore General Hospital

Limin Wijaya

Department of Infectious Diseases
Singapore General Hospital

Lai Gwen Chan

Department of Psychiatry
Tan Tock Seng Hospital

Wei Leong Goh

HealthServe Community Clinic

Shawn Vasoo

Lee Kong Chian School of Medicine
Nanyang Technological University
Department of Infectious Diseases
Institute of Infectious Diseases and Epidemiology
Tan Tock Seng Hospital

Migrant workers form an important part of Singapore's workforce. However, they also face a number of challenges as temporary migrant workers in the city-state, including access to health care coverage. For instance, they are not entitled to medical subsidies that are often covered by healthcare coverage for citizens. They also face risks of injury and infectious diseases in the workplace and in accommodations, and of psychological distress. This paper is based on a 2016 survey that we conducted in order to identify the factors that affect migrant workers' access to healthcare in Singapore. We administered a survey of over 400 migrant workers at subsidised clinics, and at a foreign worker dormitory. Our findings suggest that their access to health care and psychological well-being are affected by economic and socio-cultural factors. In particular, low-wage migrant workers face economic challenges as part of the migration process, which is often debt-fuelled. The financial barriers due to indebtedness affect their health-seeking behaviour and mental well-being. Health literacy can also be a factor. For instance, several workers had insurance, but had limited to poor understanding of its inpatient and outpatient coverage. The information provided to them regarding insurance was also not in their native language. These factors interplay with their living, social, and work conditions in Singapore.

While some progress has been made in the last decade in healthcare provision for migrants, the COVID-19 pandemic has brought these issues to the fore again. In particular, the spread of infections in migrant dormitories challenged Singapore's response to the pandemic and underscored not only the importance of preventive medicine, but also the need to improve migrant workers' access to healthcare and social protection, and better living and working environments [Yee et al., 2021]. Due to the outbreak in dormitories, migrant workers accounted for majority of Singapore's cases [ChannelNewsAsia, 2021]. This galvanised a national conversation on improving standards for housing migrant workers, such as reducing the density of living quarters. Moreover, it brought attention to the provision of healthcare for migrant workers, not only in relation to communicable diseases of public health concern like COVID-19, but also chronic diseases and the mental health of migrant workers. COVID-19 is also an acute reminder that the health and well-being of migrants in a community are intertwined with and can affect the general populace as well.

Aside from the vaccination of migrant workers, including those residing in dormitories, there have been some policy changes underway. For example, in early 2021, the Ministry of Manpower started reviewing medical insurance coverage for migrant workers, and an update is expected later into the year [Sin, 2021]. The Ministry is also planning a new primary healthcare system for migrant workers [Kok and Ng, 2021]. As COVID-19 is unlikely to go away in the short-term, and given the possibility of future epidemics, it is imperative for a migrant-receiving country like Singapore to learn from this pandemic, in ways that can contribute to better public health policies and healthcare delivery for migrant workers.

References

ChannelNewsAsia. (2021, 8 March). Singapore to vaccinate migrant workers against COVID-19, starting with 10,000 dormitory residents. Retrieved from https://www.channelnewsasia.com/news/singapore/covid-19-vaccination-migrant-workers-dormitories-moh-14360202

Kok, Y. and Ng, K. G. (2021, 30 June). New healthcare system to be set up for migrant workers in S'pore; 6 medical centres planned. *The Straits Times*. Retrieved from https://www.straitstimes.com/singapore/health/new-healthcare-system-to-be-set-up-for-migrant-workers-in-spore-6-medical-centres

Sin, Y. (2021, 4 March). Better access to primary healthcare for migrant workers. *The Straits Times*. Retrieved from https://www.straitstimes.com/singapore/better-access-to-primary-healthcare-for-migrant-workers

Yee, K., Peh, H. P., Tan, Y.P., Teo, I., Tan, E. U. T., Paul, J., Rangabashyam, M., Ramalingam, M.B., Chow, W. and Tan, H. K. (2021). Stressors and coping strategies of migrant workers diagnosed with COVID-19 in Singapore: A qualitative study, *BMJ Open*, Vol. 11, No. 3, pp. e045949. DOI: 10.1136/bmjopen-2020-045949. PMID: 33741672; PMCID: PMC7985935

Chapter 7b

Healthcare-seeking Behaviour, Barriers and Mental Health of Non-domestic Migrant Workers in Singapore*

Jia Wei Ang,[1] Colin Chia,[2] Calvin J. Koh,[3] Brandon W. B. Chua,[4] Shyamala Narayanaswamy,[5] Limin Wijaya,[6] Lai Gwen Chan,[7] Wei Leong Goh,[2] and Shawn Vasoo[1,8]

Background: Low-wage migrant workers are vulnerable to healthcare inequities. We sought to identify potential barriers to healthcare and risk factors for mental health issues in non-domestic migrant workers in Singapore, and identify high-risk subgroups.

Methods: A cross-sectional, interviewer-administered survey of 433 non-domestic migrant workers was conducted at subsidised clinics and a foreign worker dormitory from July to August 2016. Questions assessed healthcare usage patterns, affordability issues, barriers to care and psychological distress using a validated screening scale (Kessler-6).

---

*This article was originally published in *BMJ Glob. Health*. Vol. 2, No. 2, pp. e000213. DOI: 10.1136/bmjgh-2016-000213.
Correspondence to Dr Shawn Vasoo; shawn_vasoo@ttsh.com.sg

Findings: Bangladeshi workers surveyed were more likely to be single, have more financial dependents, a lower level of education and salary and pay higher agent fees ($p < 0.01$). 61.4% of workers reported that they had insurance, but had poor understanding of whether it covered inpatient/outpatient expenses. The majority of workers had not, or were not sure if they had, received information about company-bought insurance (72.4%). Among those who had, most reported that information was not in their native language (67.7%). Non-specific psychological distress was found in 21.9%, as estimated by the Kessler-6 scale. Multivariate analysis found that psychological distress was independently associated with Bangladeshi nationals (OR 2.98, 95% CI 1.58 to 5.62; $p = 0.001$) and previous experience of financial barriers to healthcare (OR 3.86, 95% CI 2.25 to 6.62; $p < 0.0001$).
Interpretation: We identified gaps in non-domestic migrant workers' knowledge of healthcare coverage, and substantial financial barriers to healthcare. The Bangladeshi population in our study was at higher risk of such barriers and psychological distress. These represent areas for further research and intervention.

Key Questions

What is already known about this topic?

- Migrant workers are at risk of disparities in accessing healthcare, and a lack of access to services may be associated with poorer psychological well-being.
- There are scant data on healthcare-seeking behaviour, associated barriers and the mental health of migrant workers in Southeast Asia, including 'tiger economies' like Singapore, which have large migrant worker populations. It is also unknown if there are subgroups who may be at higher risk of healthcare barriers and poorer psychological health.

What are the new findings?

- Migrant workers working in Singapore, of Bangladeshi origin, compared with those from India or China and other countries, supported more persons in their home country, incurred higher agent fees, had a lower median salary and were more likely to report psychological distress as measured by the Kessler scale.

- Workers who reported financial barriers to accessing healthcare were also more likely to experience psychological distress.
- We found a great degree of indebtedness due to agent fees among migrant workers (~35% incurred agent fees of >SG$5000).
- There was poor knowledge, in general, among migrant workers with regard to eligibility to healthcare coverage and variability in sick leave policy among employers.

Recommendations for policy

- More transparent and regulated frameworks in sending and receiving countries may help diminish migrant workers indebtedness.
- Interventions should be directed towards improving the knowledge of migrant workers with regard to their entitled healthcare coverage, and also diminishing financial barriers to accessing care (inpatient and outpatient).
- Subgroups of migrant workers at higher risk of healthcare barriers and psychological distress, such as the Bangladeshi population in our study, should be paid special attention for further research and when formulating health policy and interventions.

Introduction

The United Nations (UN) estimates that international migrants reached 244 million in 2015, with Asia adding 26 million migrants between 2000 and 2015, more than any other region in the world in the same period.[1] Half of all international migrants are born in Asia, with India having the biggest diaspora of 16 million persons in 2015. China and Bangladesh had 10 and 7 million persons, respectively.[1] Most international migrants are of working age, and developing countries were estimated to have received remittances of US$441 billion in 2015.[2] Recognising this trend, and the important contribution of migrants to home and receiving countries, migration issues, such as achieving universal health coverage and the promotion of a safe and secure working environment for all workers, have been included in the UN 2030 Agenda for Sustainable Development (UN Sustainable Development Goals 3 and 8).[3]

At the crossroads of Asia, Singapore has seen tremendous growth over the past 50 years, with migrant workers essential in fuelling this growth. Many are low or semiskilled workers employed under a short-term contractual basis, performing jobs either in the domestic sector or non-domestic jobs deemed by the local population as 'dirty, dangerous and demanding' — the three Ds.[4] Most migrant workers in Singapore enter on a 'Work Permit' (for those in the construction, manufacturing, marine, process or services sector) or a 'S Pass' (for midskilled technical staff). In 2015, migrant workers holding Work Permits or S Passes made up 20% of Singapore's population of 5.54 million people.[5]

Migrant workers health has been a challenging topic deeply intertwined with the history of Singapore, which has seen major regional migratory flows in the past century.[6] Indeed, most Singaporeans trace their roots to economic migrants who started arriving in the early 1800s, and migrant workers continue to play an important role in the city–state's economy.

While improvements have been made over recent years with regard to healthcare coverage for migrant workers in Singapore, several gaps still remain. A number of sociocultural and economic factors limit healthcare accessibility and increase vulnerability of low-wage migrant workers in Singapore. They are also subject to increased risk of work-related injury and infectious diseases.[7–9] Migrant workers do not qualify for medical subsidies and are not covered by the healthcare financing schemes that citizens fall under.[10] Instead, employers of low and semiskilled workers, holding Work Permits and S Passes, respectively, are legally required to provide inpatient and day surgery medical insurance coverage of ≥$15 000 a year.[11] In addition, workers who sustain work injuries or occupational diseases with resulting permanent incapacity or death are liable to compensation under the Work Injury Compensation Act.[12]

The few local studies on migrant workers health have focused on describing commonly faced medical issues such as workplace accidents and infectious diseases.[7–9] A large study on mental health in this vulnerable population in Singapore found an increased rate (62%) of psychological distress in migrant workers facing injury claims and salary disputes.[13] In the larger Asian region, the few studies on the effects of economic migration on mental health have largely focused on the 'left-behind' families of migrant workers.[14 15] One study that did examine the mental health migrants themselves found poorer psychological well-being among Cambodian migrant workers in Thailand who reported poverty, debt and a lack of access to services.[16] Little has been investigated on perspectives of migrant workers in accessing healthcare. In 2014, Lee *et al*[17] described health-seeking behaviours of male migrant workers found that inadequate finances may impede healthcare-seeking behaviour and also identified low rates of awareness of insurance policies, but did not explore this in depth. In collaboration with a local non-profit organisation, HealthServe, we conducted an observational cross-sectional anonymous survey among low-wage non-domestic migrant workers to better understand the potential barriers they face in accessing healthcare, and their mental health. We also sought to identify subgroups at higher risk of facing healthcare barriers and psychological distress.

Methods

Ethical approval

This study was approved by the National Healthcare Group's Domain Specific Review Board (DSRB Reference Number: 2016/00499).

Survey design

Survey questions (see online supplementary appendix A) were designed in consultation with various stakeholders, including doctors, volunteers and HealthServe. Four domains of health-related knowledge, attitude and practices were assessed: current healthcare usage patterns, affordability, other barriers to access and psychological well-being. The Kessler-6 scale,[18] a validated screening tool, was used to estimate the prevalence of psychological distress. Demographic information was also included for the assessment of risk factors.

The survey was translated into the native languages of respondents: Bengali, Mandarin and Tamil, and was piloted among migrant workers to ensure feasibility of the questions.

Research site and study population

Interviewer-administered surveys were administered to workers who visited three HealthServe clinics in Singapore. Migrant workers staying in a dormitory were also recruited to ensure broader representation. Singapore Citizens and workers holding Permanent Residency and Employment Passes (skilled professionals with medium to high wages) were excluded. Informed consent was obtained verbally from participants and confidentiality assured as no personal identifiers were collected.

Training of volunteers and data collection

Volunteer interviewers were recruited to assist in the surveys, and training was conducted to reduce interinterviewer bias. Interviewers were provided with briefing slides of instructions on survey administration. Completed forms were checked after each session to minimise transcribing errors.

Statistical analysis

We estimated that a sample size of 400 would afford a CI of +4.9%, at a confidence level of 95% (http://www.nss.gov.au/nss/home.nsf/). Data analysis was performed using SPSS software (V.24.0). χ^2 test, Fishers' exact test and Hodges-Lehmann's median difference test were performed. Backwards-stepwise logistic regression was performed for factors associated (univariate analysis $p < 0.20$) with psychological distress as estimated by a Kessler-6 score of ≥13. The Hosmer-Lemeshow test was used to assess goodness-of-fit. A p value of <0.05 indicated statistical significance.

Results

Over a 5-week period from July to August 2016, 489 low-wage non-domestic migrant workers were invited to participate in the study. Of these, 433 (88.5%) agreed to participate. Three hundred and twenty-nine (76.0%) were clinic visitors and 104 (24.0%) were non-clinic visitors from a dormitory.

Sociodemographic characteristics

The median age of workers surveyed was 31 (IQR, 27–38) (table 1). The majority were men (99.1%), Bangladeshi (67.7%) and employed in the construction industry (71.7%). Two per cent were unemployed (n = 11).

Comparing the Bangladeshi and non-Bangladeshi workers, the proportions of Bangladeshis who were single (OR 1.9, 95% CI 1.2 to 2.9) and supported ≥7 people (OR 6.96, 95% CI 3.12 to 15.5) were significantly higher. They were also more likely to work in the shipyard/marine industry (OR 2.80, 95% CI 1.45 to 5.38), were less likely to have received a postsecondary education (OR 0.46, 95% CI 0.30 to 0.71), had a lower median salary of SG$700 (IQR, 571–900; $p < 0.0001$) and paid higher amounts of agent fees.

Healthcare usage patterns and self-reported insurance coverage

Most workers had seen a doctor in Singapore before (83.8%), with Bangladeshi workers more likely to have performed so (OR 2.35, 95% CI 1.39 to 3.96), and to have visited four or more healthcare facilities in the past year (OR 2.14, 95% CI 1.38 to 3.31) (table 2). Only 61.4% of workers were certain they had medical insurance coverage, while 20.9% were unsure. Sixty-three per cent were unsure if their insurance covered outpatient expenses; 10% reported that their coverage excluded outpatient costs.

Barriers to healthcare and perception of healthcare financing

Twenty-two per cent of workers surveyed reported having ever experiencing financial barriers in accessing healthcare in Singapore (respondents answering in the affirmative to survey questions C1a, C1b or C1c, see online supplementary appendix A; indicated in table 3 as those who cited cost as a reason for ever (1) not seeking medical care, (2) avoiding referrals to a specialist/tertiary medical centre or (3) not filling a prescription). This was associated with having paid agent fees of >SG$10 000 ($p = 0.01$).

When asked whether any information was provided regarding their company-bought insurance policies, only 15.2% responded 'Yes'. Among these, 32.3% received it in their native languages. Bangladeshi workers were significantly less likely to receive this information (OR 0.49, 95% CI 0.29 to 0.84) and have it in their native language (OR 0.32, 95% CI 0.11 to 0.94).

More workers perceived that in the event of a hospitalisation, they would have to self-pay if it was not work injury-related (32%), than if the expenses were incurred from a work injury (6.8%). Fewer respondents (19.9%) reported insurance playing a role in the payment of non-work injury-related, compared with work injury-related (40.3%), expenses. Most workers (63%) were also unsure if their medical insurance covered outpatient costs.

A majority reported that their employers recognised sick leave in the form of medical certificates (MCs). However, 12.5% said that only MCs from their company doctors were accepted. In addition, 26.5% and 7.5% of workers reported that withholding and deduction, respectively, of daily wages (even with a valid sick/outpatient MC) was practiced in their company. The reported wage withholding and deduction rates for respondees with hospitalisation leave were 24.9%, and 4.5%, respectively.

Psychological distress

Twenty-two per cent of workers surveyed were at higher risk of psychological distress as indicated by a Kessler-6 (K6) score of ≥13. This was associated with age, nationality, employment status, basic monthly salary, amount of agent fees, type of entry visa and experience with financial barriers to healthcare (table 4). However, it was not associated with gender, number of people supported, marital status, highest education completed, working hours, number of rest days, duration in Singapore, current agent fees owed or presence of chronic medical problems.

Multiple logistic regression analysis showed that factors independently increasing the risk of psychological distress were Bangladeshi nationality (OR 2.98, 95% CI 1.58 to 5.62) and previous experience of financial barriers to healthcare (OR 3.86, 95% CI 2.25 to 6.62) (table 5). Online supplementary appendix B details the breakdown of K6 scores.

Table 1. Sociodemographic information of non-domestic migrant workers, HealthServe clinics and foreign worker dormitory, 23 July–28 August 2016*

Characteristic (number of respondents, n)	Bangladeshi† (N = 293)	Indian (N = 85)	Chinese (N = 52)	All (N = 433)	Bangladeshi vs non-Bangladeshi (reference category)†	
					p Value	OR (95% CI)
Age						
Median (IQR)	30 (26–35)	30 (26–36)	45 (41–49)	31 (27–38)	<0.0001‡	—
Gender						
Male, no. (%)	293 (100)	84 (99)	50 (96)	429 (99)	0.011§	—
Marital status (n = 432)						
Married, no. (%)	170 (58)	48 (57)	50 (96)	269 (62)	0.008	0.56 (0.36 to 0.86)
Single, no. (%)	123 (42)	36 (43)	1 (2)	162 (38)	0.005	1.9 (1.2 to 2.9)
Separated, no. (%)	0 (0)	0 (0)	1 (2)	1 (0.2)	0.32§	—
Number of people supported, median (IQR) (n = 431)	5 (4–7)	5 (3.5–5)	4 (2–4.8)	5 (4–6)	<0.0001‡	—
Number of people supported (n = 431)						
3 or less, no. (%)	54 (19)	21 (25)	24 (46)	100 (23)	0.001	0.47 (0.29 to 0.74)
4 to 6, no. (%)	159 (55)	61 (71)	24 (46)	246 (57)	0.11	0.73 (0.49 to 1.1)
7 or more, no. (%)	78 (27)	3 (4)	4 (8)	85 (20)	<0.0001	7.0 (3.1 to 16)
Work industry (n = 431)						
Construction, no. (%)	**208 (71)**	**61 (72)**	**40 (78)**	**309 (72)**	**0.76**	**0.93 (0.59 to 1.5)**

(Continued)

Table 1. (*Continued*)

Characteristic (number of respondents, n)	Bangladeshi† (N = 293)	Indian (N = 85)	Chinese (N = 52)	All (N = 433)	Bangladeshi vs non-Bangladeshi (reference category)†	
					p Value	OR (95% CI)
Shipyard/marine, no. (%)	61 (21)	11 (13)	1 (2)	73 (17)	0.002	2.8 (1.5 to 5.4)
Maintenance, no. (%)	14 (5)	11 (13)	2 (4)	28 (7)	0.038	0.45 (0.21 to 0.97)
Others¶, no. (%)	9 (3)	2 (2)	8 (16)	21 (5)	0.012	0.34 (0.14 to 0.82)
Currently unemployed, no. (%) (n = 433)	7 (2)	0 (0)	4 (8)	11 (3)	0.75§	0.83 (0.24 to 2.9)
Highest education completed (n = 433)						
Primary or less, no. (%)	31 (11)	9 (11)	9 (17)	49 (11)	0.48	0.80 (0.43 to 1.5)
Secondary, no. (%)	195 (67)	33 (39)	33 (64)	262 (61)	<0.0001	2.2 (1.4 to 3.3)
Postsecondary, no. (%)	67 (23)	43 (51)	10 (19)	122 (28)	<0.0001	0.46 (0.30 to 0.71)
Basic monthly salary (SG$), median (IQR) (n = 420)	700 (570.5–900)	800 (600–1000)	1950 (1600–2000)	800 (600–1000)	<0.0001‡	—
Average working hours/week, median (IQR) (n = 417)	60 (54–70)	60 (48–66)	64 (60–70)	60 (54–70)	0.34‡	—
Number of rest days/month, median (IQR) (n = 417)	4 (2–4)	4 (2–4)	4 (2–4)	4 (2–4)	0.11‡	—
Duration in Singapore (years), median (IQR) (n = 429)	6 (4–9)	6 (3–9)	5 (3.3–9)	6 (4–9)	0.21‡	—
Type of entry visa (n = 429)						
Work permit	279 (96)	80 (94)	42 (86)	403 (94)	0.041	2.3 (1.0 to 5.0)

S Pass	5 (2)	5 (6)	5 (10)	16 (4)	0.001	0.20 (0.07 to 0.59)
Special pass	6 (2)	0 (0)	2 (4)	8 (2)	1.00§	1.4 (0.28 to 7.1)
Multiple journey visa	2 (0.7)	0 (0)	0 (0)	2 (0.5)	1.00§	—
Amount of agent fees paid to come to Singapore, no. (%) (n = 421)						
None	29 (10)	8 (10)	7 (14)	45 (11)	0.68	0.87 (0.46 to 1.7)
SG$1000 and less	6 (2)	4 (5)	0 (0)	10 (2)	0.74§	0.73 (0.20 to 2.6)
SG$1001–SG$5000	123 (44)	61 (73)	26 (51)	211 (50)	<0.001	0.44 (0.29 to 0.66)
SG$5001–SG$10 000	98 (35)	10 (12)	13 (26)	122 (29)	<0.001	2.5 (1.5 to 4.2)
SG$10 001 and above	13 (5)	1 (1)	5 (10)	19 (5)	0.91	1.1 (0.39 to 2.9)
Unsure	14 (5)	0 (0)	0 (0)	14 (3)	0.006§	—
Current amount of agent fee owed, no. (%) (n = 421)						
None	232 (82)	61 (73)	48 (94)	344 (82)	0.84	1.1 (0.63 to 1.78)
SG$1000 and less	7 (2.5)	3 (4)	1 (2)	11 (3)	0.76§	0.85 (0.24 to 3.0)
SG$1001–SG$5000	27 (10)	10 (12)	1 (2)	38 (9)	0.60	1.2 (0.59 to 2.5)
SG$5001–SG$10 000	9 (3)	9 (11)	1 (2)	19 (5)	0.059	0.42 (0.17 to 1.1)
SG$10 001 and above	1 (0.4)	1 (1)	0 (0)	2 (0.5)	0.55§	0.49 (0.03 to 7.8)
Unsure	7 (2)	0 (0)	0 (0)	7 (2)	0.10§	—

*p Values by Pearson χ^2 test except otherwise indicated. Reference population used for p values and OR are non-Bangladeshis.

†Non-Bangladeshi group include Indians (n = 85), Chinese (n = 52), Malaysian (n = 1), Burmese (n = 1) and Vietnamese (n = 1). The χ^2 test/Fisher's exact test was performed comparing Bangladeshis versus non-Bangladeshis (the latter being the reference category).

‡p Values by independent-samples Hodges-Lehmann's median difference.

§p Values by Fisher's exact test.

¶Others include: gardening (n = 4), manufacturing (n = 3), food and beverages (n = 3), ad hoc workers (n = 2), other miscellaneous jobs (n = 9). SG$, Singapore dollars.

Table 2. Healthcare usage and self-reported insurance coverage of non-domestic migrant workers, HealthServe clinics and foreign worker dormitory, 23 July–28 August 2016*

Characteristic (number of respondents, n)	**Bangladeshi (N = 293)**	**Indian (N = 85)**	**Chinese (N = 52)**	**All (N = 433)**	**Bangladeshi vs non-Bangladeshi (reference category)†**	
					p Value	**OR (95% CI)**
No. seen by a doctor in Singapore before besides pre-employment examination (%) (n = 431)‡	256 (88)	60 (71)	44 (85)	362 (84)	0.001	2.4 (1.4 to 4.0)
Number of visits to healthcare facilities in the past year, no. (%) (n = 431)						
0	20 (7)	32 (38)	0 (0)	52 (12)	**<0.0001**	**0.59 (0.14 to 0.46)**
1	66 (23)	19 (22)	16 (31)	103 (24)	0.39	0.82 (0.51 to 1.3)
2	42 (14)	7 (8)	10 (19)	60 (14)	0.66	1.1 (0.63 to 2.1)
3	34 (12)	9 (11)	6 (12)	49 (11)	0.77	1.1 (0.58 to 2.1)
4 or more	129 (44)	18 (21)	20 (39)	167 (39)	0.001	2.1 (1.4 to 3.3)
Hospitalised before in Singapore, no. (%) (n = 432)	46 (16)	6 (7)	8 (15)	60 (14)	0.11	1.7 (0.89 to 3.2)
Has insurance, no. (%) (n = 430)						
Yes	172 (59)	55 (65)	36 (71)	264 (61)	0.46	0.81 (0.47 to 1.4)
No	53 (18)	11 (13)	11 (22)	76 (18)		
Unsure§	66 (23)	19 (22)	4 (8)	90 (21)		

Insurance covers for inpatient expenses, no. (%) (n = 354¶)						
Yes	96 (40)	26 (35)	10 (25)	132 (37)	1.0**	0.53 (0.06 to 4.7)
No	5 (2)	0 (0)	1 (3)	6 (2)		
Unsure§	137 (58)	48 (65)	29 (73)	216 (61)		
Insurance covers for outpatient expenses, no. (%) (n = 354¶)						
Yes	70 (29)	20 (27)	6 (15)	96 (27)	0.88	0.93 (0.39 to 2.3)
No	26 (11)	6 (8)	3 (8)	35 (10)		
Unsure§	142 (60)	48 (65)	31 (78)	223 (63)		

*p Values by Pearson χ^2 test except otherwise indicated. Reference population used for p values and OR are non-Bangladeshis.
†Non-Bangladeshi group include Indians (n = 85), Chinese (n = 52), Malaysian (n = 1), Burmese (n = 1) and Vietnamese (n = 1). The χ^2 test was performed comparing Bangladeshis versus non-Bangladeshis (the latter being the reference category). This section consists of questions to which answers were 'Yes', 'No' and 'Unsure' except when stated otherwise. 'Unsure' responses were not included in the statistical analysis.
‡These include healthcare visits to public and private hospitals/clinics, specialist centres like the National Skin Centre and other non-profit clinics.
¶Excluded those who answered that they have no insurance (n = 76).
§'Unsure' responses were not included in the χ^2 test.
**p Values by Fisher's exact test.

Table 3. Barriers to healthcare and self-reported perception of payment of inpatient expenses among non-domestic migrant workers, HealthServe clinics and foreign worker dormitory, 23 July–28 August 2016*

Characteristic (number of respondents, n)	Bangladeshi (N = 281)	Indian (N = 84)	Chinese (N = 51)	All (N = 419)	Bangladeshi vs non-Bangladeshi (reference category)† p Value	OR (95% CI)
Did not seek medical care because of cost (n = 432)						
Yes	57 (20)	9 (11)	14 (27)	81 (19)	0.58	1.2 (0.69 to 2.0)
No	235 (81)	75 (88)	38 (73)	350 (81)		
Unsure‡	0 (0)	1 (1)	0 (0)	1 (0.2)		
Did not get prescription medications because of cost (n = 432)						
Yes	34 (12)	3 (4)	10 (19)	47 (11)	0.47	1.3 (0.65 to 2.5)
No	257 (88)	82 (97)	41 (79)	383 (89)		
Unsure‡	1 (0.3)	0 (0)	1 (2)	2 (0.5)		
Did not get specialist care or referral to tertiary hospital because of cost (n = 432)						
Yes	40 (14)	5 (6)	10 (19)	56 (13)	0.50	1.2 (0.67 to 2.3)
No	249 (85)	80 (94)	41 (79)	372 (86)		
Unsure‡	3 (1)	0 (0)	1 (2)	4 (0.9)		
Insurance policy/information provided (n = 429)						
Yes	34 (12)	23 (27)	8 (16)	65 (15)	0.009	0.49 (0.29 to 0.84)
No	215 (74)	55 (65)	38 (79)	311 (73)		
Unsure‡	41 (14)	7 (8)	5 (10)	53 (12)		
Insurance information in native language§ (n = 65)						
Yes	7 (20)	12 (52)	2 (25)	21 (32)	0.034	0.32 (0.11 to 0.94)

No	27 (79)	11 (48)	6 (75)	44 (68)		
Who pays for work-related injury hospitalisations¶ (n = 429)						
Self only	16 (6)	2 (2)	10 (20)	29 (7)	0.16	0.58 (0.27 to 1.2)
Insurance has role	125 (43)	29 (34)	18 (35)	173 (40)	0.10	1.4 (0.93 to 2.2)
Unsure‡	15 (5)	2 (2)	2 (4)	19 (4)	—	—
Who pays for non-work injury-related hospitalisations¶ (n = 428)						
Self only	82 (28)	19 (22)	35 (69)	137 (32)	0.018	0.59 (0.38 to 0.92)
Insurance has role	64 (22)	16 (19)	4 (8)	85 (20)	0.08	1.6 (0.94 to 2.8)
Unsure‡	30 (10)	6 (7)	8 (16)	44 (10)	—	—
Employer recognises MC from company doctor (n = 256)**						
Yes	163 (90)	53 (96)	12 (63)	229 (90)	1.0††	0.71 (0.14 to 3.5)
No	7 (4)	1 (2)	1 (5)	9 (4)		
Unsure‡	11 (6)	1 (2)	6 (32)	18(7)		
Employer recognises MC from private general practitioner (n = 427)						
Yes	209 (73)	67 (79)	29 (57)	307 (72)	0.73	0.91 (0.53 to 1.6)
No	54 (19)	12 (14)	11 (22)	77 (18)		
Unsure‡	25 (9)	6 (7)	11 (22)	43 (10)		
Employer recognises MC from HealthServe clinic (n = 427)						
Yes	194 (67)	59 (69)	27 (53)	282 (66)	0.49	0.82 (0.46 to 1.5)
No	54 (19)	9 (11)	11 (22)	74 (17)		
Unsure‡	40 (14)	17 (20)	13 (26)	71 (17)		
Employer recognises MC from government polyclinic/hospital (n = 427)						
Yes	**236 (82)**	**71 (84)**	**31 (61)**	**340 (80)**	**0.57**	**1.2 (0.62 to 2.4)**

(Continued)

Table 3. *(Continued)*

Characteristic (number of respondents, n)	Bangladeshi (N = 281)	Indian (N = 84)	Chinese (N = 51)	All (N = 419)	Bangladeshi vs non-Bangladeshi (reference category)†	
					p Value	OR (95% CI)
No	28 (10)	8 (9)	7 (14)	43 (10)		
Unsure‡	24 (8)	6 (7)	13 (26)	44 (10)		
Only MCs from company doctors are accepted (n = 255)**						
Yes	24 (13)	7 (13)	1 (5)	32 (13)	0.67	1.2 (0.51 to 2.8)
No	137 (76)	45 (82)	10 (53)	192 (75)		
Unsure‡	19 (11)	3 (6)	8 (42)	31 (12)		
Daily wages held if on sick/outpatient MC (n = 426)						
Yes	68 (24)	17 (20)	28 (55)	113 (27)	0.025	0.60 (0.38 to 0.94)
No	208 (73)	62 (73)	18 (35)	290 (68)		
Unsure‡	11 (4)	6 (7)	5 (10)	23 (5)		
Daily wages held if on hospitalisation MC (n = 426)						
Yes	69 (24)	11 (13)	26 (51)	106 (25)	0.37	0.81 (0.50 to 1.3)
No	192 (67)	64 (75)	18 (35)	275 (65)		
Unsure‡	26 (9)	10 (12)	7 (14)	45 (11)		
Had pay deducted even with sick/outpatient MC (n = 426)						
Yes	22 (8)	4 (5)	6 (12)	32 (8)	0.92	1.0 (0.48 to 2.3)
No	258 (90)	78 (92)	42 (82)	380 (89)		
Unsure‡	7 (2)	3 (4)	3 (6)	14 (3)		

Had pay deducted even with hospitalisation MC (n = 425)						
Yes	12 (4)	1 (1)	6 (12)	19 (5)	0.67	0.81 (0.31 to 2.1)
No	259 (91)	81 (95)	40 (78)	382 (90)		
Unsure‡	15 (5)	3 (4)	5 (10)	24 (6)		
Knows someone with pay deducted even with sick/outpatient MC (n = 424)						
Yes	55 (19)	6 (7)	10 (20)	71 (17)	0.043	1.9 (1.0 to 3.4)
No	208 (73)	75 (88)	35 (69)	320 (76)		
Unsure‡	22 (8)	4 (5)	6 (12)	33 (8)		
Knows someone with pay deducted even with hospitalisation MC (n = 423)						
Yes	38 (13)	4 (5)	8 (16)	50 (12)	0.14	1.7 (0.84 to 3.3)
No	218 (77)	77 (91)	36 (71)	333 (79)		
Unsure‡	28 (10)	4 (5)	7 (14)	40 (10)		
Afraid of losing job or being sent home if fall sick (n = 422)						
Yes	76 (27)	9 (11)	12 (24)	97 (23)	0.010	2.0 (1.8 to 3.4)
No	202 (71)	72 (86)	38 (75)	315 (74)		
Unsure‡	6 (2)	3 (4)	1 (2)	10 (2)		

*p Values by Pearson χ^2 test except otherwise indicated. Reference population used for p values and OR are non-Bangladeshis. This section consists of questions to which answers were 'Yes', 'No' and 'Unsure' except when stated otherwise. 'Unsure' responses were not included in the statistical analysis. MC, medical certificate.

†Non-Bangladeshi group include Indians (n = 85), Chinese (n = 52), Malaysian (n = 1), Burmese (n = 1) and Vietnamese (n = 1).

‡'Unsure' responses were not included in the χ^2 test.

§Three hundred and sixty-five who answered 'No' and 'Unsure' to having been provided a copy of their health insurance policy were excluded.

¶Respondents were given scenarios and asked for who (among company, insurance and self) they thought was responsible for payment of medical bills, multiple selections were allowed.

**One hundred and seventy-one respondents who have no company doctor were excluded.

††p Values by Fisher's exact test.

Table 4. Characteristics of non-domestic migrant workers with psychological distress assessed by Kessler-6 score of 13 or higher, HealthServe clinics and foreign worker dormitory, 23 July–28 August 2016*

Characteristic (number of respondents, n)	Kessler-6 score of 13 or higher (N = 92, 21.9%)	Kessler-6 score of 12 or lower (reference group) (N = 328, 78.1%)	p Value	OR (95% CI)
Age, median (IQR) (n = 420)	29.5 (26.0, 34.5)	32.0 (27.0, 38.5)	0.047†	—
Gender, no. (%) (n = 420)				
Male	91 (99)	325 (99)	1.0‡	0.84 (0.09 to 8.2)
Nationality, no. (%) (n = 420)				
Bangladeshi	75 (82)	208 (63)	0.001	2.6 (1.4 to 4.5)
Indian	8 (9)	75 (23)	0.003	0.32 (0.15 to 0.70)
Chinese	9 (10)	42 (13)	0.43	0.74 (0.35 to 1.6)
Others	0 (0)	3 (0.9)	1.00‡	—
Marital status, no. (%) (n = 419)				
Married	59 (64)	201 (62)	0.64	1.1 (0.69 to 1.8)
Single	33 (36)	125 (38)	0.68	0.90 (0.56 to 1.5)
Separated	0 (0)	1 (0.3)	1.00‡	—
Number supported, median (IQR) (n = 418)	5 (4, 6)	5 (4, 6)	0.91	—
Work industry, no. (%) (n = 418)				
Construction	66 (73)	234 (71)	0.71	1.1 (0.65 to 1.9)
Shipyard	18 (20)	52 (16)	0.35	1.3 (0.73 to 2.4)
Maintenance	4 (4)	24 (7)	0.33	0.59 (0.20 to 1.7)
Others	2 (2)	18 (6)	0.27‡	0.39 (0.09 to 1.7)
Unemployed (n = 420)	8 (9)	1 (0.3)	<0.0001‡	31 (3.84 to 253)
Highest education completed, no. (%) (n = 420)				
Primary	11 (12)	37 (11)	0.86	1.1 (0.52 to 2.2)
Secondary	58 (63)	196 (60)	0.57	1.2 (0.71 to 1.9)
Postsecondary	23 (25)	95 (29)	0.46	0.82 (0.48 to 1.4)
Basic monthly salary(SG$), median (IQR) (n = 409)	700 (546.5, 900)	800 (600, 1100)	0.10†	—

Average working hours a week, median (IQR) (n = 407)	60 (54, 71)	60 (52, 70)	0.46†	—
Number of rest days/month, median (IQR) (n = 407)	4 (2, 4)	4 (2, 4)	0.26†	—
Duration in Singapore, years, median (IQR) (n = 417)	6 (4, 9)	6 (3, 9)	0.85†	—
Agent fees (SG$), no. (%) (n = 420)				
None	8 (9)	37 (11)	0.48	0.75 (0.34 to 1.7)
1000 and less	2 (2)	8 (2)	0.88	0.89 (0.19 to 4.3)
1001–5000	40 (44)	170 (53)	0.16	0.72 (0.46 to 1.1)
5001–10 000	29 (32)	93 (28)	0.55	1.2 (0.71 to 1.9)
10 001 and above	9 (10)	10 (3)	0.011‡	3.5 (1.4 to 9.8)
Current amount owed (SG$), no. (%) (n = 420)				
None	71 (77)	272 (83)	0.21	0.70 (0.40 to 1.2)
1000 and less	2 (2)	9 (3)	1.00‡	0.79 (0.17 to 3.7)
1001–5000	11 (12)	27 (8)	0.27	1.5 (0.72 to 3.2)
5001–10 000	5 (5)	14 (4)	0.58‡	1.3 (0.45 to 3.7)
10 001 and above	1 (1)	1 (0.3)	0.39‡	3.6 (0.22 to 58)
Type of entry visa, no. (%) (n = 417)				
Work permit	82 (89)	311 (96)	0.017	0.37 (0.16 to 0.86)
S Pass	4 (4)	12 (4)	0.76‡	1.2 (0.37 to 3.8)
Special pass	6 (7)	0 (0)	<0.0001‡	—
Multiple journey visa	0 (0)	2 (0.6)	1.00‡	—
Chronic medical problems, no. (%) (n = 419)				
Yes	10 (11)	24 (7)	0.26	1.6 (0.72 to 3.4)
Financial barriers reported§, no. (%) (n = 420)				
Yes	39 (42)	54 (17)	<0.001	3.7 (2.3 to 6.2)

*p Values by Pearson χ^2 test. Reference population used for p values and OR are those with Kessler-6 score 12 or less.

†p Values by independent-samples Hodges-Lehmann's median difference test.

‡p Values by Fisher's exact test.

§Respondents who answered 'Yes' to the following questions: during your time in Singapore, was there any time when, because of cost (a) you did not seek medical care; (b) needed prescription medications but did not get them or (c) needed specialist care but did not do so?

SG$, Singapore dollars.

Table 5. Multiple logistic regression model for risk factors associated with psychological distress as measured by Kessler-6 score 13 or more among non-domestic migrant workers*

Variable	Coefficient (β)	SE	p Value	OR (95% CI)
Nationality (Bangladeshi†)	1.09	0.32	0.001	3.0 (1.6 to 5.6)
Financial barriers reported‡	1.35	0.28	<0.0001	3.9 (2.3 to 6.6)

*Variables included in backward stepwise logistic regression analysis: age, nationality, unemployed status, basic monthly salary, amount of agent fees paid, type of entry visa, financial barriers. This model was well fitted with a Hosmer–Lemeshow statistic of 0.97.

†Bangladeshi versus non-Bangladeshi (reference group).

‡Respondents who answered 'yes' to the following questions: During your time in Singapore, was there any time when, because of cost (a) you did not seek medical care; (b) needed prescription medications but did not get them or (c) needed specialist care but did not do so?

Discussion

A substantial number of workers appeared to have poor understanding of healthcare expenses financing. Despite policies protecting migrant workers financially in the event of hospitalisation,[11] many workers still thought that they had no insurance, or were expected to pay the bills completely. Many had misconceptions that insurance cannot cover non-work-related hospitalisations. Furthermore, it appears that a majority of the workers surveyed were unclear about the payment of outpatient medical bills, in particular whether this was covered by their insurance policies. Current medical insurance guidelines for employers of migrant workers in Singapore stipulate a coverage of SG$15 000/year to cover inpatient care and day surgery, including hospital bills for conditions that may not be work-related,[19] but are silent on outpatient coverage.

A possible cause for the deficiencies in knowledge is the widespread practice by employers of not providing information on insurance policies. Even when provided, this was rarely in their native language. Bangladeshis were most commonly affected by this in our study. This is not surprising as the native languages of the two other large ethnic groups of non-Bangladeshi migrant workers, Tamil (for most Indian migrant workers) and Mandarin (for Chinese migrant workers), are official languages in Singapore.

Overall rates of psychological distress (21.9%) were slightly higher than what was previously found among non-injury or salary claim workers (13%).[13] Only 3% of our survey population were unemployed (eg, due to an injury-claim). In addition, we identified Bangladeshi nationality and previous financial barriers to healthcare to be independent significant risk factors. Though payment of a high agent fee was a variable identified in our univariate analysis and Harrigan *et al*,[13] it was not statistically significant in our multivariate model.

The Bangladeshi workers surveyed, who were three times as likely to have a Kessler score ≥13, had other significant differences from workers of other nationalities, including lower salary and educational levels, more financial dependents and higher agent fees. Lower salaries and having to financially support more people were previously identified by Lee *et al*[17] as risk factors for not seeking care within 3 days of illness, though nationality was not an independent risk factor. In our study, although Bangladeshi workers appear to have risk factors for not seeking care, they were a group which sought healthcare more frequently. This could be due to their cultural influences on illness beliefs, or a greater level of anxiety over health problems, as a manifestation of the greater psychological distress faced by this group.

Another factor relating to psychological distress (Kessler Score ≥13) was the presence of financial barriers to healthcare (OR, 3.8). Almost a fifth of respondents reported having ever not sought care because of cost. In 2008, the Ministry of Manpower, Singapore, introduced compulsory medical insurance for migrant workers. In 2010, the minimum coverage for medical insurance (inpatient and day surgery) was raised from SG$5000 to SG$15 000/year. While these represent positive improvements in healthcare coverage for migrant workers, our findings suggest that significant gaps may remain. While not directly addressed by our study, feedback from various stakeholders (migrants, non-governmental organisations and healthcare providers) indicates that a significant proportion of migrants (especially those with chronic illnesses) do not have outpatient insurance coverage, and may not be able to afford outpatient medical fees. In addition, the ceiling of SG$15 000 for inpatient/day-surgery fees may be easily breached in the event of catastrophic illness/injury. These factors, along with concern over losing their job/repatriation in the event of illness,[17] may contribute to reluctance to seek medical care. Future studies should explore in greater depth the healthcare economics among low-wage migrant workers in Singapore.

Lee *et al*[17] found that a perception of inadequate finances hindered healthcare access (specifically, self-reported health-seeking behaviour) among male migrant workers. We found a significant degree of initial and current indebtedness incurred due to agent fees among migrant workers in our study. Indebtedness (specifically, agent fees >SG$10 000) was associated with self-reported financial barriers to seeking healthcare and poorer mental health (as indicated by a Kessler-6 score of >13) on univariate analysis. Our findings that self-reported financial barriers had a significant effect on mental health (multivariate analysis, $p < 0.0001$) corroborate those from recent survey by H.O.M.E, a Singapore-based non-governmental organisation for migrant workers, which found that debt significantly affected the mental health of Filipino migrant domestic workers.[20] Debt-financed migration adds to the inherent precarity associated with migrant labour,[21] impedes health-seeking behaviour and adds to mental stress faced by migrant workers.

Regarding sick leave policies, 12.5% of workers with company doctors said that their employer only recognised medical leave from their company doctors. According to employment regulations for work permit holders in Singapore, all sick leave must be endorsed by a company or a government (public institution) doctor. Salary deductions are permissible for unauthorised absence from work or if sick leave is not authorised and the employer suffers loss as a result (eg, from having to employ a replacement). This sometimes leads to a conflict in the doctor–patient relationship (eg, authorising an inadequate duration of sick leave) when there is a contractual relationship (formal or otherwise) between healthcare providers and the employer.[22] In our study, 26.5% and 24.9% of migrant workers reported that their daily wages were not paid, for outpatient and hospitalisation sick leave, respectively, even if they had documentation from a doctor (whether company, government or others). A further 7.6% (with outpatient sick leave) and 4.5% (with hospitalisation leave) reported having salary deductions (on top of wages being withheld for day(s) of absence).

Limitations

First, as we surveyed mostly healthy workers who never faced catastrophic illnesses, our study may not represent the full spectrum of healthcare experiences and beliefs of migrant workers. In addition, most of those surveyed had access to low-cost outpatient care at HealthServe clinics; potentially biasing (underestimating) responses about care limitations and healthcare usage patterns. However, interviewing workers in this setting, without the presence of employers, provided a more private setting for respondents to be open in sharing their experiences.

In addition, there could be some degree of interinterviewer bias, and misinterpretation due to language barriers. These were minimised by having translated surveys, and interpreters were available during the conduct of the survey. Training and supervision for interviewers were also provided.

There were no validated Tamil and Bengali translations of the Kessler-6 scale available which may affect the assessment of psychological distress. We sought to overcome this limitation by having our translated versions independently verified by native-speakers.

Finally, this study was conducted in Singapore, which is a high-income, non-OECD country. Facets of the migrant healthcare experience described in this study might be specific to Singapore; however, we believe that the Singapore experience might mirror other midincome to high-income receiving countries.

Implications

Our results reflect a degree of information asymmetry which can result in workers avoiding seeking care, or preferring to be repatriated for fear of unaffordable healthcare. This is a possible area where intervention to increase policy awareness could be carried out. In addition, we identified subgroups of migrant workers at higher risk of poor mental health, for which further research is needed to determine root causes and effects. Self-reported rates of errant practices (eg, salary withholding or deductions despite outpatient or hospitalisation leave) potentially highlight an area where tighter enforcement is necessary. Based on findings from our study, we propose several key areas policymakers in sending and receiving countries, healthcare providers and other non-governmental organisations should focus on to improve migrant health (table 6).

Table 6. Suggested priority areas for study and interventions to improve migrant health and deliver

Area	Notes
1. Migrant worker indebtedness and job security	▸ Improving regulatory framework and transparency in the sending countries vis-à-vis the application process and related fees for prospective migrant workers seeking jobs ▸ Receiving countries, in collaboration with sending countries, may consider direct-hiring, or hiring via more regulated process(es) ▸ Improve protective framework for the job security of migrant workers, including protection from arbitrary repatriation/dismissal, lack of income while awaiting case settlement/after loss of work permit and improved avenues for redress
2. Migrant worker healthcare coverage	▸ Improve migrant worker knowledge about healthcare coverage. Specifically they should be provided information, in their native language, re: specifics of company-bought medical insurance coverage ▸ Improve clarity in, and enforcement of, what constitutes lawful (and unlawful) salary deductions by employers ▸ Expanding regulatory guidance for compulsory insurance coverage to cover outpatient visits and procedures beyond day surgery ▸ Insurers may consider expanding insurance coverage for migrant workers, for example, by voluntary purchase of riders which raise coverage ceilings. These are anticipated to be especially helpful in the event of catastrophic illness ▸ Migrant workers contribute to the economy of sending and receiving countries. While in many countries, they are not included in the universal healthcare coverage afforded to citizens, policymakers/regulators may consider creating alternate parallel health systems for low-wage migrant workers
3. Migrant worker mental health	▸ Specific subgroups of migrant workers may be at risk of mental health issues and other healthcare barriers, and should be the focus of further research and interventions

Although the focus of this study was on healthcare accessibility and mental health, we recognise that there are other factors, such as beliefs, lifestyle and preventive measures, which influence population health. Further work should be performed on these other health determinants in migrant workers.

Conclusions

We identified potential barriers to healthcare among low-wage non-domestic migrant workers in Singapore. These include knowledge gaps and financial barriers. The reasons for these are probably multifaceted and merit further study. The Bangladeshi workers in our study are possibly at higher risk of psychological distress and poor knowledge, and might represent a more vulnerable subgroup for intervention.

Author Affiliations

[1]Lee Kong Chian School of Medicine, Nanyang Technological University, Singapore
[2]HealthServe Community Clinic, Singapore
[3]Division of Gastroenterology and Hepatology, National University Hospital, National University Health System, Singapore
[4]Department of Pharmacy, KK Women's and Children's Hospital, Singapore
[5]Department of Pharmacy, Singapore General Hospital, Singapore
[6]Department of Infectious Diseases, Singapore General Hospital, Singapore
[7]Department of Psychiatry, Tan Tock Seng Hospital, Singapore
[8]Department of Infectious Diseases, Institute of Infectious Diseases and Epidemiology, Tan Tock Seng Hospital, Singapore

Handling Editor

Seye Abimbola.

Acknowledgements

The authors would like to thank the volunteers who helped to administer this survey: From the Class of 2018–2021, the Lee Kong Chian School of Medicine, Aishwarya Narayanan, Ang Wee Kiat, Chew Yi Rong, Claudia Tong Ren Hwee, Joel Wong, Joshua Tan, Kiang Wen Wei, Justin Liu Shuang, Melissa Chia, Moses Ko, Poon Yee Jun, Toh Wen Shien, Wong Chun Jie and Yap Hong Wan; Volunteers from HealthServe: Carissa Lim, Christine Toh, Colin Seow, Lim Kang Le, Lim Ying Fu, Ruthra, Seow Han Cong, Shane Wu, Sherilyn Chew, Sumitha Grace Pandjaraja, Utthra, Wong Kit Yarn and Yi Xin. The authors also record their thanks to Musfiqul Islam, Dong Muyun and Manavala Reuben for translating the survey into Bengali, Mandarin and Tamil, respectively, and also the staff and volunteers of HealthServe for their support for this study. Above all, the authors acknowledge and thank the migrant workers who participated in this survey, without whom this study would not have been possible.

Contributors

JWA and SV designed the study and survey questions, managed the data set, performed the statistical analysis and wrote the first and subsequent drafts of the report. CC, BWBC, SN, LGC WLG, CJK and LW contributed to the study and survey design, reviewed and commented on the drafts of the report. CC and WLG facilitated the conduct of the survey at the HealthServe clinic and its outreach programme. All authors approved the final submitted version of the manuscript. SV had full access to all the data in the study and assumes final responsibility for the decision to submit for publication.

Competing Interests

None declared.

Ethics Approval

National Healthcare Group Domain Specific Review Board F.

Provenance and Peer Review

Not commissioned; externally peer reviewed.

Data Sharing Statement

The data collected from the surveys described in this manuscript can be shared by the authors on request.

Open Access

References

1. United Nations, Department of Economic and Social Affairs, Population Division. Population Facts. Trends in international migration, 2015. Dec 2015; No. 2015/4. http://www.un.org/en/development/desa/population/migration/publications/populationfacts/docs/MigrationPopFacts20154.pdf (accessed 1 Mar 2017).
2. World Bank Group, Global Knowledge Partnership on Migration and Development. Migration and remittances fact book: 2016. 3rd edn. http://siteresources.worldbank.org/INTPROSPECTS/Resources/334934-1199807908806/4549025-1450455807487/Factbookpart1.pdf (accessed 1 Mar 2017).
3. United Nations, Transforming our world: the 2030 Agenda for Sustainable Development. https://sustainabledevelopment.un.org/post2015/transformingourworld (accessed 30 Sep 2016).
4. Yap MT, Koh G, Soon D, *et al*. *Migration and integration in Singapore: policies and practice*. Chapter 1, Immigration and intergration in Singapore, Page 27. London, New York: Routledge, 2015.

5. Ministry of Manpower, Singapore. Foreign Workforce Numbers. 2016. http://www.mom.gov.sg/documents-and-publications/foreign-workforce-numbers (accessed 10 Sep 2016).
6. Amrith SS. Migration and health in Southeast Asian history. *Lancet* 2014;384:1569–70.
7. Ngo CS, Leo SW. Industrial accident-related ocular emergencies in a tertiary hospital in Singapore. *Singapore Med J* 2008;49:280–5.
8. Ong VYK, Habibah AK, Lee FCY. Safety among foreign workers and impact on emergency medicine services in Singapore. *Singapore Med J* 2006;47:121–8.
9. Lee GK, Tan KW, Goh KT, *et al.* Trends in importation of communicable diseases into Singapore. *Ann Acad Med Singapore* 2010;39:764–70.
10. Guinto RLLR, Curran UZ, Suphanchaimat R, *et al.* Universal health coverage in 'One ASEAN': are migrants included? *Glob Health Action* 2015;8:25749.
11. Ministry of Manpower, Singapore. Employment of Foreign Manpower (Work Passes) Regulations. 2015. http://www.mom.gov.sg/legislation/employment-of-foreign-manpower-act (accessed 10 Sep 2016).
12. Ministry of Manpower, Singapore. Work Injury Compensation Act Singapore. 2009. http://www.mom.gov.sg/workplace-safety-and-health/work-injury-compensation (accessed 10 Sep 2016).
13. Harrigan N, Koh CY. *Vital Yet Vulnerable: Mental and Emotional Health of South Asian Migrant Workers in Singapore*. Research Collection School of Social Sciences. Paper 1764. 2015. https://centres.smu.edu.sg/lien/files/2012/03/Vital-Yet-Vulnerable.pdf (accessed 30 Sep 2016).
14. Graham E, Jordan LP. Migrant parents and the psychological well-being of left-behind children in Southeast Asia. *J Marriage Fam* 2011;73:763–87.
15. Wickramage K, Siriwardhana C, Vidanapathirana P, *et al.* Risk of mental health and nutritional problems for left-behind children of international labor migrants. *BMC Psychiatry* 2015;15:39.
16. Meyer SR, Robinson WC, Chhim S, *et al.* Labor migration and mental health in Cambodia: a qualitative study. *J Nerv Ment Dis* 2014;202:200–8.
17. Lee W, Neo A, Tan S, *et al.* Health-seeking behaviour of male foreign migrant workers living in a dormitory in Singapore. *BMC Health Serv Res* 2014;14:300.
18. Kessler RC, Barker PR, Colpe LJ, *et al.* Screening for serious mental illness in the general population. *Arch Gen Psychiatry* 2003;60:184–9.

19. Ministry of Manpower, Singapore. Medical insurance requirements for foreign worker. http://www.mom.gov.sg/passes-and-permits/work-permit-for-foreign-worker/sector-specific-rules/medical-insurance (accessed 10 Sep 2016).
20. Humanitarian Organisation for Migration Economics (H.O.M.E.). 'Home sweet home? Work, life and well-being of foreign domestic workers in Singapore'. Research Report. 2015. http://www.home.org.sg/wp-content/uploads/2015/07/HOME_2015_Home-sweet-home_short.pdf (accessed 20 Dec 2016).
21. Platt M, Baey G, Yeoh BSA, *et al.* Debt, precarity and gender: male and female temporary labour migrants in Singapore. *J Ethn Migr Stud* 2016;43:119–36.
22. TODAY. Doc suspended over inadequate MCs for foreign worker. 12 May 2016. http://www.todayonline.com/singapore/landmark-ruling-against-doctor-ngos-say-inadequate-mcsmigrant-workers-still-problem (accessed 1 Oct 2016).

Section III

Social Connections, Personal Lives

Chapter 8a

Urban Liveability and Low-wage Migrants in Pandemic Times*

Tim Bunnell

Department of Geography
National University of Singapore

Laavanya Kathiravelu

Division of Sociology
Nanyang Technological University

The outbreak of COVID-19 in migrant worker dormitories across Singapore has brought issues of everyday liveability as well as the larger structural conditions under which migrants' labour has come under sharp scrutiny. What has been impossible to ignore is that the well-being of this migrant group is intrinsically connected to the larger public health of the nation-state [Kathiravelu, 2020]. Yet, the urban experience of pandemic has been divergent, disconnected, and differentiated by socio-economic and immigration status, signalled by the distinctions drawn between these 'migrant dormitories' and the larger 'community.'

---

*Reflections on Bunnell, T. and Kathiravelu, L. (2016). Extending urban liveability: Friendship and sociality in the lives of low-wage migrants, *Int. Dev. Plan. Rev.*, Vol. 38, No. 2, pp. 201–220. DOI: 10.3828/idpr.2016.12.

This paper, published in 2016, was driven by a desire to see official discourses of 'liveability' applied equally to all city inhabitants, and not just those deemed highly-valued and skilled migrants. Because COVID-19 has exposed how far we are from such an ideal vision of equality, the pandemic is an important point for revisiting the factors that make low-wage migrant workers' lives more 'liveable.' The concerns of this paper are thus even more exigent within the changed context of living and working conditions for migrant men. We suggest its continued relevance in three aspects.

Firstly, our paper's focus on the importance of affective and emotional social networks is even more prescient now that mental health issues of physically isolated migrant men in locked down dormitories have come to light as important and urgent concerns [Phua and Min, 2020]. This chapter points to the need to invest in strengthening migrants' own networks and social capital. There are high levels of trust within the migrant community, particularly within co-ethnic groups of friends. These networks of trust and friendship are almost always the first points of contact for migrant workers when seeking information about keeping safe from potential infection, or seeking emotional and psychological support. They can serve as key resources in empowering the migrant community to better cope with the effects of the pandemic; whether it is in normalizing the adoption of new social distancing habits or acting as informal support groups.

Secondly, our paper finds that investing in the infrastructures of friendship and sociality for low-wage migrants is significant in generating positive outcomes in terms of liveability for this group. In response to the pandemic, issues concerning migrants' health and living conditions have been primarily relegated to discussions of the materiality of residential spaces, such as amount of floor space per migrant worker within dormitories. Our findings, however, suggest that such discussions should be expanded to include considerations of migrants' freedom of mobility within the city, in ways that do not isolate migrants further and preclude them from interactions with other urban residents.

Finally, this contribution demonstrates that the possibilities of building stronger and more cohesive cities lie in the ability to foster a 'culture of hospitality.' Collective wells of sympathy are so important in providing spaces for low-wage and marginalized migrants to develop solidarities with the wider public. These swelled during the initial stages of the pandemic with the increased awareness of the difficulties that low-wage migrant men face. Our paper suggests that developing such civic pride in being welcoming of distant others fosters a sense of collective responsibility for shared urban futures. As we pointed out in our paper, friendships and migrant hospitality can be a resource for a city's liveability. Urban spaces that foster conviviality, friendship, and hospitality towards migrants can cross the social divides that separate local residents and migrant groups. These resonate with ideas of shared spaces — including urban spaces — as sites of difference and encounter [Valentine, 2008], but also for potential sociality and meaningful relationships. In pandemic times, a culture of hospitality and welcome towards migrant workers can also strengthen a city's collective response to a crisis.

References

Kathiravelu, L. (2020, 11 November). COVID-19 exposes the Singapore migrant worker experience. *East Asia Forum*. Retrieved from https://www.eastasiaforum.org/2020/11/11/covid-19-exposes-the-singapore-migrant-worker-experience/

Phua, R. and Min, A. H. (2020, 12 September). In focus: The long challenging journey to bring COVID-19 under control in migrant worker dormitories. *ChannelNewsAsia*. Retrieved from https://www.channelnewsasia.com/news/singapore/in-focus-covid19-singapore-migrant-worker-dormitories-lockdown-13081210

Valentine, G. (2008). Living with difference: Reflections on geographies of encounter, *Progress in Human Geography*, Vol. 32, No. 3, pp. 323–337. DOI:10.1177/0309133308089372

Chapter 8b

Extending Urban Liveability: Friendship and Sociality in the Lives of Low-wage Migrants*

Tim Bunnell† and Laavanya Kathiravelu

'Liveability' continues to attract considerable attention internationally, in the media, among urban policymakers and from academics. In this paper, we extend consideration of liveability beyond the elite, professional migrants who are the primary target of inter-urban competition to low-wage migrants in two different urban contexts in Asia. Drawing upon narratives of South Asian men in Dubai and Singapore, we highlight friendship and sociality as vital components of quality of life – in emotional and affective as well as practical or material terms. We highlight investments in spaces, times and technologies of friendship, and also in cultures of welcome and hospitality, as key ways of extending urban liveability. While recognising important critiques of liveability as

*This article was originally published in *Int. Dev. Plan. Rev.*, Vol. 38, No. 2, pp. 201–220. DOI: 10.3828/idpr.2016.12.

†Tim Bunnell is Associate Professor in the Department of Geography at the National University of Singapore, 1 Arts Link, Kent Ridge, Singapore 117570; Laavanya Kathiravelu is Assistant Professor at Nanyang Technological University, Division of Sociology, HSS 05–45, 14 Nanyang Drive, Singapore 637332; email: geotgb@nus.edu.sg; laavanyak@ntu.edu.sg

seemingly irredeemably bound up with neoliberal inter-urban competition, we consider how such competitiveness and the 'discursive power' (McCann, 2004) of liveability may be steered towards the making of more welcoming and friendly cities.

Keywords: liveability, friendship, sociality, migration, Asia, ethnography, cities

Introduction

City authorities in Asia, as in many other regions of the world, have become increasingly concerned with issues of liveability. In part, the relatively new attention being given to the idea of 'liveable cities' in Asia is to be welcomed as a corrective to strictly economic pursuits, particularly in contexts that experienced environmental degradation and new social challenges in achieving rapid economic growth (Douglass, 2002). At the same time, the concept of liveability itself clearly now forms part of economic growth strategies – ones that are based on highly-skilled service sector and creative industries, rather than low-end manufacturing. Most cynically then, the emergent object of concern may be less about the lives of ordinary city residents than about a place being *seen* to be liveable by the mobile professional elites whom policy makers wish to attract or retain. Perceptions of the relative liveability of cities are shaped in large part by business indices that circulate in the international media, and which are explicitly designed to allow cities to be compared and ranked. To the extent that being (seen to be) liveable has thus become a matter of scoring well in such international rankings, liveability has been reduced to aggregate city data sets which are strongly skewed to the priorities and preferences of elite migrant (or would-be migrant) populations.

This paper seeks to extend critical analysis of city liveability in two key ways. The first concerns the application of issues of liveability to non-elite, international migrant groups. Given that existing business rankings of liveability are oriented to elite migrants, perhaps the more obvious corrective would be to consider non-elite 'local' citizen populations. However, we believe that a focus on non-elite international migrants is important because they tend to be excluded from deliberations on city liveability on grounds of both citizenship (at least in conventional political and territorial conceptions of that term) and labour market position (in that they are at the other end of the socio-economic hierarchy from the kinds of transnational workers whose skills and credentials are prioritised in economic policy). Second, we extend analysis of liveability beyond existing preoccupations with aggregate city-wide data sets and their discursive effects. High-profile liveability rankings along with academic analyses that critique their less-than-socially progressive effects, or that seek to reconceptualise liveability for less elite-centred policy agendas, share a tendency to obscure the important role that intimate social relations such as friendships play in making cities liveable. Moving away from measures of aggregate city characteristics and audits implies a corresponding shift towards individual and collective human lived experiences which, somewhat ironically, have not featured prominently in either popular media discourses or academic analyses of liveability.

The paper is comprised of three main sections. The first reviews existing critical approaches to city liveability and outlines our own approach which is centred upon social lives and associated urban spatial practices. We suggest that geographies of friendship, conviviality and other forms of positive sociality may form the starting point for rethinking urban liveability from the bottom up. In the second section, we turn to the lives of low-wage South Asian migrant workers in Dubai and Singapore. Drawing upon ethnographic fieldwork in these two urban contexts, we detail the importance of friendships and conviviality among other factors of city liveability. The third and final section is concerned with ways in which such resources of urban sociality may be developed. In particular, we point to possibilities for investing in 'infrastructures' of friendship, and extending cultures of hospitality.

Critical Approaches to City Liveability

Liveability is an increasingly common term around which cities are compared and ranked. To the extent that such comparisons and rankings – and, by extension, the criteria of evaluation that underpin them – are taken seriously by city authorities and policy makers, they can have real transformative effects on cities from 'above'. It is in part for this reason that 'liveability' has been subjected to critical academic scrutiny. In what follows in this section, we review existing scholarship on the less-than-socially-progressive effects of discourses of liveability – and on efforts to recuperate or reorient the term towards more progressive and socially inclusive agendas – before sketching our own critical approach in which we seek to build 'upwards' from the social lives of economically-marginal migrants.

First, and perhaps unsurprisingly, the business-oriented city liveability indices and rankings which we have mentioned have attracted both popular and academic critique. In part, this concerns quibbles over the methods that are employed – the criteria and factors that are (not) included and the relative weight accorded to them – in compiling the likes of the Economist Intelligence Unit's Global Liveability Reports or the Most Liveable cities Index, which is published by *Monocle* magazine. More significant, for us, are those academic critiques that examine the material effects or 'discursive power' (Mccann, 2004) of city rankings. However inadequate, flawed or 'un-scientific' are the methods through which they are generated, popular rankings influence decision-making among multinational firms and policy makers, as well as by mobile professionals. Associated efforts to make cities more liveable – or, more precisely, to satisfy whatever criteria of liveability will allow any given city to ascend influential rankings – serve to orient public policy towards particular directions (Mccann, 2000). Public policy thus comes to be shaped by the priorities and preferences of professional elites and creative classes,[1] precluding alternative, possibly more socially-progressive, policy directions (see Peck, 2005 with regard to 'creative city' strategies). Relatedly, as Eugene Mccann has shown, liveability ranking processes are not merely reflective of competition between cities, but more actively reproduce and reinforce senses of cities as singular and homogenised actors that are in competition with one

[1]The *Liveable Cities: Challenges and Opportunities for Policy Makers* report, the first of two reports commissioned by Philips and published by the Economist Intelligence Unit for example, sought to address what city residents wanted from their cities and how city leaders could deliver on citizens' requirements. Yet these residents/citizens were in fact 575 'urban professionals' from around the world, 'the majority from the financial and professional services, IT and technology, energy and natural resources, manufacturing, education and healthcare, publishing and media, and retail' (EIU, 2010, 1).

another. cities are compared and positioned on league tables according to their ability to attract, retain and pander to professional classes. As such, discourses of liveability may be critiqued for obscuring the wider diversity of people who live and work in any given city and, in particular, for their lack of concern for the lives of more socio-economically marginal members of urban populations.

A second, and rather different, existing critical approach seeks precisely to reorient the term liveability towards the realisation of more inclusive and socially-progressive policy agendas. Scholars such as Mike Douglass recognise that dominant discourses of liveability reduce the term to the interests of professional classes and matters of intercity competition (Douglass, 2002). In an article on experiences in Pacific Asia, for example, Douglass noted that the kinds of strategies being deployed in the name of liveability were 'catering to the lifestyle needs of investors', in the form of amenities such as golf courses, international schools and 'exclusive, high-security residential communities with parks and greenery' (62). However, rather than seeing 'liveability' as irredeemably associated with such inequitable outcomes, Douglass has been concerned to push towards more inclusive liveability policies. Accordingly, he has prescribed intercity cooperation (as opposed to competition) such that resources that were being used to compete for investors and elite workers could be redeployed to realise 'cities for citizens' (Friedmann and Douglass, 1998). The problem with this mantra is that 'citizens' could be read in opposition to non-nationals, thus perpetuating the exclusion of low-skilled, low-wage international migrants who are not the kinds of transnationals prioritised in existing liveability policies. As such, the progressive force of 'cities for citizens' arises from it being read alongside wider efforts to delink citizenship itself from conventional understandings of national territorial political membership (Holston, 1999), most notably in work on 'the right to the city' (Purcell, 2003). In his own more recent collaborative efforts to steer liveability in more progressive directions, Douglass has pointed to the need for the concept to take into consideration inclusive urban life spaces (Douglass et al., 2008). Socio-cultural 'life-worlds', and the extent to which cities or urban regions afford spaces for convivial interaction and associational life, are thus added to the list of indicators conventionally used to evaluate liveability.

Our own approach to city liveability recognises important contributions made by the two sets of approaches that we have reviewed above, but begins from a different starting point: the everyday lives and social relations of people in cities. There is no doubt that dominant discourses of liveability can be critiqued for reproducing (rather than merely representing) elite-centred city policy nor that efforts to recuperate the concept must seek to make it more inclusionary, including through extending conventional notions of citizenship and the right to the city. Similarly, we acknowledge consideration of socio-cultural lifeworlds as a valuable addition to conventional measures of liveability. However, what these existing contributions share – somewhat paradoxically in the case of the proposal to incorporate sociocultural lifeworlds into liveability research and comparison – are views of the city in discourse and policy rather than through the lives and experiences of city dwellers. It is thus in contrast to either the critical urban discourse analyst or progressive planners' view of the city that we seek to build up from ground-level anthropological engagement with the lives of city dwellers. In doing so, we are particularly concerned to examine friendship, conviviality and other forms of positive sociality as resources that render cities liveable.

Until recently, friendship had received surprisingly little attention in work on urban social life and, indeed, in the social sciences more broadly. Sociologists have often trivialised friendship as having little or no wider structural significance (Eve, 2002), and even highly influential work on social capital (Putnam, 1995) has taken social networks as its primary unit of analysis, thereby overlooking the interpersonal spatial dynamics of friend-like relations. Anthropologists, meanwhile, have largely associated sociality with kinship ties although there have been important strands of urban anthropology (such as the Manchester School) which considered unstable and unbounded networks of intimacy (including friendships) that are unrelated to kinship ties (e.g. Mitchell, 1969). However, in urban studies, there has been growing interest over the past decade in friendship as a form of intimacy that appears increasingly important in our urbanising, mobile and interconnected world. Nigel Thrift, for example, sketched the role of friendship and conviviality in 'keeping cities resilient and caring' (Thrift, 2005, 146). According to Thrift, unlike loving couple relationships, friendship offers a 'light-touch' model of intimacy and compassion, which appears to be realistic and achievable today, not least in a world of increasingly mobile urban populations.

There is also work that has pointed to the importance of friendships in the urban lives of migrant populations, albeit (and revealingly) often emerging from research projects that were not explicitly framed around the concept of friendship. In an article on British expatriate professionals in Dubai, for example, Katie Walsh begins by examining transient heterosexual intimacy only to end by noting the prevalence of platonic (friendship) ties; 'the fun associated with performances of transient heterosexuality is not only in sex itself, but also in the practices of drinking, dancing and socialising that occur among friends in this context' (Walsh, 2007, 527). The young men and women who formed the focus of Walsh's ethnographic study often found (mainly same-sex) friendships to be more meaningful and dependable forms of intimate attachment than those with their sexual partners.

If friendship is thus important for the urban social lives and psychological wellbeing of professional migrant populations who are actively sought by and catered to by city authorities, then what more for migrants at the other end of the socioeconomic spectrum? Yasser Elsheshtawy's (Elsheshtawy, 2008) work, also on Dubai, examines the 'forgotten' urban spaces of low-income migrant communities in the city. Although intimate social relations are not central to his concerns, Elsheshtawy's informants from both India and the congo make mention of friendship in elaborating the significance of urban public spaces to their lives in the city. Perhaps especially for low-income migrants who do not feature prominently in the minds of those who formally plan and shape the material infrastructure of the city – the kinds of migrants who would rarely, if ever, be considered in efforts to render cities 'liveable' – social relations assume additional importance as a kind of 'infrastructure' in its own right (see Simone, 2004). In the next section, we turn more explicitly to consideration of the role of friendships and other forms of positive sociality in the liveability of Dubai and Singapore for low income migrant workers.

Friendship and Conviviality Among South Asian Migrant Workers

Both Singapore and Dubai are highly dependent on transient labour populations. Authorities in both cities are also concerned with being or becoming (seen) as liveable, with Singapore even establishing a centre for

Liveable cities (cLc) in 2008. Although the cLc connects liveability more squarely to the lives and concerns of national citizens in Singapore than is the case in Dubai – in part a reflection of the fact that Singapore is a city-*state* – the two contexts also have in common a clear disconnect between discourses of liveability and low wage migrant populations. Flows of low-wage migrants are controlled within restrictive regimes that limit who can enter and for how long (Yeoh, 2006; Keane and McGeehan, 2008), and that are entirely separate from promotional city liveability strategies. In the popular media as well as in academic analyses (Ali, 2010; Beaverstock, 2002; Yeoh, 2006), both cities have been portrayed primarily as spaces for the affluent, and while comfortable middle class lifestyles are possible for professional migrants, low wage workers are regularly marginalised and live compromised lives. In both cities, low wage workers account for the overwhelming majority of migrants.

Our focus is on lives of temporary migrant men, primarily from South Asia, who work on construction sites, factories and shipyards in low paid jobs. We argue that in both Singapore and Dubai, friendships and other forms of sociality are important aspects of these migrants' articulations of everyday sustenance, pleasure and ease of living in the city. Before turning to the empirical evidence for our argument, it is important to make two key points of methodological clarification. First, the ethnographic and interview material that we draw upon in what follows does not emerge from a single research project comparing Dubai and Singapore. Rather, the material that we cite is drawn from two research projects that were conducted separately: (1) in the emirate of Dubai over a period of eight months in 2008 and (2) in the city-state of Singapore between 2011 and 2013.[2] As such, our analysis is not comparative – at least not as that term has conventionally been understood in urban studies (though see Robinson, 2011) – but draws out ground-level commonalities in understandings and

[2]Data collection in Dubai was part of a larger project on city-building strategies examining the lives of low wage migrants in Dubai whilst it attempted to position itself as a 'global city'. The Singapore data emerges from a larger comparative study that interrogated socio-spatial patterns of 'diversity' in the neighbourhood of Jurong West. Although low wage migrants were not the singular focus of the research, they were one of the largest groups of residents in the area.

conceptualisations of what makes cities liveable for non-elite migrant groups in the two cities. This is significant because Dubai and Singapore are in many other ways very different cities and have rarely been drawn into a single frame of analysis, at least in part because of the ways in which knowledge is often spatially compartentalised (they are located in Western Asia or the Middle East and Southeast Asia respectively). In both locations, ethnographic observations, interaction and interviews with low waged migrants were carried out in spaces such as labour camps, low wage migrant spaces of consumption and leisure such as shopping streets and malls, coffee shops, street corners and parks.[3] Interviews allowed for the development of in-depth and private understandings of how friendship ties are established, maintained and even broken, as well as insight into their significance for enjoyable and effective urban living. Together, these ground-up methods starting from migrant narratives and quotidian performance provided means of understanding the importance of friendship and other forms of sociality to low waged men in the two urban contexts.

Second, as with the work of Walsh and Elsheshtawy referred to in the previous section, friendship was not, at the outset, central to the two research projects from which our empirical material is drawn. In both projects however it became quickly apparent, not only that most low-wage migrants developed a range of coping strategies and discourses that enabled them to deal with the nature of their marginalised lives overseas; but also that, amongst these, the development and maintenance of close relations between working class co-ethnics, as well as friendships that transcended the divides of ethnicity, socio-economic class or of local/foreigner, were highly significant.

The most obvious ways in which friendship networks were important to low wage migrants concerned the practical aid and support that they availed, especially in financial matters. No or late payment of wages is

---

[3]The enactment and performance, especially of the affective registers of friendship and sociality, were regularly observed in these everyday spaces of the city. For working class groups such as low wage migrants in Singapore and Dubai, there is little private or personal space to meet friends given limited days off, restricted mobilities and shared living spaces. Within this context, ethnography of public spaces was important as a means of understanding how the material configurations and constraints of the city shaped possibilities for positive sociality and the development of convivial relations.

commonplace for low wage migrants employed on large construction projects in both Dubai and Singapore. In these instances, borrowing cash from fellow migrants was a means of survival as well as a way to keep remitting cash back to home country family members, who are dependent on these regular flows. Rotating credit unions were another means through which friendship networks were utilised to maximise the financial returns of migrant work. These informal groups were most often composed of five to seven men and loosely formed around ties of friendship, common place of origin and shared language. Through the pooling of capital, low-wage migrants had access to large lump sums of money which would have been otherwise unavailable to them. These are especially useful when paying for dowry or marriages of family members in home countries and maximise remittances by sending in bulk. In specific instances of need, friends would even organise a 'collection' of funds. For example, an informant working as a messenger for a Dubai-based company described how during the amnesty period in 2007 (when irregular migrants could leave the country without incurring any penalties), ten of his friends put money together to buy air tickets for two men to go back to India, when they could not afford to themselves. Friends here fulfilled the role of more formal financial institutions such as banks and credit unions that cater mostly for citizens and middle class migrants.

The often taken-for-granted ways in which middle-class and elite migrants learn to negotiate cities are less available to working class migrants, particularly those who have previously never left their hometown or country. It is not only the everyday knowledge about a place, but the actual process of 'urban learning' (Lofland, 1973) that needs to be acquired. Friendships are often crucial to this process for low wage migrants. While elite transnational migrants moving to a new location often have human resource departments to manage the transition, and assistance in the form of access to serviced apartments and comprehensive information packs, low wage migrants must learn about a foreign space on-the-go, with little formal support. Ram, a construction labourer from a small town in Tamil Nadu, described in an interview how he was instructed how to manage his way on the urban rail network in Singapore; the mundane details of which stop to get off at, where to change to a different line, for example, to get to Little India from his dormitory in Jurong, at the far west of the island. For many low wage migrants, the technology of swiping cards, topping them up with credit at an automated machine, and even withdrawing money from an ATM are all everyday urban skills they have not encountered in their home countries and must learn from prior or new acquaintances on arrival.

Another important form of tangible advice that gets passed on to new migrants, often by co-ethnics, is to do with how the body must be disciplined in the context of a highly regulated state like Singapore. Speaking of an older migrant friend who had given him advice upon his arrival, Ram said: 'He told me I have to dress properly, not spit anywhere, not be a nuisance to other people. This place is not like India he told me. We cannot just do as we please. When we live here we have to follow the rules here'. Friendships are thus useful in quickly learning skills or codes of behaviour that enable better 'fitting in', so as not to stand out or transgress established social and cultural expectations of urbanity. For low wage migrants whose position within a migrant context is precarious and can be revoked at the whim of an employer, there is a strong imperative to quickly become competent at being a city resident. It is here that the quotidian reminders and nudges from friends work to regulate behaviour and body-language of low wage migrant men and teach the effective performance of docile, compliant workers.

Friendships with non-co-ethnics, particularly if they are members of the middle-class 'host' population, are generally seen as highly valuable forms of social capital. Although commonly attributed more influence or *wasta* than they actually exert, friendships with citizens or long-time residents are seen as possible sources of job recommendations or routes to other forms of social mobility. Often situated within a hierarchical configuration of employer–employee or researcher-informant, these friendships sometimes also extend to everyday pleasurable socialities of eating together and visiting each other's homes. With little other opportunity to meet 'locals', these friendships then also become a key way through which marginalised migrants accumulate knowledge about the host environment. Amin, a Bangladeshi who had been working in Singapore for seven years, became unhappy with his job when he was moved to a different section of the factory where he worked, which entailed harder manual labour that had a detrimental effect on his health. After a week on the new job, he called an ex-employer, an older Singaporean chinese man who owned a chain of food courts, amongst other businesses. This well-connected former employer had previously proffered his help to Amin. He was immediately invited to dinner at a seafood restaurant near his ex-boss's home. Although the meeting did not eventually result in the creation of an alternative job for Amin, he was pleased by his ex-employer's warmth and felt that it was a connection that was mutually valued, as well as suggesting possibilities for alternative employment opportunities in the future. Friendship here is invoked by the willingness to meet, share food, and extend an offer of future help, despite differences of nationality, class and status position. Beyond acting merely as a form of capital that Amin can access, his former employer's performance of concern over his well-being was read by Amin as an indication of how Singaporeans, and by extension Singapore itself, is not a completely alienating or uncaring place. Interpersonal friendship ties performed in specific microgeographical sites can thus come to make the wider city appear more hospitable and convivial.

Through such interactions with 'locals' outside and beyond the space of the worksite or shipyard, migrant men are made to feel valued as more than just workers. Within urban political contexts where they are valued only for their productive labour, friendship – even if not deep-rooted or sustained – functions as one of few contexts in which these migrants are recognised as unique individuals. It is important to stress here that friendship is not just a means of accessing social capital, nor should it be seen only in the context of 'bonding' and 'bridging' capital. Beyond the utilitarian, friendship also functions as an extremely important form of affective and emotional connection that can help to foster social and psychological belonging. Friendship networks can also be seen as one of the key modes through which low wage South Asian men 'network' in the migrant context, seeking social mobility alongside the pleasures of companionship.

Friendships (especially in conditions of tight, shared living spaces) are integral in dealing with depression and alcoholism, which appear to be widespread amongst low wage migrant men (Dervic et al., 2012).[4]

[4]In Singapore, more comprehensive statistical data is not available, but see http://twc2.org.sg/2012/02/28/88-of-migrant-workers-caught-in-limbo-show-signs-of-climical-depression/ (accessed 1 October 2014).

Alcohol consumption as a form of escapism is often sustained and encouraged by friends, but, as the following vignette demonstrates, friendships can conversely take on rehabilitative qualities in such situations. Friend relations here are especially important as low wage migrants in cities like Singapore or Dubai have little means of accessing trained social workers, psychiatrists or self-help groups. Being away from the usual support networks of extended family and long-time friends, friendships forged within the migrant context take on increased significance.

Jairaj is a young man from India, recently married, but who was having marital issues with his wife, whom he suspected of having an affair while he was in Dubai. In addition, he was still repaying the large debt he had incurred in coming to Dubai to work in the hospitality industry.

> I owed an 8 lakh loan[5] and was feeling terrible about not being able to pay it off. So I used to drink bottles of rum although there is no history of drinking or alcoholism in my family. … I started abusing alcohol a lot more. I used to drink and then sleep exhausted. It began to affect my work. I wouldn't turn up for work regularly. I used to drink one or two bottles a day. That's how much fury I had. A superior at work who was concerned for me asked me what was going on. He told me to leave it (drinking). It's not good for you he said. But I told him I can't stop. … One time when I was drunk, I bought a 250 ml bottle of poison (with the intention to kill myself). I thought, how could I live like this? With so much debt. I felt pressured by all those issues – like they were pressing on me. (Translated from Tamil, Dubai, 2008)

Jairaj goes on to describe how other workers with whom he shared a room smelt something amiss and found him unconscious. He was brought to a hospital and survived the suicide attempt. With the support and vigilance of his friends, he also managed to bring his excessive drinking habit under control.

Migrant worker deaths on and off the worksite are one of the key indices that are regularly cited by human rights organisations and civil society groups in shaming city authorities into imposing tighter

---

[5] 8 lakhs refers to 800,000 rupees, which is approximately equivalent to US$12,550 at the exchange rate of US$1 = 63.74 Indian Rupees.

regulations in the employment and welfare of migrants working in dangerous jobs such as in the construction and ship building sectors. While tangible measures to reduce worksite accidents can be more easily instituted, preventing depression-led suicides is far more complicated. Here, the supportive role of positive sociality amongst friends should be acknowledged as playing a significant part in its management. For example, Gulf States Abu Dhabi, Dubai and Qatar have garnered much negative publicity in the last few years – because of the exploitative conditions under which low-wage migrants labour on high profile projects such as the building of the Guggenheim in Abu Dhabi and the stadiums that will host the next football World cup in Qatar. High numbers of self-inflicted migrant deaths that are attributed to attempts to escape debt bondage situations or obligations to family back home have also reached the mainstream international media. Governments and urban authorities keen to avoid such negative characterisations could learn from emphasising and creating space for the kinds of effective self-management that friendship networks enable. Friendships then do not just characterise more liveable spaces, but create conditions to sustain life itself.

Friendship and other forms of convivial sociality act not just as social glue, but also as a kind of balm that helps soothe and heal the everyday stresses and difficulties of low wage labour in highly stratified cities like Dubai and Singapore. As we have shown, it is not just effective support networks, but practical advice and social capital that low wage migrants depend on friendships for. Much of this sort of emotional 'labour' is discounted by states that presume the non-elite migrant is merely a worker, devoid of the myriad needs of a rounded individual human being. The regenerative effects of modes of sociality such as friendship should not be discounted in measures of liveability, both for highly marginalised populations and for authorities concerned about their cities gaining a reputation for being threatening and uncaring places for their most vulnerable residents.

Extending Positive Sociality for More Liveable Cities

These vignettes have thus far demonstrated how non-elite migrants describe and draw on friendships and utilise friend-like relations to create a more liveable city space for themselves. How do these everyday acts of friendship, support and positive sociality scale up to macro-scale urban notions of liveability? In unpacking the larger social relevance of interpersonal and group relations, it is imperative to understand friendship as a kind of sociality that is performed within the private, personal sphere, but that is simultaneously shaped by the politics outside it (Kathiravelu, 2013). Many of the friend relations and productive social networks that we have discussed in this article draw from and are based on existing forms of social capital between migrants, such as a shared ethnicity, immigration status and often gender. The larger political and social spaces of Singapore and Dubai, generally unfriendly to low wage migrants, enable and even encourage the dependence on such forms of affinity and social capital. The existence of productive capital and networks alone, however, were not the markers of a liveable space, but their enactment and utilisation engendered forms of friend relations. These modes of employing and deploying friendship can be seen as a form of the 'tactical learning' suggested by McFarlane (2011a) as a means through which marginalised migrants learn to negotiate dense spaces of the city, or akin to the 'tactical cosmopolitanism' of African traders that Landau (2009) describes, allowing for productive commercial exchanges across highly politicised barriers of nationality and ethnic difference. Through these forms of learning, negotiation and sociality, the urban is not just seen in particular ways by urban inhabitants, but constantly remade and meaningfully reinscribed (McFarlane, 2011b). In this way, friendship demonstrates not just the existence of a more compassionate and caring city, but also provides a way in which migrants themselves can generate the types of relations that they deem important as low waged workers. Additionally, we have demonstrated that beyond the practical ways in which these networks or relational resources are utilised, their surplus as affective intangible ties is significant in sustaining notions of liveability. Established concepts such as social capital and networks do not encompass the emotional and larger affective aspects of friend relations that were central to our migrant informants in their everyday negotiations, or in their perceptions of what constitutes a satisfactory and 'liveable' urban life. The dynamism and precarious temporality evoked by notions of friend-like socialities are also more appropriate to the kinds of ties that our informants described.

It is important to note that our ethnographic evidence of how friendship can serve as an affective and social resource for low-wage migrants in Dubai and Singapore carries several risks. One which is largely beyond the scope of this article is the risk of casting friendship itself in a wholly positive light. Friendship can certainly have a 'dark side' not least because the trust placed in friends opens vulnerability to deception or exploitation (Bunnell et al., 2012; Lindquist, 2012). Insofar as friendship is a positive resource, the second risk of our necessarily selective vignettes in the previous section is that they can be read as implying that possession of such social resources is itself sufficient to make a city liveable. Positive forms of sociality may be important, perhaps even necessary, for any individual's experience of a city as 'liveable', but this does not mean that friendship and/or conviviality can wholly supplant other environmental or material factors (including many that are already included in conventional liveability rankings). Friendship is mobilised as a means of accessing other resources, such as paid employment, precisely because these are valued in their own right. Third, and relatedly, there is a risk that the apparent capacity of even – perhaps especially – the most economically and politically marginal of city residents to mobilise friendship as a resource is taken to infer that wider forms of progressive political intervention and socio-spatial transformation are unnecessary. In contrast, we ask to what extent can planning and development interventions work through existing friendships and provide conditions for the formation and flourishing of new ones in order to make cities more liveable? In what follows, we answer this question in two interrelated ways.

Investing in Infrastructures of Sociality

First, and perhaps most simply, it is important to consider the kinds of infrastructure that make possible the formation and sustenance of friendships, so as to identify how (and where) appropriate developmental investments may be made. The existing critical planning literature has focused largely on material spatial aspects. Especially for migrant workers whose non-work living quarters are highly spatially-confined – whether in dormitories or labour camps, as in the case of many of the male migrant workers considered in the previous section, or in employers' homes in the case of (usually female) domestic workers in Dubai and Singapore – spaces of associational life can play significant roles in making cities liveable. These can be public spaces, as in the case of the land at the junction of Orchard and Paterson roads in Singapore where Indonesian domestic workers gathered at weekends before this space was enclosed for the private sector commercial development of what is today ION Orchard (Yeoh and Huang, 1998). But privately-owned, commercial spaces can sustain friendships and associational life among migrant workers too, as Kitiarsa's rich ethnography of Thai migrant men in Golden Mile complex (2014) or descriptions of the night-time economy (Yeo et al., 2012) in Singapore's Little India demonstrate. Mike Douglass and Amrita Daniere have suggested that rather than focusing on the conventional distinction between public and private spaces, attention be given to 'civic spaces' which can be either public or private, and the defining features of which are 'a high degree of autonomy from state and commercial interests and inclusiveness in being open to people from all walks of life' (Douglass and Daniere, 2009, 8). There is, by now, a robust literature pointing to the importance of providing and protecting civic spaces, not only for the social well-being of the most marginal migrant members of city populations but as a more general component of the progressive city.

We contend that civic spaces are a necessary but insufficient component of urban social infrastructure: interventions also need to attend to *time* as a resource as well as to *technologies* of interaction. Various studies have noted how migrant groups appropriate civic spaces at particular times (Yeoh and Huang, 2003; Elsheshtawy, 2013). What has less often been explicitly remarked upon in such situations is that time is itself a necessary resource in order for material spaces to support friendships and other forms of sociality. This, in turn, compels consideration of legal infrastructures of labour laws, employer responsibilities and their enforcement. In Singapore, the recently instituted (2014) ruling of giving female foreign domestic workers one mandatory day off every week is an example of the kind of enabling legislation that allows for migrants to meet and form friendship communities outside the spaces and times of work. However, effective enforcement of such laws is often severely lacking. Many migrant men, such as those described in our above vignettes, do not have a cap on daily working hours and do not get mandatory days off in the week, despite coming under the remit of national labour laws that institute such limitations (Kitiarsa, 2014; Yea et al., 2014). In other words, investments need to be made not just in material spatial infrastructure but in legislation associated with providing migrants with the time to make use of spaces of sociality, and in efforts to enforce any such legislation.

Relatedly, technologies of transportation and communication can be important components of friendship infrastructure. Even if civic spaces do exist, to what extent can they be reached affordably and safely? And in what ways can co-presence in civic spaces be enabled among people for whom time is often in very short supply? For many migrant men housed in worker dormitories in the far western, highly industrial, corners of the island of Singapore, or in Dubai in the labour camps of Sonapur, a wholly migrant zone set far away from the main arteries of the city, meeting friends and accessing resources in other parts of the city can be an expensive and time-intensive affair. The emergence of localised time-spaces of sociality is one outcome of this transportation deficit and associated difficulties of accessing more distant civic spaces. The role of technologies of communication, such as telephone, SMS and, increasingly, internet-based applications, is more complex. At one level, such technologies can result in withdrawal from the city given extended possibilities for real-time participation in family and friendship networks extending to distant elsewheres; to the extent that such technologies are increasingly accessible through personal devices, there may not even be the need to visit areas of a city which have traditionally provided long distance communication services to migrant populations. But communication devices can also foster sociality in the city – facilitating face-to-face encounters rather than replacing them, enabling synchronisation of schedules for meetings in civic spaces and even helping to turn more fleeting time-spaces into opportunities for social interaction (such as when domestic workers synchronise their scheduling of mundane tasks such as grocery shopping or dog walking) (Thompson, 2009). Given the significance of mobile technologies of communication in the social lives of (often spatially-dispersed and time-scarce) city migrants, access to them is arguably as important to their wellbeing as mandatory time off work and the provision of civic space in wider infrastructures of sociality.

Extending Cultures of Hospitality

While our suggestions about investment in basic infrastructures of sociality were concerned with social relations between migrants, perhaps even migrants with shared regional backgrounds and/or who occupy similar positions in the urban labour market, our second set of suggestions for intervention involves possibilities for friendships between migrants and non-migrant populations. As noted in the previous section, friendships can bridge such divides, but in most cases, as can be seen from our work in Dubai and Singapore, they do not. To what extent can this be attributed to the institution of friendship itself ? Conversely, to what extent might it be because existing infrastructures of interaction among migrants separate them socially and spatially from wider urban populations, and even seek to contain them within specific spaces, times and networks? While influential sociological literature has often cast friendships as being of minor significance precisely because they mostly fail to cross social boundaries such as class and ethnicity (e.g. Rawlins, 1992), more recent anthropological work has pointed to possibilities for relations of friendship to 'transcend the divisions imposed by such collective mechanisms of inclusion and identity as kinship ties, settlement membership, or ethnic affiliation' (Santos-Granero, 2007, 13; see also Johnson and Werbner, 2010).

The boundary-crossing potential of friendships is another resource for city liveability, holding potential for cities to be made more welcoming and hospitable to migrants, rather than containing them in separate social spheres. One city that has received considerable recent academic attention in this respect is Sheffield in the UK. Here, drop-in centre spaces such as 'The Talking Shop' have sought to foster the development of personal relationships between 'local' people on the one hand, and asylum seekers and refugees on the other (Darling, 2011). While cautioning against romanticised notions of a place-based community transcending boundaries of difference and status, Jonathan Darling has described the drop-in centre as 'a site of complex relations through which ideas of care were performed and momentary feelings of welcome articulated'. Such relations certainly include conviviality and friendship: 'For individuals often waiting for decisions on asylum status for months and even years in some cases, the structure offered by a twice weekly drop-in centre, together with the friendships developed here, proved central in offering an informal support network and the strength to carry on from day to day' (Darling, 2011, 415). Friendships developed in specific sites can thus extend across divides between long-time city residents and even the most vulnerable of migrant populations, making cities more liveable in practical and affective terms.

The Talking Shop and other drop-in centres form part of wider efforts to build a 'culture of hospitality' in Sheffield, which has, in turn, come to form part of a wider 'city of sanctuary' movement (Squire, 2011; see also Darling, 2010). Building a culture of hospitality has meant not only presenting or envisioning Sheffield as a 'welcoming place' but promoting civic pride in that vision, so much so that city residents and institutions actively contribute to efforts to extend urban hospitality. Although public reaction is reported to have been mixed, institutional success is evidenced by the fact that other towns and cities have followed Sheffield's initiatives to form a network of cities of sanctuary in the UK. The notion of Sheffield 'leading the way' (Darling, 2010, 128) is itself another resource for bolstering civic pride and encouraging more active popular participation. central to a diverse range of public activities in Sheffield has been the objective of 'encouraging thought and interaction as a means to develop friendships across difference and tackle some of the myths readily associated with asylum seekers' (Darling, 2010, 129). While this clearly includes 'myths' and issues that are specific to the politics of asylum in the UK, Darling's work on the city of sanctuary has much wider conceptual purchase. In particular, relational reframing of the city through promotion of awareness of its entanglements with distant 'elsewheres' invokes a need for non-territorially-bounded geographies of responsibility, and serves to challenge boundaries of inside(r) and outside(r), hosts and guests.[6] Perhaps especially in the case of a city-state such as Singapore where city boundaries are also national ones, notions of urban inside(r) and outside(r)

[6] In Sheffield, practices of friendship, too, were not merely about locals extending hospitality to migrants, but variously inverted and extended beyond the 'host' versus 'guest' dichotomy that is conventionally implied by that term. The dichotomy is (temporarily) inverted when asylum seekers offer tea or food to longer term residents visiting drop-in centres (Darling, 2011; Squire, 2009), and arguably transcended altogether when befriending is understood as a reciprocal process of sharing and learning.

may be particularly resistant to blurring. In such a context there may be more potential for forging migrant/local friendships and solidarities through commonalities (e.g. we are both Hindus or Muslims etc). Nonetheless, the city of sanctuary movement serves as a reminder of the possibilities that friendship holds for making cities more welcoming, hospitable and 'liveable' to even the most marginal of others.

Conclusion

'Liveability' continues to attract considerable attention internationally, not only in popular media and among urban policy-makers, but also from academics. Existing academic work on liveability includes some important critiques of the concept, especially in terms of its class bias. We have sought to extend consideration of liveability beyond the elite, professional migrants who are the primary target of inter-urban competition to low-wage migrant men in two different urban contexts in Asia. We have also sought to extend critical analysis of 'liveability' beyond readings of discourses and indices, by starting from the lives and narratives of the men concerned. It was from this starting point that we identified positive forms of sociality, and especially friendship, as significant to the everyday urban experiences and quality of life of the men concerned. Friendship is important not just in material, practical and even instrumental terms, but also emotionally and affectively. While low-wage migrants are resourceful in recognising and realising what friendships can offer to their quality of life, we have also highlighted some possibilities for wider intervention. Investments in spaces, times and technologies of friendship, and also in cultures of welcome and hospitality can make for more liveable cities.

Why consider low-wage migrants' lives and friendships, and wider developmental efforts to nurture or sustain them, in terms of 'liveability' given ways in which the term has already been problematised and shown to be (seemingly irredeemably) bound up with neoliberal inter-urban competition? First, our very use of the term in the context of groups and lives that are conventionally beyond the purview of liveability is a strategic one, intended to draw attention to inequalities that may inadvertently be reproduced by scholarly conceptual partitioning. There are dangers associated with a tendency to examine certain kinds of migrant experiences in relation to merely 'acceptable' or 'bearable' conditions, while other migrants feature in the discourses and spaces of liveability. Second, and more pragmatically, we engage with liveability as a concept that is already invested with considerable 'discursive power' in public policy circuits (Mccann, 2004) and which looks to be here to stay, at least for the foreseeable future. Liveability is very much part of interurban competition in many parts of Asia, as elsewhere. We argue that it may be possible to make progressive use of this reality rather than seeking to wishfully critique it from existence. We have already noted important existing academic attempts to expand the definitional criteria of liveability to be more inclusive (Douglass et al., 2008). To what extent can such expanded criteria be worked into competitive agendas? To what extent can inter-city competition be shifted away from the current preoccupation with being friendly to business and transnational professional elites and correspondingly towards friendliness to/liveability for the kinds of low-wage migrants that are central to our interests in this paper? The short and simple answer to that naive-sounding question is probably: not much. Entrenched geographies of uneven development and the associated abundant supply of 'cheap' unskilled labour internationally mean that it is highly unlikely that relatively affluent cities are going to have to compete to attract such workers any time soon. However, city authorities most certainly are concerned with image, and although imaging strategies are themselves oriented to being seen as 'investible' (Sidaway and Pryke, 2000), the image of being inhospitable or unwelcoming to migrants is surely not one that city authorities would wish to foster (not least because it might inadvertently make them less attractive to transnational elites).

Finally, then, we wonder about progressive possibilities of the very kinds of liveability rankings and tables which were the initial object of our critical attention. While their discursive power has been unmasked and subjected to deserved critique for promoting neoliberal business-oriented agendas (and so obscuring or even widening associated inequities), much less effort has been made to mobilise the power of rankings for more progressive agendas. In contrast, inspiration may be derived from strands of research on policy mobilities that show how best practice urban models that travel and are replicated elsewhere are not limited to those that are most conducive to big business or elite economic interests, but can include non-mainstream and even socially-progressive urban policies (Mccann, 2008; see also Bunnell, 2015). Of course, in the case of liveability, the main existing rankings and the very criteria of evaluation upon which they are based are bound up with corporate media interests, and this, in large part, accounts for their power. But especially in an era of digital interconnection and social media, there are surely possibilities for alternative rankings to travel, especially if aligned with networks of NGOs and/or international labour organisations who could tap the comparative urban evaluations of mobile low-wage migrants. An important challenge, then, may be to devise and popularise rankings that could make cities want to be more friendly – and even to compete to be (seen to be) more friendly – to the kinds of migrants who do not usually feature in discussions of liveability.

References

Ali, S. (2010) *Dubai: gilded cage*, New Haven and London, Yale University Press.

Beaverstock, J. V. (2002) 'Transnational elites in global cities: British expatriates in Singapore's financial district', *Geoforum*, 33(4), 525–38.

Bunnell, T. (2015) 'Antecedent cities and inter-referencing effects: learning from and extending beyond critiques of neoliberalisation', *Urban Studies*, 52(11), 1983–2000.

Bunnell, T., Yea, S., Peake, L., Skelton, T. and Smith, M. (2012) 'Geographies of friendships', *Progress in Human Geography*, 36(4), 490–507.

CLC (centre for Liveable cities) (2008) 'centre for Liveable cities, Singapore http://www.clc.gov.sg/ (accessed 10 October 2015).

Darling, J. (2010) 'A city of sanctuary: the relational re-imagining Sheffield', *Transactions of the Institute of British Geographers,* 35(1), 125–40.

Darling, J. (2011) 'Giving space: care, generosity and belonging in a UK asylum drop-in centre', *Geoforum*, 42(4), 408–17.

Dervic, K., Amiri, Amiri, L., Niederkrotenthaler, T., Yousef, S., Salem, M. O., Voracek, M. and Sonneck, G. (2012) 'Suicide rates in the national and expatriate population in Dubai, United Arab Emirates', *International Journal of Social Psychiatry*, 58(6), 652–56.

Douglass, M. (2002) 'From global intercity competition to cooperation for livable cities and economic resilience in Pacific Asia', *Environment & Urbanization*, 14(1), 53–68.

Douglass, M. and Daniere, A. (2009) 'Urbanization and civic space in Asia', in A. Daniere and M. Douglass (eds), *The Politics of Civic Space in Asia: Building Urban Communities*, Abingdon, Routledge, 1–18.

Douglass, M., Le, T.Q., Lowry, c.K., Nguyen, H.T., Pham, A.N., Thai, N.D. and Yulinawati, H. (2008) 'The livability of mega-urban regions in Southeast Asia – Bangkok, Ho chi Minh city, Jakarta and Manila compared', in G. Jones and M. Douglass (eds), *Mega-Urban Regions in Pacific Asia*, Singapore, NUS Press, 284–319.

EIU (Economist Intelligence Unit) (2010) *Liveable cities: challenges and opportunities for policymakers*, London, Economist Intelligence Unit.

Elsheshtawy, Y. (2008) 'Transitory sites: mapping Dubai's "forgotten" urban spaces', *International Journal of Urban and Regional Research*, 32(4), 968–88.

Elsheshtawy, Y. (2013) 'Where the sidewalk ends: informal street corner encounters in Dubai', *Cities*, 31, 382–93.

Eve, M. (2002) 'Is friendship a sociological topic?', *European Journal of Sociology*, 43(3), 386–409. Friedmann, J. and Douglass, M. (1998) 'Editors' introduction', in M. Douglass and J. Friedmann (eds), *Cities for citizens: planning the rise of civil society in a global age*, chichester, John Wiley and Sons, 1–6.

Holston, J. (ed) (1999) *Cities and citizenship*, Durham and London, Duke University Press.

Johnson, M. and Werbner, P. (2010) 'Diasporic encounters, sacred journeys: ritual normativity and the religious imagination among international Asian migrant women', *The Asia Pacific Journal of Anthropology*, 11(3), 205–18.

Kathiravelu, L. (2013) 'Friendship and the urban encounter: towards a research agenda', *MMG Working Paper*, 13–10, http://www.mmg.mpg.de/publications/working-papers/2013/wp-13-10/ (accessed 10 June 2015).

Keane, D. and McGeehan, N. (2008) 'Enforcing migrant workers' rights in the United Arab Emirates', *International Journal on Minority and Group Rights*, 15(1), 81–115.

Kitiarsa, P. (2014) *The 'bare life' of Thai migrant workmen in Singapore*, chiang Mai, Silkworm Books.

Landau, L. B. and I. Freemantle (2009) 'Tactical cosmopolitanism and idioms of belonging: insertion and self-exclusion in Johannesburg', *Journal of Ethnic and Migration Studies*, 36(3), 375–90.

Lindquist, J. (2012) 'The elementary school teacher, the thug and his grandmother: informal brokers and transnational migration from Indonesia', *Pacific Affairs*, 85(1), 69–89.

Lofland, L. H. (1973) *A world of strangers: order and action in urban public space*, New York, Basic Books.

Mccann, E. (2000) 'A nice place to live? The role of urban livability rankings in the construction of public policy', in J. Benson and M. Roe (eds), *Urban lifestyles: spaces-places-people: proceedings of an international conference on cities in the new millenium*, Newcastle upon Tyne and Rotterdam, Balkema, 211–18.

Mccann, E. (2004) '"Best places?" Interurban competition, quality of life and popular media discourse', *Urban Studies*, 41(10), 1909–29.

Mccann, E. (2008) 'Expertise, truth and urban policy mobilities: global circuits of knowledge in the development of Vancouver, canada's "four pillar" drug strategy', *Environment and Planning A*, 40(4), 885–904.

McFarlane, c. (2011a) 'The city as a machine for learning', *Transactions of the Institute of British Geographers*, 36(3), 360–76.

McFarlane, c. (2011b) *Learning the city: knowledge and translocal assemblage*, Oxford, Wiley-Blackwell.

Mitchell, J. c. (ed.) (1969) *Social networks in urban situations: analyses of personal relationships in central African towns*, Manchester, Manchester University Press, for the Institute of Social Research, University of Zambia.

Peck, J. (2005) 'Struggling with the creative class', *International Journal of Urban and Regional Research*, 29(4), 740–70.

Purcell, M. (2003) 'citizenship and the global city: reimagining a capitalist world order', *International Journal of Urban and Regional Research*, 27(3), 564–90.

Putnam, R. (1995) 'Bowling alone: America's declining social capital', *Journal of Democracy*, 6(1), 65–78.

Rawlins, W. K. (1992) *Friendship matters: communication, dialectics, and the life course*, New York, Aldine de Gruyter.

Robinson, J. (2011) 'cities in a world of cities: the comparative gesture', *International Journal of Urban and Regional Research*, 35(1), 1–23.

Santos-Granero, F. (2007) 'Of fear and friendship: Amazonian sociality beyond kinship and affinity', *Journal of the Royal Anthropological Institute*, 13(1), 1–18.

Sidaway, J. D. and Pryke, M. (2000) 'The strange geographies of emerging markets', *Transactions of the Institute of British Geographers*, 25(2), 187–201.

Simone, A. (2004) 'People as infrastructure: intersecting fragments in Johannesburg', *Public Culture*, 16(3), 407–29.

Squire, V. (2011) 'From community cohesion to mobile solidarities: *the city of sanctuary* network and the *strangers into citizens* campaign', *Political Studies*, 59(2), 290–307.

Thompson, E. c. (2009) 'Mobile phones, communities and social networks among foreign workers in Singapore', *Global Networks*, 9(3), 359–80.

Thrift, N. (2005) 'But malice aforethought: cities and the natural history of hatred', *Transactions of the Institute of British Geographers*, 30(2), 133–50.

Walsh, K. (2007) '"It got very debauched, very Dubai!": heterosexual intimacy amongst single British expatriates', *Social and Cultural Geography*, 8(4), 507–33.

Yea, S., Mohsin, A. K. M. and Fordyce, D. (2014) *A thousand and one days: stories of hardship from South Asian migrant workers in Singapore*, Singapore, Banglar Kantha Publications.

Yeo, S. J., Hee, L. and Heng, c. K. (2012) 'Urban informality and everyday (night)life: a field study in Singapore', *International Development Planning Review*, 34(4), 369–90.

Yeoh, B. S. A. (2006) 'Bifurcated labour: the unequal incorporaton of transmigrants in Singapore', *Tijdschrift voor economische en sociale geografie*, 97(1), 26–37.

Yeoh, B. S. A. and Huang, S. (1998) 'Negotiating public space: strategies and styles of migrant female domestic workers', *Urban Studies*, 35(3), 583–602.

Yeoh, B. S. A. and Huang, S. (2003) 'civil space in a city-state: foreign domestic workers in Singapore' in R. Iredale, c. Hawksley and S. castles (eds), *Migration in the Asia Pacific: population, settlement and citizenship issues*, Northhampton, Edward Elgar, 341–54.

Chapter 9a

Migrant Workers and Mobile Communication in Pandemic Times*

Arul Chib

Wee Kim Wee School of Communication and Information
Singapore Internet Research Centre
Nanyang Technological University

Rajiv G. Aricat

Wee Kim Wee School of Communication and Information
Nanyang Technological University

In this 2017 article, we examined the mobile communication practices of low-skilled South Asian male migrant workers living and working in Singapore. In a global city where low-wage migrant workers are paradoxically admitted for their labour but excluded in local society, these migrants have turned to mobile phones as a way of dealing with their marginalised position in Singapore.

Mobile phones are embedded in their lives and livelihoods in complex ways. Our research found that mobile communication between co-ethnic

*Reflections on Chib, A. and Aricat, R. G. (2017). Belonging and communicating in a bounded cosmopolitanism: The role of mobile phones in the integration of transnational migrants in Singapore, *Inf. Commun. Soc.*, Vol. 20, No. 3, pp. 482–496. DOI:10.1080/1369118X.2016.1168470.

workers resulted in productivity gains at work and enhanced social bonding. In negotiating their marginalised social position, these migrants gained a degree of empowerment by improving their knowledge and technical skills, while extending their social network to include peers from other cultures/countries. In this sense, the rise of digital technologies, social messaging apps, and data connectivity have become a platform for migrant workers to grow in their personal and professional lives. However, our study also found limitations in their digital engagement, in that despite the transformative impact of ICTs on migrant workers' lives, they still have to contend with restrictive spaces and issues of alienation and discrimination that mark their lives in the global city.

Our research is relevant to the role of mobile phones and communication technologies on the lives of migrant workers in the context of COVID-19, particularly during the outbreak in migrant dormitories. The structural characteristics of these densely packed dormitories, coupled with congestions at worksites and spaces for gatherings, created hotspots for widespread infections amongst male migrant workers [Sim & Kok, 2020]. A nationwide circuit-breaker to mitigate infections extended to these dormitories, where migrant workers were placed under strict quarantine and movement restrictions. Media reports covered the dormitory cases, distinguishing them as a major challenge vis-à-vis community spread.

We highlight two observations from the case of the outbreaks in migrant dormitories. First, mobile communication acted as a lifeline for quarantined workers, both for frequent interaction with left-behind families as well as for tracking the evolving pandemic situation. Social media applications provided a source of social support, and as a means of forging friendships despite movement restrictions [Chua, 2020]. However, the isolation of quarantine further bounded their engagement with mainstream society, resulting in the dispersal of myths and misinformation about the virus via social media. Secondly, social media arguably increased both local and foreign public attention towards the problems affecting migrant workers during the pandemic — poor dormitory infrastructure and workplace hygiene challenges — leading to action from both non-profit organisations and the government, and raising awareness among locals. On the other hand, the outbreak has also stirred debates about the rise of prejudice fuelled by social media discourse. The infodemic of fake news combined with online prejudice has been linked to rising anti-immigrant sentiment globally, and Singapore is no exception.

Singapore will continue to rely extensively on immigrants in all categories to remain economically competitive. The immediate challenge, however, is to manage immigration from neighbouring countries ravaged by the pandemic. Mobile technologies have a role to play for individuals and their relationship with society. Firstly, the use of digital communication technologies for health and safety, such as the *TraceTogether* application, should be reviewed for their effectiveness and also in relation to privacy concerns, given that these are also technologies of governance and surveillance [Das and Zhang, 2020]. Government agencies can partner with research institutions and non-governmental organisations (NGOs) to harness the embeddedness of these technologies in migrants' lives. Secondly, improved digital literacy of migrants at the bottom of the economic pyramid is required to minimise risks from misinformation. We recommend technology-supported solutions — mobile applications, interactive kiosks, etc. — to tackle the menace of any future outbreaks, and to ensure physical and psychological well-being. Finally, investigation of the prevailing social media discourse can be a means to manage favourable public perception of foreign workers, with counter-attitudinal campaigns acknowledging migrants' social contributions and aiding the economy in medium-term recovery and long-term prosperity.

References

Chua, E. (2020, 26 October). Staying plugged in: Video app TikTok gives migrant workers a means to stay connected for support. *The Straits Times*. Retrieved from https://www.straitstimes.com/singapore/staying-plugged-in-video-app-tiktok-gives-migrant-workers-a-means-to-stay-connected-for

Das, D. and Zhang, J. J. (2021) Pandemic in a smart city: Singapore's COVID-19 management through technology & society, *Urban Geography*, Vol. 42, No. 3, pp. 408–416. DOI: 10.1080/02723638.2020.1807168

Sim, D. and Kok, X. (2020, 17 April). How did migrant dormitories become Singapore's biggest coronavirus cluster? *South China Morning Post*. Retrieved from https://www.scmp.com/week-asia/explained/article/3080466/how-did-migrant-worker-dormitories-become-singapores-biggest

Chapter 9b

Belonging and Communicating in a Bounded Cosmopolitanism: The Role of Mobile Phones in the Integration of Transnational Migrants in Singapore*

Arul Chib[a,b,c] and Rajiv G. Aricat[a]

[a]*Wee Kim Wee School of Communication and Information, Nanyang Technological University, Singapore*

[b]*Singapore Internet Research Centre, Nanyang Technological University, Singapore*

[c]*arulchib@ntu.edu.sg*

The unabated influx of transnational labour migrants has been accompanied by complex societal fissures, from differential policies to the creation of isolated cultural geographies. In Singapore, citizens voice their aggravation caused by transients' lack of acculturation, and the resultant risks posed to the cosmopolitan vision of the state. We examine the

*This article was originally published in *Inf. Commun. Soc.*, Vol. 20, No. 3, pp. 482–496. DOI:10.1080/1369118X.2016.1168470.

intersection of transnational acculturation with mediated communication via mobile phones within the domains of life and work. Data from in-depth qualitative interviews (75) allowed for thick descriptions. We find that, despite encountering heterotopic practices, transnational migrant workers engage in a phenomenon we label 'bounded cosmopolitanism', or the ability to engage in learning, enjoy economic growth, and embrace cultural hybridity, to escape the shackles of race, class, and gender. Mobile phones play a significant role in providing open participatory spaces; yet; this phenomenon signifying openness, innovation, and acceptance is restricted to organizational workspaces. We therefore conclude with comments on the implications of applying management perspectives to broader societal challenges, and propose shifting of the discourse from the bounded confines of the organization to that of society.

Keywords: ICT; mobile phone; migrants; acculturation; cultural identity; organizational commitment; cosmopolitanism; integration

One of the few uplifting narratives within the migrant crisis unfolding across the globe concerns mobile phones. In Europe, the media reports on the life-saving influence of the refugees' use of smartphones for gaining information about route-maps, border restrictions, transportation and accommodation and most recently, real-time updates on parliament proceedings regarding legislation (Brunwasser, 2015). In Singapore, mobiles phones aid blue-collar foreign workers to keep in touch with distant friends and family (Thompson, 2009). There is a rich literature on migrants in Singapore, ranging from financial remittances (Sundararajan, Sirajudin, Jinnah, & Chib, 2015), trans-national mothering (Chib, Malik, Aricat, & Kadir, 2014), resisting employer control (Thomas & Lim, 2011), and for gender empowerment (Nguyen, Chib, & Mahalingam, 2016).

This research study aims to investigate the role of mobile phones in alleviating or deepening the marginalization and alienation experienced by migrant workers. We further existing research by parsing the impact of information and communication technologies (ICTs) on significant life domains of firstly, personal well-being, and secondly, professional livelihood attainment. A secondary objective is to build upon existing research conducted within the respondent group, triangulating results of quantitative analysis with qualitative data to provide thick descriptions of the lived experience, and discuss possible explanations from a critical perspective.

To achieve these objectives, we situate the analysis within the theoretical lens of acculturation as a bi-dimensional model encompassing both home and host cultures. We argue that the impact of mobile phones needs to be examined as a complex social phenomenon, with differences across, in this specific case, gender, life domains, and cultural belonging and diversity. Finally, we comment on the impact of the intersection of transnational mobility with mediated communication on the Singaporean cosmopolitan ideal.

Migration

The unprecedented movement of peoples across and within national boundaries has been accompanied by societal fissures between glimmering megapolises and abandoned villages, between suave cosmopolitan urbanites and hard-hat donning construction workers, between the documented and the illegal. Hitherto largely dormant, these stresses are being catalysed by the global market-based system's insatiable demand for growth. Of a total global migrant stock of 232 million (United Nations, 2013), labour migrants constitute 105 million (IOM, 2014), the sheer numbers causing substantive pressure on host country societies. A developmental success story, Singapore has historically encouraged labour inflows from South and Southeast Asia to combat local labour-force declines (Yeoh, 2007), with the consequence that non-citizens now constitute 40% of the population of the tiny island-state of 5.4 million (Sing Stat, 2014).

Singaporean policy, guided by open market principles, has historically emphasized multiculturalism (Noor & Leong, 2013), because of, and despite, ethnic Chinese comprising almost three-quarters of the population. Multiculturalism as a discursive and policy tool for ethnic harmony amongst residents has since been expanded to incorporate cultural hybridity to attract international financial investment and human talent. A broader and longer term imagining of the vision has added globalization and sophistication to arrive at cosmopolitanism as a discursive tool for the promotion of the island (Yeoh & Soco, 2014). While these neo-liberal principles have performed remarkably efficiently for those citizens and highly skilled 'foreign talent' at the upper income strata, the social compact in Singapore has faced considerable challenges when faced with an influx of transient low-skilled migrant workers (Jones, 2012).

We are particularly interested in the ensuing societal stresses within the context of transmigration across home and host national boundaries, expanding the examinations to relationships in multiple domains of life and work (Basch, Glick Schiller, & Szanton-Blanc, 1994). Labour migrants, or working-class cosmopolitans (Yeoh & Soco, 2014) with limited education in the liberal arts or exposure to multicultural settings, already face a multitude of adaptation difficulties, culminating in psychological alienation and, often, depression (Swagler & Ellis, 2003), to which is added the burden of a far from welcoming environment. The systematic differential treatment of immigrants has ranged from preferential government policies (Lei & Li, 2012) to employment entitlements (Aldashev, Gernandt, & Thomsen, 2012) for locals and long-term residents. Being employed in low-income, blue-collar occupations (Low, 2002; Rahman & Lian, 2005), and segregated into distinct cultural geographies (Law, 2001), transnational migrant workers face marginalization in terms of limited legal, financial, political, and social status versus citizens (Yeoh, 2004).

The systemic marginalization of migrants has recently extended to social exclusion and public resentment (Jacobs, 2012; 'Singapore's angry', 2013). In the midst of a recession, and unable to match wealth levels of a global elite class arriving on their shores, citizens reacted negatively to the perceived pressure put on their wages and public services by these highly visible migrant workers. Typical sentiments expressed include,

> … foreigners feed our sense of insecurity. If that sounds like a poor reason for our mistrust of foreigners, we can lay claim to the second: Foreigners, through no fault of their own, cannot partake in a strong and pulsating Singapore identity. (Chang, 2010)

Similar to the immigration backlash being witnessed globally in migration-recipient nations, civil society in Singapore offered staunch resistance to a White Paper on Population, aimed at enhancing migration, promulgated by the government (Goh, Yong, & Sim, 2013).

Acculturation

As a basis for research on the impact of communication on cultural belonging (Kim, 2007), the concept of acculturation is defined as 'phenomena which result when groups of individuals having different cultures come into continuous first-hand contact' (Redfield, Linton, & Herskovits, 1936, p. 149). Migrants are faced with a conundrum, having to align their existing relationship with the home culture with the new, and largely unfamiliar, host culture encountered (Berry, 1997). This pluralistic-typological approach to acculturation has been used to describe the problems migrants face in the new culture (Liu, 2007; Piontkowski, Florack, Hoelker, & Obdrzálek, 2000). We operationalize the bi-dimensional acculturation indicators as *cultural identity*, which determines the loyalty felt towards a home culture, and *multiculturalism*, which denotes the level of affinity and favourable attitudes exhibited towards other cultures. Prior research finds that cultural identity negatively affects acculturation (Jeffres & Hur, 1981), and is often evoked in response to discriminatory practices and policies (Rumbaut, 2008), while multicultural attitudes have a positive effect on adaptability (Chae & Foley, 2010; Frankenberg, Kupper, Wagner, & Bongard, 2013).

The bi-dimensional model has faced criticism for being fragmentary in explaining the totality of human experience (Skuza, 2007). Prior studies have noted that migrants are treated differentially by the host society depending on demographics such as socioeconomic and gender backgrounds (Luque, del Carmen García Fernández, & Tejada, 2006; Yeoh & Huang, 2015). Furthermore, scholars find that migrants acculturate differently to distinct life domains such as work, social life, religion, and politics (Arends-Tóth & Van De Vijver, 2003; Navas et al., 2005). After establishing the progression of our research on male migrant acculturation across gender and class, we extend the application of the bi-dimensional model of acculturation to analyse migrant adaptation outcomes across specific life domains. We operationalize the two adaptation outcomes as migrant *life satisfaction* within the personal domain and *organizational commitment* to professional organizations in the work domain. The concept of life satisfaction was derived from the series of studies associated with the Mutual Intercultural Relations In Plural Societies (MIRIPS) (Berry, 2010), and comprises proficiency in the host society language (Berry, 2005) adaptation to host society rules, and overall comfort in the host society (Skuza, 2007). Organizational commitment denotes employees' attachment to an organization, and is comprised of three constructs – compliance, identification, and internalization (Claus, Lungu, & Bhattacharjee, 2011; O'Reilly, Chatman, & Caldwell, 1991). In this study, we examined for both cultural identification and engagement within both personal and professional domains.

Mobile Phones

There is a substantial research tradition examining the usage of modern ICTs such as mobile phones by migrant groups. From a functional perspective, mobiles have aided in the maintenance of relationships with the home country (Thompson, 2009; Vertovec, 2004) and are associated with remittance transfers (Singh, 2010; Sundararajan et al., 2015). From a professional perspective, mobile phone usage enabled economic benefits garnered in the host culture (Qiu, 2009), and has facilitated job networking (Fortunati, Manganelli, Law, & Yang, 2008; Ngan & Ma, 2008). There is evidence that communication with informal social networks acts as a significant source of emotional, informational, and instrumental support for migrants (Aroian, 1992; Hernández, Pozo, & Alonso-Morillejo, 2004; Leslie, 1992; Lynam, 1985), enabling both personal well-being and professional growth.

At this point, we depart from the extant literature and focus on Singapore, first in terms of differential gender effects of technology adaptation. For women, we find that mobile phone usage acts as both a constraining technology and a liberating technology, with employers of domestic workers limiting usage and using it as surveillance tool (Anderson, 2000; Lin & Sun, 2011), and as a means of resistance to overcome employer control (Thomas & Lim, 2011), respectively. In their personal lives, foreign domestic workers use mobile phone strategies to balance the dialectic tensions arising from transnational motherhood (Chib et al., 2014). An earlier study amongst Bangladeshi male and Filipino female migrants (Chib, Wilkin, & Mei Hua, 2013) found that for women, mobile phone usage alleviated stress by increasing social support; in particular, emotional support positively influenced psychological well-being.

Our second point of departure from the extant literature regards the 'blurring of lives and livelihoods' framework developed by Donner (2009). He argues that motivations of using the technology have resulted in a blurring of boundaries between personal and professional life domains. Continuing from the study described in the preceding paragraph (Chib et al., 2013), we found that, in contrast to women, the stress experienced by male migrant workers increased with mobile usage, particularly whilst receiving increased emotional support. We argued previously (Chib & Aricat, 2012) that the increased stress caused by calls from friends and family was a reason for the distinct separation of mobile phone usage in personal and professional social spaces by male migrant workers. In this research study, we aim to distinguish between well-being in these two life domains for male migrants, caused by their acculturation orientations and mobile phone calling practices.

To further investigate these phenomena, we conducted quantitative analysis (Aricat & Chib, 2014) to determine the influence of acculturation (cultural identity and multiculturalism) and mobile phone usage (calls to home and host cultures) on adaptation outcomes of life satisfaction and organizational commitment in personal and professional life domains, respectively. We found that multiculturalism positively affected life satisfaction and organizational commitment, while cultural identity positively affected only organizational commitment. This paper illuminates the quantitative investigation with an in-depth triangulation of qualitative data. Building upon the argument derived from the literature, the research question interrogates the role of the mobile phone in professional and personal setting in the process of acculturation for migrants within host societies that aim, as a discursive ideal, for multiculturalism and cosmopolitanism.

Methodology

We conducted 75 in-depth interviews among male blue-collar workers from Bangladesh and India in Singapore. The aim of the exercise was to triangulate the quantitative results in terms of an enriched understanding of migrants' communication strategies in the two life domains, and their influence on adaptation outcomes. Following the bi-dimensional model, qualitative data were analysed under the themes of (i) differential impact of cultural identity and multicultural thinking in organizational setting on migrants' adaptation to personal and professional domains and (ii) migrants' mobile phone communication to members of home and host cultures as pertaining to social and work life. We recorded a series of narrative descriptions and present a thick description of the lived experiences of the respondents, drawn from interviews and ethnographic methods, including participant observation in migrants' day-to-day activities. The interviews were conducted in English, Hindi, and Malayalam, and were translated and transcribed for analysis and presentation. In order to preserve the integrity of the data and capture the lived experiences of the respondents, the quotations have retained the particular intonations and cadence of the respondents. We have elaborated upon the interpretations only where necessary. The minimum age of participation was established at 21, following approval from Nanyang Technological University Institutional Review Board.

Findings

Belonging and communication

The quantitative results (Aricat & Chib, 2014) suggest that migrants' multicultural outlook has a positive influence in the context of both organizational and personal life, while their identification with ethnic culture was positively related only to organizational commitment. Mobile phone calling to the home culture had no influence in either the personal or the professional realm, though mobile phone calling to members from other communities in the host country was related positively to organizational commitment. Migrants who were older and more educated experienced greater life satisfaction. The remainder of the section presents the qualitative findings to support, and explain, the results of the quantitative analysis.

Professional domain

First, the strict distinction between personal and professional domains described by Chib and Aricat (2012) is repeated. Migrant workers often have to comply with industrial work place regulations which limit their ability to answer mobile calls. Furthermore, the risk of their professional identity being compromised, as well as safety concerns, leads to self-control.

> I was in refinery earlier. There no one is allowed to use mobile phones. It's the specialty of the area. Safety issue.
>
> Work time, I on top go … working high … but I cannot take hand phone. Because this time my mind is 'I working'. If I take hand-phone, then drop … then it's problem. Because I go the ladder, this time call I take one … one hand no enough … after fall down … that's why I cannot.

The resistance to personal mobile use in the workplace can also be attributed to the heightened anxiety felt by recipients of potentially urgent calls from the home culture, failure to respond to which led to increased stress. This reiterates the finding that increased emotional support via mediated mobile communication leads in turn to greater stress (Chib et al., 2013). We further argue that migrant workers increasingly identify with the professional nature of the organization that characterizes Singapore, and modify their behaviours accordingly.

> Work time my house any problem, eh … [family] call 'missed call'. Important time, eh … many many call. Normal time one time call, ok. Two time three time. So, two three missed call means something urgent. I asked them, 'This time, this time you call me, I know. This time this time my work time. Don't disturb.' Not family members alone, but everyone knows, all my friends, everyone.

As a consequence, migrants create distinct rules that isolate personal and professional mobile usage. Certainly, there is instrumental value in the mobile phone usage, with acquisition of knowledge about advanced uses of the mobile phone to address migrant workers' inadequacies in English.

> There is internet [on mobile phone] now. Many things can. I don't know some English vocabulary. I don't know its meaning. I can searching my phone, eh … My phone dictionary I can get from very soon. Last time eh.. I waiting, go to room and see dictionary. This one taking a long time. Because, sometime I go to room also I forgot this word. Actually, I hear this word, eh.. I cannot [understand]. This is happens many times. Because, somebody talked to me, some higher officer also talked to me. Some they give me a letter, or something eh … project details, something. Because, some words I don't know. Then I need to check this: 'what is the actual meaning of this one'. Now I am very easy. I can use this some Android app, eh … That way it's very helpful. English is very much required to go up in my career. Exactly.

The use of the mobile enables micro-coordination at work (Ling & Yttri, 2002), further occurring within the organizational hierarchy, allowing for a mediated space for multicultural interactions.

> I use mobile phone during work to discuss work related matters with co-workers and company professionals like supervisor and engineer. Calls are related to work, like arranging materials … in my case, my duty is to take measurement. For matters related to these, we call the supervisor and engineers always on mobile phone. On mobile phone, this communication becomes easier. Without mobile phone this coordination will not happen.

Migrant workers realize the value of the mobile phone communication within the multicultural job environment, to the extent that they are willing to accept infrequent exceptions to the barrier established between personal and professional mobile usage. Migrant worker's personal subsidization of work calls points to the perceived value of mobile phone usage to their organizational commitment.

> Work-related calls is only at the time of work. Outside work sometime only.
>
> We use mobile to call our boss and to call our colleagues. Yes, I receive job-related calls in the mobile. The company does not pay me for that. It doesn't pay because, we're not making jobrelated calls always.

> Sometimes … during work, if one falls sick, I call the manager … .then the manager himself will take us [to the doctor].

Migrant workers' organizational commitment was enhanced by perceived shared cultural values with the organizational management. The following narratives contrast the treatment of workers in Singapore versus prior work engagements; note the mediation of the mobile phone in both intense personal situations occurring within the professional environment.

> Once a call came from home saying my grandfather passed away. They did not call me, but my manager. The manager called to our work site and conveyed the news. He asked my supervisor to allow me to sit in the canteen for 10 to 15 minutes or to make arrangements to go to the room, if I wanted so. This was in between my work. He permitted me to call home, if I wanted to, or to go back to my room and call home, whatever I chose to.
>
> When I was in Saudi, I was not even informed when my father passed away. The company didn't inform me. Some firms are like that, especially in Arab countries. They don't inform, thinking that we will leave immediately. So, I didn't know about my father's demise. I got to know after a few months. Everything was through letters then. Now, we call daily.

Co-ethnic professional networks aid migrant workers in adapting to the professional behaviours and routines required in Singapore, and in furthering their career ambitions.

> You should see this place in the morning, when everyone awaits their transport to work. It becomes a sea of workers. We do coordinate between ourselves using mobile devices. We wake up early in the morning setting alarm in it.
>
> Actually speaking, I'm trying to get into a better job than the current one.. sometimes.. [while working in the religious organization] I can get introduced to many Malayali friends. With them I sometimes enquire whether there is a good chance.. I ask them about it often … then I can get to know about many people.

Personal domain

Telecommunication has long been identified as an important means of maintaining regular contact with distant friends and family in the home culture (Metykova, 2010; Vertovec, 2004). Within Singapore, migrants reached out to familiar co-ethnics for companionship and social support, particularly informational, as related to their workplace (as described in the precious section). From an instrumental perspective, as seen in the professional domain, mobile phones allow for micro-coordination (Ling & Yttri, 2002) with co-ethnic migrants.

> Mobile phone has helped me many things in my Singapore life. Example, one day my friend called me 4.30: 'Hey, do you have any information of the particular movie – Deiva Thirumagal.' I want to see movie. That time I don't have the newspaper, magazine anything. So, I come to see the shop, there also no stock. Then I go to my mobile, just browsing the time I find out the timing – 6 o'clock. … . We could save time and coordinate properly.

Mobile phone calling to the home culture, however, acted as double-edged sword. Migrants need to struggle with the dialectical tension (Baxter & Montgomery, 1996) caused as a consequence of mediated communication. On the one hand, communication alleviated feelings of loneliness and provided much-needed succour.

> Sleep time I talk to my mother … because every people mother very important … fathermother. I talk to night time one minute, two minute, five minute … And I sleeping, I very happy.

Yet, on the other hand, the brief snatches of mediated contact accentuated these very same feelings and acted as a reminder of the vast distances between the home culture and the departed migrant. Mobile calling to the home culture was found to have limited (quantitative) effects, with frequent mediated communication with family creating dialectical tensions for migrant workers.

> Sometimes I use internet on mobile, but most of the time I go to the cybercafé. And through Google and through Internet Explorer I read

> news ... I want to make them [fellow countrymen] concern what's going on in my country just now. I make them aware. I talk to them about these matters. We earn money here, but we sacrifice our times. You know, I left my family, my friends. All I miss it here, so much. But I have nothing to do. Because here life is very difficult.

The cultural identity of the migrant is often juxtaposed versus that of the local culture, whose practices remain a source of mis-alignment for the new arrival.

> So many people have some or other things do ... some people have girlfriends, like this ... Singapore[ans] also have, right? But I don't like this one ... Saturday Sunday coming, many people drinking, I don't do that ... I don't' spend money on these things.

The heightened cultural identity of the migrant, often reinforced via mobile phone communication, also acts as a cocooning force within limited geographical locations, such as the factories, ports, and construction sites constituting the workplace, the dormitories where they reside, and ethnic ghettos such as the Little India neighbourhood. Yeoh and Soco (2014) point out the irony of these pioneers of transnational mobilities being constrained within fixed boundaries of cultural experiences within cosmopolitan environments created upon the premise of cultural diversity and difference. These cultural geographies, often cordoned away from the local populace in outlying locations, become an echochamber of cultural identity, with activities ranging from the mundane and daily, such as cooking ethnic meals (Law, 2001), to the special, such as religious or social events.

> In Singapore I have more than 50 friends from my own community [Tamil]. I have their numbers, I contact them regularly. No specific purpose, just friendship.
>
> There is no socially oriented activity to involve. No such organization has approached us, nor have we been informed that there is any such activity going on. We don't know about it. The usual activity outside job is to chat with people from our Malayali culture, go shopping along with them ... nothing else.

Nonetheless, we find that the lived experience of the worker in a diverse workplace increasingly marks a shift from partaking in a confining cultural identity to a nascent multiculturalism; however, much of this arises from opportunities presented at the dormitories and the workplace. For some migrants, interaction with other cultures from their own nation was a novel experience. The presence of fellow nationals from states other than one's own offered a common experience in a foreign environment that led to emergent bonds of friendship.

> I have lot of friends from my own [Tamil] and also from Malayali community. Around 15 of them. We have life outside work … for instance, tomorrow they have arranged for a trip to Marina Bay. They called me and informed me.

The multicultural make-up of the Singaporean workplace led to close proximity with both local and foreign, other than the migrant's own, cultures. We further note that the communicative practices, and therefore locations for multicultural engagement, occurred not merely with peers at the bottom of the hierarchy, but within the organization structure as well (as noted above). As migrants from South Asia collaborated during work-hours and developed language skills, social relationships formed. The mobile facilitated these nascent practices of cosmopolitanism that achieved cultural diversity and incorporated difference into daily practices.

> I don't have very close friends from other cultures. But, things are going fine. I communicate to them using English. I am comfortable communicating with them. They understand my English …
>
> I do communicate with other communities, especially at work – to Burmese, Bangla and Thai. I call them sometimes, outside work also. With some I do talk outside work also … . Say, when he goes home for leave then also I maintain contact.

Whilst we acknowledge that experiences of migrants may lead to a growing cosmopolitanism in the workplace, we cannot deny broader societal trends, and specific events, that act as a brake on these ideals of openness and inclusion. Against the backdrop of a global economic recession, and a concomitant hardening of conservative opposition to a variety of migrants, Singaporeans attitudes towards migration have coalesced, catalysed by a rare 2013 riot[1] by South Asian migrant workers numbering around 400. The resultant, often incendiary, debate revolved around the complications of harbouring a significant population of non-acculturated migrant workers, focusing on their lack of socialization with Singaporeans, labour grievances, alcoholism, behavioural issues, and xenophobic sentiments triggered by the riot (Heng, 2013).

> These bunch of ingrates must be repatriated. We had [sic] not had a riot since the early days n [sic] we r [sic] not going to have one due to foreign elements. I want my old country back. Someone up there must do something swift. ("Not the Singapore", 2014)

Some (Mei Hua Raman, 2014) suggest deeper underlying motivations to the phenomenon of migrant flashpoints, in contrast to existing viewpoints attributing these incendiary events to particular circumstantial factors. Given the discussion here, it is worth noting that the event occurred in a social space appropriated by migrant workers as a cultural geography, and not in a workplace setting. For the general mass of migrant workers, the associated discrimination and incrimination created alienation (separation within the bi-dimensional acculturation model) (Berry, 2005), possibly making it relatively easier to adapt within the confined organization culture than broader Singaporean society. Perceived discrimination by the host society causes reluctance of migrants to interact with locals, as well as makes them less willing to see themselves as intercultural (Chen, 2010)

> Singapore culture is OK. Each one will have his own opinion about it. What I feel is that those in high status do not have any connection with us. They are in their own level. People like us are in our own groups.

Beyond the longer term imperatives of acculturation with the host society, in the face of resistance and discrimination, the primary purpose of short-term employment with a focus on economics is a constant reminder by distant relatives. Those left behind are often financially dependent on the migrant's remittances and often burdened by the debt incurred to ensure passage and employment.

> In any case, we will not be able to go home. We have to stick to it somehow. When I call home they say, 'Whatever it is, you stay there for two years. Look for another job.' That's what they say. There is nothing to be done after going home. So, I'm thinking of sticking to it for two years.
>
> I don't use mobile during work. I don't try to do that … because, when I do my work, if a call comes from home, then I would be tensed. Then saying that if the matter to be conveyed over the call is likely to cause tension, then I would be tensed, I never use the mobile [during work]. I have told my family not to call during this time.. Urgent calls during work … but I leave behind my mobile in the room. When I work, if something negative comes to my knowledge, then I feel tension. Then the attention goes there.

For migrants on temporary work permits, the migrant experience necessarily remains of a transitory nature, intensifying cultural identity and exacerbating the problem of ghettoization (Ryan, Sales, Tilki, & Siara, 2008; Weiss, Nincic, & Nolan, 2005).

> Comparing working here and in our homeland, I can be close to my family if I work in Kerala. Not only that, there family means, everyone has a connection with one another. I don't see it here. Other cultural differences … here it's modern, whereas our place is not that modern. I don't have any interest to mix with the culture here. If I get a good benefit from the job, I will stay here for long-term. But to stay here permanently as a citizen, I'm not interested.

While the observed emergent practices of multiculturalism suggest a shift towards a working-class cosmopolitanism arising out of a lived experience, these forces nonetheless remain limited and bounded.

> I have friends from local cultures also – Malay, Chinese, Singaporean. The local friends are sometimes my colleagues and also those who are staying here. I have the numbers of all of them. I don't call them regularly, but only if necessary.

Conclusion

The next chapter in the Singaporean growth narrative as a cosmopolis (Reid, 2004) is premised, beyond integration in the global capitalist enterprise with concomitant flows of goods, services, and people, on ideals of multiculturalism and cultural hybridity (Turner, 2010). The ideal cosmopolitan state, as opposed to the nation with notions of boundaries, hierarchies, and citizenship, is designed to embrace diversity and difference as extended to openness and acceptance of the Other. As a space for openness, these ideals unleash the forces of creativity, innovation, sustainable growth – all situated within an inclusive participatory environment.

This discourse has piqued the interest of a global elite, substantial proof of which is readily available in the form of the foreign capital and foreign talent that has arrived on these shores as the global economic malaise forces them to scour the planet for growth opportunities. Yeoh (2004) argues that the transient and transnational migrant slides in-between the discursive spaces, not so much forgotten as systematically excluded as a legitimate participant in the cosmopolitan ambition. We counter-argue that, instead of being marginalized, the differences of the subaltern allow for the practice of a 'bounded cosmopolitanism', aided partially by the advent of global ICTs such as mobile phones. It is important to note that we conceptually distinguish 'bounded cosmopolitanism' versus the 'bounded solidarity' (Ling, 2008; Ling, Bertel, & Sundsøy, 2012), which argues that mobile phones may reinforce close ties at the expense of weaker ties in our social networks. In fact, we find the reverse phenomenon to be true in the case of migrants, for whom mobiles open up opportunities in both personal and professional realms.

The research problem was premised on an emergent social situation in Singapore – an otherwise multicultural society in which multiple ethnicities reportedly live in harmony – wherein transnational migrants are increasingly becoming target for host society's negative sentiments, antipathy and even resentment. Current practices engaging transnational migrant workers operate via the production of difference (Witteborn, 2011). Laws and policies differentially determine economic, legal, and socio-economic status for migrant labour versus citizens and the elite guests. Witteborn (2011) describes the heterotopias, or places for social deviants, for asylum-seeking migrants to Germany as 'material places and social places which represent exclusion' (p. 1148). The physical cultural geographies (work-sites, dormitories, ethnic ghettos, and even the open vans incessantly shuttling between them) of Singapore mirror these heterotopias, extended to the discursive heterotopia of the 2013 riots, which applies to every South Asian transnational migrant worker. The formerly quarantined spaces of physical being no longer afford the migrant worker the protection of anonymity and distance – the stain of heterotopia as a source of social instability is now carried by each individual.

This is not to argue solely for the existence of such a dystopic reality beneath the veneer of an elite cosmopolitanism created for citizens and foreign talent. We find succour in the knowledge that a 'bounded cosmopolitanism' is simultaneously being negotiated by transnational migrant workers, aided by mobile phones. For this subaltern labour, there is an optimism and a focus in economic empowerment via the acquisition and execution of technical skills; there is pride and effort expended in the attainment of language and knowledge proficiency; there is the creation of multiple new relationships that transcend ethnicity, nationality, and hierarchy. Migrants are using their transnational experiences mediated by technology to transcend limitations of class, race, education, and gender. In effect, the ideals of cosmopolitanism are alive and well, although bounded.

We argue that ICTs provide open participatory platforms for learning and growth. Mobiles in particular subvert the closed boundaries of restrictive spaces, cutting across the cultural geographies to allow communication with a variety of others, and providing access to information. We find that the influence of these technologies is greater in the professional sphere than in the personal environment – social transformation seems to be limited to the organizational context. An examination of the broader social context finds that technology usage is determined by the power structures in the society as well as the social practices of the users. In view of this multifaceted critique of acculturation and technology's role in the process, we propose redrawing the contours of the concept of 'societal challenge' from a management perspective to a political praxis, shifting both the discourse and the practice from the bounded confines of the organization to that of society.

Note

1. An Indian migrant worker was killed in a bus accident in Little India, a busy business district in the country. The driver of the bus was a Singaporean.

Disclosure Statement

No potential conflict of interest was reported by the authors.

Funding

This work was supported by the International Development Research Centre under the SIRCA Grant.

Notes on Contributors

Arul Chib is an Associate Professor at Wee Kim Wee School of Communication and Information, and Director of the Singapore Internet Research Centre, Nanyang Technological University, Singapore. [email: arulchib@ntu.edu.sg]

Rajiv G. Aricat was a graduate student (at the time of writing) at the Wee Kim Wee School of Communication and Information, Nanyang Technological University, Singapore. [email: aric0001@ntu. edu.sg]

References

Aldashev, A., Gernandt, J., & Thomsen, S. L. (2012). The immigrant-native wage gap in Germany. *Jahrbucher fur Nationalokonomie und Statistik*, *232*(5), 490–517.

Anderson, B. (2000). *Doing the dirty work? The global politics of domestic labour*. London: Zed Books.

Arends-Tóth, J., & Van De Vijver, F. J. R. (2003). Multiculturalism and acculturation: Views of Dutch and Turkish–Dutch. *European Journal of Social Psychology*, *33*(2), 249–266. doi:10. 1002/ejsp.143

Aricat, R., & Chib, A. (2014, December 14). *Social integration of male migrant workers in Singapore: The enabling and constraining roles of mobile phones.* Proceedings of the association for information systems special interest group for ICT in global development (SIG GlobDev), Auckland, New Zealand.

Aroian, K. J. (1992). Sources of social support and conflict for Polish immigrants. *Qualitative Health Research*, *2*(2), 178–207.

Basch, L., Glick Schiller, N., & Szanton-Blanc, C. (1994). *Nations unbound.* Langhorne, PA: Gordon and Breach.

Baxter, L. A., & Montgomery, B. M. (1996). *Relating: Dialogues and dialectics.* New York, NY: The Guilford Press.

Berry, J. W. (1997). Immigration, acculturation, and adaptation. *Applied Psychology: An International Review*, *46*(1), 5–34.

Berry, J. W. (2005). Acculturation: Living successfully in two cultures. *International Journal of Intercultural Relations*, *29*(6), 697–712.

Berry, J. W. (2010). *Mutual Intercultural Relations in Plural Societies (MIRIPS).* Retrieved January 28, 2012, from http://cacr.victoria.ac.nz/projects/research-projects/mirips

Brunwasser, M. (2015, August 25). A 21st century migrants checklist: Food, shelter, smartphone. *The New York Times.*

Chae, M. H., & Foley, P. F. (2010). Relationship of ethnic identity, acculturation, and psychological well-being among Chinese, Japanese, and Korean Americans. *Journal of Counseling & Development*, *88*(4), 466–476.

Chang, R. (2010, July 5). Life is tough at 24 with us and them. *The Straits Times*, p. A2.

Chen, W. (2010). Internet-usage patterns of immigrants in the process of intercultural adaptation. *Cyber Psychology, Behavior & Social Networking*, *13*(4), 387–399.

Chib, A., & Aricat, R. (2012). Seeking the non-developmental within the developmental: Mobile phones in the globalized migration context. In R. Parker & R. P. Appelbaum (Eds.), *Emerging economies, emerging technologies: Can technology make a difference in development?* (pp. 153– 167). New York, NY: Routledge.

Chib, A., Malik, S., Aricat, R. G., & Kadir, S. Z. (2014). Migrant mothering and mobile phones: Negotiations of transnational identity. *Mobile Media & Communication*, *2*(1), 73–93. doi:10. 1177/2050157913506007

Chib, A., Wilkin, H., & Mei Hua, S. (2013). Singapore migrants workers' use of mobile phones to seek social support. *Information Technologies & International Development*, *9*(4), 19–34.

Claus, L., Lungu, A. P., & Bhattacharjee, S. (2011). The effects of individual, organizational and societal variables on the job performance of expatriate managers. *International Journal of Management*, *28*(1), 249–271.

Donner, J. (2009). Blurring livelihoods and lives: The social uses of mobile phones and socioeconomic development. *Innovations: Technology, Governance, Globalization*, *4*(1), 91–101.

Fortunati, L., Manganelli, A., Law, P.-L., & Yang, S. (2008). Beijing calling … mobile communication in contemporary China. *Knowledge, Technology & Policy*, *21*(1), 19–27. doi:10.1007/ s12130-008-9040-1

Frankenberg, E., Kupper, K., Wagner, R., & Bongard, S. (2013). Immigrant youth in Germany: Psychological and sociocultural adaptation. *European Psychologist*, *18*(3), 158–168. doi:10. 1027/1016-9040/a000154

Goh, C. L., Yong, C., & Sim, W. (2013, January 31). White paper on population: Reactions – coping with a rise in numbers; S'poreans' fears. *The Straits Times*.

Heng, R. (2013). Little India riot: Learning the right lessons from this episode. *The Straits Times*. Retrieved from http://www.straitstimes.com

Hernández, S., Pozo, C., & Alonso-Morillejo, E. (2004). The role of informal social support in needs assessment: Proposal and application of a model to assess immigrants' needs in the south of Spain. *Journal of Community and Applied Social Psychology*, *14*(1), 284–298.

International Migration Organization. (2014). *Labor migration*. Retrieved from http://www.iom.int/

Jacobs, A. (2012, July 27). In Singapore, vitriol against Chinese newcomers. *The New York Times*. Retrieved from http://mobile.nytimes.com/

Jeffres, L. W., & Hur, K. K. (1981). Communication channels within ethnic groups. *International Journal of Intercultural Relations*, *5*(2), 115–132. doi:10.1016/0147-1767(81)90003-1

Jones, G. W. (2012). Population policy in a prosperous city-state: Dilemmas for Singapore. *Population and Development Review*, *38*(2), 311–336.

Kim, Y. Y. (2007). Ideology, identity, and intercultural communication: An analysis of differing academic conceptions of cultural identity. *Journal of Intercultural Communication Research*, *36*(3), 237–253. doi:10.1080/17475750701737181

Law, L. (2001). Home cooking: Filipino women and geographies of the senses in Hong Kong. *Cultural Geographies*, *8*(3), 264–283.

Lei, K., & Li, L. (2012). Discrimination against rural-to-urban migrants: The role of the hukou system in China. *PLoS ONE*, *7*(11), 1–8.

Leslie, L. A. (1992). The role of informal support networks in the adjustment of Central American immigrant families. *Journal of Community Psychology, 20*(3), 243–256.

Lin, T. C., & Sun, H. L. (2011). Connection as a form of resisting control: Foreign domestic workers' mobile phone use in Singapore. *Media Asia, 37*(4), 183–192.

Ling, R. (2008). Exclusion or self-isolation? Texting and the elderly users. *The Information Society, 24*(5), 334–341.

Ling, R., Bertel, T. F., & Sundsøy, P. R. (2012). The socio-demographics of texting: An analysis of traffic data. *New Media & Society, 14*(2), 281–298.

Ling, R., & Yttri, B. (2002). Hyper-coordination via mobile phones in Norway. In J. Kaz & M. Aakhus (Eds.), *Perpetual contact: Mobile communication, private talk, public performance* (pp. 139–169). Cambridge: Cambridge University Press.

Liu, S. (2007). Living with others: Mapping the routes to acculturation in a multicultural society. *International Journal of Intercultural Relations, 31*(6), 761–778. doi:10.1016/j.ijintrel.2007.08.003

Low, L. (2002). The political economy of migrant worker policy in Singapore. *Asia Pacific Business Review, 8*(4), 95–118.

Luque, M. N., del Carmen García Fernández, M., & Tejada, A. J. R. (2006). Acculturation strategies and attitudes of African immigrants in the south of Spain: Between reality and hope. *Cross-Cultural Research, 40*(4), 331–351. doi:10.1177/1069397105283405

Lynam, M. J. (1985). Support networks developed by immigrant women. *Social Science and Medicine, 21*(3), 327–333.

Mei Hua Raman, S. R. (2014). New Singapore law will not keep peace in Little India. *The Diplomat.*

Metykova, M. (2010). Only a mouse click away from home: Transnational practices of Eastern European migrants in the United Kingdom. *Social Identities, 16*(3), 325–338. doi:10.1080/13504630.2010.482418

Navas, M., García, M. C., Sánchez, J., Rojas, A. J., Pumares, P., & Fernández, J. S. (2005). Relative Acculturation Extended Model (RAEM): New contributions with regard to the study of acculturation. *International Journal of Intercultural Relations, 29*(1), 21–37.

Ngan, R., & Ma, S. (2008). The relationship of mobile telephony to job mobility in China's Pearl River Delta. *Knowledge, Technology & Policy, 21*(2), 55–63. doi:10.1007/s12130-008-9046-8

Nguyen, H., Chib, A., & Mahalingam, R. (2016, June 3–6). *Mobile phones and gender empowerment: Enactment of 'restricted agency'*. Proceedings of 8th international conference on information and communication technologies and development, Ann Arbor, Michigan, USA.

Noor, N. M., & Leong, C. (2013). Multiculturalism in Malaysia and Singapore: Contesting models. *International Journal of Intercultural Relations*, *37*(6), 714–726. doi:10.1016/j.ijintrel.2013.09.009

Not the Singapore we know. (2014). Case study. Lee Kuan Yew School of Public Policy, Singapore. Retrieved from http://lkyspp.nus.edu.sg/

O'Reilly, C. A. III., Chatman, J., & Caldwell, D. F. (1991). People and organizational culture: A profile comparison approach to assessing person-organization fit. *Academy of Management Journal*, *34*(3), 487–516.

Piontkowski, U., Florack, A., Hoelker, P., & Obdrzálek, P. (2000). Predicting acculturation attitudes of dominant and non-dominant groups. *International Journal of Intercultural Relations*, *24*(1), 1–26.

Qiu, J. L. (2009). *Working-class network society: Communication technology and the information have-less in urban China*. Cambridge, MA: MIT Press.

Rahman, M. M., & Lian, K. F. (2005). Bangladeshi workers in Singapore: The views from inside. *Asia-Pacific Population Journal*, *20*(1), 63–89.

Redfield, R., Linton, R., & Herskovits, M. J. (1936). Memorandum for the study of acculturation. *American Anthropologist*, *38*(1), 149–152.

Reid, A. (2004). *Cosmopolis and nation in Central Southeast Asia*. Singapore: Asia Research Institute, National University of Singapore.

Rumbaut, R. G. (2008). Reaping what you sow: Immigration, youth, and reactive ethnicity. *Applied Developmental Science*, *12*(2), 108–111. doi:10.1080/10888690801997341

Ryan, L., Sales, R., Tilki, M., & Siara, B. (2008). Social networks, social support and social capital: The experiences of recent Polish migrants in London. *Sociology*, *42*(4), 672–690.

Singapore's angry migrant workers. (2013, December 27). *The New York Times*. Retrieved from http://www.nytimes.com/2013/12/28/opinion/singapores-angry-migrant-workers.html?_r=1&

Singh, B. (2010). Workers' remittances to India: An examination of transfer cost and efficiency. *International Migration*, *48*(5), 63–88. doi:10.1111/j.1468-2435.2009.00540.x

Sing Stat. (2014). *Monthly digest of statistics Singapore*. Singapore Department of Statistics. Retrieved from http://www.singstat.gov.sg/publications

Skuza, J. (2007). Humanizing the understanding of the acculturation experience with phenomenology. *Human Studies*, *30*(4), 447–465.

Sundararajan, N., Sirajudin, M., Jinnah, M., & Chib, A. (2015). Migrants, Mobile Finance and Marginalization: Exploring Remittance Processes and

"Ghettoization" in Singapore. In J. Steyn & D. Van Greunen (Eds.), *ICTs for inclusive communities in developing societies* (pp. 180– 200). Newcastle upon Tyne: Cambridge Scholars Publishing.

Swagler, M. A., & Ellis, M. V. (2003). Crossing the distance: Adjustment of Taiwanese graduate students in the United States. *Journal of Counseling Psychology, 50*(4), 420–437.

Thomas, M., & Lim, S. S. (2011). On maids and mobile phones: ICT use by female migrant workers in Singapore and its policy implications. In J. E. Katz (Ed.), *Mobile communication and social policy* (pp. 175–190). New Brunswick, NJ: Transaction.

Thompson, E. C. (2009). Mobile phones, communities and social networks among foreign workers in Singapore. *Global Networks, 9*(3), 359–380. doi:10.1111/j.1471-0374.2009.00258.x

Turner, B. S. (2010). *Vulnerability and human rights.* University Park, PA: Penn State Press.

United Nations, Department of Economic and Social Affairs, Population Division. (2013). *International Migration Report 2013.* Retrieved from https://www.un.org/en/development/desa/population/publications/pdf/migration/migrationreport2013/Full_Document_final.pdf

Vertovec, S. (2004). Cheap calls: The social glue of migrant transnationalism. *Global Networks, 4*(2), 219–224.

Weiss, J., Nincic, V., & Nolan, J. (2005). Difference and the internet: When ethnic community goes on-line. In P. P. Trifonas (Ed.), *Communities of difference* (pp. 205–213). New York, NY: Palgrave Macmillan.

Witteborn, S. (2011). Constructing the forced migrant and the politics of space and place-making. *Journal of Communication, 61*(6), 1142–1160.

Yeoh, B. (2007). *Singapore: Hungry for foreign workers at all skill levels.* Migration Information Source. Retrieved from http://www.migrationpolicy.org/article/singapore-hungry-foreign-workers-all-skill-levels

Yeoh, B. S. (2004). Cosmopolitanism and its exclusions in Singapore. *Urban Studies, 41*(12), 2431– 2445.

Yeoh, B. S., & Huang, S. (2015). Cosmopolitan beginnings? Transnational healthcare workers and the politics of carework in Singapore. *The Geographical Journal, 181*(3), 249–258. doi:10.1111/ geoj.12084

Yeoh, B. S., & Soco, M. A. (2014). The cosmopolis and the migrant domestic worker. *Cultural Geographies, 21*(2), 171–187.

Chapter 10a

Pandemic and Precarity: Migrant Masculinities in Singapore During COVID-19*

Junjia Ye

School of Social Sciences
Nanyang Technological University

Just as Third World women are positioned as being more suitable for particular types of work, social science research has shown that young, able-bodied men from developing economies are also being situated as more capable for certain types of work. Drawing upon qualitative data collected in Singapore over 14 months from 2009–2010, this paper explains migrant precarity by examining the complex, intertwined processes of class, gender, migration, and labour. Singapore's development aspirations as a global city, along with a low-birth rate and ageing population, continues to industrialise by importing a growing number of migrants to its labour force [Ye, 2016]. The majority of these labour migrants are on the work-permit system, which means they are transient, low-waged, and often brokered through labour agents, such as the Bangladeshi men in this study.

---

*Reflections on Ye, J. (2014). Migrant masculinities: Bangladeshi men in Singapore's labour force, *Gend. Place Cult.*, Vol. 21, No. 8, pp. 1012–1028. DOI: 10.1080/0966369X.2013.817966.

A close look at Bangladeshi men in Singapore illuminates the social, cultural, and economic structures that shape both their labour migrant experience as well as the ways in which they experience their transnational lives as low-waged migrant men. The men included in this paper are, however, no longer on the work permit. Brought in to carry out construction and shipyard work, these men have fallen out of employment after reporting of unpaid wages, illegal deployment, or, frequently, a workplace injury. These men have been issued a Special Pass by the Ministry of Manpower which allows them to remain in the country but without working rights while their cases are being investigated. The Special Pass therefore, highlights how precarious the work permit system is and which bodies this precarity impacts the most.

Entrenched within this precarity are the aspirations of the migrant men themselves, who, through their international mobilities, are also working to realise some deep-seated cultural norms of what it means to be a successful man. The social reproduction of masculinities thus intersects with economic production as the men exercise their own agencies that are also shaped by enduring social and cultural patterns. I hope it becomes clear in the paper that there are systemic processes working to situate these men within a particular position within the labour hierarchy in Singapore, which relies upon *and* marginalises them from economic production.

The precarities faced by migrant men on the work permit are amplified during Covid-19. Without space to socially distance in large-scale migrant dormitories where many of the men are housed, the virus quickly spread throughout their accommodations [Sim and Kok, 2020]. Migrant men have also not been allowed to leave their dorms and are subject to more intense surveillance since April 2020 as part of the measures to control the pathogen's pathways. Migrant masculinities, through regulations of Covid-19, have been rendered a medical risk, rather than being at risk [Ye, 2021].

References

Sim, D. and Kok, X. (2020, 17 April). How did migrant dormitories become Singapore's biggest coronavirus cluster? *South China Morning Post.*

Retrieved from https://www.scmp.com/week-asia/explained/article/3080466/how-did-migrant-worker-dormitories-become-singapores-biggest

Ye, J. (2016) *Class Inequality in the Global City: Migrants, Workers and Cosmopolitanism in Singapore.* (Palgrave MacMillan, UK).

Ye, J. (2021). Ordering diversity: Co-producing the pandemic and the migrant in Singapore during COVID-19, *Antipode*, Vol. 53, No. 6, pp. 1895–1920. DOI: 10.1111/anti.12740

Chapter 10b

Migrant Masculinities: Bangladeshi Men in Singapore's Labour Force*

Junjia Ye

Department of Socio-Cultural Diversity
Max Planck Institute for the Study of Religious and Ethnic Diversity
Hermann-Föge-Weg 11, 37073 Göttingen, Germany
Email: jiageog@gmail.com

Although there is a growing body of scholars who have examined the reproduction and experiences of masculinities, research on the experiences of migrant men remains relatively limited. While I continue to draw upon insights from these scholars of both migration and gender, my data show that there remains considerable potential to contribute to this research field, in particular, analysing the reproduction of masculinity through a class lens. Drawing upon migrants' own narratives and notions of class by Bourdieu, I examine how Bangladeshi men make sense of their labour migration to Singapore, particularly after they fall out of work. Their responses are not only based upon instrumental calculation, but are also powerfully shaped by a complex set of normative gendered formations that can further constrain them.

Keywords: migration; class; men; gender; intersectionality; work

*This article was originally published in *Gend. Place Cult.*, Vol. 21, No. 8, pp. 1012–1028. DOI: 10.1080/0966369X.2013.817966.

The processes and experiences of gender and movements of low-waged, documented migrants are now widely understood. Gender emerges as a significant factor in the way in which migrants experience their positions in the labour market. Indeed, it has been persuasively shown that women from developing economies are consistently constructed as particularly attractive to employers for jobs in the textile and electronics industries because of persistent assumptions such as obedience, patience and dexterity, and as a result are being paid low wages, denied job security and provided limited benefits (Elmhirst 2007; Gibson, Law, and McKay 2001; Mills 1999; Ong 1987; Parrenas 2001; Pratt 2004; Silvey and Elmhirst 2003; Silvey 2006; Tyner 1996, 2004; Wright 2006; Yeoh and Huang 1998, 1999). Yet, the impact of migration on gendered identities and experiences has been predominantly analysed from the perspective of female migrants. Although there is a growing body of scholars who have examined the reproduction and experiences of masculinities, research on the experiences of migrant men remains relatively limited (Broughton 2008; Datta et al. 2009; Jackson 1991; McDowell 2003; McDowell, Batnitzky, and Dyer 2008). While I continue to draw upon insights from these scholars of both migration and gender, my data show that there remains considerable potential to contribute to this research field, in particular, analysing the reproduction of masculinity through a class lens.

Just as Third World women are being constructed as more suitable for particular types of work, young men from the developing countries are also being situated as more capable of certain types of work (Donaldson 2009; Hopkins 2007; Jackson 1991; McDowell 2003, 2007; Ryan and Webster 2008). It has been widely noted that men's experience of paid work is directly linked to their conception of masculinity. Furthermore, these gendered normativities about work also designate which jobs are *not* masculine. These normativities, however, are not only imposed by macro-level institutions such as state actors, but are also reproduced and lived through the micro-level as well, where men themselves see certain types of work as 'not men's work'. Indeed, it has been argued that the hegemony of masculinity – albeit an incomplete and unstable one that always requires maintenance – accounts for and is reproduced through the reflexive operation of real people. Ideals of being a successful provider for the family become a principle to which people focus on their desire and aspirations (Donaldson and Howson 2009). As Ahmad (2008) and Keeler (2008) show through their respective case studies of Pakistani and Kurdish migrants in London, sewing and catering work by male migrants are sometimes not regarded as paid employment by other men but as 'women's work'. Burrell (2008) further show how gender plays a role in the downward mobility of occupational status for Polish and East African Asian male migrants who feel unable to live up to masculine ideals of material success and provision for their families. Masculinity is hence intersected by ethnicity, race and, as my focus here, class, where men from different social backgrounds experience various aspects of social life differently. Masculinity – or indeed, masculinities – is marked by hierarchy and exclusion that affect not only women but also men where the latter do not all benefit equally from, *even as they aspire towards*, the 'patriarchal dividend' (Hibbins and Pease 2009, 2). I would argue, however, that subjectivities of masculinity do not only maintain forms of patriarchy but instead go further to reproduce class inequalities through the economic practices of migration.

In this article, I illustrate that Bangladeshi male migrants are now part of a vast pool of inexpensive and mobile workers who are maintained as such because of powerful structures of inequality that require the extraction of their labour at both the global and local scales. These low-waged migrants occupy particular positions in Singapore's segmented labour market – a point that remains the backdrop of my argument. Drawing upon migrants' own narratives, I examine how Bangladeshi men make sense of their labour migration to Singapore, particularly after they fall out of work. With reference to Bourdieu's notions of class and habitus, I demonstrate that their responses are not only based upon instrumental calculation but are also powerfully shaped by a complex set of normative gendered formations that can further constrain their voices. I argue here that these masculine normativities cannot only be reduced to patriarchy but further become a means for the reproduction of class position.

This article is part of my doctoral research where I conducted fieldwork in Singapore for a period of 14 months, from October 2009 until December 2010. The primary data I present here is drawn from participant observation, semi-structured in-depth interviews and informal conversations I had with migrants, NGO workers and middle-level management at shipyards and construction companies. The Bangladeshi male migrants were between the ages of 20–35 years, with half of them married. Most of them were from Dhaka and have at least a high school certificate. For all of them, Singapore is the first place they have ever worked outside of Bangladesh, while a number of them have relatives working in the Gulf.

Migration, Gender and Work

As Hugo (2000) suggests, migration could create situations and dilemmas that disturb preexisting notions of gender, class and race. In particular, the linkages between masculinities and migration have not been as often conceptualized (Charsley 2005; Gamburd 2000; Osella and Osella 2000a). It has, however, been acknowledged that migrant men may be disadvantaged in service sector work in the UK because of the issues of skills transfer from their sending countries (Raghuram 2004). It has also been observed that analysing renegotiations in gender identities in the context of migration can demonstrate that identity is not an essential attribute (Gibson-Graham 1996; Osella and Osella 2000b). Indeed, like other social identities, masculinity is socially constructed within specific historical and cultural contexts of gender relations (Hibbins and Pease 2009). In highlighting different forms of masculinity among Kerala migrants to the Gulf, Osella and Osella (2000b) illustrate how migration and work become important frameworks through which to understand the identity project of individuals. Using a Bourdieusian perspective, they show how migrant men's failure to comply with dominant social expectations deeply impacts their gender subjectivities and class mobilities (*ibid.*). There is an articulation between contradictory everyday experiences of masculinity expressed in dilemmas (such as how much money to spend on individual consumption and how much to remit or spend on family and friends) faced by Gulf migrant returnees and in the disjunctures between their actual labour conditions in the Gulf where economic capital was accumulated and their representations of their jobs back in Kerala. This corresponds with my fieldwork data as I present below where the normative constructions of masculinity represent ideals upon which people focus their desires and aspirations to produce certain attitudes, configurations of practice and identifications.

Although I do not trace the transformations of gendered identities and relations *per se* as male migrants move from Bangladesh to Singapore, here I will illustrate how gender is reproduced through the men's experiences of their positions in the division of labour. This article contributes to the body of work that addresses the nuanced ways in which contemporary migrants adapt to their new circumstances while preserving aspects of culture and social organizations from their places of origin (Glick-Schiller, Basch, and Szanton-Blanc 1995; Rao 2013; Vertovec and Cohen 2003). I would further argue through my case study that the experience of new circumstances in the receiving area is tempered by pre-existing forms of social reproduction so that the class aspects of their gendered selves are reinforced through the labour migration process.

By integrating migrants' stories with Bourdieu's notions of class, I show that Bangladeshi men occupy a particular location within the segmented labour market in Singapore as low-waged migrants – one that reproduces class and its intersections with gender, ethnicity and nationality. In other words, I seek to show that social reproduction is always intertwined with economic production and people's positions within the latter's circuit. Further, as Lawson (2000, 174) argues, migrant narratives can 'reveal that access to labor markets, state assistance or social networks, are not merely unique individual experiences but rather, are systematically shaped by social relations of gender, class, ethnicity and migrant status'. This can return these subjects of development to the centre of theorizations about them (Silvey and Lawson 1999).

Through Bourdieu's theoretical notions of class, I interpret the social reproduction of these workers as men conditioned through their position in the division of labour, even after they fall out of work. All of the Bangladeshis I interviewed are, or have at some point during their time in Singapore been, rendered jobless and homeless. Unsurprisingly, perhaps, remittance and improvement of the lives of their families back home are the main reasons for their labour migration, the men tell me. Similar to the study of Osella and Osella (2000b), this temporary migration is for Bangladeshi low-waged migrants very much conditioned by their beliefs in becoming the economic provider of their families. Labour migration clearly cannot be understood solely in terms of economic rationality. As Gardner's (1995) ethnography on Bangladeshi migrants from Sylhet clearly shows, labour migration and the economic capital they hope to reap from it become a significant part of their identity construction as men. This is not to assume fixity in the gender regimes of Bangladeshi men but rather that migration is constitutive of the social and cultural processes of subject making.

The poignance of this aspiration comes into sharp focus when we recognize the precarity that is entrenched within these aspirations especially in the context of international mobility, work and deeply entrenched cultural understandings of what it means to be a man for these migrants and their families. I hope it becomes clear through the following that there is a systemic process working to entrench these men within a particular position within the labour hierarchy in Singapore, which ultimately marginalizes them from economic production. The dimensions of class theories I have selectively utilized, namely Bourdieu's, provide explanatory power that addresses the regeneration of inequalities through the intersections of economic production *and* social reproduction. Indeed, Bourdieu himself argued for the flexibility of his theories and the necessity of inconsistency (Bourdieu and Wacquant 1992). It was through my fieldwork that I truly grasped how unstable and fluid empirical realities and the theories that frame them can be. This was where the extended case method became a useful tool not only for making sense of our empirical world through a particular theoretical lens but also for explaining everyday practices when theoretical prescriptions start to falter (Burawoy 1998). This methodologically self-conscious way of extending, reconstructing and piecing together theories was particularly useful, indeed, even necessary in weaving together the migrants' lived realities of economic production and social reproduction.

Social reproduction takes on relations of domination that are rendered dynamic between individuals and at the same time become social formations that are mediated by objective, institutionalized mechanism to the point of being invisible. As Wacquant (2007, 51) states, 'class lies in neither structures nor in agency alone but in their relationship as it is historically produced, reproduced and transformed'. Social class, it could be argued, can only arise through the conjunction of these two partially independent forces and it bears repeating that both structure and people's agency are very much shaped by the unequal distribution of economic resources. If Marx was right in saying that economic relations are very much social relations, then this part of the discussion shows that social relations and, more specifically, habituses are themselves powerfully conditioned and differentiated by economic relations as well. Hence, it is reasonable to argue that objective differences reproduce themselves in the subjective experience of difference (Weininger 2002).

These structures, however, are also met with the active agency of the workers themselves. Indeed, corresponding with Haggis and Schech's study (2009) on low-waged male migrants to Australia, the sense of loss and frustration I felt in the migrants also collided with their own purposes for taking on the precarious, unstable work that seems to ultimately marginalize them to the peripheries of the economy. Undergirding this agency is the ongoing construction of their gender subjectivities, which is always tied with waged labour. It is also this subjectivity – South Asian, male and entering Singapore as a working-class migrant – which, when mobilized through their agency, forms a habitus of silence (Bourdieu 1998). My respondents often masked the difficulties and stresses that are encountered by these workers on a daily basis. In other words, the migrants are themselves enabling and participating in this exploitative process, reproducing certain patterns of subordination and appropriation of their labour (Burawoy 2000). The intersections of precarious work and working-class masculinity where men are unable to speak of their suffering enable the permanence of a class-based migration process in which the actual forms of capital accumulation may not correspond with their representations of it. The latter is often being materialized through specific consumption practices, as I discuss later.

Bangladeshis in the Global Economy

As Peck argues, previous forms of geographically uneven development always recreate or at least shape emergent geographies of work (1996). I assert that the economic stagnation of Bangladesh and the restructuring of Singapore's economy – discursively constructed as a cosmopolitan one – set up a highly calibrated transnational labour market for male migrants from the former to take on certain jobs in the latter. At one level, the mobility of Bangladeshi men represents another example of how the current global economy consistently relies on migrants from developing countries as the foundation of a cheap and compliant workforce. As capital gets more and more mobile, its drive to increase productivity while driving down production costs leads firms further and further afield. One result has been to shift labour-intensive industries to highly dispersed sites around the globe (Mills 1999; Kelly 2002; Dicken 2003). Another is the incorporation of different migrant bodies into low-waged, low-status work within global cities. As low-waged labour migrants elsewhere, the Bangladeshi male migrant is valued precisely for his cheapness rather than skill for the employers and at a larger scale, for Singapore's overall development.

It has been pointed out that the territory of what is now Bangladesh has always been characterized by migration, both internal and international (Siddiqui 2003; Gardner 1995, 2009). This is largely a result of its turbulent history that has created much precarity for its people, with many developing a particular fast-footedness for survival (Gardner 2009). Bangladesh has a current population of about 141 million and a labour force of 60.3 million. A total of 62.3% of its working population is in agriculture, with most farmers taking on non-farm work during the off-season to supplement their household incomes.[1] Most farmers live on farms of less than 2.5 acres and despite rich soils, ideal growing conditions and an abundant supply of labour, agricultural yields are extremely low in comparison with Malaysia and Sri Lanka. The combination of geopolitical location, ecological conditions and historical circumstances has turned Bangladesh into an exporter of cheap labour (Rahman 2000). Bangladesh's success in increasing school enrolment has been one of the most notable achievements of the last 25 years, although there still remains a significant disparity between rural and urban areas. The unemployment rate, however, remains high (United Nations report on Bangladesh).[2]

Without employment security in Bangladesh, workers seek transnational forms of employment despite, or perhaps precisely because of, the tyranny of global political economy (Gardner 2009). Work migration has therefore become a means of relieving the domestic market of unemployed or underemployed persons as well as a source of foreign exchange earnings. The amount of remittances sent back to Bangladesh from working in Singapore supports the pattern of temporary migration: between 2007 and 2008, Bangladeshis remitted some US$130.11 million. At one level then, participation in the global economy through the export of cheap labour does seem to benefit the Bangladesh economy, perhaps explaining the motivations for individuals to continue taking on this sojourn, despite the high agent fees and the hyper-exploitative work conditions.

Incorporating Foreign Labour

I now turn to the issue of labour within Singaporean space in recent years. The turn of century saw an increasing share of non-citizen population – a direct consequence of the city-state's restructuring policies to attract and rely on foreign labour (Yeoh 2004). The strategic reliance on 'foreign manpower' is part and parcel of the dominant neoliberal discourse of globalization as an 'inevitable and virtuous growth dynamic' (Coe and Kelly 2002, 348). As elsewhere, the transmigrant population grows in tandem with restructuring processes to render labour more 'flexible' in relation to capital (Yeoh 2004). The workforce has been rigorously configured to incorporate a significantly large foreign labour pool that can be broadly divided into two strands: foreign talent and foreign workers. Both strands of workers are brought into Singaporean space strategically and they are administered very differently, although there is no space for me to elaborate on their differences here (see, e.g., Yeoh 2006). The state's management of its migrant populations requires different modalities of government based on various mechanisms of calculation, surveillance, control and regulation that create a graduated system to which different migrants are incorporated (Ong 2000). I would argue that the instruments for the administration of foreigners into Singapore set in place the mechanisms for extracting particular forms of labour from different bodies, dividing labour that reproduces particular classed and gendered bodies.

The high demand for migrant workers on work permit illustrates not only the low wages but also what is deemed acceptable by these low-status workers, and consequently, what is unacceptable for Singaporean workers. They mostly take on jobs that require manual labour or shift work in the sectors such as manufacturing, construction, shipbuilding, personal services as well as domestic work (*The Straits Times*, December 9, 2009; Yeoh 2006). Gender, nationality and ethnicity profiles shape the overall form of work permit holders. The ways these factors affect female migrant domestic workers in Singapore have been well documented by Brenda Yeoh and Shirlena Huang (see, e.g., Yeoh and Huang 1998). Hard physical labour such as construction and shipbuilding is largely performed by foreign males, with Bangladeshis and Chinese nationals among the most visible, though Thais, Indians and Burmese also work in these sectors. Seventy per cent of the labour force in construction is performed by foreigners, far higher than the national 37.6% reliance rate. There are an estimated 120,000 Bangladeshi nationals working in Singapore, an increase of some 20,000 from the year 2000 (Rahman 2000). This is likely to be a conservative estimate as the actual numbers are not released to the public and also do not include undocumented Bangladeshis taking on spontaneous work under tourist visas. Of this number, 90% are on work permit and in the construction and marine industries (Bangladesh High Commission website).[3] Work permits are valid for either 1 or 2 years and, depending on the availability of work, are eligible for renewal for up to 2 years (Rahman 2000). Migrants on the work permit are also highly dependent on their employers as stipulated by the Employment of Foreign Manpower Act in Singapore. Aside from their wages, workers entering through the work permit system also rely on their employers for housing, daily meals, transportation to and from the work site, medical insurance and also eventual repatriation.

I met all 35 of my respondents through a Singapore NGO called Transient Workers Count Too (TWC2) where I had volunteered throughout my doctoral fieldwork between October 2008 and December 2009. Aside from volunteering on a daily basis at the meal programme run by TWC2 in Singapore's Little India neighbourhood, I also accompanied the men to the Ministry of Manpower and various hospitals to follow up on their case statuses and doctor's appointments, respectively. The narratives included here are drawn from both in-depth interviews and less structured conversations they shared with me during those 14 months. All of the Bangladeshis I spoke with are or have been at some point during their work journey in Singapore on a special pass.[4] This is a permit issued to work permit holders who have become unemployed as a result of work disputes, usually of the following nature: salary disputes, illegal deployment and Workmen's Compensation cases (for illnesses and injuries incurred during work). About 25 of the men I spoke with were on Workmen's Compensation – a figure reflective of the men who turn to the NGOs for help on an individual basis, highlighting not only the dangers these migrants are exposed to on the job but also how atomized they are as individual workers. Special passes are issued by the Ministry of Manpower (MOM) for foreign workers to legally stay in Singapore while their cases are being investigated. During investigations, however, special pass holders are not eligible for work unless they apply to be on a Temporary Job Scheme (TJS), which is only applicable for workers engaged in salary disputes. Applying for the TJS does not guarantee a job and all schemes are only valid for 6 months. NGO directors say that while the pass is a useful step in providing some recourse to workers who run into employment disputes, they note that MOM also seems to have taken a more stringent approach in deciding which cases are eligible for the pass during the time of economic recessions. During investigations as well, the workers I spoke with do not live with their employers – even if employers are legally bound to provide them with shelter, in particular those claiming Workmen's Compensation. Most fear the forceful repatriation carried out by 'security companies' that employers sometimes hire to keep workers in check. In essence, the Bangladeshis I spoke with are homeless and jobless workers who came into Singapore under the work permit system only to have fallen through its cracks. After investigations are over, MOM cancels the pass and repatriates workers within a week of this cancellation. The Bangladeshis I spoke with, therefore, were not examined during their productive circumstances – that is they are officially not working. They have been rendered jobless and effectively homeless as a result of their enforced transience through the processes that I will examine in the sections that follow. In other words, the situation of special pass holders is a result of the very processes that exploited and subordinated them within the division of labour in Singapore and has led many of them to become ultimately marginalized from economic production.

Working and Living in Singapore

In this section, I briefly discuss the features of how Bangladeshi men are situated within the Singaporean labour force. This will illustrate the ways in which Bangladeshi men are made a cheap, acquiescent workforce by highlighting how exploitation and subordination are maintained, resulting in much precariousness through their work lives in Singapore that eventually led my respondents to unemployment.

Although Bangladesh does not have a state-based, centralized overseas employment institution such as the Philippine Overseas Employment Administration, its strategies in sending labour migrants abroad are arguably characterized by its lack of state-based labour brokerage. These strategies continue to be legitimized by the remittances that are sent back from its overseas migrants. Remittances from Singapore, as mentioned earlier, were estimated to be some US$130.11 million between 2007 and 2008, with Bangladeshis lauded as playing an 'important role in national development' (Bangladesh High Commission, Singapore website).[5]

To mobilize a ready pool of cheap labour to take on jobs that local Singaporeans reject, firms turn to recruitment agencies in Singapore with connections in Bangladesh. This transnational assemblage of workers through agents not only reproduces the divisions of labour by reinforcing state policies on labour restrictions for Bangladeshi men in Singapore, but also through its lack of accountability to its recruits and heavy fees becomes an active process of engulfing migrants and their households in financial turmoil.

My data reveal that it is common for agents in Bangladesh to operate individually and proactively on the search for men to work in Singapore. The data revealed just how mystified the process of recruiting is, the closer it reaches the source of labour. I found no information on the sourcing process for workers on any of the websites of the recruitment agencies. My interviews with NGO directors also shed little light on the actual steps taken to source workers in the sending country. There does appear, however, a process of social networking for agents to get in touch with potential clients. The Bangladeshis I interviewed all told me that they knew the agents who first approached them about work in Singapore. For most, the recruiters are other men they knew from their village. This transnational recruiting process hence takes on a very local dimension and depends on social relationships. This was reflected in Ismail's decision to come to Singapore to work in a shipyard,

> My agent (told) me many of his relatives go to Singapore to work. He also knows that my brother-in-law also go for many years and he send money back. Agent (told) me that I can be like that also. I can make money and have good job ...

This promise of a good job in Singapore does not come cheap: each worker pays between SG$7000 and SG$10,000 to their agents for a work permit job even before they leave Bangladesh. The roundtrip air tickets cost about $700, passport fees cost $100 and job training usually cost about $1500 (personal interview with director of Humanitarian Organization of Migration Economics) – the remaining balance is unaccounted for. The NGO personnel I interviewed believe that the rest of the money goes to the employer to offset government-imposed levies, to pay for the upkeep of the worker and also to the agent's personal profit. If it is true that part of the 'agent fees' goes towards paying for the workers' levies and maintenance, this serves the employer by cheapening labour costs while at the same time creating an atomized and vulnerable worker who, in order to access work, is already in debt even before earning any wages. In this way, the worker is sucked into the exploitative social relations by material circumstances. Almost all the Bangladeshis I interviewed sold off various assets – land, homes, jewellery, savings – and took out loans from banks, relatives and/or loan sharks to pay for the agent fees. In Marxian terms, to become workers in the global economy, the men sell off their other means of livelihood, putting up only their labour power for sale in return for wages (Burawoy 1985). To convert labour power – the capacity to work – into labour – the application of effort to provide wages and profit – migrants must first pay a large fee. Clearly for these men, their exploitation and subordination begin even before they start work. I would argue that the precarity in their work lives is exacerbated as a result of having to pay off these loans (Waite 2008).

The degree of precariousness to which workers are vulnerable is heightened given their high dependency on their employers. There is a high degree of containment in the daily lives of the Bangladeshi workers that is clearly seen in their living spaces. Aside from their wages, workers also rely on their employers for housing, daily meals, transportation to and from the work site, medical insurance and also eventual repatriation. These are institutionalized within the MOM's guidelines for employers who are hiring foreign workers. Bangladeshi workers in Singapore are supposedly housed in state-approved, employer-provided accommodations – a formalized practice usually for workers from 'abroad' (i.e. non-Johorean commuters, not local Singaporean workers). Under the Employment of Foreign Manpower Act, employers must provide 'acceptable accommodations' for work permit holding workers. These come in forms of purpose-built dormitories that are commercially run, temporary quarters on worksites, harbour crafts and a smaller number of workers are also housed in Housing Development Board flats.[6]

The wages these migrants earned while they were still officially employed are also far below the national average for shipyard and construction workers. In 1996, the average starting wage for workers in these sectors was $860. This figure fell to $600 by 2006, a decrease of 30%. This trend of driving down production costs by suppressing wage increases for this particular group of workers is likely to continue. Indeed, the Labour Chief, Lim Swee Say says, 'The downward pressure on the wages of low-wage workers will continue to be there for some time as there is no shortage of low-cost, low-skilled workers in the world' ("Singapore's Dirty Secret", *The Straits Times*, July 28, 2007). This is, however, in contrast to 'semi-skilled' and 'professional' workers – all of whom had wage increases ranging between 8% and 49% within the same decade. Interviews with NGO directors and migrant workers also revealed that these low wages are further reduced by employers who charge workers for monthly room and board fees.

Migrant Selves

The economic lives of these Bangladeshi male migrants in Singapore reflect profound structural disparities and uneven development that in many ways render them more vulnerable than other workers to processes and practices of exploitation and subordination as I have elaborated above. As they enter these circuits of production, however, they also traverse critical arenas of cultural and social reproduction. The politics of class and gender goes beyond these exploitative, structural limitations within the workers' lives. In the choices the workers make, the values they share and the identities they pursue, male migrants from Bangladesh (and elsewhere) are neither passive victims of domination nor simple pawns of structures and processes beyond their control (Gardner 1995; Mills 1999). Through their own notions of fulfilment and self-expression, Bangladeshi male migrants also engage powerful meanings about what it means to be a man working in a globalized labour force. Waged work for them, thus, is intertwined with their gender and nationality, even after they fall out of work.

While Bourdieu discusses at length the cultural dimensions of class at the scale of the individual's bodily practices – most powerfully captured in the concept of the habitus – he does not leave the economy out of it. Rather, social formations and differentiations are necessarily conditioned by economic bases – the habitus is inherently a product of the various economic resources differently available to individuals in a given field. The empirical discussion of people's social class position must therefore always be linked to their economic capital. In other words, social reproduction is not only tied to the relations of economic production but is another form of entrenched social domination. If everything suggests a belief that there is a correlation between people's incomes and consumption habits, it is because taste is almost always the product of economic conditions. Attitudes of prudence and thrift, among the working class, are therefore regulated by their specific positions in the division of labour, by their own economy of means. This form of regulation and domination is arguably more deeply entrenched as domination no longer needs to be exerted in a direct way when it is 'entailed in possession of means ... of appropriating the mechanisms of the field of production and the field of cultural production' (Bourdieu 1977, 184). As Osella and Osella (2000b) show, this habitus of thrift is very much part of the construction of masculinity where the responsible migrant (idealized as the *pavam* or the mature householder) spends their money earned through their work as low-waged migrants in specific, calculated ways that can enrich their social and cultural capital in their sending areas.

Masculinity and Mobility

Whenever the men spoke of their decisions to work in Singapore, it was almost always in relation to their roles as men in their households. While I do not assume fixity in Bangladeshi gender regimes, I argue that this international mobility is conditioned by and constitutes ongoing gender and class relations. As Karim reveals:

> Bangladesh no good job for me, so I come to Singapore. I cannot ask my wife to go and work. Because it is not good! Ladies in Bangladeshi don't work – not like in Singapore. If she work, who can take care of my family? I am a man so I must take care of my family. No matter how hard the job, nevermind. I do because I know I must support my father and mother, also my wife and small daughter. And also we paid so much money to my agent so I can come to Singapore for work. He said like other men, I can also come to Singapore to make money to support my family.

Mannaf, a previous shipyard worker who has been sleeping at a parking lot intermittently for 3 months while awaiting his Workmen's Compensation Claim tells me:

> last time when I (had) a job, I (sent) maybe 80% of my $600 (monthly) salary[7] to Bangladesh. Cannot keep so much salary for myself. My family will be happy if they know I give them my salary. It is my job to my family because I am a man ... Now I cannot tell my family my situation! Sometimes they ask me why I don't send money back but I just say I give money to my friend to start a business here. If they understand my condition in Singapore, my mother and father will get heart attack and my wife will cry everyday. So I one person 'tahan'[8] no problem ... If my wife knows, then she go work in a factory – (there are) many men working in factory! What if she sees, and she (thinks), 'my husband no use, not sending money back, I want to go and marry another man', then what will happen?

This suggests that even with their having migrated, masculinity for these Bangladeshi workers continues to be readily accommodated within existing patriarchal structures, confirming their resilience and versatility rather than signalling any major shift in the sexual balance of power. Karim's emphatic claim that it is 'not good' for a woman to be working continues to reinforce the standard of a man's role as the economic provider while a woman's role is to take on reproductive labour within the household – indeed, many of the men have told me that the reason they take on work overseas is because they are men and getting used to unfamiliar territory is easier 'for a man'. This is as Bourdieu (2001, 96) argued, where

> social positions themselves (are) sexually characterized and characterizing .. . in defending their jobs against feminization, men are trying to protect ... themselves as men, such as manual workers ... which owe much, if not all of their value, even in their (own) eyes, to their image of manliness.

Consequently, a gendered moral framework is reproduced, where good men continue to take on paid work and virtuous women work within the house. This corresponds with Osella and Osella's (2000a) study of gender and work in Kerala, where gendered divisions of labour not only spatialize men and women differently but also reproduce differentiated notions of morality for men and women. Traditional patterns of masculinity and femininity may be more stretched across space, borders and scales but it would not be too far-fetched to argue that there is a persistent asymmetry of power between men and women (Jackson 1991).

This persistence can be further understood through Bourdieu's (1984) notion of the habitus – a mechanism that organizes how individuals perceive the social world but at the same time, this perception is also a result of how people are themselves produced in the division of classes. Further, the habitus is an internalization of one's conditions of existence and is 'converted into a disposition that generates meaningful practices and meaning-giving perceptions' (Bourdieu 1984, 170). This 'feel for the game' functions below conscious reasoning and deliberate will to action to the extent that gives the impression one's actions, dispositions and attitudes which are instinctual rather than conditioned by social forces (McNay 2000). In this sense, the modus operandi of habitus allows men to view their masculinity and its alleged opposition to femininity as innate. The habitus is thus a mechanism that reproduces dispositions that are durable precisely because of its pre-reflexive quality. Masculinity as an uncalculated strategy forms part of the habitus of men which is transposable to given situations to form practical dispositions and actions to everyday situations (Coles 2009).

The loss of paid employment, then, is experienced often as a threat not only to the livelihoods of the workers and their households but also to their manhood. Indeed, the transposable quality of the habitus functions to silence Mannaf from speaking about his marginalization from economic production to his family. Bearing the responsibility of remitting the money and having the capacity to do so is tied to Mannaf's gender identity. In believing the primacy granted to masculinity, Mannaf, like many other migrants, is further entrenched within masculine domination himself: limited by the lack of secure employment and exposed to certain vulnerabilities because of his job, he experiences challenges to his values as a Bangladeshi male, as a son and a husband. Similar to the female migrants in Mills' (1999) study of Bangkok's rural migrant workers, these tensions underlying the men's labour migration also prompt them to negotiate a series of linked fragile compromises – balancing personal consumption to remit most of their money to Bangladesh, having to keep their homeless and jobless situations from their families and wanting to maintain a particular form of masculine construction in relation to their wives.

The cultural dominance of gender structures illustrates that the experience of class cannot be fully understood without also understanding the permanence of other social collectivities, even in times of vulnerabilities (Bourdieu 2001). This also shows the oppressive aspect of masculinity not just towards females, but as experienced by men, as well, as they grapple with precarious lives without becoming redundant. Maintaining these delicate roles is possible because of pre-existing gender politics and also a strategy that responds to political-economic conditions and inequalities that restrict their access to material resources and opportunities in Singapore. As these men try to balance structural fractures with dominant cultural discourses and personal values, they experience these disjunctures most sharply as personal misfortune and hardship. Their silence becomes part of their dominated habitus: their hardship in Singapore cannot be seen as sheer passivity but rather actively contributes to the symbolic violence that rendered them unable to speak of these hardships in the first place. As Bourdieu (2001, 38) argues:

> the practical knowledge and recognition of the magical frontier between the dominant and the dominated that are triggered by the magic of symbolic power and through which the dominated, often unwittingly, sometimes unwillingly, contribute to their own domination by tacitly accepting the limits imposed, often take the form of bodily emotions – shame, humiliation, timidity, anxiety, guilt ...

It would also be possible to argue that these dominant discourses of gender couched within the pursuit of happiness through waged labour motivated them to come to Singapore in the first place while also obscuring how their hardship is rooted within the exploitative relations of the paid work they can access. These discourses become embodied by the migrants over time, indeed, become historicized, through their experiences informed by, and engaging with, structures of gender and economic domination (Bourdieu 2001).

Masculine Tastes

In this section, I further explore the gendered linkages between being a low-waged migrant and taste. Classed and gendered attitudes and dispositions manifest – whether consciously or not – through their consumption patterns, further complicating their class subjectivities. This does not merely entail an examination of the things they buy but also what orients their taste towards specific goods. Through these consumption choices and orientations, indeed, through their very symbolic power, Bourdieu argues that social collectivities are formed (Weininger 2002). Indeed, all of the men with whom I spoke indicated the desire to purchase 'Singaporean' goods and bring them back to Bangladesh. As Ishaak explains to me:

> Ishaak: I think I will buy some make-up for my wife and shampoo for other ladies in my house and village. For my father, I will buy torchlight.

> Jia: Why can't you buy it back in Bangladesh? I think it would be cheaper there, right?
> Ishaak: Yes, of course cheaper in Bangladesh! Even buying it at Dhaka airport will be cheaper. But no problem. I am the son that (came) to Singapore to work. People will see that I buy Singapore shampoo and Singapore torchlight. My father will be happy, my wife also happy and my villagers will also think 'He had good job in Singapore that's why can buy Singapore things'.
> Jia: And why torchlight for your father?
> Ishaak: Because my village (doesn't) have electricity 24 h a day. Sometimes at night, he want to go somewhere, he (needs) a torchlight. Bangladesh (has) torchlight also! But Singapore's torchlight is better I think. All Bangla men buy torchlight for their fathers and brothers when they go back .. . my villagers will say I am a good son.

As this above conversation shows, there is an 'economy of cultural goods, but it has a specific logic' (Bourdieu 1984, 1). That Ishaak would rather buy apparently mundane items such as shampoo and torchlights in spite of them costing more in Singapore suggests the symbolic significance of being able to purchase these goods as well as his cultural competence. Ishaak's taste for these items, while not economically rational even if it is embedded with a clear gendered rationale, is a result of his pre-existing cultural knowledge about which items to get and how to expend his wealth to get symbolic mileage. Through these items, people from Ishaak's village can imply his position in the division of labour (regardless of whether or not it is true). The symbolic properties of these items, indeed, their value, lie within their ability to illustrate conditions of acquisition and are regarded as 'attributes of excellence, constitu(ting) one of the key markers of class and also the ideal weapon in strategies of distinction, that is .. . the infinitely varied art of marking distances' (Bourdieu 1984, 66). This illustrates the power relations that create social reproduction in places (Bangladesh) outside Ishaak's economic production (Singapore). At one level, the lack of electricity in villages is a result of uneven development inherent in global capitalism – village life and, in particular here, taste are therefore linked to broader structural political economy. Similar to Gamburd's study of Sri Lankan female migrants to the Gulf, the cultural value of these gifts relates closely to that of 'personhood, agency, social relations and morality' (Gamburd 2004, 170). While it is not this article's focus to discuss the reproduction of social classes in sending areas, I argue nonetheless that this illustrates the far-reaching and salient geography of classes. As much as work migrants' class trajectories on the production side stretch from Bangladesh as a result of the global assemblage of Singapore's labour market, so do their class and masculine subjectivities in terms of their consumption. This continues to show how local encounters with global capitalism must look not only beyond the imposition of new demands and power relations from the outside but also in light of how this process may be received by workers on the ground who are themselves also occupying positions in different cultural fields.

These consumption choices are made up of people's economic and cultural capital – resources upon which individuals draw to exercise their class identities. People's class habitus – within which are couched gender subjectivities as well – then orient the expenditure of their economic and cultural capital in practical ways that give coherence to a lifestyle, most visibly seen through the notion of taste. A cultural product – the torchlight, shampoo – is a constituted taste, which is constituted through the process of objectification by the social field in which the agent (in this case, the Bangladeshi worker) occupies a position. Through his consumption of these products, he further legitimizes its objectification, assigning the product and its consumer a prestige, realizing itself as well as its consumer's class identity (Bourdieu 1984). In other words, Bourdieusian discussions of class move beyond ideas of exploitation within capitalist production and engage with social reproduction through consumption without neglecting people's positions in the realm of material production. The concept of habitus explains why an agent's 'whole set of practices (or those of agents produced by similar conditions) are both systematic, inasmuch as they are the product of the application of identical (or interchangeable) schemes and systematically distinct from the practices constituting another lifestyle' (Bourdieu 1984, 170). Simply put, different conditions create different habituses. Through the concept of the habitus, Bourdieu bridges the often (mis) used dichotomy between agency and structure within class practice. It must be kept in mind, however, that the ways in which people consume commodities and ideas reflect more than just the economy. The acquisition or at least yearning to acquire certain goods serves as symbolic measures of success.

Conclusion

On the one hand, the Bangladeshi men's labour migration highlights the powerful and complex structures of inequality in global capitalism and in Singapore's labour market through the various policies and practices that maintain their economic exploitation and subordination, as I have examined here. As workers enter these new forms of waged labour, with precarious conditions of low wages, close regulation of their (re)productive bodies, enforced transience and sheer physical dangers of their jobs, it becomes clear that their work lives are not merely economic in the narrow sense, but, deeply entrenched within, are complex social goals and cultural discourses that linger even after they fall out of work. Migration does not simply unsettle or reproduce local gender regimes but it is a vital part of the social and cultural processes of subjectivation. The theoretical framework I have utilized here illustrates how Bourdieu's notions of class – that includes but is not limited to the realm of economic production – are useful in analysing the empirical case study. Through the notion of the habitus, we see that these are individuals who operate as subjects engaging with, rather than being passive receptors of, social constructs such as class and gender. As Enloe argues, ' ... without women's own needs, values and worries, the global assembly line would grind to a halt' (1989, 16 – 17, quoted in Mills 1999). My argument shows that this needs to be extended to include discussions of masculinities and its intersections with class subjectivities as well. The intertwined subjectivities of Bangladeshi masculinity and class are constitutive, rather than a preceding fixity of the labour migrant experience. Masculinity cannot simply be reduced to patriarchy but, as I have discussed, becomes a crucial meal for the reproduction of class position. Despite and perhaps precisely because of their precarious livelihoods that eventually led them to being special pass holders, Bangladeshi migrant workers continue to grapple with dominant narratives of gender and modernity.

Acknowledgements

The author would like to thank her advisor Dr Jim Glassman from the Department of Geography at the University of British Columbia for her steadfast intellectual support since her doctoral studies. The author is indebted to the staff and volunteers of the NGOs who took her in and the workers who generously offered their time, friendship and observations that she had no right to expect but without which this study would not have been possible. She only hopes that this article and future writings that spring from this work can convey her gratitude and solidarity towards the resilience, sharpness and pain she saw during his fieldwork. The author also thanks Challenges of Agrarian Transition in Southeast Asia (CHATSEA) and the Pacific Century Graduate Scholarship whose funding made this work possible.

Notes

1. High Commission of Bangladesh website. Accessed March 5, 2010. http://bangladesh.org.sg/cms/index.php?option=com_content&task=view&id=62&Itemid=95.
2. United Nations website. Accessed March 28, 2010. http://www.un-bd.org/bgd/index.html.
3. Bangladesh High Commission website. http://bangladesh.org.sg/cms/index.php?option=com_content&task=view&id=36&Itemid=57.
4. Information on the special pass, unlike the work permit and employment pass, is not made available on the website of the Ministry of Manpower. Inquiries to the Immigration and Checkpoint Authorities have also not yielded any official statistics.
5. Accessed December 18, 2010. http://bangladesh.org.sg/cms/index.php?option=com_content&task=view&id=36&Itemid=57.
6. http://www.mom.gov.sg/publish/momportal/en/communities/work_pass/work_permit/application/requirements/Housing_Requirements/List_of_Approved_Housing.html.
7. In 1996, the official average starting wage for workers in these sectors was $860. This figure fell to $600 by 2006, a decrease of 30% (*The Straits Times*, July 28, 2007). My fieldwork data also revealed that

while this is the official monthly salary, deductions by the employer for electricity, room and board are common among many workers in this sector of the economy. Many workers receive less than $400 a month post-deductions – a wage that is far below the official national average for construction and maritime labourers.

8. This is a Malay word often used in Singapore that means 'tolerate'.

Notes on Contributor

Junjia Ye received her PhD in Geography at the University of British Columbia. She is presently a postdoctoral research fellow in Urban Geography at the Max Planck Institute for the Study of Religious and Ethnic Diversity.

References

Ahmad, A. N. 2008. "Gender and Generation in Pakistani Migration: A Critical Study of Masculinity." In *Gendering Migration: Masculinity, Femininity and Ethnicity in Post-War Britain*, edited by L. Ryan, and W. Webster, 155–170. Hampshire: Ashgate.

Bourdieu, P. 1977. *Theory of an Outline of Practice*. Cambridge: Cambridge University Press.

Bourdieu, P. 1984. *Distinction: A Social Critique of the Judgement of Taste*. Translated by Richard Nice Cambridge, MA: Harvard University Press.

Bourdieu, P. 1998. *Practical Reason: On the Theory of Action*. Stanford, CA: Stanford University Press.

Bourdieu, P. 2001. *Masculine Domination*. Stanford, CA: Stanford University Press.

Bourdieu, P., and L. Wacquant. 1992. *An Invitation to Reflexive Sociology*. Chicago, IL: University of Chicago Press.

Broughton, C. 2008. "Migration as Engendered Practice: Mexican Men, Masculinity and Northward Migration." *Gender and Society* 22 (5): 568–589.

Burawoy, M. 1985. *The Politics of Production: Factory Regimes under Capitalism and Socialism*. London: Verso.

Burawoy, M. 1998. "The Extended Case Method." *Sociological Theory* 16 (1): 4–33.

Burawoy, M. 2000. *Global Ethnography: Forces, Connections and Imaginations in a Postmodern World*. Berkeley: University of California Press.

Burrell, K. 2008. "Male and Female Polishness in Post-War Leicester: Gender and its Intersections in a Refugee Community." In *Gendering Migration: Masculinity, Femininity and Ethnicity in Post-War Britain*, edited by L. Ryan, and W. Webster, 71–88. Hampshire: Ashgate.

Charsley, K. 2005. "Unhappy Husbands: Masculinity and Migration in Transnational Pakistani Marriages." *Journal of Royal Anthropological Institute* 11 (1): 85–105.

Coe, N., and K. Kelly. 2002. "Languages of Labour: Representational Strategies in Singapore's Labour Control Regime." *Political Geography* 21: 341–371.

Coles, T. 2009. "Negotiating the Field of Masculinity: The Production and Reproduction of Multiple Dominant Masculinities." *Men and Masculinities* 12 (1): 30–44.

Datta, K., C. McIlwaine, J. Herbert, and Y. Evans. 2009. "Men on the Move: Narratives of Migration and Work among Low-Paid Migrant Men in London." *Social and Cultural Geography* 10 (8): 853–873.

Dicken, P. 2003. *Global Shift: Reshaping the Global Economic Map in the 21st Century*. 4th ed. London: Sage Publications.

Donaldson, M. 2009. *Migrant Men: Critical Studies of Masculinities and the Migration Experience*. New York: Routledge.

Donaldson, M., and R. Howson. 2009. "Men, Migration and Hegemonic Masculinity." In *Migrant Men: Critical Studies of Masculinities and the Migration Experience*, edited by M. Donaldson, R. Hibbins, R. Howson, and B. Pease, 210–217. New York: Routledge.

Elmhirst, R. 2007. "Tigers and Gangsters: Masculinities and Feminised Migration in Indonesia." *Population, Place and Space* 13 (3): 225–238.

Gamburd, M. R. 2000. *The Kitchen Spoon's Handle: Transnationalism and Sri Lanka's Migrant Housemaids*. Ithaca, NY: Cornell University Press.

Gamburd, M. R. 2004. "Money that Burns like Oil: A Sri Lankan Cultural Logic of Morality and Agency." *Ethnology* 43 (2): 167–184.

Gardner, K. 1995. *Global Migrants, Local Lives: Travel and Transformation in Rural Bangladesh*. Oxford: Clarendon Press.

Gardner, K. 2009. "Lives in Motion: The Life-Course, Movement and Migration in Bangladesh." *Journal of South Asian Development* 4 (2): 229–251.

Gibson-Graham, J. K. 1996. *The End of Capitalism (As We Knew It): A Feminist Critique of Political Economy*. Oxford: Blackwell.

Gibson, K., L. Law, and D. McKay. 2001. "Beyond Heroes and Victims: Filipina Contract Migrants, Economic Activism and Class Transformation." *International Feminist Journal of Politics* 3 (3): 365–385.

Glick-Schiller, N., L. Basch, and C. Szanton-Blanc. 1995. "From Immigrant to Transmigrant: Theorizing Transnational Migration." *Anthropological Quarterly* 68 (1): 48–63.

Haggis, J., and S. Schech. 2009. "Migrants, Masculinities and Work in the Australian National Imaginary." In *Migrant Men: Critical Studies of Masculinities and the Migration Experience*, edited by M. Donaldson, R. Hibbins, R. Howson, and B. Pease, 60–76. New York: Routledge.

Hibbins, R., and B. Pease. 2009. "Men and Masculinities on the Move." In *Migrant Men: Critical Studies of Masculinities and the Migration Experience*, edited by M. Donaldson, R. Hibbins, R. Howson, and B. Pease, 1–20. New York: Routledge.

Hopkins, P. E. 2007. "Young People, Masculinities, Religion and Race: New Social Geographies." *Progress in Human Geography* 31 (2): 163–177.

Hugo, G. 2000. "Migration and Women's Empowerment." In *Women's Empowerment and Demographic Processes*, edited by H. Presser, and G. Sen, 287–317. Oxford: Oxford University Press.

Jackson, P. 1991. "Towards a Cultural Politics of Masculinity: Towards a Social Geography." *Transactions of the Institute of British Geographers* 16: 199–213.

Keeler, S. J. 2008. "'No Job for a Grown Man': Transformations in Labour and Masculinity among Kurdish Migrants in London." In *Gendering Migration: Masculinity, Femininity and Ethnicity in Post-War Britain*, edited by L. Ryan, and W. Webster, 171–188. Hampshire: Ashgate.

Kelly, P. F. 2002. "Spaces of Labour Control: Comparative Perspectives from South East Asia." *Transactions of British Geographers* 27: 395–411.

Lawson, V. 2000. "Arguments within Geographies of Movement: The Theoretical Potential of Migrants' Stories." *Progress in Human Geography* 24 (2): 173–189.

McDowell, L. 2003. *Redundant masculinities? Employment Change and White Working Class Youth*. Malden, MA: Blackwell.

McDowell, L. 2007. "Respect, Deference, Respectability and Place: What is the Problem with/for Working Class Boys?" *Geoforum* 38: 276–286.

McDowell, L., A. Batnitzky, and S. Dyer. 2008. "Internationalization and the Spaces of Temporary Labour: The Global Assemble of a Local Workforce." *British Journal of Industrial Relations* 46 (4): 750–770.

McNay, L. 2000. *Gender and Agency: Reconfiguring the Subject in Feminist and Social Theory*. Cambridge: Polity.

Mills, M. B. 1999. *Thai Women in the Global Labour Force: Consuming Desires*. New Brunswick, NJ: Rutgers University Press.

Ong, A. 1987. *Spirits of Resistance and Capitalist Discipline: Factory Women in Malaysia*. Albany: State University of New York Press.

Ong, A. 2000. "Graduated Sovereignty in South-East Asia." *Theory, Culture and Society* 17 (4): 55–75.

Osella, F., and C. Osella. 2000a. *Social Mobility in Kerala: Modernity and Identity in Conflict*. London: Pluto.

Osella, F., and C. Osella. 2000b. "Migration, Money and Masculinity in Kerala." *Royal Anthropological Institute* 6: 117–133.

Parrenas, R. 2001. *Servants of Globalization: Women, Migration and Domestic Work*. Stanford, CA: Stanford University Press.

Pratt, G. 2004. *Working Feminism*. Philadelphia, PA: Temple University Press.

Rao, N. 2013. "Migration, Mobility and Changing Power Relations: Aspirations and Praxis of Bangladeshi Migrants." *Gender, Place and Culture*. doi: 10.1080/0966369X.2013.810600.

Ryan, L., and W. Webster. 2008. *Gendering Migration: Masculinity, Femininity and Ethnicity in Post-War Britain*. Hampshire: Ashgate.

Rahman, MdMizanur. 2000. "Emigration and Development: The Case of a Bangladeshi Village." *International Migration (USA)* 38 (4): 109–130.

Raghuram, P. 2004. "The Difference that Skills Make: Gender, Family Migration Strategies and Regulated Labour Markets." *Journal of Ethnic and Migration Studies* 30 (2): 303–323.

Peck, J. 1996. *Work-Place: The Social Regulation of Labour Markets*. New York: Guilford Press. Siddiqui, T. 2003. "Migration as Livelihood Strategy of the Poor: The Bangladesh Case." Paper presented at the Conference on Migration, Development and Pro-poor Policy Choices in Asia, Dhaka, June 22–24. http://www.livelihoods.org/hot_topics/docs/Dhaka_CP_5.pdf

Silvey, R. 2006. "Consuming the Transnational Family: Indonesian Migrant Domestic Workers to Saudi Arabia." *Global Networks* 6 (1): 23–40.

Silvey, R., and R. Elmhirst. 2003. "Engendering Social Capital: Women Workers and Rural– Urban Networks in Indonesia's Crisis." *World Development* 31 (5): 865–879.

Silvey, R., and V. Lawson. 1999. "Placing the Migrant." *Annals of the Association of American Geographers* 89: 121–132.

Tyner, J. 1996. "The Gendering of Philippines International Migration." *Professional Geographer* 48 (4): 405–416.

Tyner, J. 2004. *Made in the Philippines: Gendered Discourses and the Making of Migrants*. New York: Routledge Curzon.

Vertovec, S., and R. Cohen. 2003. *Conceiving Cosmopolitanism: Theory, Context and Practise*. Oxford: University Press Inc.

Wacquant, L. 2007. *Urban Outcasts: A Comparative Sociology of Advanced Marginality*. Cambridge: Polity.

Waite, L. 2008. "A Place and Space for a Geography of Precarity?" *Geography Compass* 3 (1): 412–433.

Weininger, E. B. 2002. "Class and Causation in Bourdieu." In *Current Perspectives in Social Theory*, edited by Jennifer Lehmann. Vol. 21, 49–114. Greenwich, CT: Emerald Group Publishing Limited.

Wright, M. 2006. *Disposable Women and Other Myths of Global Capitalism*. New York: Routledge. Yeoh, B. S. A. 2004. "Cosmopolitanism and its Exclusions in Singapore." *Urban Studies* 41 (12): 2431–2445.

Yeoh, B. S. A. 2006. "Bifurcated Labour: The Unequal Incorporation of Transmigrants in Singapore." *Tijdschrift Voor Economische En Sociale Geografie* 97 (1): 26–37.

Yeoh, B. S. A., and S. Huang. 1998. "Negotiating Public Space: Strategies and Styles of Migrant Female Domestic Workers in Singapore." *Urban Studies* 35 (3): 583–602.

Yeoh, B. S. A., and S. Huang. 1999. "Spaces at the Margins: Migrant Domestic Workers and the Development of Civil Society in Singapore." *Environment and Planning A* 31 (7): 1149–1167.

Abstract Translations

Masculinidades migrantes: hombres bangladeshíes en la fuerza de trabajo de Singapur

Aunque existe una creciente cantidad de investigadores que han estudiado la reproducción y las experiencias de las masculinidades, la investigación sobre las experiencias de hombres migrantes permanece relativamente limitada. Mientras continúo basándome en miradas de estos investigadores tanto de la migración como del género, mis datos muestran que aún hay mucho para contribuir a este campo de investigación, en particular analizando la reproducción de la masculinidad a través de un enfoque de clase. Apoyándome en las narrativas de los migrantes mismos y en los conceptos de clase de Bourdieu, estudio cómo los hombres bangladeshíes dan sentido a su migración laboral a Singapur, particularmente después de quedarse sin trabajo. Sus respuestas no están basadas solamente en cálculos instrumentales sino que están fuertemente formadas también por un complejo conjunto de formaciones normativas generizadas que pueden limitarlos más aún.

Palabras claves: migración; clase; hombres; género; interseccionalidad; trabajo

移居的男性气概：新加坡劳动力中的孟加拉男性

儘管有逐渐增加的学术研究检视男性气概的再生产与经验，关于移居男性经验之研究仍然相对有限。我虽然持续运用移民与性别研究学者的洞见，但我的资料显示，仍存有相当大的潜能可对此一研究领域做出贡献，特别是透过阶级的视角分析男性气概的再生产。我运用移民工的自我叙事以及布迪厄的阶级概念，检视孟加拉男性如何理解他们至新加坡的劳动迁徙，特别是当他们失去工作之后。他们的反应不仅是根据工具性的计算，亦同时强烈地被复杂的规范性性别化形构组合所形塑，这些规范性的性别化形构并可能进一步限制他们。

关键词： 移居；阶级；男性；性别；相互交织性；工作

Chapter 11a

Remittances, Migrant Households and Pandemic Resilience in Rural Bangladesh*

Mohammad Jalal Uddin Sikder

Department of Development Studies
Daffodil International University

Vaughan Higgins

School of Social Sciences
University of Tasmania

In 2017, we wrote an article that highlighted the impact of remittances on the capacity of rural households to respond to economic and environmental challenges. Based on a study of rural migrant households in Bangladesh, our findings suggest that remittances enhance the social resilience of households, or the ability to respond to different challenges. Our analysis shows that monetary remittances boost migrant households' ability to build other forms of economic, human, and cultural capital, which in turn contribute to the household social resilience in response to

* Reflections on Sikder, M. J. U. and Higgins, V. (2017). Remittances and social resilience of migrant households in rural Bangladesh, *Migration and Development*, Vol. 6, No. 2, pp. 253–275. DOI: 10.1080/21632324.2016.1142752. © 2016 Informa UK Limited, trading as Taylor & Francis Group.

challenges. This involves different investment strategies that are shaped by gender roles in the household, and can relate to specific forms of capital, such as access to land for agricultural production or housing construction, or education which adds to human capital. Given the current challenge of COVID-19, we reflect on the pandemic's impact on remittances and rural migrant households in Bangladesh.

There is a growing body of literature drawing attention to the COVID-19 pandemic, its impact on global and national economies, and how it has generated fluctuations in the demand for labour [Sorkar, 2020; World Bank, 2020]. These fluctuations have had a significant impact on the livelihoods of migrant workers, and the remittances they send home to support their families. In Bangladesh, remittances sent home by migrant workers abroad are critical to the country's economy, contributing to the balance of payments and the financing of imports of capital goods and raw materials for industrial development. Prior to the pandemic, remittance data suggest an increasing trend; from an inflow of USD 2 billion in 2001, to USD 13.53 billion in 2017, and further rising to USD 15.54 billion in 2018 and USD 18.35 billion in 2019 [Bangladesh Bank, 2020a]. The contribution of international remittances to gross domestic product (GDP) was 5.11 per cent in FY2017, 5.47 per cent in FY2018 and 5.44 per cent in FY2019. In FY2019, remittances also contributed 40.51 per cent of total export earnings and 29.62 per cent of import payments, and it also played a supportive role in strengthening the reserves [Bangladesh Bank, 2019].

As no organisation in Bangladesh maintains any data on internal or domestic remittances, it is therefore very difficult to measure total flow of internal remittances and its overall impact. However, the 2016 Household Income and Expenditure Survey (HIES) reported that gifts and remittances (both internal and external) accounted for 10 per cent of household income at the national level, 12.2 per cent in the rural areas, and 6.6 per cent in the urban areas [Bangladesh Bureau of Statistics, 2019]. Travel and work restrictions associated with the global COVID-19 outbreak have jeopardised remittances from both these sources. The Bangladesh Bank reports that international remittance growth fell drastically from 35.3 per cent in the second quarter to 0.15 per cent in the third quarter of FY20. This resulted in the shrinking of the bank's liquidity, which affected the overall economy [Bangladesh Bank, 2020b].

As COVID-19 spreads across the globe, migrant-receiving countries introduced lockdowns and closed their international borders — many of them stopped recruiting short- or long-term migrants from sending countries like Bangladesh. At one point, around 150,000 Bangladeshi migrants were stuck in various countries in the Middle East, and long-term migrants who lacked valid visas and were unable to work spent days without food [Siddiqui et al., 2020]. Such conditions have triggered the return of migrants to Bangladesh. The Bangladesh Wage Earners' Welfare Desk reported that from 1 April to 18 August 2020, a total of 70,427 migrants returned to Bangladesh from different countries [Wage Earners' Welfare Board, 2020]. At a national scale, there were concerns about how the country's handling of the virus can affect job losses among the local population, especially the youth [Byron, 2020]. In addition, many internal migrants, particularly low-paid workers, have lost their jobs and this has pushed a mass exodus of migrant workers from urban to rural areas [Bhuiyan, 2020; Islam, 2020]. Overall, the pandemic has had a negative impact on Bangladeshi migrant workers.

COVID-19 has also resulted in a slowdown in remittance inflows, which has already negatively impacted the national economy, as well as remittance-dependent households. Many migrant households borrowed money to cover the costs of securing jobs abroad, on the assumption that these costs would be recovered by the remittances sent back within a year. However, many of these migrants have struggled to maintain their regular jobs, or to find regular work; others have already left or lost their jobs. A number of migrants found themselves stranded, unable to send remittances to their families or fund their return home [Islam, 2020; Islam and Jahangir, 2020; Refugee and Migratory Movements Research Unit, 2020]. Instead of receiving remittances, migrant households had to raise funds to support these migrants instead [Ovee, 2020]. At the same time, these households have struggled to cover family expenses and repay loans. Rather than bringing them wealth, migrant households ended up with greater accumulated debt. Reports also suggest declining purchasing power among remittance-receiving households, which has already impacted the local market and economy [Islam and Babu, 2020; RMMRU, 2020]. The same scenario has been observed with regard to internal migrants and their families in the villages of origin.

In our study, the migrant households viewed remittances as a key strategy for coping with and recovering from their adversities. With COVID-19, however, we also call attention to how adversities like a pandemic can have serious economic consequences for migrants who send remittances to their families. This has led some researchers to argue that the current situation can negatively affect the resilience of migrants, their households, and their communities in terms of responding and adapting to future economic and environmental crises.

References

Bangladesh Bank. (2019). Quarterly report of remittance inflows: October–December 2019. Dhaka: Bangladesh Bank. Retrieved from https://www.bb.org.bd/pub/quaterly/remittance_earnings/oct-dec2019.pdf

Bangladesh Bank. (2020a). Yearly data of wage earners' remittances. Dhaka: Bangladesh Bank. Retrieved from https://www.bb.org.bd/econdata/wageremitance.php#

Bangladesh Bank. (2020b). Bangladesh Bank quarterly report: January–March 2020. Dhaka: Bangladesh Bank. Retrieved from https://www.bb.org.bd/pub/quaterly/bbquarterly/jan-mar2020/bbquarterly.php#

Bangladesh Bureau of Statistics (BBS). (2019). Report of the household income and expenditure survey 2016. Dhaka: BBS Government of Bangladesh.

Bhuiyan, A. H. (2020, 25 July). Pandemic pushes back rural migrants. *The Financial Express*. Retrieved from https://thefinancialexpress.com.bd/trade/pandemic-pushes-back-rural-migrants-1595648778

Byron, R. K. (2020, 20 August). Youth unemployment to double this year, *The Daily Star*. Retrieved from https://www.thedailystar.net/business/news/youth-unemployment-double-year-1947961

Islam, M. (2020, 11 July). Dealing with the new poor and reverse migration. *The New Age*. Retrieved from https://www.newagebd.net/article/110840/dealing-with-the-new-poor-and-reverse-migration

Islam, J. and Babu, M. U. (2020, 2 April). Bangladesh rural economy reels from shutdown. *The Business Standard*. Retrieved from https://tbsnews.net/economy/rural-economy-reels-shutdown-63994

Islam, R. and Jahangir, A.R. (2020, 2 April). Corona fallout spells disaster for millions of poor Bangladeshis: Economists. *United News of Bangladesh*.

Retrieved from https://unb.com.bd/category/special/corona-fallout-spells-disaster-for-millions-of-poor-bangladeshis-economists/48533

Islam, S. (2020, 30 May). Returnee migrants falling into hard times, *United News of Bangladesh*. Retrieved from http://www.unb.com.bd/category/special/returnee-migrants-falling-into-hard-times/52265

Ovee, S. (2020, 14 July). মালয়শেয়িায় ‘কাগজপত্রহীন’ বাংলাদশেদিরে ভাগ্যে শুধুই নরি্যাতন! (Torture is only for the fate of ‘undocumented’ Bangladeshis in Malaysia!), *The Bangla Tribune*. Retrieved from https://www.banglatribune.com/632605

Refugee and Migratory Movements Research Unit (RMMRU). (2020). The other face of globalization: COVID 19, arbitrary return of Bangladeshi migrants and their unpaid dues. Policy Brief 30. Dhaka: RMMRU. Retrieved from http://www.rmmru.org/newsite/wp-content/uploads/2020/07/Policy-Brief-30.pdf

Siddiqui, T., Rashid, S. R., Sikder, M. J. U., Azad, N. and Abrar, C.R. (2020). Protection of migrants during COVID-19 Pandemic: Situation analysis of RMMRU and tasks ahead. Dhaka: Refugee and Migratory Movements Research Unit (RMMRU), pp. 1–5. Retrieved from http://www.rmmru.org/newsite/wp-content/uploads/2020/04/COVID-19-Situation-Report.pdf

Sorkar, M. N. I. (2020, 9 July). COVID-19 pandemic profoundly affects Bangladeshi workers abroad with consequences for origin communities, *Migration Policy Institute*. Retrieved from https://www.migrationpolicy.org/article/covid-19-pandemic-profoundly-affects-bangladeshi-workers-abroad-consequences-origin

Wage Earners’ Welfare Board (WEWB). (2020). Monthly information of workers returning abroad (1 April – 18 August, 2020). Dhaka: Wage Earners’ Welfare Desk (WEWB), Government of Bangladesh.

World Bank. (2020, 12 April). Bangladesh must ramp up COVID-19 action to protect its people, revive economy. Retrieved from https://www.worldbank.org/en/news/press-release/2020/04/12/bangladesh-must-act-now-to-lessen-covid-19-health-impacts

Chapter 11b

Remittances and Social Resilience of Migrant Households in Rural Bangladesh*

Mohammad Jalal Uddin Sikder[a] and Vaughan Higgins[b†]

[a]*Refugee and Migratory Movements Research Unit (RMMRU)*
University of Liberal Arts, House No. 56, Road No. 4/A
Satmasjid Road, Dhaka 1209, Bangladesh

[b]*School of Humanities and Social Sciences*
Charles Sturt University, Elizabeth Mitchell Drive
Albury, NSW 2640, Australia

Remittances from migration have significant impacts on economic livelihoods in developing countries. Yet, to date, scholars have paid little attention to the broader ways in which migrant remittances enable rural *households* to improve their capacity to respond and adapt to economic as well as environmental challenges. This paper draws upon 'social resilience' as a conceptual tool to investigate how monetary remittances are used by households to enhance their ability to respond to challenges,

*This article was originally published in *Migration and Development*, Vol. 6, No. 2, pp. 253–275. DOI: 10.1080/21632324.2016.1142752.

[†]Corresponding author. Email: vhiggins@csu.edu.au

build economic, human and cultural capital, and plan for the future. Using data from a qualitative study of rural migrant households in Bangladesh, we provide an analysis of how different strategies for investing internal and international remittances contribute to household social resilience. Our analysis reveals that remittances in general contribute to improving the social resilience of migrant households. Remittances are important in building economic capital through accessing land for agricultural production as well as housing construction. Remittances also enable households to access education, and thus build their human capital. Nevertheless, the paper reveals an important gender dimension in the choice of investment strategies. Female-headed households tend to invest remittances in human capital, and such strategies may contribute to the reinforcement of existing gender inequalities and do little to improve resilience.

Keywords: migration; remittances; rural households; social resilience; Bangladesh

1 Introduction

Remittances, defined as the money, goods, and sharing of knowledge sent back by migrants to their families left behind in the villages of origin (Adams & Cuecuecha, 2010; Deshingkar & Grimm, 2005; Rahman & Yong, 2015), are an increasingly important livelihood strategy within developing countries. Monetary remittances in particular are argued tocontribute not only to national development, but are an integral aspect of the global development process. In 2014, the flow of *international* remittances to developing countries was estimated to be US$436 billion, a figure that is higher than total official aid and private debit and net inflows of portfolio equity to the developing world (Ratha et al., 2015, p. 1). While it is more difficult to obtain accurate information on *internal remittances*, micro-level studies estimate that internal flows are equally as significant as international remittances. For instance, the Consultative Group to Assist the Poor estimated that in 2005 rural migrants in China transferred to their families nearly US$30–40 billion (Cheng & Zhong, 2005, p. 5). Murphy (2006, p. 5) points out that this figure is more than the total amount that China or any other country receives from international remittance flows.

A considerable body of research literature has examined the economic impacts of remittances on receiving regions and households. Early research tended to focus on the negative impacts of remittances: the impacts on agricultural production with the loss of migrant labour, the increase in perceived inequality between households and within rural communities, and creating greater dependency among households on external funding (e.g. David, 1995; Khatir & Rezaei-Moghaddam, 2014; Lipton, 1980; Rogaly & Rafique, 2003). However, more recently, there is growing evidence of the positive impact of remittances. It is argued that remittances allow income diversification to create possible social and economic opportunities and preferences so that individuals can achieve an optimal balance between expected returns and exposure to risk, shocks and stress (De Haas, 2007; Deshingkar & Grimm, 2005; de Haan, 1999; Sabates-Wheeler & Waite, 2003). However, the effect of migrant remittances on receiving regions and households depends on the size and frequency of remittances and their uses. It varies according to social relations that structure the migrants' movements, the nature of their employment and income, degree of attachment to the family and willingness and motivation to share earnings, and desire to maintain links with their place of origin (Ellis, 2003, p. 4; Damon & Wisniewski, 2015, pp. 4–6; Singh, 2005, pp. 7–8; Taylor, 1999, p. 66). Guzmán, Morrison, and Sjöblom (2008, p. 128) thus stress the imperative to examine the characteristics of remittance-receiving households, and particularly the social relationships within them that may influence how remittances are spent.

While the literature to date highlights that remittances have significant potential impact on economic livelihoods, it provides limited insights into how remittances contribute to the longer-term *social resilience* of households – their capacity 'to cope with disturbances or changes and to maintain adaptive behaviour' (Maguire & Cartwright, 2008, p. 3). Migration and remittance researchers have been relatively slow in drawing upon the concept of social resilience, and when they do so, they have used the concept as a way of conceptualising recovery from hardship (e.g. Stefanovic, 2012). Moreover, while many of these references acknowledge that remittances play a role in promoting social resilience at a community level (Adger, Kelly, & Ninh, 2002; Locke, Adger, & Kelly, 2000), the link between remittances and social resilience at a household level remains under-developed.

This paper provides an important contribution to the existing literature by examining how monetary remittances promote social resilience *at a household level*. In doing so, we are particularly interested in the ways that remittances are used to build household economic capital, *as well as* human and cultural capital, thereby providing a buffer for these households against future shocks or stresses and enhancing their capacity to adapt to change. Drawing upon data collected by one of the authors from an ethnographic study of 36 remittance receiving migrant households across three rural villages in Bangladesh, the paper provides an in-depth analysis of the different strategies used by households for investing remittances and the ways in which these contribute to specific forms of social resilience. It is important to note that in this paper international and internal migration and remittances are not distinguished. This is because the only real difference is in the degree of net income returned to households; other than this, both forms of migration incur costs for households and the two types of migration follow similar patterns (Sikder & Ballis, 2013).

In the following section of the paper we examine the literature on remittances and household livelihoods in developing countries. The lack of explicit attention to social resilience in this literature provides the basis of our theoretical contribution: understanding how households use monetary remittances to improve their capacity to cope with immediate challenges and build economic, human and cultural capital. Following a discussion on how remittances can contribute to household social resilience we provide a brief overview of remittances and migration in Bangladesh. We then turn to the methods, sampling, and analytical techniques underpinning the research on which this paper is based. The subsequent section of the paper presents research findings from selected case study villages in rural Bangladesh on the relationship between remittances and social resilience. In this section we discuss three themes that emerged from the research data where remittances impact on household resilience. Finally, in the concluding section, we consider how the research findings build on and contribute to the existing remittances literature, and the significance of social resilience as a conceptual approach for understanding the complex social and economic impact of remittances on household livelihoods.

2 Remittances, Household Livelihoods, and Social Resilience

In the relevant literature, the New Economic Labour Migration theory focuses on the fact that household members have different capacities, characteristics and skills, and decisions to migrate are strategic attempts to diversify household income through the allocation of labour. Decisions to support a family member's migration are underpinned by a need to stabilise or maximise the household's income. It can also reflect a plan to minimise risk from loss of crops or sudden loss of income; unanticipated changes in income can result in a total economic disaster for the household. According to this theoretical perspective, migration provides a strategy for diversifying the sources of income and ensuring income instability. Brownlee and Mitchell (1997, pp. 46–47) note that migration can act as a strategy for overcoming immediate market constraints by enabling household members to engage in economic activities by means of migration to support family members in the migrant's place of origin.

It is also widely recognised that credit and insurance markets in the least developed countries are underdeveloped (De Haas, 2007; Rapoport & Docquier, 2005; Taylor & Rozelle, 2003; Vargas-Lundius, Lanly, Villareal, & Osorio, 2008). In the absence of a formal or informal market for credit or insurance, households have no insurance and limited or no opportunity to self-finance production or investment in agriculture and the non-agricultural sector. Remittances play a crucial role in enabling households to overcome missing or incomplete credit by providing access to capital to support production and income-generating activities (Stark, 1991; Taylor, 1999; Taylor & Wyatt, 1996). Eversole and Shaw's (2010) study of Sri Lanka, the Philippines and Indonesia found that families drawing on international remittances were asked to compare their pre- and post-departure economic status in Sri Lanka and the Philippines. Sixty-nine per cent of migrant households in the Philippines and 59% in Sri Lanka reported a 'substantial' post-departure outlook in terms of ownership of major household assets.

Afsar (2000), Siddiqui and Sikder (2009), and Siddiqui and Abrar (2002) argue that remittances are particularly important in helping migrant households to overcome credit constraints and enabling investment in agriculture-related activities. A study by Moses (2012) in rural China found that where local government officials were unable to secure investment to improve local conditions, income from internal migration provided an important alternative enabling the poorest migrant families to improve their economic circumstances. Another study by Mohanty, Dubey, and Parida (2014) on 25,578 households in India found that the cash income from internal migration resulted in the economic condition of migrant households being better than that of non-remittance receiving households, and that these remittances were used in the human capital formation and the purchase of consumer durables.

Remittances invested in agricultural land and agricultural technologies contribute to a greater economic return than other activities by increasing production levels and supporting the diversification of crops. In addition, remittances also provide landless and small migrant household cultivators with capital to gain access to agricultural land and technologies. As Quasem (2004, p. 146) argues, '[R]emittances from other working members of the family facilitate the land-poor households in trading enterprises and also to lease-in rice land, which ensures their food security'. For example, a study by Simelane (1995, p. 213) in Swaziland found that the women capitalised on migrants' remittances to hire second-hand tractors so as to maintain cultivation in household fields and improve agricultural production. In a study of Jiangxi province in China, Murphy (2006, p. 24) found too that remittances helped to support agricultural production. On account of remittances, the poorest households with migrant members no longer needed to rely on borrowing seed and fertiliser from their neighbours before the harvest and on making their repayments in grain after the harvest. These remittances were particularly important when the cash requirements were high, such as at harvest-time.

Income from remittances is therefore significant in achieving the goals of portfolio diversification and providing access to credit markets and economic liquidity to the migrants' households of origin (Rapoport & Docquier, 2005, p. 10; Vargas-Lundius et al., 2008, p. 27). In doing so, remittances can act also as 'a form of insurance' or 'risk sharing contract' (Lucas & Stark, 1985; Stark, 1991), 'security back up' and 'safety net' (Afsar, 2000), 'a private or informal social protection strategy'

(Sabates-Wheeler & Waite, 2003) and 'a self-insurance mechanism for developing countries' (Kapur, 2004).

As the discussion above reveals, the literature to date focuses primarily on the ways in which remittances contribute to overcoming credit constraints, diversifying household income, and ensuring income stability. While significant, the emphasis on financial and economic benefits overlooks the broader ways in which remittances promote *social resilience*; specifically, how the use of remittances builds the longer-term capacity of households to recover quickly from adverse events, adapt to change, and to plan for the future. The term 'social resilience' originates from the Latin word *resilire* that means 'to leap back'. The Oxford Dictionary defines resilience as 'the ability of a substance or object to spring back into shape; elasticity' and 'the capacity to recover quickly from difficulties; toughness'. Since it first came into to use in the early 1970s (Gordon, 1978), the concept of resilience has gained in popularity and has been embraced by researchers from diverse fields and with wide-ranging interests, including psychology, sociology, geography, anthropology, public health, ecology, technology and communication.

Psychologists employ the concept of resilience to describe an individual's response to psychological vulnerability and risk experiences (Rutter, 1993, p. 627; Masten & Gewirtz, 2006, p. 3). The concept has also been employed in ecology research where it is used to refer to the ability of an ecosystem to recover from environmental stress, such as fires, drought, climate change and pollution (Brand & Jax, 2007, p. 1; Handmer & Dovers, 1996, pp. 485–488). In recent years, the concept of resilience has been adopted by social and environmental scientists to highlight the impact of humans on the environment (Sapountzaki, 2007, p. 275; Umetsu, Shinjo, Sakurai, Shimada, & Yoshimura, 2010, p. 1). Folke (2006, p. 259) defines resilience as 'the capacity of a system to absorb disturbance and re-organize while undergoing change so as to still retain essentially the same function, structure, identity and feedbacks'.

The concept has been embraced also by social scientists to investigate and discuss social change in relation to the environment, individuals, households and communities. This research promotes the links between social resilience and ecological resilience (Abesamis, Corrigan, Drew, Campbell, & Samonte, 2006, p. 3; Adger, 1997, p. 1; Sutton & Tobin,

2012, p. 1). Specifically in relation to the study of communities, Maguire and Cartwright (2008, p. 3) explain that 'social resilience is the capacity of a community to cope with disturbances or changes and to maintain adaptive behaviour'. Social resilience represents the capacity of people to learn from their problems and incorporate learning into their interactions with the social and physical environment (Maguire & Cartwright, 2008, p. 5).

The different definitions and applications of the concept have a number of assumptions in common that can be summarised, as Maguire and Cartwright (2008, pp. 3–4) have done, into a number of core principles. The first is that resilience infers stability, that is, an ability to tolerate some amount of disturbance. 'A resilient community has a high threshold – it is able to absorb considerable stress before it breaches its threshold'. Second, that resilience infers recovery, that is 'ability to "bounce back" from a change or stressor to return to its original state' and do so 'relatively quickly'. The third principle that underpins the notion of social resilience is the idea that communities are dynamic and have 'capacity … to respond to a change'. The concept of social resilience is therefore an important tool for understanding how to maintain stability through both adaptation and coping in the face of social change.

Increasingly, researchers have embraced the concept of resilience as a way of understanding the economic and social impact of migrant remittances on receiving communities. Used in this way, resilience describes how remittances enhance the capacity of communities to respond to a range of negative impacts and stresses, such as changes to climate, natural disasters and development of coastal regions (Adger, 1997; Adger, Kelly, Winkels, Huy, & Locke, 2002; Locke et al., 2000). For example, in their examination of migration and resource use in coastal northern Vietnam, Adger et al. (2002) argue that migration changes the structure of both the sending and receiving communities and that migrant remittances impact on a community's abilities to continue to maintain its way of life by absorbing change and disturbance. For Adger et al. (2002, p. 358), remittances feature as the central pillar of social resilience, exerting a substantial influence on communities by 'altering economic well-being, changing the structure of the community, and affecting the natural resource base' (2002b, p. 359).[1] The positive impact of remittances on community social resilience is further demonstrated in a number of recent studies.

A study by Deshingkar (2012) on diverse communities in Western Mexico, the Central Plateau of Burkina Faso, and Eastern India reveals that migrant remittances are one of the key factors enabling agricultural intensification, and this contributes to notable improvements in the resilience of poor households to economic and environmental shocks. Scheffran, Marmer, and Sow's (2011) study in the Western Sahel shows that migration is as an important response to cope with climate change. In this context, remittances provide potential opportunities and resources that can strengthen the livelihoods and resilience of migrant communities of origin and enable the development of innovative approaches for climate adaptation. Similarly, Banerjee, Yuves-Gerlitz, and Kniveton's (2011) research in the Hindu Kush-Himalayan region found that income from migration has enabled 62% of recipient households to adapt to current water hazards, thus helping to build resilience in the migrant sending communities. Nevertheless, all of the above studies recommend that further investigation is needed on how remittances contribute to building resilience against future shock and stress at the community and particularly the household level.

To date, much of the work examining the impact of migrant remittances on social resilience has focused on communities or villages as the level of analysis. In this paper we build on and contribute to this work by focusing on the impact of remittances on *household* social resilience. This enables a more fine-grained and micro-sociological understanding of the relationship between remittances and social resilience. It also allows us to explore in greater depth how the spending of remittances on education, agricultural land, and housing construction has both short and long-term economic, social and cultural impacts which in turn contribute towards the social resilience of migrant households.

3 Context: Remittances and Migration in Bangladesh

This paper focuses on Bangladesh, a country that has become one of the major migrantsending countries in the world. Each year large numbers from Bangladesh migrate overseas, or in-country, from rural areas to cities, to engage in long-term and short-term employment in order to better their livelihoods. According to data from the Bureau of Manpower Employment and Training (BMET), from 1976 to 2015, 9.69 million

Bangladeshis travelled abroad as short-term labour migrants, with over 90% based in the Middle East and Southeast Asia (BMET, 2016). With regards to internal migration, the 1991 Census recorded that 6% of households move each year, 85% of whom move from rural to urban areas and most of whom send remittances and maintain ties with their home village (Garrett & Chowdhury, 2004, p. 15).

A result of increases in migrant flows is the growing remittance flows to households. While the amount of remittances from internal migration is difficult to estimate, empirical research conducted mostly in (urban) destination areas suggests that migrants transfer considerable amounts of their income to rural areas. For example, in Bhuyan, Khan, and Ahmed's (2001, p. 67) study, 60% of internal migrants had remitted money to their root or branch families in their village. Another study by Kuhn (2001, p. 13) of migrants' villages of origin, found that 18% of all household income and 27% of migrants' households' income came from net remittances (both urban-rural and international), and that 25% of all households received half or more of their household income from remittances.

International remittances are one of the most consistent sources of foreign currency in Bangladesh. In 1991, the total amount of international remittances received by Bangladesh equalled US$7.6 million. By 2001, the amount of remittances received had increased to US$2 billion, further rising toUS$13 billion in 2013, US$14 billion in 2014 and US$15 billion in 2015 (BMET, 2016). The Household Income and Expenditure Survey in 2010, conducted by the Bangladesh Bureau of Statistics (BBS) reported that household income from gifts and remittances accounted to 10.6% at the national level – 17.28% in rural areas and 7.75% in the urban areas (BBS, 2011, p. 32). Such research findings confirm that remittances have become one of the most consistent sources of household income in Bangladesh. The present paper endeavours to add to this research on the use of remittances in Bangladesh and the ways in which monetary remittances support household resilience.

4 Methods

The broader research underpinning this paper was informed by an ethnographic methodological approach, with semi-structured interviews used as the main tool of data collection. The villages selected for the field work were from districts located in three different regions of Bangladesh: *Kisamatpur Sherpur* village of Sadullapurupazila of Gaibandha district, in the Northwest region of Bangladesh; the *Hasail* village of Tongibariupazila of Munshiganj district, located in the central region of Bangladesh; and *Baynagar* village of Daudkandiupazila of Comilla district in the eastern region of Bangladesh (Figure 1). Since every village in Bangladesh has a level of migratory experience, villages selected were ones associated with

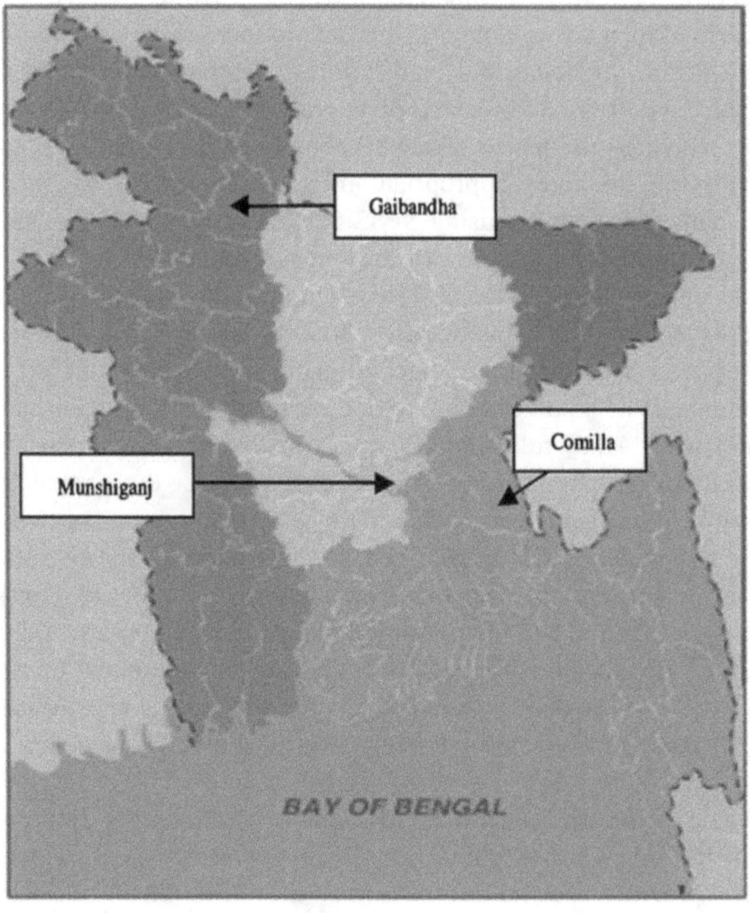

Figure 1 Location of the study sites in Bangladesh.

Source: http://www.lged.gov.bd/ViewMap.aspx

greater levels of migration and more vulnerable to natural disasters (GoB, 2009; Siddiqui & Abrar, 2002; Siddiqui & Sikder, 2009).

Migrant households were accessed and selected through three key processes. First, informal discussions with villagers enabled rapport-building and provided a crucial starting point in understanding household conditions, migration and remittance patterns in the respective villages. Second, a short questionnaire was administered in person to the heads of 480 households in the selected villages. These households had previously been identified as migrant households through earlier informal discussions. The questionnaire included questions on type of household, number of household members, number of household income earners, sources of income, pattern of household land holding, number of migrants of the household, who migrated, nature of migration, and place of destination and of receiving remittances. The 480 completed questionnaires assisted in identifying the most appropriate migrant households to interview. Survey data was analysed using SPSS software to analyse demographic data to inform the construction of the semi-structured interviews. Third, from the survey data, a total of 36 households were identified for interviews. As it turned out, the selected households proved appropriate in terms of their socio-economic backgrounds, were well informed about migration and had an understanding of their livelihood strategies and uses of remittances. A key selection principle was that households had family members with at least a two year migration experience during which time the household had been receiving remittances. The minimum of two years migration experience was considered because research on migration in Bangladesh suggests that most international migrants are on short-term contracts (2–3 years) and internal migrants are also temporary and circular. The fact that the 36 households included an equal number of male and female heads assisted in understanding the similarities and differences between men's and women's livelihood strategies and management of remittance income.

The fieldwork was undertaken over a nine month period during 2010. Each of the selected households was interviewed six times. The initial interview provided specific information on uses of remittances. Each subsequent interview provided householders opportunity to further reflect on their use of remittance funds, to gain a more detailed understanding of remittances in the context of the circumstances and needs of the migrant household, including social, economic, political and environmental factors.

The analysis of data is pivotal to ethnographic research: the key challenge is to interrogate the data, or as Goetz and LeCompte (1981) state, to 'crunch data'. This is achieved by coding, counting, comparing and summarising the findings. The interviews conducted with villagers were analysed to identify common themes in relation to remittance processes, social interactions and how villagers used the funds (Boyatzis, 1998, p. 4). The thematic analysis aimed to identify the key themes and sub-themes to gain a comprehensive view of the practices of informants. Through the thematic analysis, three core themes emerged around how migrant households use remittances and the implications for social resilience: (1) access to and purchasing of agricultural lands; (2) investing in land and housing; and (3) investing in education. These three themes are examined in detail in the following section of the paper. The names and key identifying information of participants has been changed to maintain anonymity.

5 Remittances and Social Resilience in Rural Bangladesh Migrant Households

Migrant households rely directly and indirectly on agriculture and agricultural related activities to access basic household necessities. However, agricultural earnings on their own are insufficient for most households and have to be supplemented with more than one earning source. The earnings of 26 of the 36 migrant households rely on income from farming such as the cultivation of their own and others' land, sharecropping and homestead gardening. Eight of the 26 households in this study draw income by having cattle, 19 rely on non-agricultural activities including wage labourers, farm labourers, petty trading, formal and informal jobs. Thirteen of the 26 families are supported by government benefits. Nevertheless, for each of the migrant households the main source of their income was remittances through migration. As the following sections of the paper illustrate, these remittances were invested in different ways by households, with some investments contributing in a more obvious way than others to household resilience.

5.1 *Investment in agricultural land*

Agricultural land is a scarce commodity in Bangladesh and more than 50% of rural households have become functionally landless and own less than 0.02 ha of land. The landless population is growing at a rate of 1.39% per year (BBS, 2011). Demographic pressures, the rapid expansion of urbanisation, and transformation of agricultural land to residential plots, educational institutions, industries and brickfields are reducing cultivated areas at a rate of more than one per cent per year. In addition much of the available cultivatable land is controlled by small groups of affluent land owners. In the mid-1980s, the richest 10% of the village population in Bangladesh controlled 25 to 50% of the land, while the bottom 60% controlled less than 25% (IBP, 2011, p. 53). In other words, the concentration of rural land control to a minority of the population places a great deal of power in the hands of relatively small groups of landlords (World Bank, 2011) and this in turn further increases the marginalisation of the landless poor.

The analysis of migrant household data in this paper reveals that remittances provide significant opportunities for migrant households to access agricultural land and cover cultivation and agriculture production costs. Only nine of the 36 migrant households in this study had their own agricultural land, but remittances provided the capital for landless households to invest in agriculture-based livelihood. Three international and two internal migrant households spent remittances on purchasing agricultural land, giving them access to at least three crops per year. Migrant householders explained that investing remittances in the purchase of agricultural land opened up for them additional social and economic opportunities. The land can be used for agricultural production or it can be sold in emergencies for more than its original price. Agricultural land increases in value over time and in some instances can double the original investment over a short period of time. Households can also convert the agricultural land into non-agricultural income generation. In another sense, the agricultural land provides families with 'an unwritten social certificate' to promote the family's reputation and status. Gardner (1995, p. 65), for example, explains that 'social hierarchy in rural Bangladesh is generally understood in terms of people's access to land'.

This is evident from the situation of Nazma Alam in *Baynagar* village, who owns 15 decimals of agricultural land near the *Baynagar* bazaar, which her internal migrant husband bought through his remittances. The land was used for growing vegetables. They had once planned to dump earth and build a small bazaar to rent out, but had failed to do so due to a shortage of capital. Two years ago, officials from the Grameen Bank, a well-reputed micro-finance institute in Bangladesh, had been searching for a small undisputed plot of land next to the bazaar on which to open a new branch in their locality. Since her husband was a government officer and owns land there, the officials offered to lease the seven decimals of property for five years, with the option to extend the contract. Nazma Alam and her husband considered it a good proposal as this land was currently being used by other cultivators who were paying less for it. Nazma Alam signed a contract. The lease agreement was lucrative, but in addition the arrangement contributed to enhancing the family's social standing in the locality. The arrangement enabled her to establish a good relationship with the Grameen Bank, which in turn accepted her as 'a guarantor' for poor rural households seeking to access micro-credit from the bank. The villagers also respect her voluntary support, which further enhances her standing in society. Nazma Alam explains: 'When I go out, people say *salam* (Muslim meaning 'peace be with you') to me … I know why they do so … I like to see it very much'.

It is worth noting that migrant households in a position to purchase land were comparatively richer among migrant households. These better off households had other income sources to secure their livelihood, and their remittances were spent on asset accumulation. Lipton (1980, p. 11) argues that positive remittances go to the financially better off, and international remitters who send back large sums to their families are seldom from the poorest village groups. Lipton also points out that, by comparison, internal remittances are very small relative to the total rural income in the villages and in most cases are unproductive. A study by Adams (1998) of internal and external remittance receiving migrant households in rural Pakistan also found that external remittances have a more important impact than internal remittances, leading to a process of rural physical asset accumulation by richer families.

Nevertheless, rural asset accumulation, such as land, depends on the nature of the village economy and opportunities. The interviews with householders revealed that the local agricultural land tenure system in Bangladesh meant that remittances created opportunities also for poor, landless and small-scale cultivators to access land, leading to the growth of agricultural production and income. The basis of such a land tenure system is largely determined by the local customs, the relationship between the landholders and cultivators, the fertility of the land and the local market price. These arrangements are based not on paperwork but on verbal agreements. In the villages, four types of agricultural land tenure system were identified. One is *borgadars* (sharecroppers), a system of cultivation with an agrarian arrangement between the landholder and the cultivator to share the production between them. The cultivator takes the land for a year or for one cropping season (that is for three to four months) without making any cash payment. Sometimes they cultivate part of the land with the help of family members or hired labourers who are paid in cash or kind and also through free board and lodging. The cultivator spends money on cultivation and, after the harvest, gives 50% of total production to the landholder. However, if the crops are destroyed by flood, rains, heat or insects, both parties will share the loss. A second type of land tenure is *barshikjoma*, or annual deposit. With this type of land tenure the cultivator leases the land for a year in return for a cash payment, depending on the location and fertility of the land. A third type of land tenure is *ordhobarshikjoma,* a six monthly deposit. This means that the cultivator leases the land for one cropping season. Then there is (fourth) the *bondhok* or mortgage, where the land is obtained for a year or for an indefinite period of time.

The visits to migrant households revealed that seven internal and two international migrant households in 2010 had spent remittances on leasing agricultural land. Five of these (one male headed and four female-headed internal migrant households) were located in the *Kisamatpur Sherpur* village. Three (one male-headed internal and two female-headed international migrant households) were located in the *Baynagar* village and one female-headed internal migrant household resided in *Hasail*. However, the households had entered into the leasing arrangements for different amounts and for a variety of periods.

Four international migrant households, one male-headed one in *Kisamatpur Sherpur* village, and two male-headed and one female-headed ones in *Baynagar* village, spent their remittances on buying back their mortgaged agricultural land. The migrant households had mortgaged their land to fund the cost of their family member migrating abroad; the costs of international migration are very high. Mortgaging one's land is a reliable method of generating immediate income and can be done easily and quickly. Nuru Sarkar in *Kisamatpur Sherpur*, and Sohid Niazi, Mojibullah Khandakar and Ashia in *Baynagar*, for example, had mortgaged their land of 66, 75, 50 and 50 decimals respectively, received Taka 50,000 (US$722), 150,000 (US$2166), 100,000 (US$1444) and 50,000 (US$722) respectively from the leaseholders. All of them were able to release their mortgaged land within two to three years after the migration of their family member. At the time of the interviews, one of the householders, Nuru, reported that he had released 33 decimals and was waiting for his son's remittances to cover the rest. Buying back their mortgaged land was a priority for households because households' income mostly depended on it. De Bruyn and Kuddus (2005, p. 35) state that using remittances to buy back mortgaged land is important in the rural context as it re-establishes the right of the individual to cultivate the land.

Analysis of household data also reveals that a number of internal and external factors can influence migrant households' decisions to spend remittances on agricultural production. An immediate challenge for many is the priority to provide food for their families while also generating income from production. A majority of migrant households report that most of their land was used for rice cultivation, as rice is the main staple food for the family. Recent increases in the retail price of uncooked rice provided the incentive for households to devote more effort to rice production. The ADB (2011, pp. 6–7) notes a trend in food cultivation in Bangladesh against the backdrop of a global hike in grain prices. The global price of rice increased by 16.8% between June 2010 and February 2011, while the domestic rice price in Bangladesh rose by 21.4% during the same period.

The actual returns to households for their investments in agriculture are by no means constant. The householders report that there are many layers that manipulate the price at which rice is sold. Paddy traders, wholesalers and retailers are responsible for the hoarding of food grains, and they manipulate the prices to rise in their own favour. The gains from the price increase of rice can be reduced by the costs for agricultural inputs such as seed, fertiliser and insecticide. For these reasons local farmers now tend to keep rice at home, transplanting it into seed beds and then collecting the seedlings to transplant on their own land. This situation influenced Sabour Miah's family in *Baynagar* village to start a small business producing seedlings for cultivation or sale. Sabour Miah's wife explained that she and her daughter-in-law saved some money from the internal migration remittances. Normally, Sabour Miah was the head of the household and he received and spent the remittances, but occasionally when his son visited them his wife and daughter-in-law received extra money from him. Over the last six months, the two women had saved Taka 500 (US$7.22). Sabour Miah's wife persuaded a rich landlord (who was also a member of her lineage) to lend her a small plot of fallow land (5 decimals) for a month for free. She bought ten kilos of rice from a villager to grow rice seedlings on this land, and had planned to give the seedlings to her husband to cultivate, but a local villager offered her a twentieth of his total production if she gave him the seedlings. She thought that her husband would need only a few seedlings since he leased merely a few decimals of land and she would not get the same price if these seedlings were sold at the local market, so she agreed to the proposal, as she did not need to bear any cost. She reported that her husband would get rice from his cultivation and she would also receive rice from the agreement, which would increase their total rice reserve and so contribute to the food security of her large family (with ten members).

The data presented above shows that far from being a random gesture of spontaneous and occasional migrant generosity, remittances are the visible manifestation of a rational process, a process that was jointly planned and carefully managed by family members. It highlights the strategic importance of remittances in enabling migrant households to invest in a variety of income-generating agricultural related activities. The migrant family members used remittances in different ways to access land for agricultural activities. Such utilisation of remittances boosts food production and consumption, and contributes to greater security of food supply, thereby improving household social resilience.The rural poor generally struggle to find sufficient food for their families, whereas rural households receiving remittances are able to protect their food supply, for example, they can sell their crops at any time or earn extra income. Therefore, having food supply or selling crops to earn money is an indicator of social resilience that provides the highest chance of coping with unexpected shocks or adapting to changed economic circumstances. While land can be used for food production, it can also support household social resilience in other ways by providing a site for secure housing.

5.2 *Investment in housing land and construction*

LaGory, Fitzpatrick, and Ritchey (2001, p. 633) argue that a home is a basic need and a matter of status that directly affects human lifestyle and quality of life in terms of comfort and privacy. The empirical literature reveals that the spending of remittances on home construction is a priority for migrant households because it is a basic need item, an income-generating asset that contributes to securing, diversifying and improving livelihoods, and it provides better living conditions and protection from natural calamities (Taylor, 1999; Savage & Harvey, 2007; Watkins, 2004). Mohapatra, Joseph, and Ratha's (2009, pp. 12–13) study in Ghana suggested a positive role for international remittances in preparing houses for natural disasters and in coping with the loss afterwards. Ghanaian households that received international remittances tended to have concrete houses that were more disaster resilient. Traditional mud and bricks houses were less able to survive destruction in the event of a disaster. Spending on building and improving houses is also a sign of prestige, prosperity and development. Gardner's (1993, p. 3) study of Bangladesh, Gamburd's (2000, p. 125) study of Sri Lanka, and Cohen and Rodriguez's (2004, p. 10) study of Mexico, highlight that there are a number of ways for migrant households to qualify as prosperous and that spending remittances on housing provides the most visible index of family accomplishment and the success of migration.

Consistent with the existing literature, villagers reported devoting remittances to purchasing land for housing; four male-headed internal and one female-headed international migrant household in *Hasail*, one male-headed internal and one male-headed international migrant household in

Kisamatpur Sherpur and one female-headed international migrant household in *Baynagar*. In addition, a female-headed internal migrant household in *Kisamatpur Sherpur* who bought land and also set aside funds to build a house, and a male head of an internal migrant household in the *Kisamatpur Sherpur* village who already had agricultural land allocated remittances to constructing a house. In other words, having land and a secure home are priorities and nine of the 36 households report capitalising on remittance income for this purpose.

However, decisions to buy land or to build a home were not automatic responses, as if the migrant villagers had entered into these arrangements without any planning. All of the householders reported weighing up their priorities before buying land or engaging in construction. Some of the villagers considered investing in land and a home as future insurance in the village, while others saw it as a necessity for the migrant households. The interviewed householders reported that their migrant relatives anticipated returning to their homeland and transferring remittances to ensure their social identity in their place of origin. Lucas and Stark (1985, p. 902) argue that individual migrants have more than one motivation for sending remittances home and that securing a property may be a way of keeping the option open to return home ultimately in dignity. Lucas and Stark add that a mutually beneficial agreement made between the migrant and their family back home is also an expression of their regard for their family members and a way of fulfilling their obligations and commitment to their family.

Sada Miah's three migrant sons from *Kisamatpur Sherpur* told that life in Dhaka is not easy and that they were unable to save very much of their earnings for their families because of the high cost of renting a house and commodities. Their limited income also prohibited the possibility of taking their families to Dhaka, and they therefore worried for their families, particularly their children. They were prepared to struggle to ensure a better future for their children. Until recently it was difficult for them to consider sending their children to better schools but recently a few local educated people and national non-government organisations (NGOs) had opened good schools in the village, including English language schools. The establishment of private and community clinics and a government hospital in the Upazila administrative area have dramatically improved the quality and availability of medical services. These developments in the village have prompted migrants to think about returning. In the previous year the three brothers had sent Taka 160,000 (US$2317) to their father (Sada Miah) to buy 16 decimals of land beside their homestead, from their uncle. The land is located beside the main village road. They now are weighing up their options: whether to extend the family home or build shop space to rent out or to establish a mobile phone accessories business when they return.

Plans to return home can vary between migrants as do plans to secure their family's future. What is shared by all is a common hope of a better future for the migrants' children and the households' survival in the village. In this sense remittances are not an end themselves, but the means for achieving goals of purchasing land and constructing homes – critical investments for the future. The husband of Hamida, a female head of an internal migrant household in *Kisamatpur Sherpur* had plans to buy land and settle in Dhaka city to provide a better future for their children but he deferred to his mother who was not willing to leave the village. He bought 4.5 decimals of land in Gaibandha city, about 30 min drive from their home in the village and built a semi-pucca building with the intention of relocating there so that his two children could attend college. Aziz Sardar and Lina Akhter had properties in the *Hasail* village that were unprotected from riverbank erosion. Each year they bought and dumped earth to protect their homes from the floods. The availability of international remittance income enabled Aziz and Lina additional land alongside their current homes. They purchased these properties which were prone to flooding so that they could remove soil and dump it on the homestead and capitalise on the small ponds that they had created on the new land to breed fish and to dredge the ponds for more earth during the winter. Therefore, instead of annually repairing their homes and properties from damage caused by floods, Aziz and Lina drew on their remittances to consolidate and protect their properties in anticipation of future flooding.

For other migrant households, the decision to invest remittances in their place of origin was influenced by participation in local development plans and programs. Hajji Abdul Motaleb, for example, felt he had to invest in the local community so as to enhance his family's reputation and fulfil his ambition to be a national leader in the region. His household already owned land in the village but he wanted to buy additional land in the central city of Gaibandha district to increase his visibility. With his two sons working overseas, Hajji Abdul Motaleb had the resources to buy additional land and a house to enhance his identity as a 'local' so as to avoid the criticism that he was a *bideshimanush* – a foreign male.

In combination, the vignettes of the respondents capture the various ways that villagers enhanced their household social resilience by investing remittances in housing construction. However, each migrant household had a different reason for using remittances to build and improve their home. Some did so in response to natural calamities. For others, investing in a home was a means of improving the family's social status in the community. The socio-economic circumstances of the village setting are also a factor driving investment in homes; modern buildings signpost social position and prosperity. The interviews reveal that the hardships and challenges of migrant life were motivation to use the remittances to build a home for themselves and in anticipation of their sons' return to the village, or to build a future for the next generation. In this way, remittances acted 'as a private or informal social protection strategy' at the household as well as individual level (Sabates-Wheeler & Waite, 2003, p. 17). These diverse reasons for investing remittances in housing construction point to the significance of economic *as well as* cultural capital in promoting household social resilience. They also show that while remittances are often invested in economic capital such as agricultural land or housing construction, remittances can also be used to support *human capital*, an issue discussed in the next section of the paper.

5.3 *Education opportunities*

According to The World Bank (2006), remittances from migration enable the family members of migrants to pursue education as a means of social mobility. In resourcepoor populations, schooling has acquired symbolic value as the prime means of escaping household poverty and realising ambition for social mobility (Boyden, 2013). Adams (2005) notes that in Guatemala, households receiving remittances spend between 45 and 58% of the funds on education. Ngoma and Ismail's (2013) study on 89 developing countries reveals that on average an increase in migrant remittances inflows by one per cent contributes to a two per cent in rise years of schooling at both secondary and tertiary levels. The findings suggest that income from remittances have the potential to relax liquidity constraints and effects on human capital formation. Studies by Acosta (2006) in El Salvador, Mansuri (2006) in Pakistan, Ullah (2010) in Bangladesh and Prabal and Ratha (2012) in Sri Lanka also note that remittances contribute towards investment in children's education. This increased expenditure on education thus represents investment in human capital. As Taylor and Y'unez-Naude (1999, pp. 16–19) point out, investment in education has positive outcomes for rural households by enabling illiterate parents to access information about agriculture, obtain new technologies, market inputs and credit, and providing them with access to information for improving family nutrition and health. However, Rao (2010, p. 137) argues that the investment in education is not automatic, and depends on the nature of the immediate needs of the migrant households, the pattern of local investment, the quality of available education and the likely returns from investing in education. What is less clear from the available research is how migrant households invest remittances in education so as to enhance social resilience for migrant household members.

Our research shows that nineteen migrant households spent remittances specifically on educational purposes, including institutional fees, private tutor fees, books and stationary, and accommodation and transport costs for school, college and university. Among the households, twelve were internal migrant households and seven were international. Of the former, three female-headed households resided in the *Hasail* village, four female-headed in the *Kisamatpur Sherpur* village and two male headed and three female headed households in the *Baynagar* village. The three female headed and one male headed international migrant household were located in the *Baynagar* village and another three female-headed ones were in *Kisamatpur Sherpur*. In the present study, 44 family members of the 19 migrant households examined were students; 19 were boys and 25 girls, with the majority enrolled in classes V to X and only one enrolled in a postgraduate Master's program. Female-headed migrant households were more likely to allocate remittances to education than the male-headed households, perhaps because the latter had other sources of income to spend on education. In eight of the

16 femaleheaded households the migrants were the primary income earner and so the children's education in those households depended entirely on remittances. While the other households had additional income to draw on, a considerable proportion of remittance income went into supporting their children's education.

The size and structure of the family, social circumstances and past experiences are factors influencing decisions to use remittances for education. Lina Akhter, a femalehead of an international migrant household in the *Hasail* village, for example, spent remittances on supporting her son's higher education studies. Her son gained a Bachelor's degree in Business Administration (BBA) from a private university in Dhaka. Higher education at private universities is very expensive; Lina Akhter bore the cost because she dreamt that her son would get a better job in Dhaka, then take responsibility for the family and bring them to settle in Dhaka. The son's education was a corollary to protecting the family from riverbank erosion; every year they spend money dumping earth and rebuilding to secure the house. Since completing his BBA was not enough to get a better job, her son wanted to study for a Masters in Business Administration (MBA). Lina was spending an extra Taka 25,000 (US$362) every month to support her son's extended degree. Her husband and oldest son, both international migrants, struggled to send extra but did so in the hope that one day this second son would return to the family double this amount. They believed that the educated son would bring additional social value as well as contribute income to the family.

Hasna and Ashia, female heads of international migrant households, had different reasons for using remittances to fund their children's education. Ashia considered education to bring social prestige. Since other households send their children to school, she feared that she and her family would lose respect if they did not send their children to school. Her goal was limited to Secondary School Certificate (SSC), and she wanted her son to work in agriculture after completing the SSC examination. She had intended to support the continuation of her daughter's education, but had stopped this when her daughter finished her SSC. She had no more interest in furthering her daughter's education and informed the interviewer that the villagers saw her daughter going to school and asked her why she had not arranged her marriage. She explains:

> Many people say many things … Some ask why I don't marry off my daughter … People think my daughter is not getting married … We don't receive any good proposals … They speak even more when they see my daughters outside the house … I asked my daughter to stay at my home and do no more studying.

When Hasna was interviewed in October 2010, she indicated that the family was now preparing for her daughter's marriage. When told that early marriage is prohibited by the government, she asked not to inform anyone otherwise the villagers will stop the marriage. Hasna explained that the sole reason for continuing her daughter's studies was in order to obtain an educated husband. 'An educated person looks for an educated girl' explained Hasna. She had not planned to marry her daughter off early but agreed to do so because she found a good husband who worked for a private company in Chittagong. An added incentive was that the groom's family did not demand a dowry, which relieved Hasna's family from considerable financial and mental costs. She received financial support towards the wedding from her other two daughters' husbands. Hasna felt that the marriage represented a new relationship which would help them in the near future if they faced any social or financial problems.

Miller (1992, p. 317), Atkinson and Kintrea (2004, p. 452), and LaGory et al. (2001, p. 637), view education as a key strategy of upward social mobility and a means of accelerating individual aspirations and expectations. The educated are more likely to be better equipped to conduct their lives, and have a greater range of opportunities available to them. Simelane (1995) and Ansell (2000, pp. 147–148) note that in rural communities education is perceived as the best hope and most effective means for young people to access the resources needed to secure the household livelihood. Remittances allowed a majority of the migrant households in our research to access education, an investment considered important in developing human capital, building social prestige, and improving household capacity to deal with future shocks and vulnerability. De Haas (2007, p. 17) supports Sen's (1999a, p. 128, 1999b, p. 7) contention that 'basic education [is] a prime mover of change' and that improvements in the lives of migrant villagers should be considered as 'development' that enhances people's well-being and ability to lead lives that have meaning and value. Nonetheless, it is important to note that investing in education does not necessarily contribute to improved resilience for all household members. In fact, it can reinforce existing gender inequalities through investment in education for male members of the household, who are viewed as the future providers. At the same time, the example of Hasna and Ashia shows that using remittances to educate female members of the household may be a strategy for enhancing their marriage prospects.

6 Discussion and Conclusion

This paper reveals that village households endure a precarious existence, striving to cope with routine and unanticipated challenges that threaten their security and livelihood. It shows that for some rural villagers, remittances are both responses to deprivation and strategic decisions by households to diversify their capital and to develop a wider range of strategies for coping with, mitigating and absorbing shocks and stresses. Remittances are thus viewed in this paper as key livelihood strategies providing migrant households with social resilience. A significant finding of this paper is the contribution of credit and insurance, which remittances enabled migrant households to access, in building household social resilience. Credit and insurance markets in Bangladesh are not well developed, and as a consequence local NGOs mostly provide credit in rural areas. In practice, most villagers rely on local *Mohajons* to access credit, and in return, have to pay higher rates of interest than do NGOs or any private or public banks' credit programmes. Remittances overcame some of these challenges enabling migrant households, and particularly landless households, to access capital to support agricultural production. This included the purchase or leasing of agricultural land and investment in agriculture-related production costs. The investment of remittance income on these activities gave negotiating power to both land-holding and landless migrant households to access agricultural land and equipment, thus contributing directly and directly to improving their resilience. Remittances also enhance the *cultural capital* of household members (Bourdieu, 1986), providing funds to support activities that promote individual status, prestige and personal satisfaction. It is arguable that such investments in cultural capital contribute to resilience in a small way by improving the capacity of households to maintain their *social position* in the face of change.

For those households that already had some resources on which they could draw, remittances were invested in building a new home or renovating an old one. Householders drew on remittance income to repair their homes from flood damage, building soil levies to secure the home from future flooding, cladding their homes with more solid material to ensure their durability, and expanding them so as to accommodate current and additional family members. This provided privacy and shelter from natural disasters, but also contributed to the cultural capital of those who inhabited them. Along with owning land, the home is the symbol of security and stability for the migrant villagers. It is no wonder, therefore, that the home features as a primary focus of remittance expenditure. In contrast, those migrant households with minimal resources to draw on found themselves allocating remittances to meeting basic necessities, and having fewer investment choices.

Regardless of resources, this study reveals an important gender dimension in the different strategies for using remittances. Similar to the work of De and Ratha (2005) in Sri Lanka and de la Cruz (1995) in Mexico, our research shows that male-headed households tended to spend remittances on the building of economic capital – such as land for agricultural production or housing construction – while female-headed households preferred investing in activities, such as education, that enhance human capital. While investments in human capital may make an overall contribution to household social resilience, particularly in the longer-term, they do not necessarily enhance resilience for the women in those households, and may reinforce existing gender inequalities. Some researchers take for granted that remittances encourage the liberation of the women who stay behind. For example, Zachariah, Mathew, and Rajan (2001, p. 58), Jolly and Reeves (2005, p. 1), Hampshire (2006, p. 403) and DFID (2007, p. 11) argue that remittances contribute to increasing life opportunities for women who stay behind, increasing their decision-making, power, and control of household resources. Rahman's study (2009) of Bangladesh reveals that in the absence of husbands who migrated, 70% wives left behind acquire full authority to manage the family budget.

However, a contrasting view is that some women have limited control over the remittances sent back by the male migrants and that they do not automatically gain control over the financial resources or have greater authority for decision-making (Gardner, 1995, p. 226; De Haas, 2007 p. 20; Tacoli, 1998, p. 10). van Rooij's (2000) study shows, remittances from migrants have had little effect on gender roles in Morocco; migrant wives remain largely confined to housekeeping, child rearing and agricultural work. Even though they tend to have some level of control over the use of their husbands' earnings and their diversion into child rearing, this gain in authority was mainly temporary, since migrants resume their position as patriarch as soon as they return. Another aspect of the impact of remittances on women can be found in a study by Agarwal (1994) in South Asia, which found that migrant earnings may contribute to increasing male authority in the household, and to making women even more dependent on men for cash for their health care. As a result womens' bargaining power declines just as their responsibilities increase. David's (1995) study of the Sudan also reveals that although the migrants' wives made the small, everyday decisions about agriculture, most of the important decisions about the farm management were postponed until the male migrants' return. This research suggests that female-headed households in the present study who invested remittances in savings and education may not have done so if their husband was present. In other words, husbands may have otherwise directed remittances to be invested in economic capital.

In conclusion, this paper has drawn on the notion of social resilience to describe and explain the role of remittances in enhancing the capacity of migrant households to maintain stability in the face of social, economic, and environmental changes (Adger et al., 2002; Locke et al., 2000). The concept is not used as a technical formula with a check-list of measures and predictors, but more as an umbrella concept to draw attention to and describe the role of remittances in enabling migrant households to respond to challenges. Remittances do not remove all migrant households from routine and unanticipated adversities. Neither do they necessarily improve resilience for all households or individual members of those households. However, in general, they contribute to the capacity of households to rebound from natural or economic shocks, provide a wider range of options for action, and opportunities to plan for the future.

Disclosure Statement

No potential conflict of interest was reported by the authors.

Note

1. Bahadur, Ibrahim, and Tanner (2010, p. 16) argue that remittances increase a community's resilience to disturbances, but add they also could lead to unequal access to resources and thus enhance the vulnerability of some individuals within a community.

Notes on Contributors

Mohammad Jalal Uddin Sikder is an assistant professor with the University of Liberal Arts Bangladesh (ULAB). He also works as a research fellow at the Refugee and Migratory Movements Research Unit (RMMRU), University of Dhaka. His research interests are migration, remittances and development. His recent publications include: Remittances and life chances: a study of migrant households in rural Bangladesh (2013, co-authored with Harry Ballis, Migration and Development, 2(2), 261–285), Bangladesh: international labour migration and remittances (2008, Asian and Pacific Migration Journal, 17(2), 257–276); Livelihoods, informal trade at the Bangladesh border (2005, Inter-Asia Cultural Studies, 6(3), 432–445); Population movements and the threat of HIV/AIDS virus at the Bangladesh-India border (2008, Singapore: Nanyang Technological University. 144 pp.); and, Rural to urban migration for domestic work in Bangladesh (2009, chapter co-authored with Tasneem Siddiqui in Janet Seeley and Chowdhury R Abrar (Eds.). Social protection and marginalised migrant workers in India and Bangladesh, pp. 57–81, Bangladesh, Dhaka: University Press).

Vaughan Higgins is an associate professor in Sociology at the School of Humanities and Social Sciences, Charles Sturt University, Australia. His research interests are in the areas of sociology of agriculture and food, rural sociology, globalisation, and sociology of science and technology. Recent publications include: Private agri-food governance and greenhouse gas abatement: Constructing a corporate carbon economy (2015, coauthored with Jacqui Dibden and Chris Cocklin, Geoforum, 66, 75–84); Payments for ecosystem services, neoliberalisation, and the hybrid governance of land management in Australia (2014, co-authored with Jacqui Dibden, Katie Moon, Clive Potter and Chris Cocklin, Journal of Rural Studies, 36, 463–474); and, Governing biosecurity in a neoliberal world: Comparative perspectives from Australia and the United Kingdom (2012, coauthored with Damian Maye, Jacqui Dibden and Clive Potter, Environment and Planning A, 44, 150–168).

References

Abesamis, N. P., Corrigan, C., Drew, M., Campbell, S., & Samonte, G. (2006). *Social resilience: A literature review on building resilience into human marine communities in and around MPA networks*. Washington, DC: Marine Protected Area (MPA) Networks Learning Partnership, Global Conservation Program (GCP), USAID.

Acosta, P. (2006). *Labour supply, school attendence and remittances from international migration: The case of EL Salvador* (World Bank Policy Research Working Paper-3903). Washington, DC: The World Bank.

Adams, R. H. (1998). Remittances, investment, and rural asset accumulation in Pakistan. *Economic Development and Cultural Change, 47*, 155–173.

Adams, R. H. (2005). *Remittances, household expenditure and investment in Guatemala* (World Bank Policy Research Working Paper-3532). Washington, DC: The World Bank.

Adams, R. H., & Cuecuecha, A. (2010). Remittances, household expenditure and investment in Guatemala. *World Development, 38*, 1626–1641.

ADB. (2011). *Global food price inflation and developing asia*. Manila: Asian Development Bank. Retrieved February 2, 2012, from http://www.adb.org/documents/reports/global-food-price-infla tion/food-price-inflation.pdf

Adger, W. N. (1997). *Sustainibility and social resilience in coastal resource use* (CSERGE Working Paper GEC-97-23). Norwich: Centre for Social and Economic Research on the Global Environment (CSERGE), University of East Anglia.

Adger, W. N., Kelly, P. M., & Ninh, N. H. (2002). *Living with environmental change: Social vulnerability, adaptation and resilience in Vietnam*. London: Routledge.

Adger, W. N., Kelly, P. M., Winkels, A., Huy, L. Q., & Locke, C. (2002). Migration, remittances, livelihood trajectories, and social resilience. *AMBIO: A Journal of the Human Environment, 31*, 358–366.

Afsar, R. (2000). *Causes, consequences and challenges of rural-urban migration in Bangladesh*. Dhaka: University Press Limited.

Agarwal, B. (1994). *A field of one's own: Gender and land rights in south Asia*. Cambridge: Cambridge University Press.

Ansell, N. (2000). Sustainibility: Life chances and education in Southern Africa. In M. Redclift (Ed.), *Sustainability: Life chances and livelihoods* (pp. 144–157). London: Routledge.

Atkinson, R., & Kintrea, K. (2004). Opportunities and despair, it's all in there: Practitioner experiences and explanations of area affects and life chances. *Sociology, 38*, 437–455.

Bahadur, A. V., Ibrahim, M., & Tanner, T. (2010). *The resilience renaissance? Unpacking of resilience for tackling climate change and disasters* (Strengthening Climate Resilience Discussion Paper 1). Brighton: Strengthening Climate Resilience, Institute of Development Studies, University of Sussex.

Banerjee, S., Yuves-Gerlitz, J., & Kniveton, D. (2011). *Remittances as a key adaptation perspectives on remittance communities exposed to water hazard in the Hindu Kush-himalayan region*. Patan: International Centre for Integrated Mountain Development (ICIMOD).

BBS. (2011). *Household income and expenditure survey-2010*. Dhaka: Bangladesh Bureau of Statistics, Government of Bangladesh.

Bhuyan, A. R., Khan, H.-A.-R., & Ahmed, S. U. (2001). *Rural-urban migration and poverty: The case for reverse migration in Bangladesh* (Monitoring Adjustment and Poverty (MAP) Focus Study Series No-10). Dhaka: Centre on Integrated Development for Asia and the Pacific.

BMET. (2016). Country wise overseas employment and remittances 1976–2015. In *Bureau of manpower employment and training (BMET)*. Dhaka: Government of Bangladesh. Retrieved January 6, 2016, from http://www.bmet.org.bd/BMET/viewStatReport.action?reportnumber=18

Bourdieu, P. (1986). The forms of capital. In J. G. Richardson (Ed.), *Handbook of theory and research for the sociology of education* (pp. 241–258). New York, NY: Greenwood Press.

Boyatzis, R. E. (1998). *Transforming qualitative information-thematic analysis and code development*. Thousand Oaks, CA: Sage.

Boyden, J. (2013). We are not going to suffer like this in mud: Educational aspiration, social mobility and independent child migration among population living in poverty. *Compare: A Journal of Comparative and International Education, 43*, 580–600.

Brand, F. S., & Jax, K. (2007). Focusing the meaning(s) of resilience: Resilience as a descriptive concept and a boundary object. *Ecology and Society, 12*(23), 1–16.

Brownlee, P., & Mitchell, C. 1997. *Migration research in the Asia Pacific: Theoretical and empirical issues* (APMRN Working Paper No. 3). Wollongong: Asia Pacific Migration Research Network (APMRN) Secretariat, Migration and Multicultural Program, Institute for Social Change and Critical Inquiry University of Wollongong. Retrieved December 9, 2015, from http://unesdoc.unesco.org/images/0011/001159/115932Eo.pdf

Cheng, E., & Zhong, X. (2005). *Domestic money transfer services for migrant workers in China*. Washington, DC: Microfinance Gateway.

Cohen, J. H., & Rodriguez, L. (2004). *Remittance outcomes in rural Oaxaca, Mexico: Challenges, Options, and opportunities for migrant households* (Working Paper-102). San Diego, CA: The Center for Comparative Immigration Studies, University of California.

de la Cruz, B. E. (1995). The socioeconomic dimensions of remittances: A case study of five Mexican families. *The Berkeley McNair Journal, 3*(1), 1–10.

Damon, A., & Wisniewski, S. (2015). Migration responses to adverse household shocks: do family relationships and types of shocks matter? *Migration and Development, 4*, 4–22.

David, R. (1995). *Changing places: Women, resource management and migration in the Sahel*. London: SOS Sahel.

De Bruyn, T., & Kuddus, U. (2005). *Dynamics of remittance utilization in Bangladesh* (Migration Research Series (MRS) No-18). Geneva: International Organization for Migration.

de Haan, A. (1999). Livelihoods and poverty: The role of migration – a critical review of the migration literature. *Journal of Development Studies, 36*(2), 1–47.

De Haas, H. (2007). *Remitances, migration and social development: A conceptual review of the literature* (Programme Paper No-34). Geneva: United Nations Research Institute for Social Development.

De, P., & Ratha, D. (2005). *Remittance income and household welfare: Evidence from Sri Lanka integrated household survey*. Washington, DC: Development Research Group, The World Bank. Unpublished.

Deshingkar, P. (2012). Environmental risk, resilience and migration: Implications for natural resource management and agriculture. *Environmental Research Letters, 7*(1), 1–7.

Deshingkar, P., & Grimm, S. (2005). *Internal migration and development: A global perspective* (IOM Migration Research Series-19). Geneva: International Organization for Migration.

DFID. (2007). *Moving Out of poverty – making migration work better for poor people*. London: Department for International Development (DFID).

Ellis, F. (2003). *A livelihoods approach to migration and poverty reduction*. London: Commissioned by the Department for International Development (DFID).

Eversole, R., & Shaw, J. (2010). Remittance flows and their use in households: A comparative study of Sri Lanka, Indonesia and the Philippines. *Asian and Pacific Migration Journal, 19* (2), 175–202.

Folke, C. (2006). Resilience: The emergence of a perspective for social-ecological systems analyses. *Global Environmental Change, 16*, 253–267.

Gamburd, M. R. (2000). *The kitchen spoon's handle: Transnationalism and Sri Lanka's migrant housemaids*. Ithaca: Cornell University Press.

Gardner, K. (1993). Desh-Bidesh: Sylheti images of home and away. *Man, New Series, 28*(1), 1–15.

Gardner, K. (1995). *Global migrants, local lives: Travel and transformation in rural Bangladesh*. Oxford: Carleton Press.

Garrett, J., & Chowdhury, S. (2004). *Urban-rural links and transformation in Bangladesh: A review of the issues* (Discussion Paper, Prepared for Rural Livelihoods Program). Dhaka: CARE-Bangladesh.

GoB. (2009). *Millennum development goals: Bangladesh progress report 2008*. Dhaka: General Economics Division, Planning Commission, Government of Bangladesh.

Goetz, J. P., & LeCompte, M. D. (1981). Ethnographic research and the problem of data reduction: What do i do with the 5 drawers and fieldnotes? *Anthropology and Education Quarterly, 12*, 51–70.

Gordon, J. (1978). *Structures*. Harmondsworth: Penguin Books.

Guzmán, J. C., Morrison, A. R., & Sjöblom, M. (2008). The impact of remittances and gender on household expenditure patterns: Evidence from Ghana. In A. R. Morrison, M. Schiff, & M. Sjöblom (Eds.), *The international migration of women* (pp. 125–152). Washington, DC: The World Bank.

Hampshire, K. (2006). Flexibility in domestic organization and seasonal migration among the Fulani of Northern Burkina Faso. *Africa: Journal of the International African Institute, 76*, 402–426.

Handmer, J. W., & Dovers, S. R. (1996). A typology of resilience: Rethinking institutions for sustainable development. *Industrial and Environmental Crisis Quarterly, 9*, 482–511.

IBP. (2011). *Bangladesh business intelligence report, volume 1 strategic and practical information*. Washington, DC: International Business Publications.

Jolly, S., & Reeves, H. (2005). *Gender and migration: Overview report*. Brighton: BRIDGE: Gender and Development Research and Information Service, Institute of Development Studies, University of Sussex.

Kapur, D. (2004). *Remittances and the new development mantra*? (G-24 Discussion Paper Series, Research papers for the Intergovernmental Group of Twenty-four on Intenational Monetary Affairs) New York, NY: United Nations.

Khatir, A., & Rezaei-Moghaddam, K. (2014). Evidence from predictors of rural youth's migration intentions in agricultural communities: The fars province, Iran. *Migration and Development, 3*, 219–238.

Kuhn, R. (2001). *Understanding the social process of migration in Bangladesh* (Labour and Population Working Papers). Santa Monica, CA: Research and Development Corporation.

LaGory, M., Fitzpatrick, K., & Ritchey, F. (2001). Life chances and choices: Assessing quality of life among the homeless. *The Sociological Quarterly, 42*, 633–651.

Lipton, M. (1980). Migration from rural areas of poor countries: The impact on rural productivity and income distribution. *World Development, 8*(1), 1–24.

Locke, C., Adger, W. N., & Kelly, P. M. (2000). Changing places: Migration's social and environmental consequences. *Environment and Development, 42*, 24–35.

Lucas, R. E. B., & Stark, O. (1985). Motivations to remit: Evidence from Botswana. *Journal of Political Economy, 93*, 901–917.

Maguire, B., & Cartwright, S. (2008). *Assessing a community's capacity to manage change: A resilience approach to social assessment*. Canberra: Bureau of Rural Sciences.

Mansuri, G. (2006). *Migration, school attainment and child labor: Evidence from rural Pakistan* (World Bank Policy Research Working Paper-3945). Washington, DC: Group, The World Bank.

Masten, A. S., & Gewirtz, A. H. 2006. *Resilience in development: The importance of early childhood*. Montreal: Encyclopedia on Early Childhood Development. Retrieved September 3, 2015, from, http://www.child-encyclopedia.com/documents/Masten-GewirtzANGxp.pdf

Miller, M. A. (1992). Life chances exercise. *Teaching Sociology, 20*, 316–320.

Mohanty, S. K., Dubey, M., & Parida, J. K. (2014). Economic well-being and spending behaviour of households in India: Does remittances matter? *Migration and Development, 3*, 38–53.

Mohapatra, S., Joseph, G., & Ratha, D. (2009). *Remittances and natural disasters ex-post response and contribution to ex-ante preparedness* (Policy Research Working Paper-4972) Washington, DC: The World Bank.

Moses, J. W. (2012). Out-migration and Chinese rural development. *Migration and Development, 1*, 244–260.

Murphy, R. (2006). *Domestic migrant remittances in China: Distribution, channels and livelihoods* (Migration Research Studies (MRS) No-24). Geneva: International Organisation for Migration.

Ngoma, A. L., & Ismail, W. (2013). Do migrant remittances promote human capital formation? Evidence from 89 developing countries. *Migration and Development, 2*, 106–116.

Prabal, K. De, & Ratha, D. (2012). Impact of remittances on household income, asset and human capital: Evidence from Sri Lanka. *Migration and Development, 1*(1), 163–179.

Quasem, M. A. (2004). Changes in economic status of rural households in Bangladesh: A case study of two villages. *The Bangladesh Development Studies, 30*, 129–148.

Rahman, M. M. (2009). Temporary migration and changing family dynamics: Implications for social development. *Population, Space and Place, 15*, 161–174.

Rahman, M. M., & Yong, T. T. (2015). International migration and development in South Asia: An introduction In M. M. Rahman & T. T. Yong (Eds.), *International migration and development in South Asia* (pp. 1–21). London: Routledge.

Rao, N. (2010). Migration, education and socio-economic mobility. *Compare: A Journal of Comparative and International Education, 40*, 137–145.

Rapoport, H., & Docquier, F. (2005). *The economics of migrants' remittances* (IZA Discussion Papers-1531). Bonn: Institute for the Study of Labor.

Ratha, D., De Eigen, S., Dervisevic, E., Plaza, S., Schuettler, K., Shaw, W., … Yousefi, S. R. (2015). *Migration and remittance flows: Recent trends and outlook: Special topic for financial development*. Washington, DC: Migration and Development Brief 24. Migration and Remittances Unit, The World Bank.

Rogaly, B., & Rafique, A. (2003). Struggling to save cash: Seasonal migration and vulnerability in West Bengal, India. *Development and Change, 34*, 659–681.

van Rooij, A. (2000). *Women of Tagzoute: The effects of migration on women left behind in Morocco*. Amsterdam: MA University of Amsterdam.

Rutter, M. (1993). Resilience: Some conceptual considerations. *Journal of Adolescent Health, 14*, 626–631.

Sabates-Wheeler, R., & Waite, M. (2003). *Migration and social protection: A concept paper* (Working Paper T2). Brighton: Development Research Centre on Migration, Globalisation and Poverty, University of Sussex.

Sapountzaki, K. (2007). Social resilience to environmental risks *Management of Environmental Quality: An International Journal, 18*, 274–297.

Savage, K., & Harvey, P. (2007). *Remittances during crises: Implications for humanitarian response* (Humanitarian Policy Group (HPG) Briefing Paper 26). London: Overseas Development Institute.

Scheffran, J., Marmer, E., & Sow, P. (2011). *Migration as a resource for resilience and innovation in climate adaptation: Social networks and co-development in Northwest Africa* (Working paper CLISEC-16). Research Group Climate Change and Security, Hamburg: University of Hamburg.

Sen, A. K. (1999a). *Development as freedom.* New York, NY: Anchor Books.

Sen, A. K. (1999b). *Beyond the crisis: Development strategies in Asia.* Singapore: Institute of Southeast Asian Studies.

Siddiqui, T., & Abrar, C. R. (2002). *Contribution of returnees: An analytical survey of post return experience.* Dhaka: International Organization for Migration and United Nations Development Program.

Siddiqui, T., & Sikder, M. J. U. (2009). Rural to urban migration for domestic work in Bangladesh. In C. R. Abrar & J. Saleey (Eds.), *Social Protection and marginalised migrant workers in India and Bangladesh* (pp. 57–81). Dhaka: University Press Limited.

Sikder, M. J. U., & Ballis, P. H. (2013). Remittances and life chances: A study of migrant households in rural Bangladesh. *Migration and Development, 2*, 261–285.

Simelane, H. S. (1995). Labour migration and rural transformation in post-colonial Swaziland. *Journal of Contemporary African Studies, 13*, 207–226.

Singh, S. (2005, April 13). *Sending money home: Money and family in the Indian diaspora.* Presented at the Institute for International Integration Studies IIIS, Trinity College. pp. 1–26.

Stark, O. (1991). *The migration of labor.* Cambridge: Harvard University Press.

Stefanovic, N. (2012). *Remittances and moral economies of Bangladeshi New York immigrants in light of the economic crisis.* New York, NY: PhD, Columbia University. Retrieved October 19, 2014, from http://academiccommons.columbia.edu/catalog/ac:152481

Sutton, S. G., & Tobin, R. C. (2012). Social resilience and commercial fishers' responses to management changes in the Great Barrier Reef Marine Park. *Ecology and Society, 17*, 6.

Tacoli, C. (1998). *Bridging the divide: Rural-urban interactions and livelihood strategies*. Gatekeeper Series No-77. London: Sustainable Agriculture and Rural Livelihoods Programme, International Institute for Environment and Development (IIFD).

Taylor, E. J. (1999). The new economics of labour migration and the role of remittances in the migration process. *International Migration, 37*, 63–88.

Taylor, J. E., & Rozelle, S. (2003). Migration and incomes in source communities: A new economics of migration perspective from China. *Economic Development and Cultural Change, 52*, 75–101.

Taylor, J. E., & Wyatt, T. J. (1996). The shadow value of migrant remittances, income and inequality in a household-farm economy. *Journal of Development Studies, 32*, 899–912.

Taylor, J. E., & Y'unez-Naude, A. Y. (1999). *Education, migration and poverty: An analytical approach and evidence from rural Mexico*. Paris: Development Centre of the Organisation for Economic Co-operation and Development.

Ullah, A. K. M. A. (2010). *Rationalizing migration decisions: Labour migrants in east and southeast Asia*. London: Ashgate.

Umetsu, C., Shinjo, H., Sakurai, T., Shimada, S., & Yoshimura, M. (2010). *Resilience of rural households in Africa: An introduction* (FY2009 FR3 Project Report). Kyoto: Research Institute for Humanity and Nature, Inter-University Research Institute Corporation, National Institute for the Humanities.

Vargas-Lundius, O., Lanly, G., Villareal, M., & Osorio, M. (2008). *International migration, remittances and rural development*. Rome: International Fund for Agricultural Development (IFAD).

Watkins, F. (2004). 'Save there, eat there': Migrants, households and community identity among Pakhtuns in Northern Pakistan. In K. Gardner & F. Osella (Eds.), *Migration, modernity and social transformation in South Asia* (pp. 59–82). Thousand Oaks, CA: Sage.

World Bank. (2006). *Global economic prospects: Economic implications of remittances and migration*. Washington, DC: The World Bank.

World Bank. (2011). *Bangladesh: Priorities for agriculture and rural development*. Washington, DC: The World Bank.

Zachariah, K. C., Mathew, E. T., & Rajan, S. I. (2001). Social, Economic and Demographic Consequences of Migration on Kerala. *International Migration, 39*, 43–71.

Section IV

A Migrant's Eye View

Chapter 12

"The Death of Wishes"

Joy Ho and Md. Sharif Uddin

"I WANT TO GO TO MUSTAFA MINIMART AND EAT TWO PLATES OF BRIYANI AT FAKHRUDDIN
Kissing hot tea & blowing smoke
CHAT ON THE FOURTH FLOOR OF CITY SQUARE."

"I WISH TO SIT IN THE FRONT SEAT IN THE TOP DECK OF BUS NUMBER 67 AND WALK AROUND THE NARROW STREETS OF THE CITY THEN BUY A THREE DOLLAR BIG SWEEP TICKET."
"I WISH TO CLIMB THE GRASSY HILLS OF MARINA BAY AND BOTANIC GARDENS!"
"I WANT TO DIVE INTO THE MURKY WATERS OF THE EAST COAST LAGOON!"
Fly in the sky of dreams
"I WISH TO READ POETRY SITTING IN THE NATIONAL LIBRARY. I WANT TO GO TO JEWEL. I WISH TO LISTEN TO THE SONG OF THE FOUNTAIN WHILE LYING DOWN!"

BUT WISHES ARE LOST IN THE CITY.
ALL DESIRES ARE BLOCKED
BY FOUR WALLS.

I am a monk
at night

The
day
is
dust.

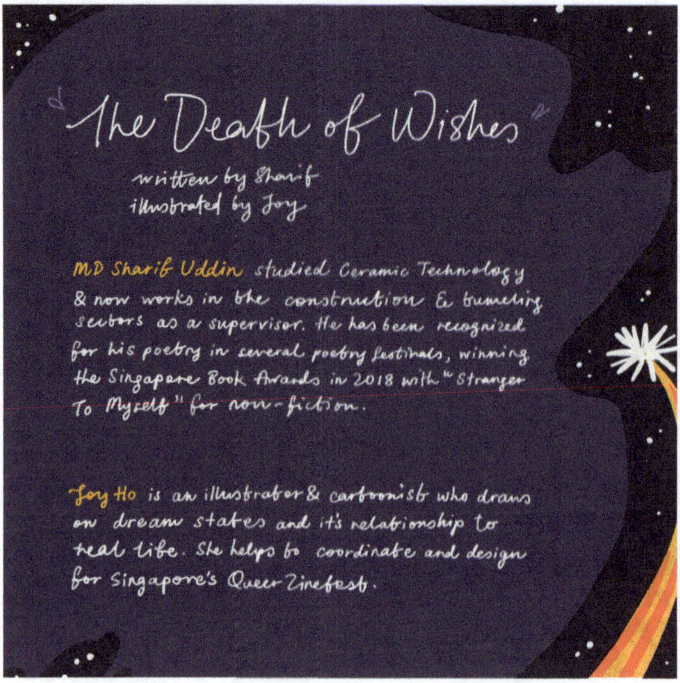
"The Death of Wishes"
written by Sharif
illustrated by Joy
MD Sharif Uddin studied Ceramic Technology & now works in the construction & tunneling sectors as a supervisor. He has been recognized for his poetry in several poetry festivals, winning the Singapore Book Awards in 2018 with "Stranger To Myself" for non-fiction.
Joy Ho is an illustrator & cartoonist who draws on dream states and it's relationship to real life. She helps to coordinate and design for Singapore's Queer Zinefest.

www.ingramcontent.com/pod-product-compliance
Lightning Source LLC
LaVergne TN
LVHW010328220926
848484LV00004BB/859